ALEXANDRE MILLERAND: THE SOCIALIST YEARS

Issues in Contemporary Politics

Historical and Theoretical Perspectives

4

Mouton · The Hague · Paris

Alexandre Millerand

The Socialist Years

LESLIE DERFLER
Florida Atlantic University

Mouton · The Hague · Paris

LC - 77 467617

ISBN: 90 – 279 – 7991 – X

© 1977 Mouton & Co., The Hague, The Netherlands

Printed in Hungary

For my mother and
to the memory of my father

Preface

At precisely 2 p.m. of June 26, 1899, Paul Deschanel, its presiding officer, declared the French Chamber of Deputies in session. Every sign pointed to an exceptional meeting. After thirteen days without a government, almost a record even for the strife-ridden Third Republic, a new cabinet had been assembled and was seeking a vote of confidence. The excited deputies awaited the man appointed Premier, the conservative lawyer-politician, René Waldeck-Rousseau. They awaited even more intently the two most controversial members of his ministry: the Marquis de Galliffet, the general whose troops had crushed the Paris Commune almost thirty years before and who was anethema to the left; and Alexandre Millerand, the chief of the parliamentary socialists, who, if not a revolutionary, was a self-avowed collectivist, a man whose very name sent a chill through the more conservative elements of the bourgeoisie. If approved the cabinet would be the first of the Third Republic to contain a socialist, and Millerand would be the first socialist, with the exception of Louis Blanc, ever to sit in a European government. The deputies speculated that only the urgent need to discipline the army, distraught by Dreyfusard attacks on its integrity, and to ensure socialist support for the ministry could have prompted such a combination. But they could not contain their hostility to one or the other of the two men.

As the new ministers filed into the Chamber the deputies were on their feet and shouting. From all sides of the amphitheater there came waves of abuse; hisses, cat-calls and curses; the outcry resembled the sudden release of pent-up steam and reminded observers of the discordant beating of tin kettles. At the sight of Galliffet the clamor from the left intensified; cries of 'long live the Commune', 'down with the murderer' and 'assassin' could be heard. The imperturable, mocking Galliffet saluted and said 'Assassin, present', whipping the rage of his detractors to a new frenzy.[1]

Accustomed to the orderly proceedings of the courtroom, where he specialized as a corporation lawyer, Waldeck-Rousseau appeared stunned by the reception. He was interrupted repeatedly during the reading of his ministerial statement and occasionally trembled so strongly that the paper seemed to jump in his hands. In a low voice he read: 'In the first rank of the interests most compatible with the preservation of the dignity of a nation we place those of the Army, the Army that the Third Republic has rebuilt on foundations so strong and extensive that it is the expression of both the security and pride of France. Together with its chiefs, its most illustrious guides, we think that an inviolable attachment to discipline is the first and most essential guarantee of its special grandeur. We mean to defend it, with the same energy, against the attacks that will be directed against it. ...'[2]

At that point a major interruption broke out. Some leftwing deputies were beside themselves at seeing on a government bench, soon a spokesman for the Republic, the general whom they considered covered with republican blood. They could no longer curb their emotion. Conservatives were hardly less indignant at the sight of Millerand. How, they asked, could a head of government select a socialist for his cabinet?

That Waldeck could and did select a socialist revealed both the growing importance of the movement, as attested to by its many representatives in national and local government, and its greater willingness to rely on legal mechanisms to bring about social change. For in the last decade of the nineteenth century a number of dissidents in not only French but European socialism had taken an ever more independent position and, as a result of their efforts to 'correct' Marx, fundamentally altered the strategies and structural forms previously relied upon. Those in France became known as 'reformists', and they had managed to cone vert a majority of their colleagues to the view that the predictions madd by Marx had not come to pass and that greater benefit was to be derives by working for reform within the framework of the existent state. A: a definition of reformism I have accepted that offered by Carl Landauer-'...in contradistinction to the dialectician the reformist sees no fundamental reason why circumstances should not be so altered as to make revolution unnecessary.'[3]

My study is centered on the early life of the leader of the socialist contingent in the Chamber of Deputies, Millerand, because his career so aptly illustrated the problems faced and the tactics devised by an important socialist politician forced to reconcile the imperatives of party doctrine and the problems of daily political life. Millerand's public life may be traced to his political origins as Clemenceau's protégé and as a young lawyer defending unpopular worker and socialist causes. It reached to the conservative senator critical of the domestic and foreign policies pursued before the outbreak of World War II. The left has rejected him as a traitor, able to rise in the world only by betraying the French working class; for the right, his fundamental patriotism could not be stifled indefinitely by the alien doctrine of Marxism.

The conflict between orthodox Marxism and reformism is well illustrated by Millerand's entry into the government during the Dreyfus affair. In agreeing to participate in a coalition cabinet of 'republican defense', he exposed himself to charges of spurning the principles endorsed by all socialists, and the dispute that followed once more sundered the party and set back its unification. Millerand was expelled from socialist ranks and stands indicted as an opportunist who made use of French workers, and of their aspirations, to advance his career.[4] He served as Minister of War shortly before and during the opening year of World War I and as Premier and then President of the French Republic in 1920. These performances were irrelevant to events before 1904, the year of his expulsion. Still, they appeared to justify completely his condemnation as renegade and traitor to the socialist cause.

While reading the speeches given by Millerand during his 'socialist years', I was struck by the way in which themes presented in the 1880s resembled those advanced even after the turn of the century. I was similarly impressed by the gyrations of most French socialists during the same period of time. And my research suggested that Millerand, during his socialist years, was fundamentally consistent in his reformist approach, which as a matter of record dates from his entry into public life. Furthermore, evidence mounted to show that even militant socialists like Jules Guesde and Edouard Vaillant became almost wholly reformist in the 1890s but returned to the revolutionary stand held during the early years of the Republic. Simply put, it would seem that it was not so much Millerand who moved to his right at the beginning of the present century but rather French socialism, first Marxists and then Independents, that reverted to its left.

My choice of subject was suggested by Boris Blick and Aaron Noland. Early research was encouraged and guided by Shepard Clough, who has exerted greater influence on it and me than he probably suspects. Travel to and research in France was made possible by the financial aid rendered by the American Council of Learned Societies, the American Philosophical Society, and Franco-American Commission for Educational Exchange and Carnegie-Mellon and Florida Atlantic Universities. In addition to Professors Clough and Salomone, I wish to thank John R.

Coleman, Irving Bartlett, Jack Suberman and Carl Landauer for their help here.

In France the kindness of those to whom I turned provided much pleasure during long periods of research. M. Jacques Millerand provided every opportunity for me to acquaint myself with his father's life. He made available the latter's unpublished memoirs and the important correspondence still in his possession. He granted the necessary authority to consult the previously untouched and still unsorted and uncataloged Millerand Papers at the Bibliothèque Nationale. He arranged meetings with others in the family, friends and colleagues of his father; and here I am expecially grateful for the assistance and friendship of M. and Mme. Jean-Paul Alfassa, née Marthe Millerand.

I am also grateful to the holders of two other private collections of Millerand papers, Mme. Madeliene Rébérioux and M. Pierre Vidal-Naquet, for granting me access to them. A number of historians found the time to share their views of Millerand with me and to suggest or facilitate access to archival materials. Those in France included Maurice Baumont, J.-B. Duroselle, François Goguel, Ernest Labrousse, Jean Maitron, H. I. Marrou, Jacques Néré, the late Alexandre Werth, Denise Fauvel-Rouif and Madeleine Rébérioux. Professor Robert Colodny made possible several interviews; Peter Larmour suggested some useful sources; David Watson and Leonard Bushkoff, in numerous conversations, provided insights and approaches. Carl Landauer consented to read the manuscript and saved me from some errors and misinterpretations. It need hardly be added that none of the people mentioned in these remarks is in any way responsible for those that remain.

A work based on historical research is original in the degree to which archival resources are made available. Archivists and librarians who smoothed my way to the sources included M. Marcel Thomas and Madame Cordroc'h of the Manuscript Division of the Bibliothèque Nationale; Madame Jacqueline Chaumié of the section moderne, Madame Chantal de Tourtier-Bonazzi of the section des archives privées and Madame Reynaud, of the Archives nationales; M. Roger Cautarel and Mme. Jeanne Harburger of the Department of Archives at the Paris Préfecture de Police; M. Célier of the Bibliothèque de l'Institut de France; and Mme. Denise Fauvel-Rouif of the Institut français d'histoire sociale. I am also grateful to the staffs of the Columbia University, New York Public, Carnegie-Mellon, University of Massachusetts and Florida Atlantic University libraries. Finally, my especial appreciation for the patience of my wife, Gunilla, which as perspective lengthens, appears ever more remarkable.

Contents

List of illustrations

1. The beginnings

A legal career was open to the ambition and talents of the poorest, and led to the very highest positions in society.

ELIE HALÉVY

1. The rue de la Jussiene in Paris is a narrow non-residential street, one block in length, emerging from rue Etienne Marcel and ending in rue Montmartre. The busy markets of Les Halles were only moments away. Millerand's first years were spent in these neighborhoods, where the sun was rarely visible during the day, and the quarter was depopulated in the evening after the workers and shopkeepers returned home.

Alexandre Millerand's family originally came from the village of Roche-sur-Vannon in the region once known as Franche-Comté, today in the Haute-Saône Department. Designated as 'la province reputée étrangère', this eastern region was renowned for its independence and attachment to local liberties and was not wholly incorporated into France by the time the Revolution began. One of three surviving children of a family decimated by tuberculosis, François Millerand emigrated with a brother to Paris, probably about 1825.[1] The two found employment in a wine depot in the great market of Bercy, in the southeastern corner of the city. Its owner, a childless widow, ultimately left the business to them, but not before she had introduced François to his future wife, Marie Boucher. The young couple maintained the depot which, doubtless with much hard work, provided a comfortable income before François died in 1865.

He left two sons: Jean-François, born in 1826 in the suburb of Gentilly, who became the father of Alexandre Millerand; and Alexandre-Severine. The latter established himself as a winebroker *(courtier-gourmet)*, and Millerand later credited the 'numerous and solid friendships' made by his uncle as an important reason for his election to the Chamber of Deputies in 1889 from the Bercy quarter of the XIIth *arrondissement,* the district he was to represent for thirty years.

In the milieu of retailers and craftsmen of the Sentier district, just
north of Les Halles, Jean-François met and lived with Amélie-Mélanie
Cahen, daughter of Cerf Cahen, a Jewish shopkeeper of Alsatian origin.
The couple dwelt in an apartment house on the boulevard Sebastopol and
was supported by the income of their small fabrics shop at 9, rue de la
Jussienne. On February 9, 1859 a son was born, Etienne-Alexandre. The
boy was baptized the following year and made legitimate by the marriage
of his parents on April 11, 1861.[2] At that time Amélie-Mélanie was converted to Catholicism. There soon followed two daughters, Amélie, who
ultimately married an architect named François Bourgin, and who, except
for occasional visits, spent the remainder of her life in Brittany; and
Marthe, whose death as a child came as a shock to her ten- or eleven-
year-old brother. He carried her photograph with him throughout his
life and was to name his younger daughter after her.

The son was much influenced by his father, although the early course
of events was shaped by the mother. His short beard, rimless eye glasses
and black frock-coat gave Jean-François a scholarly appearance. He was
one of those men, Millerand later wrote, whose lives are spent at a trade
in which little pride was taken but 'who worked in shadow and in silence
to enlighten himself'.[3] He had definite convictions stamping him as republican and agnostic but, aside from sharing them with his son, kept
his views largely to himself. The baptism of his children and conversion
of his wife presented only an apparent contradiction, for opinion and
ceremony were then more widely separated. Baptism invariably facilitated things, while conversion served to quiet doubtful in-laws. Millerand
remembered him as 'the most tender and surest of counsellors for my
sister and me'. He recalled clearly the spring day in 1870 when his father took him to the small lycée at Vanves, later the lycée Michelet. At
a newsstand in the Gare Montparnasse they read the account of Pierre
Bonaparte's acquittal of criminal charges by the High Court of Blois. The
Bonapartist prince in a fit of rage had murdered a staff member of the
radical newspaper, *La Marseillaise,* and, for exasperated opponents of
the regime, the *affaire* shrivelled the already-waning prestige of the Second Empire. The elder Millerand expressed proper republican indignation at the apparent denial of justice under the Empire, and the incident left a vivid impression on the son.[4]

Amélie Cahen was short and stout with hair kept tightly pinned. The
severe appearance matched her ambition for her son and her determination to provide him with the best education available to her means. Years
later, members of the family recall, when the son became a minister, she
said with pride: 'My work, my intelligence'. The interests of Jean-François helped shape his choice of career; Millerand's ability to work hard

and steadily came from his mother. Millerand's younger contemporary, Georges Mandel, had a strikingly similar background. His mother has been described as 'one of those women, so many then, of the Jewish bourgeoisie of Paris who sought to make her home comfortable, who consecrated themselves day and night to their children' and whose ambition it was to advance them in social rank.[5]

That the family was close and its members concerned with each other's welfare was demonstrated during the Franco-Prussian War, and particularly during the hardships endured in the siege of Paris and the Commune. Early in August 1870, Jean-François sent his wife and children to spend the summer near Dinard in Brittany, then a village and not today's resort. He expected to join them shortly, but the siege was to keep them apart until the following February. For the next six months letters were exchanged almost daily. Young Alexandre and his sister usually wrote on the last page of the mother's letters, which were precise and detailed. Those of Jean-François, his brother, Alexandre-Severine, and Amélie's sister, Valérie, were later despatched by balloon. They described the worsening military situation and general uncertainty of the news. Prices were rising steadily. Food supplies were being stocked in anticipation of a siege, expected to last 'one or two months'.[6]

Play was interrupted by excursions through the surrounding countryside. Alexandre carefully reported his activities, making observations and criticisms of neighborhood chateaux and churches. However, the boy devoted two hours every day to schoolwork, at the insistence, we may assume, of his mother. At one point his sister had to reassure a worried Jean-François that he was not working too hard. On September 2 Valérie sent the first news of the imminent proclamation of the Republic. She stressed the calm with which statues and emblems of the Empire were pulled down, but with 'smiling faces everywhere in sight'. Millerand's chief memory of the period was that of the poster he read containing Gambetta's proclamation of the new Third Republic. He said that 'the stirring words: Français, élevez vos âmes et vos résolutions à la hauteur des effroyables perils qui fondent sur la patrie... shattered the image of a conquered and harassed France; [they] enflamed his imagination, and solidified [his] republican faith'.[7] With the Prussians expected in Paris at any moment, her worried family begged a hesitant Amélie not to return and warned that the flow of mail would most certainly be cut. For the sake of her children she agreed. Jean-François was pressed into the 6th Company, 11th Battalion of the National Guard, but repeatedly assured his wife that he was not 'exposed on the ramparts'. On September 16 he promised his son that he 'loves him too well to be imprudent', but that he would do his duty. 'The rest', he said, 'is not within our power', and there was no need to fear things one could not avoid. A letter written four days later intimated it would be the last because the city was virtually isolated and its suburbs deserted. His tone, however, was generally cheerful, reassuring his family that he lacked nothing and that his health was good.

In Dinard, Alexandre completed his vacation work and wished to return to school. By the end of the month he was attending classes, with pleasure according to his mother, but fretting that the village school was inadequate, that work was being repeated and time wasted. He was also 'very disturbed', according to Amélie's letter of September 26, on reading the Prussian conditions for an armistice. The family was heartened, spiritually and materially, when letters leaving Paris, however irregularly, by balloon began to arrive, and when Jean-François' business partner, Brazier, in Elbeuf for the duration, replenished Amélie's depleted finances. Alexandre worked throughout the winter – school in the afternoon with local children and a handful of other young Parisians and, because a teacher had been found, Latin and Greek at home in the morning. He followed the war news closely. The announcement of Gambetta's arrival at Tours cheered him, but notices of defeats followed each other, and on December 5 he was saddened to learn of the evacuation of Orléans.

Letters were written, if not delivered, every day. The father regretted that he could not play with his children and urged them to care for their mother until their ordeal should end. On December 23 he expressed sympathy for 'our poor France' and said: 'Our revenge, unfortunately, will be only too legitimate.' He described the cold winter and the regularity of the Prussian bombardment, by January coming once at mid-day and again at night, and the first threats and rumors of impending revolution. Then, by the beginning of February news came of the armistice and its terms. Jean-François received permission to go to Dinard and bring his family back to Paris. According to the *laisser-passer* issued February 4, he gave his profession as that of *négociant,* his age as forty-four and residence as 147, boulevard Saint-Michel.

The family thus reassembled at Paris almost coincident with the outbreak of the Commune. Their fifth-floor apartment was near the dance hall Bal Bullier, frequented by Latin Quarter youth, and Alexandre was placed as a day-student *(externe, en septième)* in the nearby lycée of Louis-le-Grand. There he met Maurice Paléologue, who after long service at the Quai d'Orsay would be asked by Millerand to serve as Secretary-General of the Ministry of Foreign Affairs in 1920. One event at Louis-le-Grand stood out. The young chaplain of the nearby Saint Geneviève church, the future Cardinal Lavigerie, was asked to lead a communion service. He greatly impressed the young Millerand with his eloquence, and the latter credited him with his 'beginning in the art of oratory'.[8]

The faith which had been so 'naive and sincere' 'evaporated' on the day he 'devoured' Renan's *Vie de Jésus*. The exposure to Renan appeared as powerful justification of his father's views and dramatically ended all spiritual involvement. If Millerand continued regularly to take a first prize at catechism, the two presiding priests 'held no illusions about the solidity of [his] religious convictions'.[9] When he married, the ceremony was a civil one, and none of his children was baptized. Although, because of his wife's influence, he was to drop his early hostility toward the church, even pleasing her with a religious marriage ceremony late in life, he would die as he had lived, an agnostic.

The Paris Commune of 1871 interrupted Millerand's schooling and provided several striking images: Jean-François constrained from helping to erect a barricade; a hunted Communard seeking shelter in the family shop; a stray bullet imbedded in the apartment wall.

His education was resumed in October, briefly at the lycée at Vanves, then at the lycée Henry IV. There is no evidence that Millerand's tuition was subsidized by a *bourse,* or scholarship. But even a modestly endowed family could meet education expenses for secondary – and higher – education in an age still foreign to inflation. If intended for a single son, then by budgeting carefully and sacrificing elsewhere, the family that so chose could invest in his education. For little over a thousand francs before the turn of the century a single man was able to live, in a constrained fashion but with all costs covered, for a year in Paris.[10] This was the decision doubtless taken by the Millerands, very much aware that the *bachelier ès lettres,* or '*bachot*', was then, as now, the necessary point of departure for any significant career or social position.

These school years were far from happy. The regimen was oppressive in terms of hours and labor, with the classics heavily stressed. Still, this basic and prolonged exposure to them was that experienced by generations of politicians and other professional men, and Millerand was probably prepared for both content and discipline. Convinced that full-time attendance would result in greater accomplishment and better grades for her son, Amélie insisted that he board – though not sleep – there as well. In describing his own warm home life, and recalling that his happiest years were those at the lycée, Albert Guerard rendered this account of the boarders at about the same period: 'Those who were to be pitied were the full boarders *(internes)*. Fortunately they were few; boys without a home in Paris, or whose home was no fit place for them. With the callousness of adolescence, we gave no thought to their loneliness and secret tragedies. They were derelicts, 'interned', incarcerated, and we took it for granted that they had deserved their fate. In return they protected themselves with an armor of rudeness. In six years I do not believe I exchanged one friendly word with an *interne*.'[11] As a day boarder, this was largely the pattern of Millerand's school life for most of the 1870s. The self-discipline and ability to labor methodically must only have intensified. In addition to the burdened curriculum prescribed, Millerand took a year of unrequired basic mathematics 'to satisfy the wishes of his parents', who had the Polytechnique and a career in engineering in mind as an alternative. He was apparently wholly unsuited for it and later wrote that, although he passed the written examination for the *'bachot'* in science, he 'happily' failed the oral.

Millerand's one reference to his personal life during this period was that he viewed his departure from the lycée as a 'deliverance'.[12] The fellow students mentioned were Gaston Bethune, who became a reputed water colorist, Maurice de Ferraudy, later of the Comédie française, and one or two others. Characteristically, Millerand spoke more of his teachers, expressing gratitude toward G. Dumas, his *'maître'* at Vanves, Reaume, who admitted him at Henry IV, and Zevort and Lavisse, who taught him history.

Rare opportunities for relief and diversion came during the spring and summer vacations. Alexandre spent several of them in the old farmhouse owned by Alexandre-Severine in the village of Coiffey-le-Bas, about forty-five kilometers north of Roche. The quiet and rural countryside provided a pleasant contrast to the teeming Paris he knew. The boy came with his books and spent long hours reading on the cracked terrace behind the house, one giving way to a brambled garden and then to tiny fields and pastures.[13]

Millerand's early interest in politics showed no signs of diminishing, but he appreciated the problems of entering public life without funds or wellplaced friends. Law, then as now, appeared as an opening wedge, and he decided on the Faculty of Law at the University of Paris. He began his studies, found a friend in Raymond Poincaré, a year younger in age, and viewed his new life as an 'enchantment'. Then, because he had passed his twentieth birthday, he interrupted them to complete a year of required military service. In November 1879, he again found himself in Brittany; at the *caserne* of the 48th Infantry Regiment at Guingamp. Unlike many degree-holding contemporaries, Millerand experienced little diffculty in adjusting to military life and welcomed the change from the repressive lycées.

The lengthy and frequent correspondence between Millerand and his family during this year reinforces the observation previously made. He wrote every other day, some letters several pages in length, and every other day a member of his family replied.[14] Usually it was his mother, and Amélie's unswerving devotion to her son was again revealed. She wrote November 8, the day she had seen him off; by the 19th, despite her son's reluctance, she was asking when she could visit. She eventually spent the last week of February 1880 in Guingamp, this in addition to two visits by Jean-François in June and September, one or two by his sister and a week's leave spent at home. The father was more reluctant to display his feelings and sought to conceal them behind a moralizing tone, causing Alexandre to complain lightly. In turn, he sent detailed descriptions of his routine, including, at his mother's explicit request, the prices charged recruits at the canteen. Several letters from Poincaré suggest that the two, in the short time they had known each other at the Faculté de droit, had grown close. The latter reported taking first place in an examination, a grandmother's death, the completion of a *thèse* and a hope that he would see Millerand at Easter.[15] Nor did the Millerands fail to remind the young soldier of their ambitions for him; a letter of May 9,1880, carried a description of an acquaintance's success in obtaining a doctorate.

In spite of the Guingamp *ambiance,* 'a small provincial village, full of convents and very quiet', and a commanding offcer 'skeptical of lycée students', Millerand soon acclimated. He found a second home in the area, that provided by the Bourgin family, either friends of his parents or distant relations. It was one of the Bourgin sons who became his brother-in-law. Millerand complained of being kept poorly informed by the local newspaper. On June 23rd, hearing of Gambetta's speech demanding an amnesty for Communards, he asked for a copy of the parliamentary text. A speech by President Grévy pleased him, he wrote July 16, except for the passage describing the army as the best school in which to build a strong citizenry. Millerand performed well in his duties. He found his tests undemanding, and working with accustomed diligence won the rank of corporal May 10, that of sergeant, November 5. He later took pride in his stripes and came to value the experience 'with people of all origins and beliefs' as 'an apprenticeship to public life'.[16]

2. The practice of law was described as 'distinguishing' and 'remunerative' and as an 'entrance to almost all elected positions, with the legislature practically its domain'. The contemporary handbook of the professions listing these attractions also stressed the high attrition rate of students, pointing out the need for 'resources and relations'. With surprising detail the same source estimated that the three years required for the *licence en droit* would cost 1,544 francs for tuition, fees and books.[17] Because he lived with his family, Millerand was spared the

costs of room and board. The Paris Faculty of Law, enlarged in 1878, occupied its present location in the triangle between the Place du Panthéon, the rue Soufflot and the rue Saint-Jacques and rue Cujas in the Latin Quarter. Millerand commuted from Passy, in the extreme western part of the city.

As was the case with numerous other politicians of the Third Republic, the legal training he received contributed greatly to the development of his approach and style. He studied Roman Law for two years, the Civil Code for three and, for briefer periods of time, criminal, commercial and administrative law. Required courses in procedure, 'political economy' (whose introduction into law schools besides that of Paris pointed to the reforming activity of the Third Republic) and the general history of French and international law completed the curriculum in the 1880s.[18]

Thus, in spite of some attempts at reform by the July Monarchy and Second Republic, legal studies in France were still regulated by Revolutionary and Napoleonic tradition. The Civil Code was viewed as a 'definitive monument', its articles held essentially as theorems; and it was the task – basically a deductive one – of the law student to learn to interpret it, to show how it related to cases under consideration and to derive the necessary consequences. The authors of the Code had intended that it should be viewed in the light of its own provisions and definitions. An early commentator, Bugnet, had said: 'I know nothing of civil law; I only teach the *Code Napoléon*.' Professors saw their role as such, and students learned by heart considerable portions of this 'intangible expression of justice' in order to find the right law for a particular problem. Examinations were designed to encourage and perpetuate this approach. An observer noted that whereas the English [or American] lawyer, seeking to interpret a legal principle, first looks for its precedent, the French lawyer first looks for its 'policy' and concluded that an important consequence of this difference of attitude was that of tending to smooth away, instead of fostering exceptions to general rules.[19]

Millerand made no reference in his *Mémoires* to the curriculum. However, if the example of other lawyer-politicians so trained is at all useful, it is likely that few of his teachers made much of an impact. They doubtless imparted a thorough knowledge of the law but also handed down an excessive concern for particulars and helped fashion a legal mentality characterized by a precise and cold outlook, as much in evidence at the Palais Bourbon as at the Palais de Justice. Lawyer-politicians like Waldeck-Rousseau, Poincaré and Millerand, trained during the last years of the Second Empire or early in the Third Republic, differed from their predecessors of a generation or two before. Lawyers like Armand Dufaure and Bethmont had received a similar education and had gone on to brilliant careers. However, they came from prestigious bourgeois families and possessed sufficient leisure and wealth to cultivate themselves and enjoy politics as a favorite pastime. In the courtroom they preferred to defend motives and stress causes. The facts, they presumed, were known; no great precision in argumentation was required. Lacking resources and already more attuned to the world of business, their successors built upon their training to emphasize financial detail and tight argumentation. Their *plaidoirie,* or summation, was carefully prepared in advance: it was no longer a question of pleasing a jury or denouncing a government but of percentages gained or lost. Cold and mechanical in delivery, devoid of sentiment, Waldeck-Rousseau was setting the tone for a generation of lawyers. As legislators they tended to regard an institution as founded, or a reform accomplished, when inscribed in a rigorous text.[20]

In addition to his courses, Millerand attended occasional *conférences* with fellow students to discuss various legal questions in simulated courtroom conditions. This exposure was intended to aid in the development of ideas and further the art of improvisation. He found himself inadequate in public speaking and, dissatisfied with what instruction there was available, sought outside help. He began to study rules of rhetoric, 'the indispensable instrument in the battles of public life', and with a small group of friends, including Poincaré, attended a course in diction offered by Talbot, a member of the Comédie française.

With several students from the various schools, Millerand frequented the Pension Laveur, on the rue Serpente, a Latin Quarter restaurant celebrated for the generosity of its credit to non-affluent students. Upon their eventual receipt of clients, patients or government offices, they repaid the sums previously borrowed. Millerand, with the two Poincarés, Raymond and Henri, Gabriel Hanotaux and others, sat at large tables, and they argued endlessly politics, philosophy and religion . There is evidence of real and warm friendliness with Raymond Poincaré. They occasionally went out together, *tutoied* and called each other *maître.* Their intimacy, as extensive as was possible for two such essentially shy and withdrawn people, encouraged confidences. Poincaré had written to Millerand at Guingamp to describe his disappointingly slow progress in an *affaire de coeur* then underway and to ask for suggestions. He dedicated occasional poems to Millerand.[21]

The latter looked capable of offering advice on such matters. A photograph shows him dressed in the high-buttoned coat of the period, hair cut short, slight mustache and already wearing a pince-nez. The characteristics later to distinguish him were present. Even so, the difference between the slender student and the massive President of the Republic was remarkable. There is no evidence, however, to suggest that he was then, or ever would be, much of a ladies' man. In his younger years, opportunities, at least, were rare; he lived with his parents and worked much too hard. Later, unlike many political contemporaries, Millerand's private life would also be very much centered in his home.

As the nature of the discussions at the Pension Laveur suggest, Millerand did not limit his reading to his studies. Lessons learned in and out of the Faculty were to serve as the 'solid base' for the political career of which he 'never ceased to dream'. Books were to supply him with general ideas of 'undeniable validity'. A technique of critical examination, one that could meet the strictest demands, was being forged. Diverting but secondary issues would be stopped by an inflexible barrier: – 'this is not the question'. He described how he would walk, book in hand, along the paths of the Bois de Boulogne and 'submit the conceptions of his authors to severe critical examination'. John Stuart Mill and Herbert Spencer were at first his favorites. From the standpoint of content, economic as well as political liberalism initially appeared most appealing.[22]

The only surviving source yielding an account of Millerand's first political views is a draft of a talk given to a local study group during the election campaign of 1881. Taking issue with his idol, Gambetta, whose speech of March 20 held the state responsible for providing guarantees against 'sickness, misery, and unemployment', the speaker held that progress no longer consisted of daily increases of state regulation. Citing his authorities, who included the liberal economist Bastiat, he said that greatest happiness is best ensured by heightening individual responsibility. Growing reliance on government and the dream of nine-tenths of the French to enter government service evoked the possibility of a 'mandarinized' France. The Republic was to prevent the exaggeration of state powers and so protect the individual from them. The twenty-two-year-old speaker reviewed Mill's arguments defending the free flow of opinion and cited Spencer to justify restraints on government intervention. A growing dependence on government could only produce a 'less virile' citizenry. He denounced Bismarckian Germany for its essays in social legislation and said there were too many Bismarcks in France.[23]

The lecture lacked originality and style, but certain characteristics in format and – despite its anti-statist message – in content were to persist. Millerand had stated his objectives at the outset of a speech. He had rejected the tendency of a political party to stifle dissenting opinion within its ranks. Concomitantly, he had urged political independence in order to resist these pressures and so enable one to pursue his ideas. As an alternative to state assurances of working-class security, Millerand pointed to the latter's collective efforts and to profit-sharing, the attainment of which required full liberty of association. Trade union solidarity and a hazy corporatism were solutions he would return to many times.

There is little evidence to reveal why Millerand soon revised this laissez-faire outlook. His memoirs suggested chiefly intellectual reasons, an awareness of the 'excesses' of economic liberalism, with its possibly 'inhuman consequences'. In an interview given years later he told of the early influence exerted by the writings of Bastiat, who in 1848 had fought socialism as ardently as he had previously fought protectionism. Millerand claimed that he saw the consequences of extreme individualism in an old class-conscious society and so was made aware of the necessity of a 'reparative' justice.[24] Still, there is no sign he was concerned with anything resembling the concept of the class struggle before his second term in the Chamber of Deputies, and his remarks here must be regarded with caution. It is more than likely that, as so often in his life, it was the presence of external events – in this case courtroom defenses of workers and radicals and association with others who defended them, in newspaper offices and on the Paris Municipal Council – that is, new situations and changed conditions rather than isolated intellectual processes, that produced changes in ideas and attitudes. For those of a strongly bourgeois background, it is a basic sense of reality and a pragmatic outlook that most often explain changes of mind. During his school years and professional training Millerand doubtless lacked any developed and consistent view of society.

There were indications that he was already planning, certainly considering, his political career. Poincaré had already begun to contribute to a Paris newspaper. He complained to Millerand in November 1881, however, that he was unable to write freely and merely 'copied and put together stupid sentences'. Nevertheless impressed, his friend asked him to inquire into the possibility of finding him a place on the staff. Poincaré replied that Millerand exaggerated his influence and that, in any case, the owners did not manage the paper.[25]

3. Millerand was introduced to the world of politics and journalism – the two were then almost wholly synonomous – when Georges Laguerre took an interest in him. Laguerre was only a year older and appeared destined for a brilliant career. A Radical lawyer who specialized in defending socialists and editor of the legal column in Georges Clemenceau's newspaper, *La Justice,* he was to be elected to the Chamber of Deputies in 1883 at the age of twenty-five and sat at the extreme left. He was regarded by his admirers as 'the prince' of the younger opposition both at the Palais Bourbon and Palais de Justice.[26]

Hardly had he finished his studies, in May of 1881, when Millerand sought out other young people interested in politics. One bridge between the two 'palais' was 'la Conférence Molé', an informal discussion group of lawyers and politicians in which Laguerre was prominent. All shades of republican opinion were represented; besides Laguerre, Millerand met Joseph-Paul Revoil, later the diplomat who served with distinction as Governor-General of Algeria in 1901–1903.

The following year Millerand made his first acquaintance with the clientele he was largely to represent for the next two decades. During the summer of 1882 there were spasmodic outbreaks of violence in the mining district of Montceau-les-Mines (Department of the Puy-de-Dôme) in the Midi. Secret societies *(bandes noires),* striking out at what they regarded as the harsh rule of the great mining companies, committed acts of sabotage, dynamited churches thought to be siding with the companies and threatened potential witnesses. Wholesale arrests were made, and anarchist and socialist doctrine – the two being totally confused – was considered the source of the trouble. Laguerre was named chief attorney for the defense, and he selected Millerand to assist him.

The two lawyers were no older than most of their twenty-some-odd clients. Laguerre appears to have done most of the questioning, Millerand's contribution consisting of a long summary on behalf of the accused. An observer recalled the latter as black-robed, determined and severe in expression. He spoke in a toneless voice without gestures or style, in sharp contrast to the elegant Laguerre, who moved continually between jury and spectators. The name of Montceau's anarchist society, 'l'Avenir de Santa-Maria', was often repeated; Laguerre chanted it in Italian, while Millerand hammered it out like a blacksmith. Millerand advised the jury to ignore any 'socialist' theories that may have prompted the defendants' actions and to concentrate instead on the evidence available. The paramount question was whether a particular defendant committed an act recognized by law as constituting a crime. He methodically reviewed each case and, while acknowledging some degree of guilt, concluded that the social order had not been endangered and asked equal justice for all. The solidity and clarity of the argument made a favorable impression on legal circles and gave its author a certain repute. The case was the first of several in which he defended strikers, socialists or both. At Lille, in June of 1884, he successfully defended the socialist, Emile Basly, held on defamation charges. Strikers at Carmaux, Decazeville and Vierzon were to be represented by Millerand during the next few years. A decade later he reviewed the lesson first learned at Montceau; the trial had demonstrated how an employer could 'yoke his workers with servitude and moral slavery'. It also revealed how the government, when so inclined, might successfully intervene to protect those same workers.[27]

Circumstances were thus working to incline Millerand toward the left. He later wrote that 'the opposition strongly seduced my spirit of contradiction' as well as satisfying 'the ideas about political liberty and economic intervention that had won me over'. Radical-Socialists then fought the opportunism of Ferry-led moderate republicans. Millerand convinced himself, naively he admitted, that the latter's regime of favoritism would come to an end once Clemenceau and the Radicals won power.[28] In any case, when Laguerre introduced him to Clemenceau and invited him to contribute to his legal column in *La Justice,* Millerand welcomed the opportunity. When Laguerre was elected to Parliament and decided to leave the staff, Millerand replaced him. Headed, 'Journal du Palais', the column contained descriptions of the more interesting cases heard. During the two years he wrote it, Millerand displayed a growing awareness of social problems but expressed few political opinions. He wrote no front page articles until 1885, when, after his election to the Chamber, he became a political editor.

4. Association with Laguerre broadened Millerand's range of contacts in politics, particularly with men on the left. His early career may be seen as a series of identifications with and attachments to older politicians; and by seeking to learn from them, he easily accepted a subordinate role of apprentice or protégé. This was demonstrated in part by brief acquaintanceships with Jules Roche and Henri Rochefort, more importantly with Jehan de Bouteiller and Georges Clemenceau and ultimately with the man whose example would serve as a guiding force for the remainder of his life, René Waldeck-Rousseau. Whether because of ambition or independence, or a combination of the two, Millerand was able to detach himself from one self-chosen mentor and move on to another. Until the death of Waldeck-Rousseau, he would continue to relate to figures of authority, and this capacity for detachment proved an aid in upward mobility.[29]

It was through Rochefort, archcritic both of the Empire of Louis Napoleon and the Republic of Adolphe Thiers, that Millerand met his first real patron and was in turn introduced to practical politics and the woman he later married. The deputy of the XVIth *arrondissement* in Paris, a M. Marmottan, had resigned, and Jehan de Bouteiller, the President of the city's Municipal Council and member of its group for communal autonomy, was one of three candidates seeking to replace him. The Radical-Liberal committee sponsoring De Bouteiller looked for a young lawyer to act as his secretary. Rochefort recommended Millerand, and the committee approved his choice.[30]

Following a campaign rally, where he gave his first political speech,

Millerand went to De Bouteiller's home on the rue de la Tour. Here he met his future wife, Jeanne le Vayer, recalled as a 'most delightful girl' and 'highly cultivated' but, because of family reverses, by no means wealthy. At the time she was working as a social assistant *(dame visiteur)*. There is no available photograph, but doubtless she was tall and attractive, slender in her youth, and found wholly appealing by the young Millerand. According to the *Mémoires,* however, his 'absorption' by politics caused him to take no further notice of her, and it was only by 'astonishing fortune' that fifteen years later he again found and married Mademoiselle le Vayer.[31] This rendition differs from the verbal account offered by two of Millerand's children, Jacques and Alice. For them it was a combination of natural timidity, lack of funds – strikers not being the most affluent of clients – and a wish first to become established that caused him intentionally to wait. There also appears to have been some objections on the part of Amélie, who, while finding no fault with the girl's background, preferred that her son marry greater wealth.

The following year, with De Bouteiller's help, Millerand successfully ran for the Paris Municipal Council on a Radical program. He represented the Muette district of the XVIth *arrondissement.* The election had been scheduled for January 1884 but, to make that in Paris coincide with other municipalities, the Minister of Interior in the Ferry cabinet, Waldeck-Rousseau, had it postponed to May. Millerand thus found himself eligible, having attained the minimum age limit of twenty-five the preceding February.

He had to meet some campaign expenses, but they were hardly exorbitant. Printers' bills, including stationery, flyers and posters, as well as the costs of distribution, amounted to less than 750 francs. On two or three occasions he rented a theatre for speeches, the single greatest expense of which was the lighting, perhaps a total of another 500 or 600 francs. At each of these rallies Millerand hired firemen from a neighboring batallion to act as doormen and ushers, usually an officer, a corporal and two men, all four costing six or seven francs for the evening. There also had been 'contributions' to newspapers; *La Lanterne* had received 4,700 francs and *L'Intransigeant* 1000 francs; but the overall cost of the campaign could not have exceeded a few thousand francs. He had received authorization from the Prefecture of Police to establish a campaign organization, the Cercle républicaine radical libéral of the XVIth *arrondissement,* naming himself secretary.[32]

Millerand credited his small (ninety-vote) majority to the heavy support of workers' districts around the Passy cemetery and to the split of the conservative vote in the wealthier sections of the constituency. He pointed to working-class support as having contributed greatly to his formation in political life and said that he continued 'to find more generosity, disinterest, and devotion to an ideal among those less favored by nature'. But his victory was due less to any working-class idealism than to an unemployment crisis in 1883–84, regarded as especially severe and held responsible for a number of Radical victories, as well as for increased anarchist propaganda.[33]

The years 1881–83, part of a world-wide economic depression, were especially bad in Paris. The building trades were hurt in 1883, and with carpenters, masons, and other construction workers numbering 80,000, unemployment in the city was widespread, sometimes reaching ten percent. Numerous strikes and a wholly inadequate relief system only exacerbated working-class discontent. In March 1883 the Bourse dropped suddenly. Failing to appreciate the movement of larger economic forces and of a society in transition, the government attributed the crisis to short-run speculation. Aware, however, that their unemployment was not of the workers' own making, and to encourage responsible working-class leadership, Waldeck-Rousseau intervened in the Senate to help assure the enactment in 1884 of a law establishing the legality of trade unions, outlawed since 1792.[34]

5. Legislation enacted on June 16, 1859, had enabled the municipality of Paris to annex several outlying communes and to reorganize the newly enlarged city into twenty *arrondissements*. Each was divided into four *quartiers,* and the law of April 14, 1871 provided that the city's Municipal Council was to consist of eighty members, one from each *quartier*. Together with those from the suburbs of Saint-Denis and Sceaux, the councillors were at the same time members of the General Council of the Seine Department. Because they also comprised part of the electoral college for the French Senate, Millerand was called on to participate in senatorial elections shortly after his victory. The experience brought him side by side with deputies of the Department, also Senate electors, and strengthened his determination to regard the Council as a stepping stone to the Chamber.[35]

The new Council contained two acknowledged socialists, the Blanquist and former minister in the Paris Commune, Edouard Vaillant, and an engraver named Chabert. In keeping with the tradition of the Commune, it leaned toward the left and the previous April had heard for the first time the suggestion to subsidize striking workers. Of the sixty-eight republicans elected in 1884, forty-five were Radicals, or independents barely distinguishable from them. Others, not so icluded, held definite anticlerical opinions. Vaillant's election had been hailed by the ex-Communard, Jules Vallès, in *Le Cri du Peuple,* as a 'brilliant triumph of socialism in the Père Lachaise quarter... because of the entry into the Hôtel de Ville of a former member of the Commune who stood for revolution'. A column subsequently appeared in a leading socialist monthly, *La Revue socialiste,* under the heading, 'Socialism in the Municipal Council'. There such proposals as Vaillant's call for a maximum eight-hour working day on city projects, a council labor committee and rent-control legislation were applauded and discussed.[36]

The Council was much influenced by the Commune-inspired movement for administrative decentralization. Since the disappearance of the original Revolutionary commune after Robespierre's fall, executive power over the city remained in the hands of the Prefect of the Seine Department and, consequently, the Minister of Interior. Any small town in France thus enjoyed more independence, and Communard demands in 1871 for municipal autonomy drew a sympathetic response. Since 1875, according to Prefecture of Police reports and the memoirs of the Prefect, an already tense situation had worsened. Led by the Moderate Yves Guyot, most councillors demanded the establishment of a central mayor and the subordination of the Prefect of Police to city hall. They stiffened these demands during the city's economic crisis in 1883, and Waldeck-Rousseau considered removing the few checks on the Prefect still held by the Council, in the minister's view led by extremists.[37] The Radical press, contemptuous of the 'Republic of Peasants', justifiably accused the government of seeking rural votes to compensate for the defection of Paris and other large cities. The degree to which these socialist and autonomous ideas influenced Millerand remains a matter of conjecture, but it was as a member of the Municipal Council of 1884–85 that he received first-hand exposure to them.

Millerand did not speak formally during his first few months as councillor. He supported various administrative proposals such as Stephen Pichon's to institute a committee authorized to compile a summary of the campaign promises made by successful candidates. More realistic was his support of a general amnesty for those having been convicted of political crimes. He became a member of the Council's public assistance committee, and as his first public act drafted a bill calling for the purchase by the city of a strip of land near the rue Molitor.[38] Subsequent acts reflected one or both of the themes with which Millerand was becoming concerned, anticlericalism and social legislation. On July 28, 1884, during discussion of a bill to improve conditions in a municipal home for the aged, Millerand recommended that wherever possible religious personnel be replaced by laymen. He objected particularly to the number of religious objects, crucifixes and statuettes found in a lay institution and in the name of 'liberty of conscience' asked for their removal and replacement with 'republican equivalents'.[39]

In his first major speech, on November 13, he opposed the reintroduction of a tax on bread as a mere expedient and urged the Council to study instead the prospect of municipal bakeries. An example had already been set in Angoulême, and Paris 'could not afford to remain indifferent to the destinies of her less fortunate citizens'. However, Millerand recommended a step-by-step policy. Although the municipality needed to intervene, it was to do so only by degrees in order to ensure some definite gain. 'We are, in fact', he said, 'in an era where whoever holds a parcel of power or influence, as minute as it may be, has an imperative duty to do everything possible to prepare by practical means, by detailed solutions, within the sphere of his powers, the solution to social questions.'[40] Hence a gradual and piecemeal approach to the solution of social problems appeared at the very outset of his career.

On December 3 he supported Vaillant's resolution denouncing the police brutality both men maintained had been shown at a meeting of jobless workers. Millerand claimed that the threats made, used by the police to justify their intervention, was the work of *agents provocateurs*. This smacked of imperial tyranny but was understandable; it was similar to the government's need to bribe the press. Amidst stirrings and murmurings from the right, he urged the Council to pass a resolution reminding the police of its responsibility to the public. The previous July, along with fifteen other councillors, he had petitioned for the establishment of a labor exchange *(bourse du travail)* in Paris. It would provide workers with placement services, meeting halls and statistics relevant to their working conditions.[41]

Millerand demonstrated his commitment to deliberate and detailed tactics most strikingly during the Council's annual debate on the budget of the Prefecture of Police. Long resentful of what it viewed as the chief symptom of unwarranted centralized authority in municipal affairs, the relevant committee, following tradition, demanded that the budget be rejected in its entirety. Millerand suggested that tradition be broken, that advantage be taken of improvements offered in the new budget, and thus separated himself from his Radical colleagues.

He admitted that the budget for 1885 failed to satisfy fully Radical demands but said that the ideal of a republicanized police force would not be realized by 'the wave of a magic wand'. The present budget, he argued, provided significant change and amelioration, the existence of which, while not to be exaggerated, was nevertheless incontestable. Progress was being made. 'We would not be statesmen if we did not take account of it. ... We are offered something, as little as it may be, let us take it'. He then listed the political and administrative reforms scheduled.[42]

To a protest that such compromise would appear ignoble, Millerand replied that it was more than a question of a politician taking a noble part; it was also necessary that he consider and weigh the consequences of his decisions. That solution judged most desirable, not from the point of view of the legislator or his particular interests but for the collective interests of those he represented, was correct. Millerand denied he was compromising a principle in as much as autonomists had previously gone on record as willing to vote for a modified budget. Rejection was therefore a question of tactics imposed by circumstances, and, when circumstances change, tactics must vary as well in order for principles to be realized. For 'we are not doctrinaires discussing a thesis. We are representatives of the people with its interests to defend, and when shown that without touching a principle, without breaking a promise, we can give it some satisfaction, we must not hesitate'. The right thus found itself in agreement with Millerand and gave him its support. But the Radical majority persisted in its refusal and voted to transfer the police budget to municipal control. As anticipated, the vote was annulled by ministerial decree.

During the council's second session and as a member of the committee concerned, Millerand dealt mainly with educational problems. He especially protested against the rigorous and classical regime demanded of lycée students. One of his last acts was a measure creating a course in the history of the French Revolution at the University of Paris. Largely a political response to Radical complaints that the Revolution had been attacked in recent years by reactionaries and pedants, the proposal was approved by the Minister of Education.[43] The historian, Alphonse Aulard, was selected to hold the first chair.

With the notable exception described above, Millerand supported the Radical program, and his articles in *La Justice,* by now political in content and on page one, reflected Radical hostility toward clericalism and colonialism. That he held no socialist views at this time was best demonstrated by his rejection of certain measures designed to enlarge the sphere of the municipality's economic activity. In June of 1885, for example, he voted with the majority against Vaillant's proposal to have the city expropriate the private telephone networks.[44] He showed concern, moreover, for the general health of the local business community. Millerand actively participated in a group of councillors seeking a municipal subsidy for the Paris Chamber of Commerce to improve general business conditions. On an earlier occasion, in support of a merchandise mart, he had identified republicanism with municipal support for business. In aiding merchants, presumably like his father, the proposed market would alleviate the financial crisis, and Millerand objected to Vaillant's denunciation of the project as a tool of the great financial interests. He said that in order for society, and the workers who belonged to it, to benefit, overall production must increase.[45]

6. Millerand began to slip into the increasingly heavier schedule that proved so characteristic and created the impression of a *burro de travail*. While a councillor he completed his initiation into the organization of lawyers to which he would remain attached, the Ordre des avocats of the Paris Court, a group dating its origins at least to the time of Saint Louis. Membership allowed him to practice in the Paris Court of Appeals.[46] Every graduate was required to complete three years of probation before being entitled to defend clients at this court. The probationers, or *stagiaires,* were members of a body called the Conférence de l'Ordre des avocats and were required to attend its meetings, although in practice not all did. The Conférence originated after the French Revolution as a weekly study seminar. Its membership came to include only probationers, although their elders in the profession often attended its opening ceremony and other events. Millerand went to every session both as probationer and practicing lawyer and voted in every election. His love for the profession and for the independence it afforded, and his respect for its fraternal organization, only grew with time. Years later he was to be named a member of the Ordre's twelve- to fifteen-member governing body, the Conseil de l'Ordre des avocats, a post of high esteem. As a beginning lawyer Millerand described his acceptance by it: 'I was no longer alone. From that day I was part of an old illustrious corporation. The gates of the Palais de Justice were open to me.'[47]

Reflecting the competition that was so much a part of the French educational structure, the Conférence had its two to three hundred *stagiaires* vie for twelve secretaryships on the basis of their respective performances. The candidates were given hypothetical cases and told to defend or prosecute; during the course of a year all but twelve were eliminated. The procedure shed luster on the profession, and designation as secretary was regarded as a coveted honor and rewarded in prizes and prestige. The title ancien secrétaire de la Conférence assured its holder a splendid future, with election to the Order's Council a virtual certainty in fifteen or twenty years.[48] Millerand was immensely gratified to be named seventh secretary; first was Raymond Poincaré.

Sometime in the spring of 1883 he became a freemason. According to an observer's account of his reception, Millerand impressed his future brethren as an exceptionally radical young lawyer. Questioned during the initiation ceremony, alone and blindfolded, he unhesitatingly labelled the government as 'rotten'. This and similar replies aroused protests and head-shaking among the more moderate elements — the case was ultimately sent to the Grand Lodge and only decided by its litigation committee in a complicated ruling the following June. With the support of progressive groups he was admitted. However, freemasonry appears to have played no significant role in Millerand's life; it was then conventional for politically minded young men with progressive views to join the Order. This was more true of Radicals than socialists, and in the 1890s Millerand was suspended by his lodge for failure to pay dues.[49]

Despite a certain success and gradually increasing prominence in the Municipal Council, Millerand's ambitions lay in the Chamber of Deputies. As the general legislative elections of 1885 drew near, he decided to run and sought a constituency. In the company and under the auspices of Tony Revillon, a leading leftwing Radical deputy and journalist, he made a brief 'expedition' to the Midi. The trip convinced Millerand that, as a novice, he could not hope to win a provincial seat; and he selected instead the Seine Department, the electoral system having been changed from single-member constituencies to departmental-wide voting for 1885.[50] *Scrutin de liste* was the system under which Millerand went to the Chamber in 1885 and which he continued to support the remainder of his political life.

Millerand credited the Montceau trial as having helped him make a name for himself. He had also gotten exposure as a councillor and from his articles in *La Justice*. He received 90,000 votes on October 4 and attributed his 'unexpectedly' good showing to a number of speeches delivered in Paris and its suburbs. However, the total was insufficient to allow him to qualify for the run-off vote. Two months later he ran again in a by-election in the Department. The system of multiple candidacies then in effect required that a number of deputies elected in more than one department select one to represent, calling for complementary elections to fill the gaps thus created. On December 27, supported by the Radical press, Millerand was sent to the Chamber of Deputies on the second vote.[51] The following day he participated in the reelection of President Jules Grévy and on Tuesday, December 29, took his seat. He was twenty-six years old and had seen his ambition fulfilled.

2. The Radical years

...nous l'avons dit à plus d'une reprise. Nous n'avons point changé d'avis. Encore est-il sage de tirer le meilleur parti possible d'une situation même mauvaise.

MILLERAND, *La Justice,* March 16, 1886

The elections of 1885 had returned about sixty Radicals to the Chamber. Like other republicans, however, Millerand was shocked by the success of the monarchist opposition. Profiting from their newly found unity after the death of the Comte de Chambord, royalists were able to offer single lists in many departments. Millerand attributed the division among republicans and their several alternate lists to the dissent raised by Jules Ferry's aggressive colonial policy.[1] Some deputies supported the government's drive to expand French influence in Indochina; others, notably the Radicals, saw it as detrimental to France's European interests. This noisy but effective minority subscribed to the principles of the Revolution as set forth in 1789. However, while more 'moderate' republicans repudiated the egalitarian ideas and practices of 1793, Radicals, rallied under the leadership of Clemenceau, admired the Revolution as a 'bloc' and demanded its complete acceptance.[2]

By the time Millerand met him in 1882, Clemenceau had already played a part in the momentous events of his time. Now his well-timed interventions were upsetting Opportunist governments and establishing his reputation as *tombeur de ministeres.* He had founded *La Justice* in 1880 – taking the name of the newspaper run by the great Jacobin of the Commune, Delescluze – and would manage it until it ceased publication in 1893.[3] Millerand remained associated with Clemenceau until 1889, and we shall see that many of the views taken, as well as much of the style displayed, both as Radical and socialist paralleled those of *La Justice* in the 1880s. The seven years spent as journalist on Clemenceau's newspaper and as member of Clemenceau's party served as his apprenticeship in national politics.

1. Millerand was of course familiar with the recent Radical past and, specifically, with the political line of *La Justice*. In 1880 (and expanded the following year), Clemenceau presented his program at Marseilles. The political and civil reforms sought ranged from constitutional revision, meaning the elimination of the Senate and Presidency of the Republic and separation of church and state, to administrative decentralization and the abolition of capital punishment. Social and economic demands included a progressive income tax; the regulation of working hours and conditions along with the participation of labor in managerial decisions affecting these conditions; old-age and sickness insurance; and extension of *prud'homme* (local arbitration council) jurisdiction. The program also aimed at providing trade unions with a 'legal personality' to facilitate the conclusion of legally binding collective agreements and to assure greater security for union funds. It went so far as to ask for the nationalization of such 'alienated public property' as mines, canals and railroads. Clemenceau said he wanted 'to destroy the monarchical principle in all our institutions and to prepare for the great social transformation which will be the coronation of the French Revolution'. The term 'socialist' was added to the party name precisely to distinguish it from its more moderate ancestry.[4]

In London, Karl Marx hailed the Marseilles speech. It introduced, he said, 'something wonderful' into the Radical party, and he welcomed Clemenceau, along with Jules Guesde and Benoît Malon, as 'a leader of French socialism'. Clemenceau was described as 'the champion of socialism' by the movement's most prolific historian, until a handful of socialist deputies entered the Chamber in 1885.[5] Still, the Radical chief differed from most socialists, certainly from Marxists, in three important respects. He rejected their references to class struggle; he repudiated any recourse to revolutionary action and dictatorship of the proletariat; and he opposed collectivization as 'the organization of humanity into convents and casernes'. This last was a foremost demand in the platform of Guesde's Socialist Workers party.

In explicitly rejecting collectivization, Clemenceau had separated his party from that of Guesde, although he did not rule out the likelihood of mutual cooperation. His approach, furthermore, was reformist; he supported (political) change that would at once improve the condition of the working man. Concerned with that which he deemed realistic, Clemenceau maintained that goals were reached by 'successive conquests within the law', and he defended rebulican institutions as necessary requisites for social reforms. In a debate with Guesde, Charles Longuet, then on the staff of *La Justice* and Clemenceau's spokesman, suggested the possibility of significant social change under a bourgeois regime.

Guesde rejoined flatly that Radicals had pirated part of the socialist program only in order to improve their political standing with workers, more of whom were now voting, to weaken socialists at the polls and to impede growing class division. In 1882 he called on workers to dissociate themselves fully from 'all bourgeois factions', thus completing the break between himself and Clemenceau.[6] Throughout his socialist years Millerand would never subscribe to the separation demanded here by Guesde. But during these years neither would most socialists, including Guesde himself.

Radicals, then, indicated real concern for working-class interests. But they lacked any meaningful economic program, certainly one based on even the most general analysis of social and economic change. They envisaged solutions primarily in political terms and consequently directed efforts to reversing the Opportunist ministries that succeeded each other in dreary procession during the 1880s. Clemenceau had ended his Marseilles speech with the admission that the party's program did not get at the root of the problem.[7] Millerand's own economic program would be similarly criticized.

Conservative, or monarchist, support was required for one of the two opposing republican groups to defeat the other, and the tactics followed by the right reflected full awareness of its favored position. Both Radicals and Conservatives repudiated Opportunism and sought to alter the existing constitution, although in totally different ways. Both denounced Ferry's imperialism, which they said would divert French interests from their proper European sphere. The monarchist and Radical press – the latter in the best Jacobin tradition – went so far as to accuse Ferry of seeking an alliance with Germany. On September 22, 1884, *La Justice* called him 'Bismarck's protégé'; on the 29th it held that 'Ferry's colonial ventures left Bismarck master in Europe'. Millerand was especially critical; French overseas expansion distracted attention from Germany and the return of Alsace-Lorraine and diverted resources better engaged in the pursuit of social legislation. At a meeting of the Radical League of Paris, he moved that the organization 'condemn and censure any compromise with Germany'.[8] The blunt language may be taken as part of the Radical effort to bring down the Ferry ministry. Still, Millerand never lost sight of the defeat of 1871 and, we shall see, never belittled patriotic sentiment, either as a Radical or as a socialist.

Another belief instilled during these years and solidified as political truth centered on the advantages of political union. Although he sat with the Radicals surrounding Clemenceau, Millerand shared Jaurès' view that, if the right, given its tactical advantage, was not to become 'arbiter of the Republic', the need for republican unity was vital.[9] Throughout the following two legislatures he was to work for Radical reform and for accord between Radicals and other republicans – and to pursue consensus both as socialist and nationalist.

2. Millerand began to write political articles in 1885 and soon averaged four to seven a month. By 1888 and 1889, the last years of his association with the staff, his monthly output had increased to about ten. The articles resembled his speeches: clear, terse, sometimes ironic, almost always logical. Clemenceau's editor-in-chief was Camille Pelletan, whose radical outlook so perfectly matched his own. The latter's capacity for work was prodigious; besides administrative duties he usually wrote one, often two, long articles a day, in addition to serving actively in the Chamber. *La Justice* had a limited circulation of slightly over 10,000 copies – Pelletan dubbed it a *journal confidentielle*. Still, it wielded considerable influence in the world of politics. Millerand later attributed its authority to Clemenceau's talent. And Clemenceau, he wrote, was surrounded by talented journalists, most of whom became longtime friends.[10]

The staff occupied tiny offices at 10 rue Faubourg Montmartre. A dark stairway indicated the entrance, and the walls were covered with caricatures made of each other by the editors. Generally Clemenceau arrived between eleven and midnight, elegant, with cigar and groomed mustache. His men gathered about and in the office or in a neighboring *brasserie* listened to his account of the day at the Chamber. There was Pelletan, poorly dressed, inky fingers, coarse and already a legend among newspapermen; Gustave Geoffroy, who edited an *avant-garde* literary and art column; Durranc, 'round and exuberant', for Millerand the 'finest parliamentary reporter', and generally credited with the classic line, 'the Republic was so beautiful under the Empire';[11] Mullem, brother-in-law of Paul Claudel, a small man with a big stomach and bad character, who attacked everyone but Clemenceau. There was Charles Longuet, 'the best and one of the most absent-minded of men, who once took the evening train home to Argenteuil forgetting the son he had left on the sofa in the newspaper's front office'; Georges Laguerre; the grave Charles Martel, the drama critic; Stephen Pichon, Clemenceau's future Minister of Foreign Affairs, who, together with Millerand and Laguerre, was a favorite of Clemenceau; and a few others. The spirit and *camaraderie* of the group was long recalled by its members. One said later that it almost resembled a family adopted by Clemenceau.[12]

Clemenceau held a certain rough affection for his three protégés, as he called Laguerre, Millerand and Pichon. He described Millerand as the leader and added: 'He has been one of the three colts in my stable, *La Justice*, along with Laguerre and Pichon. ... Laguerre was the most brilliant; Pichon, the most faithful; Millerand, the most shallow; but the hardest worker, obstinate and methodical. He will go far, if the little pigs don't eat him on the way.' An Opportunist critic, Yves Guyot, regarded Millerand as Clemenceau's student and stressed the efforts often made by the Radical chief to further the careers of his colleagues. Alexandre Zévaès likewise credited Clemenceau with Millerand's victory, as well as that of others on the Radical list, in the by-election that first sent him to Parliament, and he viewed Clemenceau as a 'great Parisian elector'.[13] Closer examination, however, limits Clemenceau's role in introducing Millerand to national politics. At the time of the regularly scheduled election of 1885 *La Justice* scratched the names of Abel Hovelacque, another Radical councillor, and Millerand in order to consolidate its list and make it 'as representative as possible'. Two other Radical newspapers continued to support him. That Millerand achieved notoriety, as a contemporary pointed out, was due less to Clemenceau than to his own efforts, as demonstrated by his good showing of 90,000 votes. Only after this proof did Clemenceau agree to support his candidacy in the following December's complementary election.[14] It would take additional proof, Millerand's performance as High Commissioner for Alsace and Lorraine, to persuade Clemenceau to name him his successor in 1920.

Millerand's articles, like his speeches, reflected either the Radical-Socialist position on political questions or such pre-political occupational skills and experiences as education and legal reform. Nearly everything written and said criticized the government in power. *La Justice* fiercely opposed Ferry's intervention in Tunis and Tonkin, and Millerand's abuse was unrelenting. That he still showed no sympathy for revolutionary socialism was revealed in his coverage of a municipal by-election in which a socialist competed. In supporting the Radical candidate, the young writer condemned as 'useless and dangerous the application of revolutionary means in our epoch. A class insurrection one hundred years after the Revolution appears as the worst of errors'. Writing of a general council election in the Nord Department, Millerand declared that no serious and influential party could adopt an 'all or nothing' policy and that revolution was not a political principle. Conversely, he imbued the act of voting with almost sacred significance. 'To abstain', he said, 'was to desert'. And when he demanded state intervention to alleviate 'the miseries of the worker', the solution for Millerand lay as much in administrative action as in additional legislation.[15]

As the shelter of democracy and the best guarantee for social reform, the Republic obviously required protection. At the moment of a war scare from Germany, Millerand urged that additional funds be allotted to the military budget as the best means of ensuring peace. When out-lining his program for 1887, he placed preparedness for war high on his list. 'Everyone seeks to maintain peace', he said on another occasion, but other military budgets are growing, and France must follow suit, for national defense is the highest preoccupation.' It was not for France, however, to take the initiative in revising the Treaty of Frankfurt. Overly zealous organizations like the League of Patriots served only to embar-rass the government. Echoing Gambetta's famous injunction, Millerand urged that the lost provinces be thought of, not spoken of, and that the League restrict itself to gymnastic activities. Gabriel Hanotaux later recalled, with obvious hindsight, that Millerand 'already seemed elegant and remarkable in his prudent socialism'.[16]

His schedule was a heavy one. He regularly contributed lead articles to *La Justice,* and he continued to practice at the Palais de Justice, in addition to attending sessions at the Chamber and familiarizing himself with its procedure. On January 12, 1886, as one of its six youngest mem-bers, he was named provisional secretary. Millerand gave his first speech the following month when he intervened in the amnesty question then under discussion. The format used, the same as that of speeches he delivered in the years to come, reflected the style already developed at the Bar. His remarks were devoid of passion; he hoped instead to appeal to reason by thorough and logical argumentation.[17]

Many former Communards had been reprieved by presidential pardon in 1879 and, thanks to Gambetta's efforts, granted amnesty the following year. There was no lessening of the sympathy felt by the far left for those still imprisoned. In 1886 it requested amnesty for the anarchists Louise Michel, Prince Kropotkin and Cyvoct. The Premier, Charles Freycinet, was ready to pardon the offenders; but Henri Rochefort, then allied with Clemenceau, and Millerand demanded that legislation be enacted to that effect.

The latter rejected a pardon as insufficient and, compared to statute, inadequate. He examined the reasons offered by the government for its opposition and criticized each in turn. If public opinion had not de-manded an amnesty, it was precisely because so few culprits were involved; consequently no one would be frightened by their release. If no insurrectional movement had occurred to justify a law, the Chamber was reminded of numerous amnesties granted by previous regimes, including the Empire, without there having been a previous uprising. The measure, moreover, was one of clemency, a necessary prelude to any new program, especially one of social reform. The amnesty enacted in 1880 had been one of the first measures agreed upon by republicans; a new law would preserve and cement their union. Amnesty, then, like many of

Millerand's subsequent proposals, was also seen worthy of enactment because it would foster republican unity and so facilitate the passage of long-needed social legislation.[18]

3. Millerand did not speak again in the Chamber until the following October. He had plunged into the events at Decazeville, the strike that focused attention on social issues and led to the formation of a 'workers' group' of deputies.

A history of the affair reads like the draft of a Zola novel. Early in 1886, in the 'black country' of the Aveyron (in south central France), the miners went on strike. They complained of the change from weekly to monthly salaries and of the company's refusal to pay the price initially agreed upon if a vein became too productive. Two long-standing grievances were especially denounced: compulsory use of the *économat,* the company-controlled store with its invariably higher prices, and pressure exerted on behalf of conservative candidates at election time. A reduction in salaries was blamed on a new foreman . After the strike broke, an enraged mob beseiged the company office in which he had taken refuge and, as happened to Maigrat in *Germinal* which had been published two years before, threw him out the window to be torn to pieces by those outside. A tremor ran through the country, and troops were sent to the area.[19]

The handful of socialist deputies immediately brought the issue to the Chamber floor, and Emile Basly denounced the 'truck system' of individual negotiation. In a stormy session repeatedly called to order, he submitted a resolution calling on the government to establish reforms, including enactment of an eight-hour day, suppression of the *économat* and a minimum wage. Only scattered and isolated applause broke the great silence that followed.[20] Then Basly, Camélinat, Clovis Hugues and Boyer, along with some newspapermen, left Paris for Decazeville.

Shortly after, two Paris newspaper editors were arrested: Ernest Roche of *L'Intransigeant,* whose detailed reports on the strike had won notoriety, and Duc-Quercy of *Le Cri du Peuple.* The authorities invoked Article 414 of the Penal Code, providing penalties for attacks made on the right to work. On April 17, the two were brought to the Correctional Tribunal of Villefranche. Duc-Quercy was defended by Laguerre; Roche by Millerand. The defendants were specifically accused of publishing false news in an effort to prolong the strike and of attempting to transform it into a socialist insurrection.

The defense rejected these charges and questioned the local court's competency to try the case. Article 414, the two attorneys argued, applied only in cases of actual threat or violence, either of which only an assize court was competent to judge. Millerand also questioned the competence of witnesses who through a closed door reportedly heard Roche tell a group of workers that he approved of the murder. None of the facts submitted in the indictment, he charged, constituted fraudulent proceedings. Moreover they infringed upon the freedom of the press guaranteed in 1881. If false news had in effect been printed, it was necessary first to prosecute the management, and the present defendants only as accessories. However, this too fell under the jurisdiction of an assize court.

Millerand also objected to the prosecutor's lack of courtesy to Laguerre, the 'first' such instance in their five years of collaboration. Seizing upon the prosecutor's question 'what is socialism'? Millerand maintained that even under the Empire no magistrate had found it necessary to ask. However, the Tribunal declared itself competent, reprimanded Laguerre for his behavior and sentenced both defendants to fifteen months imprisonment plus costs.[21]

An angry Radical and socialist press denounced the decision. In Jules Vallès' newspaper, *Le Cri du Peuple,* Guesde called it an outrage. Socialists gathering to select a candidate in the special election required by Rochefort's resignation – he had quit the Chamber after its rejection of his amnesty bill – named the newly condemned Roche. The Paris Municipal Council voted a resolution calling for his release to allow him to campaign, and Roche was given a safe-conduct on April 20. Receiving only socialist support, he was defeated on May 2 but compiled a surprising 100,000 votes. The election was later, and prematurely, described as 'the last victory of Radicalism in the Seine Department'.[22]

The strike ended June 12, four and a half months after it began, and work was resumed two days later. The company granted an increase in wages but demanded reprisals. Eight men, including a thirteen-year-old boy, and two women were accused of premeditated murder. Once again, Millerand and Laguerre comprised the defense, this time at the Assize Court of the Sâone-et-Loire Department. They insisted that the particular charge pressed against each defendant be thoroughly scrutinized but, to employ the sympathies of the jury, made no objection to raising the relevant social issues. And when the two lawyers charged the company with all responsibility, the affair took a decidedly political turn. Breaking with the tactics used at Montceau, Millerand oriented his defense along social lines and pointed to the poverty of the district as the real culprit. Although a *Figaro* editorial found this position decidedly revolutionary, the jury quashed the premeditated murder accusation and freed six defendants. It acknowledged extenuating circumstances for the others, and they received five- to eight-year terms.[23]

Decazeville was important both for French socialism and Millerand, although in 1886 his tie to the movement was at most one of general sympathy. His defense won the attention of politicians and the admiration of socialists. And socialists took a first step toward forming a unified party. A Central Assistance Committee representing all socialist factions had been created during the strike by Vaillant, and it lasted for the duration of the crisis. The strike and its aftermath exposed inadequacies in labor legislation. It had marked the first time that elected deputies, socialists to be sure but nonetheless deputies, had traveled to the scene of a strike, and the act set a precedent. The Paris Municipal Council had voted funds for the strikers and their families, and other councils sent different forms of assistance.[24]

More deputies turned to what they now considered neglected social problems. Although not responsible for turning Millerand in this direction, the Decazeville strike undoubtedly quickened his speed on the road taken. In the parliamentary debate over import duties on grain, in March 1887, Millerand and Jean Jaurès asked that benefits of agricultural tariffs be more widely distributed to assure greater protection for share-croppers and tenant farmers and that higher wages be paid to rural workers. Born the same year as Millerand, Jaurès was elected to the same legislature. Millerand's newspaper article that followed, warm with admiration for Jaurès' speech, was his first to mention the deputy from the Tarn. Some deputies, representing all shades of republican opinion and including Millerand, Jaurès, Hanotaux and Poincaré, later asked that the Chamber set aside two sessions a week for debate on economic and social legislation . *La Revue Socialiste,* a leading socialist monthly, was exultant. Because of deputies well disposed toward socialism, though unaffiliated with the existing small group, it predicted the rise of a parliamentary socialist party.[25]

A labor coalition had first been formed in the Chamber following the election of 1885. It included the six socialist deputies and a handful of others. Apart from the essential demand for the progressive nationalization of ownership and the emphasis placed on workman's insurance and compensation, the group's program resembled that of the Radical-Socialists, who largely ignored it. That amorphous and undisciplined contingent of deputies calling themselves Radicals, we have seen, defended all liberties, including economic ones.[20] In December of 1887 a new and larger Groupe ouvrier was created. Listed among the names of its original members were those of Millerand and Laguerre. The Declaration of Principles retained traditional Radical demands like additional individual rights, a national militia and separation of church and state. It also called for the transformation of monopolies into public services administered on a corporate basis under state control and for 'the progressive nationalization of ownership, the individual enjoyment of which was to be made available to all workers'.[27]

Exposure to the ideas and personalities of the socialist leaders encountered during and immediately after the strike assuredly influenced Millerand's thinking. It was to continue to do so. When, for example, he began to publish his own newspaper, *La Voix,* before the election of 1889, he invited Basly to serve as an editor. But it would be an error to call Millerand a socialist by the end of his first term as deputy. The labor group in the Chamber contained not only collectivists but those who favored extensive Radical reform and who sought increased public ownership only in utilities. In common with other short-lived parliamentary coalitions, it offered no firm methods or ready solutions and, because of its small size and loose organization, was practically powerless. Yet its presence sufficed to arouse the opposition of the Senate and fears of the government.

4. In mid-October 1886, Millerand joined in an interpellation of the Freycinet Government for its use of *gendarmes* at a strike in Vierzon. An industrial crisis had forced the Societé française de Materiel agricole to reduce the number of its employees. Workers resented the apparently arbitrary procedure used and went on strike. Troops were ultimately despatched and used to break up a demonstration called by strike leaders. Deputies and socialists again appeared at the scene; the government was questioned; and Camélinat submitted a resolution censuring 'the ministry's use of armed force in a strike'. Jean Sarrien, Minister of the Interior, acknowledged the right of the workers to strike but justified the presence of troops to maintain order.

Military intervention was criticized by Millerand as, first, unnecessary and, second, clumsily executed. The strikers, he said, had asked only for equal conditions, had, during the six weeks of the strike, conducted themselves in perfect calm; and thus disorder had to be attributed to the behavior of the authorities. Turning to the ministers present, Millerand asked if they considered themselves as serving the Republic when they continued under its name the abuses of the Empire. He stressed the importance of the labor question to the regime and repeated Gambetta's admonition of 1870 that governments must remain neutral in times of strike. Far from provoking the strikers as accused, Eugène Baudin, the district's General Councillor, had in fact calmed them by promising impartial justice, only to be repudiated when the government ordered in troops. How were workers to trust the Republic which had told them to rely upon the ballot and not upon violence? In deceiving them, the government had hindered the cause of social peace. Together with two other Radicals, Henry Maret and Laguerre, Millerand moved that the Chamber censure 'the inopportune intervention of the authorities'. Camélinat's resolution varied only in language, and the incident revealed that tactical differences then separating Millerand from the parliamentary socialists were primarily those of degree.[28]

Millerand again achieved notoriety when he articulated the opposition of the Radicals to the Rouvier ministry. Installed the end of May 1887, it was viewed with alarm by some deputies in the center as well as by those on the left. It was the first, since republicans had won parliamentary control a decade before, formed and able to survive only with the support of Conservatives. Opponents feared that the all-Opportunist cabinet had entered into a secret alliance with them, promising to impede the development of a progressive republic and perhaps even work for the return of the monarchy in return for their support. Millerand, one of the first to question the new government, rejected Rouvier's explanation of 'republican concentration' – the tendency of French governments in the period to try to bring together the centers of the opposed republican factions – on the grounds that the far left, successful in sending Radical deputies to the Chamber, was not represented. The cabinet, he charged, was in reality one of 'republican division', preferring to represent 'the forces of reaction'. Rouvier was invested but survived as Premier only five months.[29]

In less than two years as deputy, then, Millerand had established a reputation as a spokesman for the far left. A witness recalled a lively corridor discussion in the Palais Bourbon at the end of 1887 over proposed Radical support for a Ferry-sponsored cabinet. Two leading Opportunists, Gabriel Hanotaux and Deluns-Montaud, complained about the refusal of *La Justice* to back Ferry. It was Clemenceau and Millerand who defended the Radical decision. With other deputies Millerand demanded the prosecution of President Grévy's son-in-law, Daniel Wilson, for trafficking in Legion of Honor decorations; and he questioned the attitude of the Minister of Justice in the affair. A leading supporter of Grévy, Bernard Lavergne, opposed prosecution of the President of the Republic fearing it would set a precedent and argued that a decree of 'no contest' would suffice. Millerand told him this would satisfy the far left.[30]

Interest in such pre-political concerns as education had by no means diminished, but neither were they in any way incompatible with Radicalism. Aside from wishing to free state schools of church influence, his concern here stemmed directly from his faith in the Republic. A democracy required a well-educated public, and dozens of articles appeared in *La Justice* urging potential reforms. They ranged from supporting

Lavisse's efforts to reform the *baccalauréat* to demanding greater regional diversification and a more modern curricula. He applauded the work of the Radical René Goblet, Minister of Education in the Freycinet cabinet and Premier in 1887, beginning the affiliation between the two that was to prove so momentous for the political future of each.[31]

As reporter for the Penitentiary Budget, Millerand asked for and received additional funds for penal reform – although the Senate later modified the Chamber's figures. He opposed what he called the 'bourgeois conception' of the best prison as 'the one in which the prisoner wants to spend the least amount of time'. The speech held 'misery and ignorance' as the fundamental cause of crime and consequently viewed the penitentiary as a place of education and social reparation. He suggested for consideration an Irish scheme by which prisoners associated according to the degree of their rehabilitation, advancing until liberty was ultimately gained. Special training for prison officials was obviously necessary, and, anticipating the great expense and unlikelihood of departmental action, he called for national legislation.[32]

Other legislative interests need not detain us; they also reflected attitudes he held while on the Paris Municipal Council. We are obliged to note only that Millerand's concern with social reconstruction grew ever-stronger during the Radical years. Strengthened also was his esteem for the instrument seen necessary to further it, the Republic. And when the Republic appeared to totter momentarily under the onslaught of Boulangism, Millerand reoriented his politics to join in the struggle to ensure its preservation.

3. To socialism:
The Boulangist interruption

Quand je vois le parti républicain s'engager dans
une voie que j'estime mauvaise, si modeste que
soit ma personnalité, je remplis mon devoir en le
disant à mes amis.

MILLERAND, to the Chamber of Deputies,
March 2, 1889

As Millerand immersed himself in the study of social questions and the
varied responses they evoked, he understandably widened his association
with socialist and labor leaders. And as it gained in strength, the French
socialist movement showed greater concern for social problems and their
immediate solutions. Like two converging lines, the movement, by turning reformist, and Millerand, by drawing closer to socialism, were finding themselves in agreement on aims and tactics. The meeting, however,
was delayed because of their different responses to Boulangism.

However crude his analyses in the columns of *La Justice* and however
simplistic the lines of action proposed, Millerand's articles permit us to
follow his evolution. His frequently sensational language was not intended
for publication in a theoretical review aimed at experts but for the
political-minded readers of a daily newspaper always interested in holding and enlarging its circulation. On January 25, 1886, for example, he
told his readers why he supported legislation providing miners with a national retirement-benefits plan. A change in employers would not result
in the loss of premiums already paid. Company-sponsored plans, like
that observed at Montceau, were dismissed as fraudulent. Mines differed from other types of property in that they were originally concessions
granted by the state. Therefore, the state, as with civil service employees, possessed particular rights and obligations with regard to miners.
Through elected delegates, grievances could be aired, and the government kept informed. The principle of workers' delegates – or shop stewards – established for miners by Basly, captivated Millerand and served
as the basis for industrial legislation submitted in the future.

The outbreak of the Decazeville strike had prompted his strongest
statement on industrial relations. The need to examine the circumstances

permitting such an atrocity was clear. The incident, he wrote, was not an isolated one; there were other, if less ghastly, outbreaks of violence; and they all stemmed from the intolerable relations between workers and their employers. Millerand compared the miner of 1886 and his employing company to the medieval serf and his suzerain. Even after quitting the pits, workers could scarcely be considered free when, as at Montceau, crowds of them and their families were 'led with lowered heads to mass and the confessional'.[1]

In articles anticipating its anniversary, published on July 20 and 23, 1887, Millerand praised the Revolution as ultimately making possible 'a regime of law and justice' and as providing the necessary instruments of social change. But political action required party structures. Millerand's voluntary separation from his colleagues on the Paris Municipal Council and his subsequent dissociations from other political groups suggests that he experienced considerable personal discomfort with anything resembling party discipline. Even so, he insisted on the need to unite and to work within a party framework in the 1880s, as a socialist in the 1890s and as a spokesman for national self-preparedness before World War I. In this intermediate period between radicalism and socialism, he urged workers to organize politically and so viewed parties as suitable expressions of class interests. In a fashion similar to Marx, Millerand saw no contradiction when at the same time he envisaged as the ultimate change, in the series of changes ushered in by the French Revolution, the abolition of all classes rather than the triumph of any one. The fact, he said, that one class temporarily profited at the expense of others only revealed the complexity of the task at hand.

These ideas, however incomplete, served as working principles, and Millerand turned to the more explicit study of needed social reforms, an area in which he doubtless felt more at ease. The many projects proposed, if not always developed and seldom original, were concrete and consistent. Support for nationwide municipal workshops, an example already set by Paris, included him, he said, among those 'who recognize the right of the state to limit the number of working hours, and who would make it its duty to do so'. He invoked the need to improve factory conditions, to grant further assistance to abandoned children and to enact legislation aiding the formation and growth of cooperatives. In each case the involvement of the state was emphasized, the 'pseudo-scientific' justification of its non-interference repudiated. In addition to citing humanitarian reasons, Millerand often appealed to the national interest in support of his proposals. Thus he regarded abandoned children, cases of which he had experienced at the Bar, as a 'diminution of national capital' and a weakening of the 'vital forces' of the country.[2]

casion, at Saint-Denis, he was shouted down by the same people who had voted for him only two years earlier.[18]

All were taking sides in the controversy regardless of previous political allegiance, and a schism developed in the Radical party. When *La Justice* at last joined the opposition, Millerand, now with approval, wrote that the excessive popularity of any general, despite his merit and service, revealed a state of mind dangerous in a republic. He had come to these views after being shocked by the adulation of a crowd; Jaurès may have arrived at them by more intellectual routes. Both men, however, correctly considered Boulangism an expression of 'deep and legitimate discontent to be met with reforms and not repression'.[19]

Deserted by most of his Radical sponsors, yet unwilling to resign himself to obscurity, Boulanger visited and won support from the Prince-Imperial in Switzerland, the Duchess d'Uzès, and perhaps the Duke of Orléans, the royalist pretender. However, Boulangism was scarcely a conservative phenomenon. It gathered much of its popular, if not financial, support from the left. Leading Radicals like Alfred Naquet and Georges Laguerre remained two of his staunchest defenders, while Rochefort and *L'Intransigeant,* as well as some socialists, also endorsed Boulanger.[20] He allowed his supporters to enter his name for a parliamentary vacancy in the Dordogne, and Millerand wrote that it was inadmissible for a general to take vengeance on his superiors in this manner. To resort to the plebiscite was to forget the lessons of history, and the young Radical found it 'distressing', that his friends had let themselves become the apologists of a military candidate. No doubt Millerand was thinking of Laguerre when he implored them to remain faithful to their principles.[21]

Millerand was especially disappointed by the readiness of socialists to support Boulanger. Many were self-styled, lacking theory and responding to emotions. Others, however, at least initially, included Brousse and Allemane, and some Blanquists and Marxists. Impressed by the mass support and working-class backing that Boulangists had won, Paul Lafargue, an important Marxist writer and organizer, suggested that Guesdists cooperate with them in the legislative election of 1889. An alliance was sealed in Bordeaux, and three Guesdists were returned as 'socialist-Boulangists'. Like Guesde, Engels was highly critical and warned that Boulangist nationalism represented a threat to French socialism. The General's defeat, he said, would not only preserve and perhaps widen the civil liberties enabling socialists to fight more effectively but would prevent other parties from posing as defenders of the Republic. By 1890 the 'Marxist flirtation' with Boulanger was over. But socialists had shown themselves as willing to join a movement 'based upon the wild, irrational politics of chauvinism and dictatorship'.[22]

Millerand continued to oppose Boulanger and as a result separated himself from his new parliamentary associates. On April 11, 1888, he noted in *La Justice* that the General had refused to comment on separation of church and state and on the role of the Senate. When the Boulangist question was brought before a meeting of the Workers group in the Chamber, Millerand sided with the minority that considered him a menace to the regime and asked the group to drop its support. Laguerre and the majority refused, and Millerand regretfully announced his resignation. The event marked the second time he dissociated himself from his colleagues in a legislative body, and it checked his formal acceptance of socialism. The next day he applauded the Paris Municipal Council for voting a resolution condemning Boulanger as a national threat.[23]

3. No longer affiliated with parliamentary socialists, Millerand continued to defend socialism in the columns of *La Justice*. In a book review published June 11 he agreed with Georges Renard on the necessity of state intervention in the economy. Socialist ideas, he said, 'were bearing fruit and so much the worse for those who fail to understand them'. On July 5 Millerand criticized an antisocialist tract as jeopardizing the freedom of labor and seven days later denounced an employers' association that had replied to a strike by a lockout. He viewed both strike and lockout as 'traditional weapons denoting bad social organization' and as pointing out the need 'to remove anarchy from industrial realtions'. On July 29 he referred to those antisocialists who continually praised English liberties and observed that the practical English realized by degrees theories once held as subversive. Later in August he called for an international labor organization to ensure the simultaneous initiation of social legislation in all countries.[24] On November 3, for the first time, he called himself a 'republican-socialist'. He told his readers of an invitation he had received to attend a meeting of the Federation of Socialist Republican groups in the Seine Department. At the previous meeting, however, he had found a Boulangist majority and would not return until the Federation clarified its position, in terms of both program and tactics. The real battle, he wrote, was that over the preservation of the Republic. On November 12 Millerand asked socialists to join the Radicals opposing Boulanger.

Thus there was every indication that Millerand would have openly embraced socialism if not for the presence of socialists at Boulanger's side. He had already rejected the alternative of Christian socialism, denouncing Boulangist attempts to confound socialism and Catholicism. He

agreed with Albert de Mun – a Boulangist – on the need for state inter-
cession between capital and labor but could not admit the church as a
regulatory agency. The church, he said, struggles only for her own interests and supports all who come to her aid, whether Bonapartist, royalist, or now, Boulangist. His relationship with anti-Boulangist socialists,
on the other hand, grew closer. In the election of 1889, Guesde ran for
the Chamber and fought a hard campaign for a Marseilles seat. On the
first ballot he out-distanced his chief opponent, the Blanquist candidate
and former Communard, Protot. However, the latter refused to yield
on the second vote and in a bitterly contested campaign took sufficient
votes from Guesde to ensure the victory of the Opportunist candidate.
Guesde charged defamation, retained Millerand and was successfully defended by him.[25]

After Boulanger's victory (and *coup manqué*) in a January 1889 Paris
by-election, the staggered republicans began to pull themselves together.
Opportunists particularly thrashed about for means to repress the movement. One proposal would designate as a 'prince' – and therefore make
subject to exile – any French citizen aspiring to 'personal power'. Other
propositions rested on equally shaky legal grounds. Convinced that extraordinary measures were required, the Tirard ministry sought to dissolve the League of Patriots which had backed Boulanger. The Chamber
debated the return to single-member constituencies and the abolition of
multiple candidacies to avoid decisions by plebiscites. It then charged
the General with jeopardizing national security. So weak was the case,
however, that the chief state prosecutor refused it, and a more politically
attuned magistrate, Quesnay de Beaurepaire, had to be found. On realizing the imminency of a trial, and to the dismay of his supporters, Boulanger fled to Brussels and so put on end to his career.[26]

As early as October 1888 Millerand had noted with alarm that moderate republicans wished to return to the *scrutin d'arrondissement*. Although list-voting was traditionally supported by the left, even Pelletan
acknowledged that departmental-wide constituencies could serve would-
be dictators. In December the Floquet ministry stated its intention to
revise the voting law accordingly. It was hoped that smaller districts
would enlarge the influence of local dignitaries and, in so doing, check
Boulangist candidates. Millerand said he was 'amazed' to find the government supporting the change and vowed his opposition. He recalled
the long struggle to have the departmental-wide vote adopted in 1885 and
how its adoption had subsequently slowed the growth of Opportunism.
Its disappearance would further that growth. Why then give it up?
Single-member constituencies, he argued, would be no more, and probably less, helpful in combating the alliance of Boulangists and reaction-

aries. Their combined appearance on a list would impose an embarrassing promiscuity upon anti-republican candidates.[27]

Millerand noted that Jaurès shared his consternation. If outspoken against Boulangism at Castres, the latter had weighed carefully the responses available to meet it. Jaurès rejected what he called a 'negative policy' and demanded the right 'to exercise a choice'. By this he meant his refusal to see Opportunism as the only alternative to Boulanger, and Millerand congratulated him warmly on his stand. The two deputies were drawing closer. Millerand said later that it was their common ideas, mutual sympathies and similar ages that brought them together and Boulangism that provided them with the opportunity to affirm their *entente* publicly.[28]

Both Millerand and Jaurès fought what the former dubbed the return to *le scrutin de la peur*. In so doing he separated himself from the majority of the left that approved it. Floquet's bill establishing single-member districts overcame considerable resistance to pass with a forty-vote majority. It was at once approved by the Senate and became law on February 13. Goblet, also opposed, later wrote that only the strong pressure exerted by the government made its adoption possible. Millerand never ceased to regret the *scrutin d'arrondissement* that, aside from the elections of 1919 and 1924, marked voting procedures during the remainder of the Third Republic, and he was to continue to fight for larger-sized constituencies. That summer the bill to abolish multiple candidacies was passed with considerably less opposition.[29]

4. On February 4, 1889, there appeared in *La Justice* the first of the several *'ni l'un, ni l'autre'* Millerand articles. He was referring to the Opportunists' condemnation of Radicals who, like himself, had refused to seal an alliance in the common struggle against Boulanger. Millerand recognized the similarity of goals but said that, while Radicals had a program, Moderates, especially those like Joseph Reinach, editor of *La République française,* merely opposed anarchism and dictatorship without offering anything but opportunism. There were other ways to remove Boulanger than by substituting Ferry, and 'if the choice is placed before us, we will continue to say, neither the one nor the other'. Millerand probably borrowed the slogan from the newspaper then edited by Jules Guesde, *Le Cri du Travailleur,* of the Workers party Federation of the Nord.[30] Unlike other socialists who became ardent Boulangists, the orthodox Guesde – as he was to do during the early stages of the Dreyfus affair – had shrugged off bourgeois quarrels and rejected distinctions among bourgeois candidates.

Boulangism, we have seen, also divided the Radical party. Like

Clemenceau the majority accepted the need for common republican action against the movement. But of those who did, some, like Millerand, opposed on grounds of principle the measures proposed to punish Boulangists and designed to prevent their reappearance as a political force.[31] This last group was convinced of the social origins of Boulangism, and Millerand's participation in it provoked his separation from Clemenceau. The winter of 1888–1889 was his last with *La Justice*.

Millerand differed from Clemenceau over the line of attack planned for the elections of 1889. Republicans had decided to cooperate against Boulangist contenders and in most cases agreed in advance on a common candidate. If there were more than one candidate, others promised to yield on the run-off vote to the largest vote-getter. Millerand's refusal to give unqualified support to Opportunists placed him in a minority position on *La Justice*. Having won representation in the government, beginning with Freycinet's in 1886, Radicals had gradually eased their demands for constitutional change. In their unaccustomed enthusiasm for a common front, few Radicals continued to speak of it, though long part of their platform, or even insist on it as a condition of their participation in electoral coalitions. Only a handful, headed by Goblet, Edouard Lockroy, the former Radical Minister of Commerce, and Millerand, André Daniel wrote in his yearly *chronique,* 'persisted in calling for intransigent revision'.[32]

The split between the two men came the day Millerand opposed Clemenceau and the Radicals on the floor of the Chamber. Laguerre questioned the Tirard ministry March 2, 1889, on its decision to prosecute the League of Patriots. In view of its anti-government demonstrations in favor of Boulanger, the League was identified as a political, and no longer purely patriotic, organization. Because political organizations were not in themselves illegal, the official indictment charged it with conspiracy and implied it was unauthorized and on both counts held it subject to the penalties provided in legislation promulgated almost half a century before and also found in two articles of the Penal Code. The legislation had fallen into disuse; the articles had been criticized even during the July Monarchy; and the fact that the government had to rely on these outdated and inappropriate statutes pointed out the weaknesses of its case.

During the debate, Millerand said he wished to explain why he could not vote either for Laguerre or for the government. Clemenceau interrupted and in a tone more bewildered than angry asked whether he wanted to apply the Penal Code.

Millerand replied that he objected to the republicans' choice of weapons. They had long criticized the arbitrary nature of Article 291 – it gave to correctional tribunals offenses which today go before juries – only now to welcome it as a weapon useful against Boulangism. The Republican party was to rely on its own arms to defend itself, not those of the parties it had always fought, those it had always repudiated.

Floquet said that he shared Millerand's objections. The former Premier recalled how he had also worked for the removal of the article in question but urged that it now be used to help defend the regime. The majority agreed; it also rejected Millerand's substitute amendment calling for the arraignment of those conspiring against the nation but not for having violated the Code.[33] In this closer vote Millerand received the support of Boulangists and Conservatives and drew the opposition of Clemenceau, the Radicals and the Workers' group. Some critics denounced him as wanting to spare Boulanger; others, like the Radical Emile Combes, accused him of sacrificing the needs of republican defense. Millerand said that he feared the arms used against Boulanger might subsequently be used against Radicals and socialists. He was to voice similar concern over the methods of the socialist-supported Combes ministry in 1904.

Millerand was defeated. However, he had taken the floor against Clemenceau and after his intervention had been congratulated by members of the right. That some Radicals, like Pelletan, began to have second thoughts about the value of the 'obsolete and inappropriate' statutes used against Boulangists and warned that a republic must respect all political associations did not alter the fact.[34] The situation paralleled that of 1885, when Millerand had opposed his colleagues on the Municipal Council and had also found himself in agreement with the right. Once again he revealed his inability – or refusal – to refrain from expanding tactical disagreements into forced departures.

Millerand's *ni l'un, ni l'autre* articles had widened the breach opened between himself and Clemenceau. On May 12, together with De Lanessan, he defended his views at Mâcon and made it irreparable. Both men reminded their audience of their early stand against Boulanger and said their position had not changed. However, they opposed the return to single-member constituencies and the move to bring together moderate Radicals and moderate Opportunists on grounds of republican defense. The combination, Millerand argued, would mean the sacrifice of Radical programs. He wanted to prevent the limitation of political options to Boulanger and Ferry and in these efforts identified as his associates Jaurès, Goblet, Lockroy and Basly.[35]

His position differed from that of *La Justice,* and Clemenceau asked him to accept the newspaper's refusal to publish those parts of the speech not reflecting its views. In a letter appearing in *La Justice* May 13, Millerand complied. He acknowledged the latitude accorded him by Clemenceau and expressed the wish not to break the 'cordial relations uniting the staff'. However, he again rejected Ferry's attempts to equate republicanism and the Constitution of 1875. Opportunists, Millerand wrote, prefer that we remain silent, but we must reorganize the judiciary, separate church and state, vote an income tax and strive for workers' legislation. Accordingly, only selected passages of Millerand's Mâcon speech appeared, without comment, on May 18. Pelletan wrote an adjoining reply, giving the newspaper's position and that of the Radical majority. He admitted that the party had long struggled against Ferry and Opportunism but noted it had never fought the Republic itself.[36] Subsequent speeches by Millerand on the subject were not reproduced in *La Justice*.

According to the *Mémoires*, Millerand 'gradually ceased' his work on the newspaper and avoided any 'pronounced rupture'. He attributed his withdrawal to his *esprit d'indépendance* and said that he retained his 'respect' for and 'gratitude' to Clemenceau. He lay stress, however, on his differences with the Radicals over the voting system and supported a candidate in a Paris by-election who was more of a socialist than the candidate endorsed by *La Justice*. A critical observer, Yves Guyot, identified Millerand's personality, now grown so strong that he could no longer remain subordinate to Clemenceau, as the cause of the separation. A future associate, René Viviani, said that Millerand tired of Clemenceau's perpetual opposition, that he held an essentially constructive attitude *(esprit réalisateur)* and despaired of seeing ministry after ministry overturned by the Radical chief.[37]

To these analyses one must add that curious disregard of political realities that we have already observed on the Paris Council. Millerand had not yet recognized, – although he was soon to do so – that Boulanger's support of constitutional revision had thoroughly discredited that part of the Radicals' platform. When his party announced its willingness to drop revision in order to join an all-republican coalition, Millerand refused to sacrifice what he regarded as principle for expediency. He had separated himself from the parliamentary Workers' group and severed his ties with socialists for the same reason. In voting for the police budget on the Municipal Council, it was a question of refusing to sacrifice expediency for principle. He was to reject a shift in tactics by socialists after the turn of the century and by the entire left at the time of the Combes ministry. He was subsequently to reject programs decided on by the groups with which he was associated as Minister of War in 1915, as Premier in 1920 and as President of the Republic after that. The reasons for these withdrawals varied; certainly advancement and satisfaction of deep-rooted ambition numbered among them. What remained constant was

Millerand's repeated assertion of independence when disagreeing with his party's tactics. It is difficult to explain his departures solely in terms of political opportunism. His ambition was scarcely served in leaving Radicalism, which in 1889 was gaining strength, and coming to socialism, which before 1893 was politically impotent. That French socialism subsequently became a viable political force was in large part the result of Millerand's own efforts; and its rapid growth could hardly have been predicted, certainly not counted on, before the last decade of the century.

Explanations for deviant political behavior often transcend politics itself. If Millerand's middle-class origins generated his ambition and required him to work strenuously to satisfy it, pressures experienced at home – and, as we shall see, in his legal profession – also imbued him with a sense of realities and an obsession with results. With this sense affronted, or the obsession frustrated, independence was sought and a change in political affiliation considered. His political life may be read as a series of withdrawals from political associations. Rather than serving either as a model of deception, on the one hand, or inflexibility and allegiance to preestablished principles on the other, it revealed a remarkable – and often mistaken – ability to adjust behavior to changed circumstances, or circumstances believed changed. Millerand was a Radical for seven years; he was to be a socialist for almost a decade and a half. He left the one when it no longer conformed to his ideal of a party; he was to come to the other when it began to so conform.

The immediate cause, then, of Millerand's departure from the Radical party was his refusal to use tactics previously denounced as deplorable, and in the summer of that year he left *La Justice* to become editor of a newly founded newspaper, *La Voix*. In an interview given at the time, Millerand said with pride that he had not abandoned the program he and Clemenceau were elected to carry out. However, he admitted to speaking at Mâcon from 'a socialist point of view'.[38] He wrote occasional articles for *La Justice* until the end of July 1889. In a short letter of resignation sent August 7, published two days later in another Radical newspaper, *L'Eclair,* Millerand explained that he had accepted an editorial post elsewhere. However he had 'forged his first arms here' and would not forget his old colleagues; they would continue to find him 'a good soldier... pledged to defend the Republic against reaction in any form'.

5. Millerand was not the only Radical objecting to an alliance with Opportunists or, more precisely, to the conditions required for it. To have dissident Radicals coordinate their criticisms, a Radical revisionist committee was established. It included Lockroy, Millerand, De Lanessan and

two Radical newspaper editors, Portales of *Le XIXe Siècle* and Eugène Mayer of *La Lanterne*. Millerand soon left because he found his new associates too liberal in their economics; conversely they saw him as a socialist. His objections to Radicalism went beyond the issue of constitutional revision. He had told the reporter interviewing him that he spoke 'from the socialist point of view' and was a 'partisan of state intervention' in such areas as accident insurance and trade-union growth. A newspaper was therefore found necessary for the forthcoming election campaign.[39]

La Voix appeared on August 20. It called itself a republican morning newspaper, sold for the customary five centimes and listed Millerand as editor-in-chief. His staff included the deputies Anatole de la Forge, De Lanessan and Emile Basly, as well as the municipal councillors Hovelacque and Alphonse Humbert. The format matched that of *La Justice* and the other fifty or so dailies then published in Paris. It contained one, perhaps two, leading articles, which reflected the newspaper's editorial position, a serial *(feuilleton)* and excerpts from the Paris press. On Mondays, however, it carried a review of socialist events and a bulletin of trade union and labor news. No evidence has survived to reveal the identity of Millerand's financial backers.

The front page of the first issue carried Millerand's editorial rejecting both Boulanger and Ferry. The voters, it predicted, would support neither the despotism of an individual, recalling the Empire, nor the domination of a clique, representing 'bourgeois reaction'.[40] Guesde's revolutionary socialist Parti ouvrier, now allied with the Blanquist Comité révolutionaire central of Edouard Vaillant, issued a similar statement. It described France as hovering between Opportunist or Radical reaction and dictatorship. However, 'the Republic', the Marxist pronouncement made clear, 'is the necessary political from of proletarian enfranchisement. At any price it must be conserved'.[41] Militant socialists and Millerand agreed then that the chief issue of the 1889 campaign was defense of the social republic.

To bring an end to Boulangism, Millerand wrote, republicans must tackle social as well as political problems and, united, find the means to resolve them. Working-class participation in politics would make democracy a reality. Because the Orleanist Constitution of 1875 organized only the powers of the bourgeoisie, constitutional revision remained a prime objective. However, he promised that in the columns of *La Voix* social questions would receive the prominence they deserved and that the answers, regardless of the need for unity, would be socialist, for 'socialism was by nature sectarian'.[42]

With the return to *scrutin d'arrondissement,* Millerand had to find himself a constituency, and the *Mémoires* reveal a shrewd analysis of the consequences of the change. Although impossible to determine how much they benefitted from hindsight, some of the ideas expressed doubtless influenced him in 1889. Millerand predicted that smaller voting districts would give 'preponderant influence' to local political organizations. He guessed that voters were aware of the skimpy record of the outgoing legislature, and he also anticipated a reaction to nationally established groupings after Boulangism and the Wilson affair. He deemed it wise, therefore, to run as an independent, and took the label 'republican-socialist', that used in 1888, as it seemed most appropriate. Millerand's electoral analysis resembled that made by the Paris Prefect of Police in the latter's report to the government. The Prefect said that an economic crisis during the summer of 1888, with accompanying high prices and strikes, especially affected the city's working-class population and would influence their voting in the coming election. He predicted their disenchantment with the Radicals and reminded his superior of a decision taken by the Broussists to end their alliance with them.[43]

Millerand considered the possibility of running in the XVIth *arrondissement,* in the Muette district where his parents now lived. Roche had written him there was some talk of it, and his letter may have accounted for Millerand's efforts to pose his candidacy there. A Radical-Socialist committee of the district on June 19 published and distributed a campaign circular on his behalf. However, Millerand decided to campaign instead in the XIIth *arrondissement* and so notified the committee organizer.[44] He estimated his chances were better in the first constituency of the *arrondissement,* an area including the wine depot of Bercy, because of his uncle's business and personal contacts. Moreover, the district was more heavily populated by workers than was the XVIth, for which Millerand must have decided he was entirely too radical.

On September 4 *La Voix* published a letter from the constituency's Republican-Socialist committee asking Millerand to serve as its candidate. It praised his independence and concern with social questions and noted that in the by-election of 1885 he had outdistanced all competitors in the constituency. He could, then, win the support of most of its republicans, progressive and moderate. In turn, Millerand observed that the district had been one of the few in Paris to resist Boulanger. There seemed, he said, no better choice and agreed to serve as the committee's candidate.[45] In the same issue of *La Voix* Millerand published his *profession de foi.* Its provisions virtually paralleled the Radical program formulated earlier in the decade. The clause most relevant to a socialist standpoint was that asking vaguely for 'regulation of contracts having alienated public ownership' – accepted as meaning the nationalization of mines and transportation.

The wine merchants of Bercy numbered among Millerand's potential constituents. He informed himself of their problems, probably in conversations with his uncle. Among his papers we find a copy of a 'complete course' in viticulture published the previous year. Millerand promised to work on their behalf for suppression of the *octrois*, the entry tax on food and beverages brought into Paris and for abolition of the recently enacted *loi Griffe*, requiring that a beverage have its contents clearly labelled. This law, he said, could not protect consumers and only endangered the livelihood of merchants. It was not long before one of his opponents acknowledged that Millerand was 'skillfully defending the major winegrowers who work the soil of Bercy'.[46]

While the anti-Boulangist Radical, Camille Dreyfus, found little competition in the second constituency of the *arrondissement*, Millerand ran against a formidable Socialist-Boulangist. Elie May, who had turned to Boulangism, was a former associate of Malon. Also running was a Radical Municipal Councillor, a Broussist and an Opportunist. Elie May emerged the winner of the first *tour* on September 22, with Millerand running a poor second. But 'republican discipline' was invoked; anti-Boulangist candidates withdrew to allow Millerand, as the leading republican candidate, to oppose the Boulangist; and they urged their supporters to follow suit. Thus on the run-off of October 6, Millerand outdistanced May by more than a thousand votes.[47] He had found his constituency and was to represent it until 1919.

'Republicans must unite', Millerand wrote in *La Voix* on October 8. Extended political liberties and social intervention comprised his program; republican unity would provide for its realization. Socialists, though few in number, were to play an important role. He envisaged them as 'the leaven of the new republican majority', the source of propulsion and leadership, taking the Chamber along the road of progress and reform. Even so, he warned, 'they will not block any of the improvements, as scanty as they may be, which present themselves'. In an open letter published October 22, he thanked his voters, promising not to forget that he won as the candidate of all the republican factions that had combined to defeat the Boulangist opponent. Millerand hoped he could represent their interests but, because reform meant change, warned that some would invariably suffer. At a victory dinner, he told his listeners that 'the Republic is socialist, and it will help the small and the weak'.[48]

The November 9 issue of *La Voix* carried a notice that it would be the last published. No reason was offered. Millerand wrote simply that 'it could not be helped', he and his associates controlled editorial and not administrative policy. Neither do the *Mémoires* present any explanation. Apparently the newspaper was intended as an ephemeral affair to give Millerand, or the position he represented, a voice in the election campaign.[49]

In coming to it from *La Justice,* Millerand had sealed his departure from Radicalism. Fifty years later, in a lecture on the Third Republic, he recalled with scorn that Radicals had fought Opportunists for twenty years – only to adopt their tactics and declare their readiness to join them. In relating the event in his *Mémoires* he reveals disillusion and a sense of betrayal.[50] The experience can only have reinforced his distrust of the principles and programs said to have distinguished one party from another. Millerand's conviction as a Radical at the end of the 1880s that his party had sold its birthright helped to ensure a minimum of ideological commitment as a socialist in the 1890s. *La Voix* gone, Millerand turned to measures of social reform and to defending the interests of his new constituents. In the process, he resumed his evolution toward the French socialist movement, now becoming markedly reformist.

4. The socialist deputy

Le génie exige la patience à travailler, docteur, et plus je vais, citoyen, moins je crois à l'efficacité des soudaines illuminations qui ne seraient pas accompagnées ou soutenues par un travail sérieux, moins je crois à l'efficacité des conversions extraordinaires soudaines et merveilleuses; à l'efficacité des passions soudaines — et plus je crois à l'efficacité du travail modeste, lent, moléculaire, definitif.

CHARLES PÉGUY, cited by Millerand in his introduction to Péguy's collected works.

1. The XIIth *arrondissement* was one of the poorer ones that formed a belt running around the outer edge of Paris, in the form of a 'U' with its open end in the west. Today, the central areas of the city, the first through the tenth *arrondissements,* are more prosperous and less industrialized than those in the outer ring – if we omit the wealthiest ones in the west. This contrast between the middle and outer parts of the city began to emerge late in the Second Empire when much of central Paris was rebuilt. Many tenements were razed and replaced by new buildings with the facilities for gas and water demanded by the middle class. The resulting higher rents forced the poorer inhabitants to move to the outlying areas then under construction.[1] The high birth rate, high infant mortality rate and alcoholism of the XIIth *arrondissement* distinguished it sharply in 1890 from a wealthy one like the VIIth, although statistics in these areas ranked it somewhat more desirable than the poorest XIXth and XXth. Its population in the early part of the decade was over 100,000, making it the tenth largest in Paris.[2]

The first constituency of the XIIth *arrondissement,* that represented by Millerand, consisted of the *quartiers* of Bercy and Quinze-Vingts. With few exceptions they contained drab and motionless neighborhoods, the monotony relieved neither by parks nor slums. The districts lay in the southeastern-most extremity of Paris and were seldom seen by tourists. Their northern boundary follows the rue du Faubourg Saint-Antoine from its origin at the Place de la Bastille to the Place de la Nation and on the south by the Seine as it runs from the Gare de l'Arsenal toward Charenton. Many of the landmarks of seventy years ago portray the area today: the furniture shops on the rue du Faubourg Saint-Antoine, the Gare de Lyon and the warehouses *(entrepôts)* of wine at Bercy.[3]

The latter is a veritable 'city of wine', consisting of sheds, cellars and small houses. It is intersected by streets and lanes named after the great vineyards of France. Adjacent is the port of Bercy with countless barrels and casks, although most wine today is shipped to Paris by rail.[4] A police officer described the area in 1895: 'That *arrondissement* was... only a sort of neutral region where Paris could disgorge and relegate her factories, hospitals, cemeteries, and prisons. The city carried on its flanks a degrading wound. ... There was much activity on the congested rue de Lyon and Faubourg Saint-Antoine, with its numerous bars and heaps of cheap furniture. Opposite was the misery of Bercy with its ramshackle warehouses, disorderly barrels... wine residue, and alcohol. Nowhere a theatre, a square, a monument to rest one's eyes; only a station, a few *casernes,* some schools, or a hospital. Not a church to house a work of art. ... In sum... there was not the least reflection of intelligent life, not the slightest appearance of charm.'[5]

The commune of Bercy, along with ten others including Passy, Auteuil, Montmartre and Belleville, was incorporated by law into the municipality of Paris June 16, 1859, assigning the city its present boundaries. The wine merchants of Bercy thus came under Paris law which required payment of the *octrois*. Because they feared the destruction of their market, the dealers were given a ten-year period of grace *(entrepôt à domicile).*[6] After he was elected to represent the area, Millerand became outspoken in his opposition to the *octrois* until its partial repeal in 1900.

Bercy and the winegrowing districts of the Midi then clashed over imitation wines and wine made from raisins. The Bercy merchants fought the legislative proposals of local distillers *(bouilleurs de cru)* to set conditions on the marketing of wine, the most notable of which was *la loi Griffe.*[7] During the decade 1880–89, phylloxera raised havoc with French wine production. To alleviate the shortage, manufacturers often resorted to cheap imitations, adding hot water and sugar to the residue in the vats. They bottled the product of the fourth and even fifth pressings. Alcoholic content was high, but when the beverage was bottled as wine, it constituted a fraud.

Millerand's first parliamentary defense of his (then future) constituents came during the summer of 1889. He opposed the Senate bill brought before the Chamber and sponsored by the Midi winegrowers. It would indicate to the consumer the contents of the wine sold, and an imitation would henceforth be clearly labelled as such. Millerand called the desire to prevent fraud only an excuse and condemned the bill, which in appearance benefited the Midi at the expense of Paris, as dangerous for both. The measure, nevertheless, became law.[8]

The following year, deputies from the Midi introduced legislation to place manufacturers of wine made from raisins under the same laws as those regulating distillers of alcohol. (Residue of raisins imported cheaply from Turkey and Greece, plus alcohol, produced the 'wine'.) Sponsors of the bill also hoped to set a higher tariff on raisins and justified their action with the need to protect national viticulture.

During the Chamber discussion on the proposed tariff, March 24, 1890, Millerand explained his opposition. While acknowledging the necessity of some protection, he failed to understand a proposal which, to protect commerce and industry, struck first at the manufacturers of a product purchased by the 'small and the poor'. The consumer would suffer, as would the worker who bought raisins to produce wine of his own. Supporters of the bill denied wishing to harm the individual consumer; their concern lay with producers of this wine, whose competition was disastrous for French vineyards. Eventually a Millerand-proposed amendment was approved by the Chamber. It limited the duration of a proposed excise tax to 1892, thus granting his manufacturers additional time.[9]

The struggle between Bercy and the Midi was fought out during the next decade, and Millerand continued to champion the cause of his electorate. The compromise legislation enacted in 1892 indiscriminately taxed all imports of raisins, regardless of their eventual use. The winegrowers managed two years later to increase the tariff on those imports destined for wine production, leaving untouched the raisins and figs intended for alimentation. Given the difficulties in determining the ultimate use of such imports, particularly in mixed shipments, the law was hardly applied. Yet Millerand time and again tried to modify it and return to a uniform tariff. In 1894, moreover, he justified the watering of wine 'in certain cases'.[10] These activities heightened his popularity in Bercy, and the influence of the wine merchants in the powerful electoral committee behind him helped to account for its energy in seeking repeatedly to return him to office.

One reason for the predominant role played by this committee, a rough but smaller equivalent to the American 'machine', was the unique makeup of the population in the area. Although it consistently registered more deaths than births, its population increase was one of the highest in the city. In 1889 the *arrondissement* contained 106,296 inhabitants; four years later the figure reached 111,665. However, during this period deaths had outnumbered births by 5,014 to 3,027, the largest such ratio in Paris. Yet by 1896 the *arrondissement* was ninth in population with 119,447, although during the previous three years there had been 1,595 more deaths than births.[11]

The extensive immigration into Paris from the countryside during the course of the nineteenth century has been adequately commented upon, although its precise impact has yet to be described. From the last quarter of the century until well into the decade before World War I, immigration into the XIIth *arrondissement* totalled approximately twenty to twenty-five percent of the existing population, ranking the district third highest in Paris in this regard. The constant inpouring of new arrivals, in a fashion similar to that of American cities on the eastern seaboard in the late nineteenth and early twentieth centuries, could only have intensified the scope of operations and influence of a well-placed political organization.[12]

Extensive immigration reinforced the prevailing economic and social structure of Bercy. Owing to its involvement with the wine industry, the area largely retained its rural character, even after annexation by Paris. One observer described it at about 1859 as 'a great store, unique, inextirpable, bordered by houses lodging a population of 10,000 souls, in addition to a transient population'. May came from Bourgogne, the Loire, the Loiret, Nievre and the Yonne (according to the electoral lists of 1872, forty percent), giving the area one of the most important provincial populations in Paris. Because of continued immigration during the next few decades, the description holds true at least until World War I. This departmental *milieu* was characterized by well-established traditions of work and life and a professional and social hierarchy which contributed to the preservation of its coherence. Politically speaking, regardless of its location and despite the fact that it sold its wine to Parisians, Bercy remained outside the nineteenth century whirlpools that agitated the neighboring Saint-Antoine district. It was an exceptional case, a quarter integrated into Paris that remained largely provincial. The tendency for immigrant masses to remain basically non-political or relatively conservative, seeking to make successes of themselves in their new surroundings rather than change them, was in this situation reinforced by the provincial make-up of Bercy. It was not radical, despite the relative poverty of most of its people, and we may assume that relatively little pressure came from Bercy to make its deputy in Parliament adopt more sweeping economic and social views.

The situation differed, but only superficially, in the other district of Millerand's constituency, that of Quinze-Vingts. It was over five times as populous as Bercy, with 47,032 inhabitants in 1891. Because of the Gare de Lyon, the area contained many railroad workers. However, it was also subjected to successive waves of immigrants seeking new employment, many of whom had not taken root or would require considerable periods of time to do so. In 1894 it was estimated that there were 4,566 tenants in the district, living in numerous rooming and boarding houses.[13] Thus, like Bercy, the presence here of an entrenched political organization would play a significant role in returning its candidate, particularly one whose incumbency became ever greater.

Millerand had already shown his awareness of the important role played by local electoral committees under the *scrutin d'arrondissement* and never reneged on the obligations he owed to the one supporting him. He reported to it at regular intervals on his legislative efforts and often used gatherings it sponsored as forums for important policy speeches. And the committee remained loyal to him, regardless of his evolution toward, and then away from, a socialist position. Committed to returning its candidate and not to any ideological preconceptions, Millerand's committee fully illustrated the comparative irrelevance of political parties and the importance of personal ties between a deputy and his constituency – constituencies that were in some cases virtual fiefs – during the Third Republic. We have seen that there were no official parliamentary groupings until 1910, and even after that time there were few threats of party discipline to curb a deputy's errant behavior. He had only to appeal to a small group of voters for reelection. In 1889 Millerand's constituency contained about 10,000 registered voters.

In his papers we find several indications of the importance Millerand attached to his committee. He carefully broke down its twenty-nine man membership according to occupation. Thus he found eleven members in the wine industry alone, including brokers like his uncle, wholesalers, retailers, distributors and a distiller, giving the industry the single largest occupational representation. The furniture industry ran a poor second with four members, including merchants and a cabinet-maker. There were three clerks *(employès de commerce),* two accountants and several shopkeepers and artisans.[14] The absence of blue-collar workers was not unusual in local politics, and Millerand was very much aware of the railroad workers living in his constituency. The presence of numerous merchants and small businessmen, however, is important in view of their relative conservatism.

There were many shopkeepers in the XIIth *arrondissement,* particularly in the Saint-Antoine district, and as a deputy Millerand looked after their interests. He facilitated licensing and bankruptcy procedures for them and submitted legislation calling for reforms in these areas. That he wished to organize the railroad workers and submitted legislation favoring trade union growth in no way contradicted his awareness of the moderate political makeup of his constituents; by permitting workers to associate in defence of their interests, he sought to make them more responsible and less prone to violence. As Millerand evolved, the constituency continued to support him. His closest call came in the election of 1902, after his reign as minister, but it returned him to office on that occasion and on six others. On his election to the Presidency of the Republic in 1920, one observer commented: 'Every four years they say Millerand will be beaten. He is never amiable, never *tutois,* never makes wild promises. Yet he served for thirty-five years as deputy in a city which takes pride in causing upsets.' The commentator called Millerand's electoral committee 'the most compact and united in France'. His partisans say they vote for him simply because he cannot be mistaken.[15]

The constituency grew accustomed to its candidate and literally shrugged off queries about his political evolution: it was, after all 'still Millerand'. As for the deputy himself, the conjunction of his voters' interests and the emphasis placed by his committee on winning elections and obtaining results reinforced the practical aspects already dominant in his makeup. Conceivably a more radical constituency might have produced a more radical Millerand. The likelihood was scarcely present in the XIIth *arrondissement.* It can be said of him, as of the American socialist, Victor Berger, of Milwaukee: 'to retain strength and support he could not be too far in advance of dominant political attitudes.'[16] The voters of the XIIth *arrondissement* did not comprise a force calculated to make Millerand more radical.

2.   Millerand began to write articles for *Le XIXᵉ Siècle* in November of 1889. It was a Radical newspaper, similar to if somewhat to the right of *La Justice,* with offices at 148 rue Montmartre. Edmond About, who became owner in 1872, had said that 'the best republicans are the most resolved conservatives', but he nonetheless grouped around him several anticlericals, including graduates of the renowned Ecole Normale.[17]
The newspaper published an article by Millerand approximately every four days. However, his affiliation with the journal was not close, and apparently he was desired as an already-respected voice in the Chamber. As for *La Justice,* he wrote on social issues, hygiene, labor and legal problems, and these articles shed light on his political activities and thoughts from 1889 to 1893. Often he outlined his reasons for granting or withholding support from legislation pending in the Chamber.

The legislature of 1889–1893 promised to be a calmer one than its predecessor. The Exposition of 1889, the opening of the Eiffel Tower and the gradual disappearance of Boulangism channeled off energy and engendered good will and prosperity. Paris had returned fewer Radicals than in 1885. Jaurès had been defeated in the Tarn, and among the new faces at the Palais Bourbon were Louis Barthou, Maurice Barrès, Delcassé and Joseph Reinach. All, save Barrès, strengthened the forces of moderate republicanism.

Hardly had the session opened when Millerand appeared to repudiate his platform by withholding support from a socialist-sponsored bill on constitutional revision. He argued that the resolution, presented so early in the legislature, would act only as a divisive force among republicans and that unless they remained united little reform was possible. By risking early defeat on a measure likely to fail, republicans further jeopardized progressive legislation. Moreover, because Opportunist withdrawals made possible numerous Radical victories, it behooved Radicals to seek those reforms under the existing Constitution. He urged a more realistic strategy – to press for less difficult reform like tax legislation. A majority ultimately shelved the bill.[18]

In rejecting constitutional revision, Millerand acted no differently from other Radicals who were no longer attempting to implement their party's revisionist demands. These demands had reached their peak in the Radicals' fierce attack on Opportunists during the 1885 campaign. Since then Radicals had served in the Freycinet and Goblet governments, and the issue had become dormant. It was scarcely raised during their struggle against Rouvier. After the latter's fall from power, the question had reemerged, was expropriated by Boulangists and subsequently discredited by the collapse of the movement. Millerand, always politically astute, probably defended it as long as he did because the issue served to distinguish his position from that held by Clemenceau.

Reporting for the year 1889, Daniel observed and commended the young deputy's ambition and prudence. 'Millerand', he wrote, 'who seemed to want to take direction of the most progressive faction on the left, announced he would not cease to support Radical programs, but carefully distinguishing propagandist from parliamentary tactics, took care to abstain rather than provoke inopportune crises.'[19] Circumstances provided him with the opportunity to reach his goal; it was during the parliamentary session of 1889–1893 that Millerand formally became a socialist. The immediate cause was his participation in the events following the shooting of workers and their families at Fourmies.

3. The Second International, born in Paris late in 1889, agreed to celebrate the first May Day the following year. The fourth Freycinet government took all precautions against possible violence. Police and army units were called out; but, as planned, the demonstrations remained peaceful. Both in this celebration and in that scheduled for 1891, the drive for the eight-hour day was stressed. In expressing its willingness to relate a major propaganda offensive with the demand for a particular piece of social legislation, the Parti ouvrier reflected its newly placed emphasis on reform. Not that the demand ran counter to Marxist teaching – the 1848 Manifesto ended with a list of reforms; but the Guesdists

had earlier down–played social legislation and would deemphasize it once more after the turn of the century.

Socialist speakers went to industrial districts to prepare the way, and on April 12, 1891, Paul Lafargue spoke at Fourmies, a textile manufacturing center in the southwest corner of the Nord Department. The area was beset by labor problems. Smaller sales had provided its manufacturers with a pretext to cut wages; and workers, to restore salaries and organize a trade union, had struck several times. In his speech Lafargue reminded them of the legacy of 1789 and equated the bourgeoisie with the feudal nobility that had preceded it. *Le Socialiste* the following day reported 'great excitement' in the crowds, 'which everywhere spoke of socialism'.

For May Day the worker and Guesdist organizer, Hippolyte Culine, organized a peaceful demonstration. His program called for a list of demands to be presented to the mayor, headed by that for the eight-hour day. At the insistence of local employers, two infantry companies had nevertheless been summoned to stand by. When some demonstrators were arrested for having urged millworkers to join them, the crowd grew noisy and demanded their release. Stones were hurled at the *gendarmes*. Troops rushed in to protect them and on order of their bewildered commander fired into the crowd from one to four minutes. Nine people were killed, and thirty were badly wounded; of the dead, four were under twenty years of age; of the wounded, twelve were under twenty-one, including several infants.[20]

The repercussions of the *fusillade de Fourmies* were heard throughout France and Europe. Municipal councils and trade unions at once voted resolutions of solidarity with the workers and promised aid. The Company that had fired, the 145th of the line, was insulted by civilians in its garrison town and finally transferred. *Chansonniers* put the event into song, and one writer pointed to a possible connection between the event and the appearance two weeks later of Pope Leo XIII's social encyclical, *Rerum Novarum*.[21]

On May 4 at the Palais Bourbon, the socialist deputies Dumay and Boyer condemned the government. Ernest Roche, reelected as a Boulangist-socialist in 1889, closed his detailed narrative of the shooting – and unleashed pandemonium – by suddenly holding aloft a blood-stained shirt with six bullet holes to demonstrate wanton murder by the soldiers. With order restored, Jean Constans, Freycinet's Minister of Interior, expressed the government's sympathy but read the prefect's report to show provocations on the part of the crowd. Supported by Albert de Mun, Millerand took the floor to reject the official explanation as insufficient and request a full parliamentary inquiry. His remarks, in that emotion-laden atmosphere, appear exceptionally cold and objective. The minister could not personally be held responsible, nor could the police be expected to behave like diplomats; but the soldiers had, after all, been sent with government authorization.[22]

Freycinet opposed Millerand's motion for an inquiry on the grounds that the government would be questioned every time it restored order. The majority agreed and approved a resolution neither blaming nor approving the action of the authorities responsible. The following day the Chamber voted to send 50,000 francs to the families of the victims. On May 8, however, it refused to consider an amnesty for those accused of exciting the crowd. The socialists and their allies dismissed these votes as *scrutins de classe,* and Millerand charged the government with working to hush up the affair.[23]

Both Culine and Lafargue were indicted for provocation leading to disorder – the former for his remarks on May 1, the latter for his speech of April 12. Lafargue wrote Engels to say that he had asked Millerand to defend him. In asking Engels to cover the costs of the trial, he referred to Millerand as the future Clemenceau of the far left and cited his influence in the Chamber of Deputies.[24] The choice may have been the result of Guesde's suggestion. We have seen that in the aftermath of the 1889 election Millerand successfully represented Guesde in court, and the Parti ouvrier leadership doubtless recalled Millerand's other defenses of socialist and labor chiefs. In a letter to Lafargue, Millerand suggested that Culine be defended by Tardiff, a young lawyer who acted as Millerand's secretary. Lafargue's defense was to be based on Marxist ideology itself, which affirmed that individual acts of reprisal, including murder, were useless within the larger context of the class struggle. The 'inevitable revolution' permitting the proletariat to seize political power would be accomplished neither by 'recourse to dynamite nor by heroic individual follies'.[25]

The trial opened July 4 at the Cour d'assises of Douai. According to plan Millerand argued that as a Marxist, Lafargue had consistently deplored the methods used by anarchists. He was upheld as a scientist – a doctor of medicine – and as a theoretician, not a mob agitator. To establish an intellectual alibi for his client, Millerand read from pamphlets written by both Marx and Lafargue in which institutions, not individuals, were held the proper objects of attack.

After close examination of the events and witnesses Millerand summed up his case and concluded with the following words: 'You accuse Lafargue and Culine; I accuse the Commissioner of Police, M. Ruche, who failed to do his duty. I accuse the sub-prefect who should have been present at the scene. I accuse the Attorney-General who did not take the necessary precautions. I accuse the mayor of Fourmies. ... I call them to the Bar to answer for their acts, and it will not be your verdict, whatever it is, which will render them innocent before public opinion.'[26] Millerand asked for acquittal and asked it in the jurors' own interests. For if the defendants were found guilty, their imprisonment would certainly stimulate the growth of socialism. The eyes of all France, he said, were on Douai; the horror of Fourmies must not be added to.

However, the jury – according to Zévaès composed of 'capitalists, industrialists, and landed proprietors' – found both men guilty as charged. Although the father of four and responsible only for organizing an entirely legal demonstration, Culine received six years' solitary confinement, Lafargue, one year's imprisonment. Socialists protested bitterly. The National Council of the Parti ouvrier called the decision a class verdict, and the party 'adopted' Culine's wife and children. The trial and its outcome sealed Jaurès' departure from the republicans with whom he had sat. Millerand seemed particularly upset. In a letter to Georges Renard, he said that as time passed his socialist convictions grew ever stronger.[27]

Three months went by. Then, in October, the Radical deputy representing Lille suddenly died, and an election was called to fill the vacancy. Guesdists, working with socialist groups in Lille, presented Lafargue as a candidate. Public opinion, they said, would be given the opportunity to judge Fourmies by acting as a national jury. If it so chose it could condemn the government's use of the army against labor.

At first glance the attempt seemed hopeless. In the vacant constituency the Parti ouvrier had polled only 1,406 votes in the previous election, republicans, 6,751 and Conservatives, 4,035. In a letter to Engels, Laura Lafargue said that a miracle was required for her husband to win. The only Paris daily to support Lafargue was Roche's *Intransigeant*.[28]

However, the Guesdists waged an all-out campaign. In a stream of pamphlets Lafargue, with Guesde's editing, treated his candidacy as providing the nation with the opportunity to judge Fourmies. Guesde and others staged thirty-four rallies in thirty-eight days. Parents and relatives of the victims participated; the women of Fourmies appealed to the women of Lille for their husbands' support. And on the first ballot Lafargue obtained a plurality. But because he failed to win a majority, a runoff was scheduled.[29]

In the Chamber of Deputies, Roche asked that Lafague be freed. Millerand, both in the Chamber and in the columns of *Le XIXe Siècle,* invoked the precedent of Louise Michel, the convicted anarchist, who had been freed by the Empire to campaign on her own behalf. Can the

Republic, he asked, appear less liberal? But his resolution to have the Chamber release the prisoner was easily defeated.[30]

On November 7, 1891, Millerand spoke at Lille on Lafargue's behalf. The latter had sought his assistance in getting out middle-class support, and Millerand's energetic repudiation of violence as a basis of socialist policy no doubt appealed to a considerable number of still-hesitant Radical voters. For the following day, with Radical candidates having stepped aside, but in spite of conservative pressure, Lafargue was elected to Parliament. Engels hailed it as a 'great victory'. The economist Leroy-Beaulieu regarded the election as the most important since 1871. 'With Lafargue', he wrote, 'son-in-law of Karl Marx, collectivism entered the Chamber of Deputies.'[31]

Within twenty-four hours of the victory, Millerand sponsored a resolution asking for Lafargue's immediate release. Rejecting the government's offer of a pardon, he invoked a law of 1875 which postponed, at least for the duration of his term in office, the detention of a deputy or senator. The resolution was adopted almost unanimously, and Lafargue took his seat in the Chamber.[32]

4. In two speeches delivered in 1903, one at Vierzon, the other before a socialist congress at Bordeaux, Millerand stated that his membership in the socialist party dated from the speech made at Lille, in November of 1891. He said at Vierzon: 'It seemed to me that it was indispensable, in the double interest of socialism and the Republic, on the one hand to discipline the still-scattered forces, and on the other to bring to the republican party the considerable contribution of the socialist party. It was under these conditions that I went spontaneously to Lille to support the candidacy of Paul Lafargue, thus publicly affirming that I meant to place myself in the vanguard of the socialist party.'[33] At Bordeaux he said: 'I present myself to the Congress just as in 1891, when I left the ranks of the Radical party to go to Lille to support the candidacy of Paul Lafargue. At that moment I came to the socialist party freely, knowing what I was doing and what I wanted. ...'[34]

Millerand's speech in the Hippodrome at Lille, therefore, was his first as an affirmed socialist. It its immediate purpose was to bring out the republican vote for Lafargue, it also illuminated his conception of socialism. Reformism was his theme. He criticized those who solicited votes from workers, made them a thousand promises and then, having succeeded, denied those same workers the right to have a candidate of their own choosing. He assured his audience that socialists sought the triumph of labor's candidates and the participation of workers themselves in the discussion and regulation of public affairs. While wishing to see in the

Chamber Guesde, Malon and other 'authorized representatives of the socialist idea', Millerand left few doubts as to the manner by which their objectives would be attained. 'That day, citizens, when universal suffrage will have become aware of its power, fears of revolution will become vain, and there will be room only for social evolution.'[35]

Millerand had not hesitated to place side by side the names of Malon and Guesde. In view of successive electoral victories, largely on the municipal level, the latter was well on his way to adopting the evolutionary tactics of the former. And it was precisely at this phase in the history of French socialism that Millerand joined the movement. Its parliamentarianism created the possibility of the republican union of which he had never ceased to dream. The next few years, he believed, could witness the fruition of the alliance between socialists and Radicals that Clemenceau had been unable to obtain – provided that French workers could be persuaded to rely upon the Republic.

Millerand did not join any particular socialist faction and continued to call himself a 'republican-socialist'. The name is most appropriate, for he wanted to identify the two as complementary. A clear exposition of his ideas was made at Calais, March 13, 1892, when at Guesde's suggestion he spoke on behalf of the Parti ouvrier. Although independent, he promised to work for a 'great republican party' and on behalf of the 'small and disinherited'. Universal suffrage was upheld as the weapon of the proletariat, and Millerand exhorted the population of the Nord to celebrate the next May Day – the first anniversary of Fourmies – peacefully. No recourse to violence was necessary, no more in 1892 than in 1886 when he had 'first expressed these ideas'.[36]

How could government fulfill its obligation of assuring everyone the right to seek maximum happiness and liberty? The answers would be found in a study of the relations between labor and capital. Millerand's survey of these relationships revealed the shape of his economic thinking.

Since 1789, he argued, certain chages in the economy had taken place. Most important was the gradual disappearance of individual ownership. Two new phenomena, the introduction of labor-saving machinery and increasing concentration of capital, were responsible. Although a considerable amount of small individual ownership survived, the phrase no longer applied to the large modern corporation. And given their growing numbers, the gulf between property and ownership was widening.

Within a century Millerand expected to see the bourgeoisie in a situation analogous to that of the nobility a century before. No longer involved with protecting his serf or directly defending his country, the nobleman continued to enjoy his privileges. Privileges without obligations could no longer be justified, and eventually he disappeared as a political force. A similar fate was predicted for the bourgeoisie, whose ownership tended to be merely representative. His property, however, did not fall to the worker. The latter continued to receive a salary, a salary rendered increasingly precarious by the introduction of competing labor-saving machinery. Unlike medieval corporate life, where a worker maintained constant rapport with a property owner, today's worker was in rapport only with his machine and ignorant of its many owners. Technological unemployment and threats to family security numbered only two of the many consequences of the industrial age. How was one to ensure that progress would bring forth happiness rather than generate misery? By studying society scientifically and relying upon the Republic to improve societal arrangements.

It provided two powerful tools in universal suffrage and the right of all to an education. By means of the ballot the worker would invariably introduce socialism into city halls and national legislatures. Hence, 'patience and perserverence' sufficed to assure a definitive victory. 'Anarchistic violence', outlawed by the Second International's Brussels Congress in 1891, constituted the greatest threat to socialism. Millerand urged his listeners to join the ranks of a great party ready to assume responsibility in public affairs. Here the speaker admitted that his ideas still differed from those of some other socialists but the difference reemphasized his independence. His strongest sources of inspiration remained the general interests of the Republic.

As Millerand had been forced to choose at the time of Lafargue's defense, so must his audience. Included was the small businessman, a victim like the worker of economic evolution and financial scandal. All formed one army against powerful financiers, the Bank of France and the church, who opposed their progress. The peroration was eloquent and emotional . Social equality must succeed political equality; a chance in life was asked for the children of the poor and for the aged.

Thus Millerand had proclaimed absolutely the priority of the rights of labor in a socialist republic founded on collectivism. In Marxist fashion, he had described it as an inevitable consequence of modern economic processes. But unlike many Marxists, he insisted that socialism and democracy complemented each other. Important in terms of the history of the movement was his acceptance of socialist thought, however simplified. That Millerand the lawyer and Jaurès the professor – who joined the movement at about the same time – both accepted it, revealed socialism's newly won respectability and emergence into the middle classes.[37]

The effects of the speech were widely felt in socialist circles. Four thousand people heard Millerand, and the future mayor and deputy of Calais, Alfred Delcluze, who had presided, cited the telegram he received from a delighted Guesde: 'What have you done with my Millerand? You have transformed him. I no longer recognize him. Bravo!'[38] Aside from reporting on his venture into Marxist economics, however, Millerand had said little that was new. The 'transformation' more properly connoted the mounting confidence in reformist tactics by Guesde and other militant socialists.

5. Millerand's energetic intervention in the famous Carmaux strike of 1892 was made as an avowed socialist. Its importance lay not so much in his reaction, similar to those he had had as a Radical, as in providing another formative experience in his evolution as a socialist. Carmaux further convinced him of the usefulness of working-class organization to achieve the legitimate goals sought by labor, and it offered additional evidence that government intervention and control provided the only solution to some of the stickier issues separating capital from labor. Finally, the recourse to national arbitration procedures and their relatively successful application in resolving this industrial conflict suggested a technique Millerand was to rely upon.

The decades following the legalization of trade unions in 1884 was a period of considerable labor unrest throughout France. Workers used their newly won right to associate in order to press demands for a more equitable share of the national product; it was precisely the frequency with which these demands were made, and the strikes accompanying them, that was so feared by employers. Agitation reached a peak in the mining industry, for three decades racked by conflict. In addition to the habitual danger, disease and lack of job-security faced by miners, profits had outdistanced wages by almost two hundred and fifty percent since mid-century. In 1893, 634 strikes took place involving over 170,000 workers. Employers were determined to stop union growth, forcing unions to struggle for their very existence, as well as for specific economic benefits. Such battles invariably took on class dimensions. Workers appreciated the usefulness of organization to win political power; so did employers who felt their interests threatened by labor-dominated municipal governments.[39]

In the summer of 1892 at Carmaux, in the Department of the Tarn, Jean-Baptiste Calvignac, a worker at the forges, socialist and secretary-general of his union, was elected by his fellow workers first as municipal councillor, then as mayor. His request to the management of the company for which he worked, one in the complex of mining and industrial holdings in the area owned by the Solages family, for permission to de-

vote two days a week to fulfill his new duties was denied. Shortly afterwards, following a brief illness that kept him from his job, the company
dismissed him. His fellow workers pointed to his nineteen years of service and asked for his reemployment. The company refused. An impassioned crowd of workers broke into the home of its director, Humblot, who had fired Calvignac, forced him to sign a statement of resignation and then went on a strike that was to last ten weeks and become a
cause célèbre. Successful arbitration by the prefect had managed to avert
an earlier strike, but the company now rejected intermediaries on the
grounds that working conditions were not in question.[40]

As Millerand followed these events, his chief concern lay in the company's apparent disregard of the wishes of the voters, the issue seized by
the miners; and in the columns of *Le XIXe Siècle* he demanded that Calvignac be rehired. The trial of the eight workers accused of illegal entry
and threats of death began October 3. Among lawyers for the defense
were Millerand and René Viviani. In his summation, Millerand censured
the employing company for having exerted economic power on a mining
population, calling it economic and political tyranny. His clients received
sentences varying from eight days to four months imprisonment.[41]

When the Chamber reconvened later in the month it heard two interpellations on the strike. Dupuy-Dutemps and Armand Després, both
leftwing deputies, maintained that the right to vote had been violated.
An elected official was not only refused office but punished for the confidence shown in him by fellow workers. They described Calvignac as a
model worker whose only fault lay in becoming involved with local politics, and they found the company's excuse of excessive absences 'intoler-
ably unjustified'. The motive, charged the interrogators, was purely political.

Millerand criticized the company's refusal to accept the arbitration
offered by the Minister of Public Works. He widened the issue by citing
a law of 1810 justifying use of the government's right of police power in
the event of a threat to public security or failure to provide for the needs
of consumers. The ownership of a mine, he argued, was recognized under
the Old Regime as constituting a privilege conceded in view of the public
interest. It remained in the hands of the concessionnaire only as long as
it was exploited in a manner conforming to that interest. This condition
had clearly been violated in the present case, and Millerand asked the
government, 'in the name of liberty and universal suffrage', to occupy the
mines and consider ultimate nationalization.

The threat worked. The President of the Administrative Council of
the Carmaux Mines, Baron Reille, surrendered and agreed to arbitration
procedures.[42] He had fought the proposal for two months. Miners put

renewed confidence in the advantages to be won by exercising political power, and socialists like Millerand were strengthened in their conviction that existing republican institutions could be made to work. Both company and strikers were to select delegates to state their cases; the decision would be rendered by the Premier and Minister of Interior, Émile Loubet.

Clemenceau, Pelletan and Millerand were chosen by the Carmaux workers. The three asked that Calvignac and the men on strike be rehired and called for the dismissal of the company director. Delegates of the mine owners wanted ratification of Calvignac's dismissal but agreed to rehire all other workers except those condemned by the Albi court.

Loubet announced his decision October 26. He found Calvignac's dismissal unwarranted. Since his new functions prevented the mayor from doing his regular work, he was to be granted a leave of absence. But the companies were held justified in not reemploying workers found guilty of violence and were not obliged to replace Humblot. The miners initially rejected this finding.[43]

In their own report, Millerand and his two colleagues expressed satisfaction with Loubet's decision on the first point but held that it contradicted the second and third. If the company was declared wrong in firing Calvignac, how could Loubet say nothing justified the dismissal of its manager?[44] The miners voted to continue the strike and 'await the verdict of public opinion' but, after lengthy discussions with their more politically attuned representatives, agreed to resume work. The three promised to seek the pardon of the condemned strikers and find them employment elsewhere, and Millerand praised the men for their difficult and emotional decision.

The outcome provided an indication of things to come. Adrien Veber, a writer for *La Revue socialiste,* told how the decision was tearfully accepted, without enthusiasm and with resignation. The workers had voted their appreciation for the 'beneficial intervention' of their delegates, but, while noting the proper parliamentary conclusion of the conflict, Veber admitted having hoped for more, for the formation of a new French left different from the old republicans who 'slid softly into the arms of the right'.[45] The article appeared as a first sign of dissatisfaction with the new reformist outlook.

Another consequence issued from the widespread opposition to Carmaux's conservative deputy. The Marquis de Solages was a member of the family owning the mines, and he resigned his seat. Jaurès, his predecessor in the Chamber who had been defeated by him in 1889, was virtually assured reelection. Millerand campaigned for him and wrote that his return to Parliament would add a logical ending to the politically motivated Carmaux strike. On January 11, 1893, he was able to congratulate the voters of Carmaux for returning Jaurès,[46] and his faith in the usefulness of republican institutions was wholly reaffirmed.

6. An admiring, yet dissatisfied, contemporary, listening to Millerand, made the following observation: 'The eloquence of M. Millerand is cold and correct. It reflects sincerity and reason, and reveals a scarcely-concealed contempt for the older generation. Listening carefully to Millerand, one is struck by the total absence of warmth and by the icy indifference in every sentence – almost every word. The young deputy shows not the slightest sign of enthusiasm for the great ideas which he sets forth and defends so persuasively and eloquently. Not the least amount of ardor for the democratic principles that he supports! He thinks what he says, and says what he thinks; and this is all. May his listeners profit from his words.'[47]

Another writer later compared Millerand's speaking style with that of various French politicians. He said that Jaurès poured forth, Clemenceau rejoined, Alexandre Ribot advised, Briand seduced, but Millerand tried to convince. His speeches, each syllable enunciated, resembled mathematical demonstrations and were characterized by solidity, clarity, sobriety and order. His object was not so much to arouse emotion as to further understanding; and they were delivered calmly, conveying a sense of reality that concealed the energy propelling them.[48] These descriptions all fitted Millerand's major speech in the 1889–1893 legislature, that given June 21, 1892, attacking the Bank of France. It offered a prime example of the demands made for nationalization of transportation, mining and finance that typified Millerand's legislative activity, when he was not defending the particular interests of his constituents.

Napoleon I founded the Bank in 1800 to 'stabilize the currency' and facilitate government borrowing. From its inception it was owned and controlled by the nation's large private banking interests. In using their position on the Bank's governing board to advise granting, or threatening to withhold, loans to the government, these financiers wielded vast political influence. In limiting the issue of paper money, they also made the franc one of the world's stablest currencies (although their tight money policy may have contributed to limiting French industrial growth). Its charter scheduled to expire in 1897, negotiations for its renewal were already underway in 1892. Anticipating an attack upon its 'privileges' the Bank had offered certain concessions. Millerand labeled all of them insufficient in his speech to the Chamber calling for its nationalization.[49]

The concessions were insufficient, he said, in exchange for the ratification of an agreement permitting the distribution of 817 million francs among only 26,517 stockholders. Millerand was seconded by Pelletan, while the economist, Léon Say, and the reporter for the bill renewing the charter, Burdeau, defended the Bank.

Millerand attacked the Bank for the privileges it received and denied the importance of its role as a credit-making institution designed to serve French commerce. In rendering the bulk of its services not to the public but to its stockholders, it had failed to provide for the needs of small business. In support of his arguments he cited the objections raised when renewal of the charter was first discussed in 1806, then in 1840 and again in 1857. Each time the opposition had viewed the Bank as a public institution, with the state and government as much involved in its transactions as its shareholders.

The speaker then described the detailed and technical procedures by which public ownership could be achieved; specifically, how an elected administrative council could replace the Bank's Council of Regency. The ideas presented revealed the rare – given the economic ignorance of most French legislators – familiarity with banking techniques acquired only after methodical study. They also attested to Millerand's implicit insistence on not destroying an old institution without suggesting a realistic replacement, in this case a state bank. Only in his conclusion did he invoke socialist concerns. In gathering and relying on data he sought to implement his objective by stressing the benefits and not the fairness of nationalization.

The *Journal officiel* reported that the speaker was repeatedly interrupted by applause from the left and center. He ended with an incantation to the bourgeoisie, inviting it to rally to the economic transformation ushering in the future. Emancipated by three revolutions and in full pursuit of its social development, labor asked only that universal suffrage have as its necessary complement universal well-being. It estimated that it was contradictory for a people to be both miserable and sovereign. The people would take possession of institutions previously exploited by a small minority. The bourgeoisie could not stop its progress and consequently must know how to make in time the necessary sacrifices.

La Revue socialiste hailed the speech as one of the best in recent years in the Chamber and published it in its entirety. The 'young and brilliant deputy of the Seine', it reported, had delivered an 'eloquent and substantial address'. A critical commentator admitted it was an 'inimitable masterpiece of a parliamentary speech' and that many deputies left that night resolved to make Millerand something of a guide. However, they were too dazzled to close debate and, fortunately for the Bank, postponed their decision. Pelletan spoke the next day, successfully muddied the issues, and support for the Bank was once again consolidated.[50]

7. Millerand did not often attain smilar heights of eloquence, but his efforts in Parliament were unrelenting. Several of the proposals first brought to the floor of this legislature, or in the columns of *Le XIXe Siècle* – or the newspaper that he began to write for as well in 1892, *La Petite République* – reappeared as the projects later undertaken as Minister of Commerce. Especially noteworthy were measures designed to establish a national retirement-benefits program and to further trade-union growth.

Like many on the French left, Millerand did not trust the Ralliement. The socialist deputy believed the church had come to the support of the Republic only to find a better means of appropriating it and had sponsored Christian socialism for the same reason. To provide an illustration, he pointed to an employers' trade association in the Nord which, with the support of the local clergy, required workers to pass by the confessional in order to retain their positions.[51] Millerand, Jaurès, other socialists and the entire French left retained a strong anticlerical republicanism. Suspected by the left, branded by the right, *rallies* remained few in number. Catholic criticisms of socialists preferring as allies the anticlerical middle class to the forces of Social-Catholicism were not without substance.[52]

The end of 1892 brought the disclosure of the Panama scandals, which indirectly precipitated a regrouping of the republican left. In December twenty deputies were charged with selling their votes to the Panama Company, and 104 others, including several ministers, were later shown to have been rewarded for securing government loans and even the right to issue shares in a public lottery. Disillusion with parliamentarianism was again widespread, but the Republic had found new defenders. The National Council of the Marxist Parti ouvrier maintained that the scandals had nothing to do with the republican form of government.[53] Reporting for the Chamber committee investigating the affair, Millerand recommended the suspension of parliamentary activity for the accused. A majority adopted the motion, and in the process one noted widespread cooperation between Radicals and socialists.[54] The latter understandably seized the opportunity to denounce capitalist corruption, and the scandal helped to return perhaps forty to fifty socialist candidates in the next year's national legislative elections. The lesson drawn by Millerand was that the need for state intervention ought to be obvious when furthering the public interest, and he repeated the call for nationalization of the Bank of France in order to prevent 'a domestic Panama'.[55]

At the suggestion of René Goblet, Radicals and socialists attempted to distinguish themselves from parties long entrenched in power and therefore more reprehensible. Accordingly, on February 16, their spokesmen presented a joint declaration of principles. Millerand and Lafargue spoke for the socialists, and André Daniel, reporting the event, noted that Radicals were invited to join forces with socialists on the grounds that it was necessary for all avant-garde republicans 'to take the same step as M. Millerand'.[56]

Millerand had foreshadowed a regrouping of parliamentary forces the previous March. In a speech delivered at Tarbes he had criticized the new Loubet cabinet as being no different from its predecessor and as revealing the need of the republican party to regroup in order to win social reforms.[57] A riot in the Latin Quarter during the summer of 1893 precipitated the realignment that was to emerge during the next legislature.

The Prefect of the Seine ordered a number of trade unions affiliated with the Paris Labor Exchange (Bourse du travail) to conform to the Law of 1884 and reveal the names of their officers. Originally designed as a placement center, the Exchange housed several unions said to be run by revolutionaries. In deciding on firm action the government had earlier closed it down to prevent a scheduled May Day celebration. Blanquists and Allemanists demonstrated in front of the doors to show their support for the unions. They had been dispersed by the police, and included among those arrested were two deputies, Eugène Baudin and Dumay. Dupuy congratulated the authorities on their action, but in Jaurès' view the government was repressing the most revolutionary unions as part of a larger and systematic effort to destroy socialism.[58] On July 4, the day the present order was to have taken effect, a mob beseiged a police station, burned kiosks and overturned buses. The Dupuy ministry sent troops to occupy and again close the Bourse and refused in Parliament to answer all questions until order was restored.

On July 8 Millerand attacked the government on its inability to handle the situation. He called its closing of the Bourse 'illegal', for the right of free association took precedence over the 1884 Law, and he accused Dupuy of 'widening the gap between workers and the bourgeois Republic'. The workers, Millerand threatened, would be the ultimate judges in the elections to come.[59]

Dupuy acknowledged instances of brutality but insisted on the need to enforce the law; if organizers of the Exchange were guilty of malpractice, the government had no choice but to close what he called 'that *foyer* of revolutionary agitation'. He defended the dispersion of the nonauthorized unions by maintaining that he had 'freed the workers from an anonymous tyranny'. And following a promise to reorganize the Paris police – he named the Prefect France's new ambassador to Austria – he received a vote of confidence. In an afternoon session held the same day, dissatisfied Radicals ironically asked that similar treatment, that is, dissolution, be accorded non-authorized religious associations. Two days later the Chamber refused to entertain any motion of amnesty for the guilty unions and proceeded to concern itself with the budget and with the state of French relations with Siam.[60]

The uproar and disorder in Paris during these days was enormous. On July 8, the city's Municipal Council published a manifesto criticizing the government's 'offense' in closing the Exchange without a court order. Rather than celebrate Bastille Day, Paris students held a day of mourning, and they received the support of the Council. In the general elections held that autumn the district was to send the revolutionary René Viviani to the Chamber, an indication of the popularity of socialism in the Latin Quarter in the last decade of the century.

Later in the summer Millerand defended the forty-four unauthorized unions before a correctional tribunal. He did not deny that the law had been broken but demonstrated the reluctance of previous governments to enforce it. Trade union officials, he argued, were justified in refusing to identify themselves, especially in the provinces where an important employer often served as mayor. The Labor Exchange itself was not a federation of unions but an education and placement center. However, the presiding magistrate decided that the law had to be accepted in its entirety, and he ordered the immediate dissolution of the offending unions.[61]

The ruling was poorly received by labor and its friends. An immediate consequence was the formation of a league of socialist journalists, and it at once issued a declaration of solidarity with the now illegal unions. It elected Malon honorary president, and Millerand served in both the league's administrative and judiciary council. That forces on the other side of the political spectrum were also beginning to group was revealed after the Chamber recessed for the summer; Dupuy then gave a speech in Albi in support of the *rallies*. He described them as 'yesterday's adversaries who today ask to join us'. In another important address, an Opportunist deputy of note, Charles Jonnart, also expressed his preference for *rallies* over radicals.[62]

This last series of Chamber debates, marking the end of the 1889–1893 legislature, helped shatter the old 'republican concentration' uniting Opportunists and Radicals against Conservatives. The next Chamber was to see moderate republicans, alarmed at the growth of a party they considered revolutionary, turn to the right in an effort to stop socialism. Radicals joined forces with socialists to further the polarization of French politics. During the course of the 1889–1893 legislature, Millerand's authority had greatly increased. Older deputies were forced out by Boulangist quarrels. Others were discredited by financial scandals and would not return. A new generation was rising to power at the Palais Bourbon, and it was to witness the emergence of Millerand as chief of the socialist left.

5. La Petite République and the Socialist Union

Nous voulons réaliser l'union de tous ceux qui
croient que la république n'est pas un mot sonore,
destiné à griser les gogos et à masquer de dange-
reuses capitulations de conscience, mais une réalité
pleine de généreuses promesses, faite de progrès
incessant.

Millerand, *Le Petit Calaisien*, March 7, 1893

Aside from scattered municipal victories in industrialized departments, at the start of the last decade of the nineteenth century Millerand's new party had yet to prove itself a meaningful force in French politics. There was still no socialist organization in the Chamber of Deputies, although 'progressive republicans' had joined forces to examine neglected social problems. Their largely Radical program, we have noted, vaguely called for collectivization and the transfer of monopolies into public services. The election of 1889 proved a republican triumph over Boulangism but weakened the extreme left.[1]

By the beginning of the 1890s, however, there were signs of a revival in socialist fortunes, conceivably preconditions of political success. There was a mild upswing in the economy after 1887 and a renewal of labor demonstrations; workers marched for the eight-hour day in 1889 and celebrated the first May Day the following year. The number of trade union members tripled in the five years following 1890, while the founding of the Second International in 1889 encouraged political regrouping. Socialist candidates began performing well at the polls, and the municipal elections of 1892 foreshadowed the legislative gains of 1893. Four municipalities returned a socialist majority; in 150 others minorities were strong enough, with Radical support, to elect sympathetic mayors. Paul Lafargue was elected to the Chamber in 1891, the political strike of the Carmaux workers took place the next summer and Jaurès was returned in a by-election early in 1893.[2]

A prerequisite for success in the national political arena, however, was united action among the diverse socialist factions and between socialists and Radicals. The coalition that was established, the 'Socialist Union', marked the first legislative, if not yet programmatic or structural, unification of French socialism and antedated by a decade the founding of a united party. Millerand worked to unite socialists as well as to unite socialists with the republican left. Invaluable in bringing about the desired accord was the newly revamped newspaper, *La Petite République*.

Designed to present socialist and Radical views, and intially publishing the contributions of both, it swerved to the former, imperceptibly at first, directly and consciously with Millerand as editor-in-chief. During the decade beginning in 1893, and until its replacement by *L'Humanité,* the newspaper served as the leading socialist daily and for several years managed to reconcile the hostile elements within the movement. By avoiding divisive issues and by stressing views held in common, the Union was maintained during the 1893–1898 legislature, although more strongly among socialists than between them and Radicals. Indeed, alliance with Radicals was made possible only by the acceptance of reformism by most socialists. Marxists abandoned their insistence on total collectivization and promised small land owners continued enjoyment of their property.

The 1893 election elicited a stunning performance by socialists. The recourse to 'gradualism' was always part of the French tradition, and French socialism was never static. Still, by offering proof of the advantages of parliamentary procedures the election crystallized the process by which they came to be relied upon. Moreover, the victory strengthened the position of moderates like Millerand within the movement, men who insisted on using the legal and constitutional machinery made available by the Third Republic and who consequently turned the movement in an evolutionary direction. It then became a viable political force and for socialists made accomodation to existing society a real alternative.

1. Léon Gambetta founded *La Petite République* in 1875, and it became the official organ of his parliamentary Republican Union. The creation of a 'serious and disciplined party' and the 'triumph of the republican idea was in large part its work'. The newspaper subsequently changed hands. From holding a left-of-center position in 1886, it turned Boulangist in 1889, and when purchased by three wealthy young lawyers – Henry Pellier, Marcel Sembat and Henri Turot – who shared an interest in politics, became Radical and socialist in 1892. They had previously founded a literary review, but, interested in acquiring a political organ, selected *La Petite République* for the memories it invoked of Gambetta.[3]

The three were introduced to René Goblet, by then a Senator and regarded as a leader and elder statesman of Radicalism, whom they asked to run the paper. He accepted and formed a management committee consisting of Paul-Louis Peytral, Jean-Marie Sarrien and Millerand. Peytral and Sarrien were long-standing Radical-Socialists, having served in the Goblet ministry of December 1886–May 1887; we have seen that as a Radical deputy Millerand had defended Goblet's educational reforms. Modest offices were taken on the rue Chauchat; and it was decided that editorials, then indistinguishable from lead articles, would be written in turn by seven prominent Radicals and socialists: Goblet, Millerand, Eugène Fournière, Edouard Lockroy, Benoît Malon, Victor Leydet and Sembat.[4]

Circulation figures, however, remained embarrassingly consistent. From 1,100 copies they climbed painfully to 1,500 or 1,600, but, according to Pellier, the newspaper was soon read in government circles. He described Millerand as rarely absent from managerial meetings. 'He came like a gust of wind, always hurried and always with excellent advice. He found *le mot juste;* he proposed the best solution.'[5] Thus it was that Millerand came to *La Petite République,* the newspaper with which he was to remain affiliated during most of his socialist years.

By opening his review to socialists of all persuasions, Malon had shown awareness of the need to bring to bear upon the *status quo* a united socialist left. His partisans agreed. On November 6, 1892, while campaigning for the reelection of Jaurès, Millerand made a strong appeal at Lyon for a consolidation of the left. He argued that success in the next year's election required an alliance between socialists and other 'progressive republicans' and called for the drafting of a minimum socialist program to attract as many workers as possible to the movement. He rejected any recourse to violence, urging his audience to rely instead upon the franchise. A general *entente,* although impossible between anarchists and socialists, could unite socialists and other republicans. The scarcely veiled preference for Radicals and the explicit repudiation of anarchists was doubless prompted by Millerand's wish to have socialism acquire respectability by decisively distinguishing itself from anarchism – and from the violence associated with it. Certainly many socialists supported a pact with Radicals for this reason; similarly, left-wing Radicals found it easier to act in concert with parliamentary-oriented socialists.[6]

Le Revue socialiste hailed the speech in its *chronique* as 'the most important political event of the past month'. It was reminded, it said, of Clemenceau's admonition to prepare for the coming of the 'fourth estate'. Likewise, modern historians of French socialism have pointed to Millerand as paving the way for an alliance of left-wing republicans and repentant Boulangists with socialists.[7] In an article published the following February, Millerand now rejected any pressing need to concentrate, a requirement explaining republican political behavior since 1875. In the Chamber of Deputies he called for an end to a now 'useless' policy and for a republican program based on 'ideas and principles' rather than interests.[8]

Millerand was taking advantage of widespread dissatisfaction with the 1889 legislature. The 'abject failure' of the Chamber to enact adequate social legislation and the 'retrograde' policies of its last (Dupuy) government were cited by a contemporary as motives inspiring a union of Radicals and socialists. Also helping to bring the left together was fear of a *rallie*-Opportunist coalition. Writing in 1901, Daniel Halévy assailed the Chamber of 1889–1893 for 'consecrating all its time to satisfying large industry and agricultural proprietors', while Boulangism and Panama had tarnished the various groupings within it. He credited Millerand with having understood the situation, taking the initiative in the election campaign and bringing together the scattered forces of the left – from revolutionaries to dislocated Boulangists.[9]

In December 1892, socialist organizations of Paris joined forces with Independent socialists. Although short-lived, their 'League of Revolutionary Action' momentarily united Guesdists, Blanquists, Broussists and Independents. Guesde had unsuccessfully sought to include ex-Boulangists.[10] An example had been set, and agitation for common socialist action soon found its voice in *La Petite République*. It was Sembat, among its publishers, who came out most strongly for a 'republican-socialist' union. Blanquist by conviction, he was an intellectual who gave of his time and fortune to socialism. Goblet acknowledged the need for reform and agreed to cooperate with socialists. Still, he rejected extreme collectivist doctrine as 'repugnant'. His understanding of the implications of nationalization was less than complete, and Pellier remembered him one day in the midst of heated discussion as having pointed to his desk and shouting: 'But this is mine!' On Sembat's insistence, however, he consented to help create a union of Radicals and socialists for the coming election. He laid down one primary condition: the anticipated union should disclaim any recourse to violence.

After prolonged debate the staff agreed upon a program. 'To accomplish social reform', it began, 'we ask the cooperation of all republicans, of all socialists, no matter how reckless their theories... provided they use only peaceful and legal means to achieve their ends'. Sembat added there would no longer be quarrels among schools; each might retain its independence but should renounce the differences that only aided their common enemy. In a manner reminiscent of Jules Vallès' *Le Cri du Peuple*, *La Petite République* promised to make itself available to the entire left and predicted the eventual appearance of two large parties: progressive reformists and conservatives. Subsequently, socialist deputies drafted a parliamentary manifesto proclaiming the existence and listing the goals of a Socialist Union. Signed by Millerand, Lafargue and eleven others, it invoked universal suffrage as the 'supreme legal resource'.[11]

On January 15, 1893, there took place the important meeting of socialists and Radicals at the Tivoli Vaux-Hall in Paris. Socialists ranging from Guesdists to Independents formally allied themselves with Radicals, and all pledged to cooperate in the election by supporting mutually acceptable progressive candidates. In a key speech Millerand implored socialists of every persuasion to unite, 'to bury past disagreements [and] to forget sterile recriminations'. Circumstances were too grave to permit the luxury of isolation. He stressed instead areas of agreement: constitutional revision by an assembly, use of the referendum, direct representation of labor interests and administrative decentralization. Invariably vague on virtually all aspects of theory, Millerand cast about for minimum means of identification for socialists in order to promote their grouping. He plainly affirmed the doctrine of the class struggle, 'the reality of which could no longer be denied', and identified as candidates for liberation from finance capitalism white-collar as well as manual workers. Cited for nationalization were credit, transportation and mining. Expropriation, however, would be carried out 'in calm, with *sang froid,* by those in control of themselves'. United, republican socialists would make universal suffrage responsive to social needs and thereby identify workers and their aspirations with the Republic. Two days later Millerand repeated these themes in the Chamber.[12]

In February 1893, together with Abel Hovelacque, the former President of the Paris Municipal Council, Gustave Rouanet and other Independents, Millerand founded the Republican-Socialist Federation of the Seine. It aimed at winning the support of the individualistic Independent socialists and moved at once to launch a campaign for the organization of *arrondissement* and neighborhood committees. The founders of the Federation, in a public statement, said they wanted to unite those socialists who 'refused to imprison their doctrinal affirmations in any narrow formulation which could not possibly contain the manifold aspirations of the modern world in full pursuit of economic, political, intellectual, and moral development'.[13] At its meeting in Zurich that summer the Second International extended formal recognition to the new Federation.

2. Late in January 1893, Millerand asked Pellier to recommend a young lawyer to act as his secretary. The latter suggested René Viviani, aged twenty-nine, admitted to the Bar in 1887 and elected a secretary of the esteemed Conférence des Avocats two years later. Viviani had turned to socialism and became known in the Latin Quarter for impromptu inflam-

matory speeches. A revolutionary, he was brusque and careless of dress and manners. Although the subsequent interview had gone badly, he thought, Millerand selected him, and he soon began to write for *La Petite République*. He always acknowledged Millerand as his *patron,* although the latter was but a few years his senior; and if Viviani often required editorial restraint, their friendship became a close and enduring one. After Jaurès returned to the Chamber on January 24, 1893, he too became a regular contributor, Sembat having ceded his turn. The editorial balance now tipped to the socialist side, and Radicals on the staff began to show concern.[14]

Great camaraderie, however, still marked staff relations. Pellier recalled there seemed to be almost continual singing and joking. A younger journalist, Edmond Claris, described the editors as working together around a great common table while 'good and friendly talk filled the air'. The newspaper launched campaigns to raise money for striking workers. Often it became involved in expensive lawsuits and, despite its legal talent, did not always emerge successfully. On one occasion, according to Claris, Goblet 'handsomely' contributed personal funds. Yet, somehow, special editions were sent to Bordeaux and Marseilles, and for a two month period *La Petite République* was published in Marseilles.[15]

As summer approached, the 'honeymoon' between Radicals and socialists continued to fade. More socialist writers were employed. In addition to Millerand, Viviani and Jaurès, there was the energetic Maurice Sarraut, a participant in many duels; André Lefèvre, a science student; and Alexandre Zévaès, a leader in the Latin Quarter disturbances during July and subsequently a lieutenant of Jules Guesde. Millerand invited Gabriel Deville to represent a Marxist point of view. Georges Renard offered to review books and write a literary column. Most of the aforementioned volunteered their services and received no salary. Moreover, such well known socialists as Edouard Vaillant and Rouanet began to contribute occasional articles. Dismayed by the shift to the left, older Radicals like Lockroy, Peytral and Sarrien had already quit.[16]

In the wake of the disorders on the Left Bank, Viviani denounced 'police brutality' in a particularly provoking article. The next day an alarmed Goblet also announced his intention to resign. He could, he said, no longer run a newspaper that called people to the barricades; and he wished to know what happened to the understanding in which peaceful tactics were promised. Although *La Petite République* disclaimed responsibility for the story, Goblet was attacked by his colleagues in the Senate. Characteristically, he refrained from mentioning his forthcoming resignation. Goblet suggested Millerand as his replacement, praising his energy, but doubtless having in mind his moderation.[17]

The admiration between Goblet and Millerand was still mutual; the two had shared speakers' platforms in 1891 and 1892 to caution against complete acceptance of the *rallies* and to emphasize the need for reform. When Pellier visited Millerand in his apartment on the Boulevard Saint-Germain and offered him the post, the latter wanted and received assurances that the newspaper could survive at least through the election. With the understanding that he would exercise full control as political director, Millerand accepted.[18]

On July 19, 1893, *La Petite République* carried on its masthead Millerand's name as editor-in-chief. The new editor wrote that there would be no change of policy and that the coalition would be preserved. Goblet's letter of resignation followed, and it is noteworthy that while Goblet spoke of 'all progressive forces', Millerand referred to 'all socialist forces'. In a later interview he described his objectives at this time: 'I am a realist, you see; a practical man . Socialism then constituted a considerable force, but one that was not being used. In taking *La Petit République* I had two aims: to implant in that mass the needed sense of discipline... then to have the Republic profit therefrom; in a word, to give socialism the shape of a political party. That, however, could be accomplished only by accepting the conditions without which there is no party; peaceful struggle and total participation in every event, every debate, and, if I may say so, every emotion experienced by the nation.'[19]

The newspaper moved briskly to the left. On July 22 Millerand wrote that in keeping with its intention to hear all socialist spokesmen, *La Petite République* would publish articles by Jean Allemane. Soon Brousse and Guesde became regular contributors. 'Millerand', recalled Pellier, 'rapidly developed on *La Petite République* a union of socialist groupings, the union so often called for, but always considered impossible to reach.'[20] The Radicals, meanwhile, were shunted aside. Of the twenty-three candidates supported by the newspaper the only non-socialist was Goblet. Union with the Radicals still existed but had taken on the trappings of a *mariage de convenance*.

3. Millerand, wrote Pellier, was a 'marvelous' editor-in-chief. He had put all socialist factions into accord. He was able to handle old militants who at first regarded him as merely one more enlightened bourgeois but soon came to acknowledge his talent. There is the legend portraying him as industrious, somber and non-communicative. He was and remained an indefatigable worker. However, he reserved time for relaxation. One heard him sing arias from the Opéra comique; he found an occasional hour to bicycle in the Bois. In 1894 after a bad fall in Brittany, he began

to exercise in a gymnasium each morning, and the habit, at least in the form of long walks, remained.[21]

Millerand possessed an ability to pass from one job to another and to apply himself to each. He prepared his dossier at home, appeared at the Palais de Justice in the morning, went to the Chamber in the afternoon either for a session or for committee work, arrived at the newspaper, Pellier recalled, 'in a flash', and in an hour or two had criticized the last issue, laid out the next and written an editorial.

His moderate approach called for the use of considerable tact among his more excitable colleagues. If an article seemed dangerous or exaggerated Millerand intervened, but gently. One day Turot wrote in favor of the general strike. Millerand published the article, but the following day, in the same spot, maintained that the strike was never to be regarded as a goal. The real objective of the socialist party rather lay in the winning of public power by universal suffrage. Often Millerand had to restrain Viviani, who attacked the government with verve.[22]

However, *La Petite République* was avant-garde, animated and aggressive. In this overheated milieu even Millerand forgot himself when especially stirred. In early December 1893 he severely criticized the Moderate Deputy of Oran and Vice-President of the Chamber, Eugène Etienne, and refused to retract his remarks. The two duelled with swords, and Millerand suffered a slight chest wound.[23] There is evidence in Millerand's papers of at least one near-duel with the Prefect of the Loire Inférieure. Undoubtedly there were others, for Pellier wrote that Viviani was almost a 'constant second', and on 'one occasion' Jaurès served. Turot, Gerault-Richard, after joining the staff late in 1893, and others were no less active in this regard. The most serious incident, one amply revealing the passions of the time, centered on a Madame Paulier. Considering herself offended by an article written by Turot, she visited the office. Finding only a copy editor, Olivier, she shot him, and within a few months of a painful operation, the young man died. In a trial similar to that of Madame Calliaux twenty years later, she was acquitted.[24]

In August 1894 the newspaper moved to larger offices, previously occupied by *Le Cri du Peuple,* at 142 rue Montmartre. Later that month the government successfully sued under a revised press law and jailed Gérault-Richard for fifteen days. On September 24 Albert Goullé was imprisoned for two months for defaming Casimir-Perier, the President of the Republic. The chief opposition to *La Petite République* came from Yves Guyot's *Le Siècle*. After serving on the Paris Municipal Council, Guyot had become a Moderate deputy and leading critic of socialism, and the two newspapers and their editors sporadically exchanged insults.[25] By January 1, 1895, the newspaper no longer made any pretense of Radical participation; that day it began running on its masthead the words: 'Journal socialiste'.

4. After the Tivoli Vaux-hall meeting Guesdists and Independents frequently campaigned together. Millerand opened the republican-socialist campaign in March 1893 by speaking jointly with Lafargue at Calais. The use of metaphor was abundant – the word 'campaign', taken literally. Millerand asked the voters to choose between a clerical and a social republic. Republican concentration was no longer acceptable because ministers, unable to agree on reforms yet afraid to displease, conciliated the opposition by granting it favors. Socialists, the speaker complained, had cooperated most loyally, sacrificing their ideas for the common good; they were nevertheless still persecuted by the republican majority.[26]

Millerand's platform was similar to but considerably shorter than that of 1889. Revision of the Republic's 'monarchical constitution', reliance on legal procedures and the need for unity of the left were predominant themes. Again, no plank supported collectivization other than for the Bank of France, mines and railroads. Millerand admitted his program was a minimum one and at Calais reassured farmers that their property was not endangered by a socialist victory. This program nevertheless resembled closely those advanced by other socialist candidates, including Marxists. On March 9 Millerand, Jaurès and Guesde spoke at Lille. The three campaigned together at Bordeaux. Millerand shared a platform with Guesde at Roubaix on July 17, and they delivered joint speeches from Calais to Montpellier.[27]

His speeches were applauded by Guesdists. They too, considered 'the Republic 'the instrument of social transformation' and praised Millerand's evolution toward socialism. It stemmed, the Guesdist organ reported, from 'his impatience with the old parties' whose politics could no longer be accommodated by his 'integrity and talent'. Guesde predicted many would follow his example. Yet, as Millerand told his constituents in a closing speech on August 6, his position remained essentially that of 1889.[28] Marxists and reformists had created a union among French socialists committed to achieving its goals by reformist tactics. The Parti ouvrier had sharply modified its position on the fundamental questions of property, and in July Guesde had stated in Paris that 'one must be ignorant or acting in bad faith to suppose that socialists mean to suppress all individual ownership'.[29] Six years later, the Marxist weekly, *Le Socialiste*, was to deny that a real union had ever existed.

Socialism's new image elicited comment by 'informed opinion'. *Le Temps* found the approach of the new allies surprising 'not for its audacity or excesses, but for its relative moderation'. To the declamation of

the Socialist Union that it embraced all 'real republicans', the newspaper pointed out that the socialist party, in contrast with a few years
before when it had yet to establish its own political identity and could
only support Radical candidates, had today 'not only achieved independence but aspires to domination. It no longer goes to the Radicals; on
the contrary, it is the Radicals who go to it'.[30]

In his speech of August 6 Millerand had identified the social question
as the key to the election. He applied the phrase previously used on the
Municipal Council and which he was to use repeatedly in the future: 'It
is not by a miracle, not by the wave of a wand or by a blow of force that
the transformation of society will be achieved; it is rather by the intelligent determination and perseverance of all who are its victims.' He also
made sure to speak directly to the particular interests of his constituents.
A flyer printed by his electoral committee, now enlarged to a membership
of eighty-four, enumerated his efforts on their behalf. It described his
support for the Bovier-Lapierre Bill favoring trade-union growth. It reminded the reader that on three occasions his deputy had questioned the
Minister of Public Works about labor abuses on the part of the railroad
companies and asked for the representation of shop stewards on management boards. Small businessmen were to bear in mind that in 1890
Millerand had denounced the 'scandalous tax reductions' proposed for
large stores and worked to prevent increases in licensing costs, import
duties and taxes. He had fought to enlarge a clinic in the Quinze-Vingts
quarter and to rebuild the Gare de Lyon and Quai de la Rapée.[31]

La Petite République cheered the election of August 20 as a 'glorious'
socialist victory. Millerand easily won on the first round receiving
seventy-two percent of the votes cast – the highest percentage in Paris.
His nearest opponent, the Guesdist Ribonier, amassed only a fifth as
many.[32] Other socialist candidates, however, triumphed only after the
run-off election of September 3, attesting the usefulness of the electoral
coalition. Nineteen of the twenty-three candidates presented by *La Petite
République* won office. Also elected were about a dozen former Boulangists running as socialists. Goblet, too, was returned. Socialist newcomers to the Chamber included Vaillant, Sembat, Rouanet, Viviani and
Guesde. The Seine Department, allotted forty-five deputies, sent twenty-
seven socialists to Parliament, and their total number in the new Chamber may have gone over fifty.[33] The new Chamber was a young one; over
thirty deputies were no more than thirty years of age. Involvement in
the Panama scandal had discredited their seniors, and the left, in particular, benefited. Ernest Labrousse pointed to the election as the first
since 1881 that the Republic felt itself secure. The right, he said, threatened in 1885, Boulangism in 1889. He attributed the success of the left

to the economic depression which struck France during the last third of the century. It had worsened in the early 1890s; liberalism seemed incapable of curing the ills of society, and Millerand had not exaggerated when he told the voters of the XIIth *arrondissement* that the social question was paramount. However, the Moderate republican majority, with the aid of the new Catholic voters, returned 310 deputies; Radicals elected 123, *rallies* 35, and Conservatives 58.[34]

In his drive for unity, Millerand had not hesitated to appeal to former Boulangists and Marxists, as well as to Radicals and Independents. Guyot reproached Millerand with accepting ex-Boulangists into the Socialist Union. The Union, he pointed out, had received the support of *L'Intransigeant,* and Boulangists elected on socialist platforms included Hovelacque, Mery, Roche and Pierre Richard. Millerand himself was accused of being a Boulangist, and the charge, totally omitting the extent of Millerand's opposition to the movement and the speed with which he began to combat it, has been accepted at face value by an historian of the Third Republic, Jacques Chastenet. Guyot's criticism, it should be noted, was leveled in the aftermath of his defeat at the hands of one of the founders of the Union, Goblet, and bore witness to its author's dismay at the growth of socialism.[35]

Marxists rejoiced in the results, and Guesde hailed the election as a 'veritable revolution'. In spite of a lifetime of revolutionary propaganda he now predicted the electoral triumph of the working class and vowed to consecrate his efforts in the legislature to securing social reform. In a letter of appreciation to his Roubaix voters Guesde anticipated a socialist majority in the next election. 'Legally, by your will becoming law', he told them, 'the social tranformation will be achieved'.[36]

Not only had the old leadership mellowed in the light of success, but newer, less ideologically oriented leadership now prevailed. Above all, for socialism the election had proved an Independent victory. They returned twenty-one deputies, the other socialist groups combined, only sixteen. And Independents won three additional seats in by-elections held the following year. If we add to their number the dozen ex-Boulangists as well as the Radicals who gravitated toward them, we find a new and significant source of influence in French socialism. This new and young leadership – the average age of the Independent deputy was about forty – preferred the efficacy of organization and the advantages of political power.[37] If the shattered hopes of 1898 momentarily turned older leaders from parliamentary paths, the new ones remained and vindicated the commitment made by French socialism to the Republic.

The psychological effect of the victory on the party was perhaps best expressed by the reformist Gabriel Mermeix. Before 1892, he said, socialists had traveled mysteriously, like outlaws. The press had seldom annoyed them, the police too often. But after the election socialist leaders became respected deputies. They lectured at the Polytechnique; they were 'amiable and available'. For Mermiex, fifteen years of intransigence by Guesde and Vaillant had achieved nothing. Daniel Halévy observed there was little in common between socialists of the 1890s and those of the 1880s. They previously had 'exerted no influence, met in backrooms, and tore each other's reputations to shreds'. They controlled only twenty municipalities and a handful of Labor Exchanges – all they could show for seventeen years of propaganda.[38] But now, for socialists, the future seemed bright.

5.   In the new parliament socialist deputies were impassioned and eager. A flurry of excitement accompanied each of their acts. The editors of *La Revue socialiste* exulted: 'On every occasion [they reported], they intervene with an exuberance of talent, a youthful ardor, a sort of need to express themselves.' The critic and literary scholar for *La Revue des Deux mondes,* Eugène-Melchior de Vogüé, described their role: they constituted 'an admirable opposition'; on certain days 'the impartial observer believes they run the Chamber. Their pressure is constant and violent; one submits to it with indignation, but one submits'. The group's leadership in the attack and its almost perfect cohesion, the writer noted, gave it a place out of all proportion to its numbers. 'Others come to the Palais Bourbon; the socialists live here.' They equalled the Irish in the art of obstruction, always enlarging the deabte. And when the tired center would leave near the end of the day, they tried to create a quorum and continue the vote. The new deputies, aglow with victory, took pride in the use of slang and vigorous epithets and scanned the old parliamentarians of the center with the joy of battles to come.[39]

The socialists found social and economic issues of greater concern than anticlericalism and constitutional revision. They questioned general policy and denounced acts of government considered arbitrary. A socialist's speech (Viviani's) was posted at bourgeois expense on the walls of all the communes in France. Publicity soared. Once the recipients of only islolated votes, socialists now constituted a force whose work became widely known through the verbatim accounts printed in the *Journal officiel* and frequently in *Le Temps* and *Le Matin.* A contemporary, Paul Louis, observed: 'All France knows about socialism, from the Breton peasant to the Savoy mountaineer.'[40]

The alliance between Radicals and socialists, waning late in the campaign, gained new strength as a result of the conservative policies of the Dupuy and Casimir-Perier governments. Leftwing deputies especially resented the repressive legislation *(lois scélérates)* voted by an angry Moderate majority to counter a wave of anarchist attacks. By the end of December the government could suppress newspapers and organizations even suspected of conspiracy or provoking violence. After the assassination of President Sadi-Carnot the following June, the government won approval of a law designed simply to crush 'anarchist ideas'. Vaguely worded, it implied that not even private meetings and correspondence were secure from state repression. Socialists and Radicals saw in this legislation a denial of civil rights and a threat to all opponents of the government. Millerand cautioned the Chamber against acting out of revenge and tried to demonstrate that only a small coterie of 'financial interests' favored it. He insisted on a clear distinction of socialists from anarchists.[41]

The animosity between the left and the Dupuy and Casimir-Perier ministries had erupted soon after the new legislature convened on November 14. Millerand and Jaurès questioned Dupuy on his 'retrograde and provocative programs'. For the better part of three sessions the debate waged, and numerous Radicals supported the socialist position. Dupuy resigned when three Radical ministers quit his cabinet, and Casimir-Perier was named to replace him as head of the government.[42] The scion of a great mine-owning family and grandson of an Orleanist minister, he seemed a poor choice in the opinion of the socialists.

Another opportunity to attack the government came within a few weeks, in the wake of a miners' strike in the Nord Department. Millerand editorially denounced the ministry for refusing to apply an arbitration law enacted the previous year. He charged it with having preferred to despatch troops instead and accused Casimir-Perier, a long-time administrator of the Anzin mines, of conflicting interests. He asked the Chamber to approve Basly's request for a committee of inquiry, but saw the proposal defeated when made a question of confidence.[43]

A Millerand-led socialist attack succeeded in revising the ministry in May of 1894. Millerand defended the right of state railroad workers to unionize – and by suddenly shifting his support to a similar resolution, but sponsored by a Conservative, he helped to divide the center. Charles Dupuy again formed a government while Casimir-Perier replaced him as President of the Chamber. The angry Goblet attacked the new ministry as no different from its predecessor and hence inadmissable in a parliamentary regime. Then Goblet made a startling declaration. Fearful of the 'considerable and persistent increase in capitalist power', he asked for state repossession of major public services. Although rejecting full collectivization, he had placed himself in agreement with the minimum socialist program. Leftwing Radicals had publicly sided with socialists

7*

on an important question of doctrine, and their joint manifesto calling for an end to 'the oppression of capitalist monopoly' gathered seventy-five signatures.[44] A number of Radicals and socialists were once again allied.

Millerand expressed shock at the anarchist assassination of Carnot but urged that his successor be someone other than Dupuy or Casimir-Perier.[45] On June 29, 1894, the latter was nevertheless elected President of the Republic, and *La Petite République* led the outcry of socialist alarm. On July 5 a Millerand article censured 'the man from Anzin' for craving power. Socialist pressure was unrelenting. They attacked him for his origins, his wealth, his continued ownership of mining interests while in public office and for his generally conservative policies. Their newspapers unearthed libels for which his grandfather had been prosecuted. Millerand's article 'L'Enemi', in *La Petite République* November 8, best expressed their resentment. Rochefort, a refugee in England since the Boulangist debacle, joined the editorial assault on his return.

The campaign to force Casimir-Perier from office was headed by *La Petite République* but precipitated, according to Pellier's astonishing story, by Gerault-Richard. The latter had been supported by *La Petite République* during the election. He was one of the more ardent and self-seeking editors of a Radical newspaper, *Germinal,* housed across the street. It became insolvent shortly after; Gerault-Richard called that same evening and began to contribute articles. He had previously served three months in prison on a defamation charge – despite a strong defense by Millerand.[46]

On September 14 at the Coq d'Or restaurant where the staff often gathered, he announced that for fifty francs he could force the President to resign. The bluff was called; the money collected. Fifteen days later there appeared a ferocious attack on Casimir-Perier in the small weekly edited by Gerault-Richard, *Le Chambord.* It obviously intended libel.[47] The government started legal proceedings October 18, and that evening, with Sembat's assistance, he asked Pellier to persuade Jaurès to defend him. A reluctant Jaurès, seconded by Viviani, comprised the defense, and the penalty decreed November 6 amounted to a year's imprisonment and a 3000 franc fine. Soon after, a smiling Gerault-Richard announced his candidacy in a Chamber by-election for the XIIIth *arrondissement,* heavily populated by workers.

On December 8 *La Petite République* began to publish subscription lists for his campaign fund. In the election of December 24 its candidate amassed a plurality and on January 6 was elected to the Chamber. The next day, under the title 'The People's Verdict', Millerand called the election a socialist victory. On January 10, speaking for the socialist group, he asked the Chamber to allow Gerault-Richard to take his seat. Dupuy momentarily succeeded in blocking the resolution, arguing that even universal suffrage could not quell a court's just decision. Two days later, however, the new deputy was seated with his friends, much to the disgust of the President of the Republic.[48]

The immediate cause of the latter's departure from the Elysée Palace issued from Millerand's attack on the Dupuy government January 14, 1895, over the resignation of its Minister of Public Works, Louis Barthou. In the railway conventions of 1883, subsidies were promised to ensure a minimum rate of return to the Orléans and Midi lines. The railroads were expected to repay the state in more prosperous times. However, the subsidies grew ever-larger; the budget of 1895 envisaged 116 million francs for the two lines. Moreover, in the absence of any terminating date, the Minister of Public Works at the time, Raynal, stated that the guarantee was to expire only with the concession itself in 1956. Barthou disagreed with his predecessor's interpretation and brought the question to the Council of State. The nation's highest administrative tribunal decreed in favor of the companies, and Barthou, despite an appeal from Dupuy, resigned the next day.[49]

Millerand seized the opportunity to argue that not only Barthou but the entire ministry was struck by the Council's decision. He asked for parliamentary censure of Raynal's 1883 judgment, while an alternative resolution called for a committee of inquiry. When the Chamber refused by twenty-two votes to give priority to the latter resolution the government resigned. Casimir-Perier regarded himself as personally attacked, avowed he could no longer be effective without a supporting majority and also resigned. Moderates regretted the act; it established a precedent and, worse, appeared as a socialist victory. And jubilant socialists viewed it as precisely that.[50] However, socialist support was insufficient to enable the Radicals to have two of their number, Henri Brisson and Léon Bourgeois, designated respectively President of the Republic and Premier. Félix Faure, an obscure if suave Havre merchant and former Minister of the Navy, defeated both Brisson and another Progressist, Waldeck-Rousseau, while Alexandre Ribot, an old-line liberal, formed a new government.

Socialists continued their opposition to what they called 'non-progressive' governments when the new ministry announced its refusal to intervene in labor disputes. During a strike of the Carmaux glass-workers in October 1895, socialists – especially Jaurès, whose interpellation lasted two days – denounced it for its policy of non-interference. Millerand attributed the presence of hostile police and the hiring of scabs to the government's refusal to act or even to send an investigating committee. Two days after Millerand's attack Ribot fell when socialists also criticized his refusal to publish an investigator's report of a railroad scandal on the Chemin de Fer du Sud, a line in Provence. A sufficient number of deputies, afraid to be compromised, voted with the left to upset the cabinet, the fourth of the legislature.[51] The reversal made possible the installation on November 1, 1895, of the first all-Radical ministry, that of Léon Bourgeois. Socialists felt their efforts were justified and looked forward to its work.

6. Socialists and Radicals thus comprised the bulk of the opposition to Progressist governments throughout the 1890s. For the former, it was Vaillant who usually spoke on labor questions, Guesde on labor and matters of socialist theory, Millerand on government and foreign policy issues and Jaurès on all these things. In spite of their success in overthrowing ministry after ministry, socialists by no means constituted a 'sterile opposition' hostile to the Republic. A program acceptable to all was slowly being shaped as cooperation strengthened among the diverse factions and as each continued to rely on reformist tactics. Millerand set a standard in insisting on legal procedures. He maintained that he was a revolutionary in so far as his goal, the disappearance of class division, was revolutionary. It was revolutionary methods, reliance on violence, that he found useless and incompatible with universal suffrage. He rejected non-parliamentary action, especially the anarchist-sponsored call for the general strike, and attached himself so strongly to the Republic that he defined socialism as its economic and social expression.[52]

Millerand worked hardest to maintain unity among socialists, anxious to keep within the movement both Independents and more aggressive elements. In October 1894, in order not to appear to favor one school over another, he formally dissociated himself from his Independent colleagues. Two months later, on the other hand, he squarely opposed the efforts of some militant socialists who criticized Guesde, Vaillant and Jaurès for their full acceptance of the Republic. Georges Renard recalled that Deville, still very much a revolutionary, in the preface to one of his books had again attacked Malon. Millerand then implored the loyal Renard, in the interests of unity, not to reply in *La Petite République*. For his pains, said Renard, Millerand was seen as senseless and as an alarmist by some former Radical friends and treated with indifference and almost hostility by the most militant of the socialists within his party. 'He tried to hold between both this *juste milieu*, which is so difficult to find and to maintain.'[53]

How Millerand justified his efforts to unify socialists, and socialists with the left, was best revealed in a lecture given to a collectivist students' group in June of 1895. He credited the Socialist Union with expanding socialist influence and defeating Casimir-Perier. Still, the actions of its members were not unlimited. Each was free 'to fire on the enemy when and how he liked; not free, however, to fire on other socialists'.[54]

The speaker found that tactical cooperation frequently led to theoretical agreement. Socialist groups differed largely because they had been out of touch with each other. Yet even these differences, from a doctrinal point of view, were not profound. Each group shared not only the same point of departure in a common critique of capitalism but also sought the same objective. For despite variations in their respective images of future society, all agreed that an individual was to receive the 'integral product of his labor' and that none was to live on the work of others. Socialists were also finding themselves in accord on the first steps to be taken. Most rejected catastrophic solutions. Collectivism remained a common strategy, but history revealed that betterment was attained by degrees. Not against small proprietors would the socialist party struggle but against nationwide enterprises like the Bank, railroads and mines, under the control of a small plutocratic minority. It would then proceed to industries like sugar refining, where private ownership was highly centralized or monopolized.

Alone, however, the worker was powerless; he needed to rely both on cooperative and political action. While trade unions defended his professional interests, only legislative representation in Parliament offered political support, hence the necessity of winning public power. And unity made that victory possible. The socialist party, he concluded, was realistic. For in a country where universal suffrage was sovereign, in principle if not in fact, the party seized all opportunities: corporate, political and legal.

Millerand's obsession with universal suffrage was not unique in western socialism in the late nineteenth century. If, within the French movement a Jaurès never ruled out revolution, as late as 1898 he was describing democracy as 'the largest and most solid terrain on which the working class can stand; ... the bed rock that the reactionary bourgeoisie cannot dissolve without opening fissures in the earth, and throwing itself into them'.[55] At the same time a revolutionary minority never ceased denouncing what it regarded as excessive reliance on the caprices of a bourgeois state, and this minority was to see its ranks swelled with former reformists disillusioned by the state's persistent unwillingness to vote a socialist majority into office. It is nevertheless true that throughout the 1890s reformist currents became ever stronger within European socialism. In France, they began revealing themselves in foreign as well as domestic pursuits. By 1896, they were to make possible the first tentative programmatic unification of French socialists. In all these activities, Millerand's part was a leading one.

6. The triumph of reformism

A consequence of reformism was socialist support of the Republic in
matters of foreign affairs. Given their newly solidified faith in the virtues
of universal suffrage, it was natural for socialists to endorse the regime
that promoted its exercise against threats both within and outside of
France. Moreover, and in the best Jacobin tradition, reformist socialists
found no incompatibility between the internationalism they preached and
the primacy of French interests they defended. What better way, they declaimed, to guarantee the success of international socialism than to have
France take the lead in its expansion! What surer way to jeopardize that
success than to weaken the one country that had introduced the principles
of liberty and equality to Europe! Moreover, for Millerand, as for most
Frenchmen, the defeat of 1871 and the loss of the two provinces had
never been forgotten. Communards, like Conservatives, retained anti-
German sentiments. If the desire for *revanche* was not always spoken, as
Gambetta had advised, it was long thought of. The statue representing
Strasbourg, draped in black on the Place de la Concorde, served as a
constant reminder. Not until a wave of militant internationalism swept
over the extreme left after 1904–1905 did many socialists temporarily
shed their hostility to the Reich.[1]

Revenge, or even adequate preparations for self-defense, remained
objects of longing until France could break out of the diplomatic isolation imposed by Bismarck. In accepting British control in Egypt, Gambetta had tried for an English alliance; the outcome, however, was not
rapprochement but increased hostility. Conflicting colonial ambitions
in the Sudan, to be dramatized by the Fashoda crisis in 1898, worsened
relations. France turned to Russia instead. A combination of French
financial and diplomatic activity, and obstinacy on the part of Bismarck's

successors, led to an *entente* between the two countries in August 1891. Earlier in the summer a French squadron had visited the base at Kronstadt, and Europeans looked on in disbelief at the tsar standing stiffly at attention while the Marseillaise was played. Both visit and reception testified to a mutual desire for an agreement. Generals and diplomats then tried to turn the *entente* into an alliance. A military convention was signed by the French and Russian chiefs of staff in August 1892, and it attained the force of a treaty by an exchange of diplomatic notes in January 1894. All negotiations were kept concealed; the treaty itself called for secrecy, and Frenchmen could only guess at its contents.

1. Millerand recalled that he began to speak on foreign affairs in the 1893–1898 Chamber.[2] Immediately before the new legislature convened he had asked, and won, socialist support for the Franco-Russian alliance on the grounds that his party could not limit itself to economic and social problems. It could not, he argued, without betraying its mission as a national party, disregard any vital public question. As far back as February 8, 1890, he had written in *Le XIXe Siècle* about the need to win Italy away from the Triple Alliance. In the same newspaper on November 20, 1890, he had welcomed the propect of an alliance between France and Russia, provided that it would not impinge upon France's internal affairs. He was to maintain this position until the end of Russian participation in World War I. The envisaged alliance, however, posed a particularly thorny problem for socialists. Although internationalist in outlook, many of them supported the Republic's efforts to find allies. Russia, on the other hand, an absolutist, authoritarian state with a long history of anti-revolutionary activity, was anathema to the left.

A victory celebration was scheduled for September 30, 1893, to honor Sembat's election as deputy. Millerand decided to make the banquet a forum for a discussion on foreign affairs and to speak on the role of socialism in the patriot-internationalist controversy in general and on the Franco-Russian alliance in particular. Ten days before it took place, he revealed his motives and the gist of his intended text to Eugène Fournière, who, he was sure, would give him 'a sympathetic hearing'. Given the views of socialists like Vaillant and Fournière on the need to support the Russian proletariat, and by implication, to do nothing to strengthen the tsar's hand, and the conflicting view that the cause of French and international socialism could be served by an alliance with Russia, Millerand considered a debate on the subject 'inevitable'. Admitting that he was speaking for himself and seeking support, Millerand wrote: 'As long as that odious abuse of force committed in 1871 lacks legitimate reparation, we must be irreconcilable toward the German Empire. For the sake of the honor and the dignity of France, which then pulled back, we must acknowledge that we are unable, by our own efforts, to wipe away the stain of that abominable abduction.'[3]

He observed that in so far as it was the War of 1870–1871 that 'upset the European chessboard', France was able 'to select the pawn that can ally the two countries'. The Russian alliance could further national security, and socialists must not hesitate to accept it. At the same time they were to make it clear that France would keep its *sangfroid* and not throw herself into the arms of Russia. It was not surprising that in 1893 the French Republic had to ally itself with a major power. Millerand recalled Engels' 'prophetic' letter of September 1870 warning against a German seizure of Alsace-Lorraine. 'We accept a situation which is not of our making', he told Fournière, 'and above all, we must protect the nation against the war-like fantasies of a Humbert as well as a William.'

His tone somewhat more circumspect, Millerand's message to the socialists gathered to applaud Sembat paralleled that sent to Fournière.[4] He told them they owed their first loyalty to France. Although not responsible for the *entente* with Russia, socialists could not ignore it; the 'cause of free men everywhere' depended on France's ability to maintain her great-power status. Accordingly, and regardless of criticism, French socialists were to remain 'good, sincere, fervent patriots'. Pacifists among them urged disarmament; but it was not for France to set the example. She had to remain alert, rifle at her side, because the disturbance of European peace depended not on her but on a king's volition. 'It is not a conquered, dismembered France that can take the initiative in disarmament and abandon herself, tied hand and foot, to the appetites of her implacable enemies. ... In such a situation, it is an imperative duty for socialists to accept, regardless of their deeprooted resentment, the twofold responsibility of universal compulsory military service and the burdens of a budget of war. ... All considerations must give way to this superior consideration, the interests of national defense.'

Socialists in the Chamber must work to control the budget and to reduce military service to two years but without enjoying complete freedom to do so. Their votes must above all be influenced by the opinion of experts. Nor were socialists completely free to act in regard to diplomatic alliances; they had to take existing circumstances into account. The Triple Alliance stands; formed in fear of France, it encircles her, and who can deny the country the right to seek forces balancing those which threaten her? No doubt it was more desirable to be guided by 'natural inclinations' in choosing allies. But similar institutions did not always provide sufficient grounds for common international action, and governments that differed in style may still establish cordial relations.

An example lay in the amiable relations between the Russian Empire and the republican United States. On the condition that France was to be neither the *protégé* nor the *obligée* of Russia, Millerand urged all socialists, like all Frenchmen, to accept the Russian alliance. He asked his listeners to welcome a visiting Russian squadron not with 'exuberant enthusiasm' but with 'courteous sympathy'. Sembat concurred and denounced 'sterile manifestations' as a possible tactic in the Chamber.

That this prosition was accepted, however grudgingly, by socialists and guided their thinking on foreign affairs for the remainder of the legislature revealed the predominance of reformism within the French movement. Marxists did not object. Guesde's consistent view of war as the natural outcome of bourgeois conflict, and his denunciation of insurrectional means to prevent it, were compatible with growing nationalist feeling on the part of reformists. France was to be defended by its proletariat; accordingly, the alliance with tsarist Russia, for socialists long the most reactionary regime in Europe, was upheld. The Eleventh Annual Congress of the Parti ouvrier, which followed in October, asked only that a distinction be made between sailors and officers when the Russian fleet arrived at Toulon. M. and Mme. Lafargue appeared at a ball held in Paris to honor the visitors.[5] The National Council of the Workers party – and français was now firmly attached to Parti ouvrier – defined the party's position with respect to the alliance: 'It is a calumny to say that socialists have no country. ... We will not let them translate our glorious cry of 'Long live the International' into the inept yelp of 'Down with France'. ... No! Internationalism is not the degredation or the sacrifice of the country. Nations are the necessary requisite for humanity ... the historic mission of the French proletariat... [requires] a great and strong France. ...' The Manifesto, signed by Guesde, Ferroul and forty others stated that the right of self-defense extended to nations as well as to workers. 'France attacked', it concluded, 'will have no more ardent defenders than socialists of the Workers party.'[6]

In London, Engels noted the Guesdists' progressive incorporation of patriotism into French Marxist thought and approved. He wrote to Laura Lafargue in June: 'The new departure of the Parti ouvrier with regard to 'patriotism' is very rational in itself; international union can exist only between *nations,* whose existence, autonomy, and independence as to internal matters is therefore implied in the very word internationalism. And the pressure of the pseudo-patriots, sooner or later, was certain to provoke an utterance of this kind, even without the alliance with Millerand and Jaurès, who, no doubt, have also urged the necessity of such an act.'[7] Very much aware of the need to cater to growing national feeling on the part of the French electorate, Guesde was to complete the fusion of patriotism and socialism and to provide an analogy. In the France of 1789, he wrote, no one said, 'Down with Picardy'. To support the Second International today, one need not denounce France. If Frenchmen then did not cease to be Normans, socialists now do not cease to be Frenchmen. Those trying to separate the two are playing into the hands of the bourgeoisie.[8]

Blanquists also defended the Franco-Russian alliance, Vaillant viewing the pact as a measure designed to keep the peace. The degree to which militant socialists thought in terms of French interests was shown by the Parti ouvrier's Montluçon Congress in September 1898. Nicholas II had proposed universal disarmament – a long-standing socialist goal. But the cautious Guesdists were caught up in the election campaign of that year. While 'in principle favorable to the proposition of the Emperor of Russia,' wrote a police observer, '[they] do not believe in its prompt realization... in the conditions envisaged until now.' The Congress rejected the proposal for use in its platform.[9] Thus it was that Millerand helped bring socialist support to the Republic, not only in terms of the reliance placed upon the state for social reform but also from the standpoint of foreign affairs.

Millerand's concern with the national interest continued to direct his thinking on foreign issues. On June 10, 1895, together with Rouanet, he questioned the Ribot government on risking French involvement in the Sino-Japanese War without parliamentary approval and under the terms of an unknown treaty. Did the alliance, he asked, commit France to support Russian territorial ambitions in Asia? Speaking 'as a Frenchman', he doubted that 'French interests' could profit from the adventure, despite the support shown for it by the Russian ally. Hanotaux admitted only that an alliance existed between France and Russia, his first such acknowledgment, and that it was in France's interest to support Russian claims. An angry Millerand and Jaurès then demanded to know the precise French commitment.[10]

Along with spokesmen from the Parti ouvrier Millerand protested the proposed French participation in ceremonies scheduled for the opening of Germany's Kiel canal. Socialists, he wrote on June 12, favored international cooperation as a means of preserving peace, but they also considered it necessary 'to hasten the moment of separation' of Alsace-Lorraine. To one observer the socialists seemed more concerned with the lost provinces than most Frenchmen. Senator Scheurer-Kestner noted that the visit of the tsar in October 1896 aroused mixed feelings. He said that if Alsatians regarded the 'moment of justice' as imminent, the 'great majority of the population' feared a disaster. Investigators in France's national intelligence organization, the Sûreté Générale, also showed surprise at the widespread acceptance of national interests by socialists. A report in September 1897 from an agent who had managed to infiltrate their ranks described fears of rumored Russian intentions to organize a 'continental bloc' against England. It was to include France and Germany, and the idea of possible French acquiescence to the loss of Alsace-Lorraine 'infuriated' socialists, rendering them all the more patriotic.[11]

Legitimate concern with defense of the Republic and with redressing a wrong they saw as having been inflicted upon France help to account for the stress laid by Millerand and other socialists on foreign affairs. A related explanation, more mundane but no less important, bore upon their decision to win political power at the polls. If success here called for increasingly attractive domestic programs, it also meant catering to the voters' sentiments on external issues. Frenchmen could hardly be expected to turn over the keys of national security to internationalist-minded Marxists, and socialist chiefs took pains to prevent repetition of the pro-German charges once leveled at Guesdists. Some socialists, notably Jaurès, never shed their hostility toward Russian autocracy. The bulk of the socialist criticism of the Russian alliance that developed later in the decade, however, stemmed from fears that a total commitment to her ally might be contrary to French interests. The reformism of French socialists in regard to foreign affairs thus appeared overwhelming.

Afraid these interests were receiving secondary consideration, Millerand continued to ask that the contents of the treaty be made public.[12] French concern with conflicting claims in Crete provided another opportunity to raise the question. The struggle of revolutionaries to have the island annexed by Greece had generated Turkish acts of repression. In keeping with its desire to maintain the enfeebled Ottoman Empire, Russian diplomacy supported the Turkish, rather than the Greek position, and Millerand lashed out at Hanotaux for having committed France to Russia. A Manifesto issued by the socialist group of deputies on March 18, 1897, stated that the government feared to divulge the real reasons for its policy and suggested that it fulfilled some secret clause or other of the Franco-Russian treaty.[13]

In February 1898 Millerand once more pointed to a possible connection between France's Mediterranean policy and a concealed portion of the alliance. If the treaty worked simply to maintain the peace and retain the *status quo,* then Germany was freed of all anxiety over France, freed to fight, at her ease, 'our influence, our commerce, our industry'.[14] In this case, his opposition to the Méline ministry, always constant, was being stepped up for the coming election. But the party-wide support given to the alliance remained unshaken. Millerand's Saint-Mandé unity program, given in 1896, had defended it, and nearly all socialists acclaimed the speech. Millerand and French socialism both displayed their patriotism in the 1890s, neither accepting as definitive the results of the War of 1870. His interest in foreign affairs was to grow: in November 1898 he was elected a member of the Chamber's Army Committee, and by 1912 Millerand was to prefer, though not to obtain, the Ministry of Foreign Affairs to that of War in Poincaré's government. When he succeeded Clemenceau and formed his own government in 1920, he installed himself at the Quai d'Orsay as France's first diplomat.

2. That part of reformist strategy calling for cooperation with progressive middle-class governments was put into practice in October 1896 when Léon Bourgeois successfully formed a Radical ministry. With a program headed by progressive income and inheritance taxes, workers' pensions and arbitration procedures in cases of industrial conflict, the new cabinet deliberately sought socialist support. While in office it reopened the Paris Labor Exchange, proposed arbitration of the Carmaux strike and announced a 'policy of confidence toward state workers'. The Minister of Commerce, Mesureur, went so far as to use the expression 'a wise and practical socialism'.

The delighted socialists returned the confidence shown in them by giving the government their full support. The enthusiasm displayed by each faction in defending a non-socialist ministry reflected the varying degrees to which socialists were committed to reformism. Independents viewed the ministry as absolutely necessary to advance the cause of reform; Marxists, if harboring greater reservations, also voted consistently to support it. In recalling their behavior during this period, Millerand said that socialists 'spared neither their approval nor their cooperation' to participate in public life. His own assistance was unqualified. Yves Guyot called him 'majority leader of the Bourgeois cabinet', with preponderent influence in the Chamber and on the public.[15]

Marxists not only accomodated Bourgeois but in November 1895, along with other parliamentary socialists, voted to retain the despised *lois scélérates* in order to prevent his fall. Although lacking any clearly formulated policy on imperialism, socialists swallowed their misgivings about granting public support for overseas ventures designed to benefit only a handful of investors. The colonialist lobby, headed by Eugène Etienne, demanded funds for a military expedition to complete the mishandled conquest of Madagascar. Socialist deputies abstained rather than deny support to the government. Hubert Lagardelle, a syndicalist-oriented and antireformist socialist, writing fifteen years later, admitted that when Millerand, on the other hand, in 1900 voted a measure inconsistent with socialist principles, he was condemned for the act. But during the 1890s all opposites seemed reconciled: class struggle with class solidarity, internationalism with patriotism. French socialists spoke in revolutionary terms only on holidays.[16]

However, Radicals and socialists could not save the cabinet when it attempted to enact a general income tax. It defended its fiscal policy on administrative as well as social grounds. As government services expanded, expenses had steadily mounted. Despite the use of such budgetary devices as 'extraordinary accounts', the need for additional taxes was clear. With the predominance of indirect taxation, the small wage-earner paid a share wholly out of proportion to his income, and more enlightened Progressists like Poincaré were well aware of it. They nevertheless opposed a direct, graduated tax on the grounds that a 'fiscal inquisition' would follow the requirement that individuals declare their sources of income. Millerand defended the proposed tax before the Chamber and, with personal reference to Poincaré, advised him to look at the company he kept.[17] The Moderate majority, although hostile in principle, estimated that the hour of fiscal reform had struck. More politically, they hesitated to reverse the government without having first gained Conservative support and reluctantly approved the tax. Both bill and ministry, however, were wrecked by the irreducible opposition of the Senate.

Observing the lower chamber's betrayal, the more conservative Senate, in order to overthrow the cabinet, chose to make life impossible for it, voting censure on three separate occasions. Each time Bourgeois appealed to, and won, a vote of confidence in the Chamber. The Senate then refused to vote necessary supplies for the troops fighting in Madagascar until there could be created 'a ministry enjoying the confidence of both chambers'. Bourgeois, whose earlier heroics had contrasted with an essentially submissive nature, refused to bypass the upper house and issue the credits by executive order. He resigned April 23 after only 170 days in office. Admittedly he lacked the support of a real majority in both houses. *La Petite République* denounced the Senate's successful attempt at blackmail. It preferred, the newspaper charged, to let soldiers perish over ministerial disputes and so betrayed the voice of universal suffrage.[18]

Jules Méline, responsible for the agricultural tariff of 1891, formed a homogeneous Progressist government and, managing Conservatives more carefully than had his predecessors, maintained his majority for over two years. Méline adopted a conciliatory attitude towards the church, continued his campaign for high protective tariffs and, with the exception of a reform in workers' accident compensation enacted in time for the election of 1898, largely ignored demands for social legislation. Although *rallies* hesitated to support a former ally of Gambetta, his program, particularly when coupled with an active defense of existing society, won their approval, and even that of some monarchists.[19]

Socialists maintained constant opposition to Méline in their press and in the Chamber. During a Goblet interpellation April 30, 1896, Millerand rejected the Moderates' charge that the Bourgeois cabinet had been the *protégé* of the socialists and denounced the present government as the *protégé* of rightwing industrial, clerical and agricultural interests. In a newspaper article he accused Méline of instigating rural against urban workers and on yet another occasion described the ministry as politically and morally 'bankrupt'.[20] Socialist criticism of the government's foreign policy, we have observed, was no less frequent. Millerand later accused the cabinet of having declared open war on collectivism in the coming election by requiring school teachers to serve as 'government spies' – a charge later made against the Radical ministry of Emile Combes.[21] In his attack on the government's general policy in 1897, a task entrusted to him by the socialist deputies, he censured it for refusing to support a national retirement-benefits plan then under discussion.[22] However, Méline retained his majority and continued to govern until caught up in the maelstrom that was the Dreyfus affair.

3.   We have seen that the Parti ouvrier agreed on the need to maintain a strong France on the world diplomatic and military scene. As a political party head, Guesde was very much aware of growing national feeling on the part of his constituents. His campaign literature, intended for the voters of Roubaix, boasted of its author's patriotism. At their Marseilles Congress in 1892, and similarly guided by electoral considerations, Marxists substituted agricultural reform for doctrinaire collectivization of all agricultural holdings. Gabriel Deville specified that without prior concentration of ownership there was to be no immediate socialization. In a speech to the Chamber in June 1896 Guesde envisaged only reformist action, urging deputies to concentrate their efforts on bringing about 'momentary attenuation of the worker's misery'. The party newspaper upheld these convictions, and the reformist viewpoint was defended doctrinally in a series of articles by a young theoretician named Joseph Sarraute. From his vantage point in the Senate, Scheurer-Kestner noted that Guesde demanded not only new social legislation but stricter enforcement of existing laws. Cited as examples of the former were the eight-hour day, the weekly rest of at least thirty-six consecutive hours and salaried absences for pregnant women workers – to begin one month before and end one month after their confinements.[23]

Admittedly, Guesde never renounced revolution. In an interview given late in 1893 he warned against expecting 'miracles' from socialist deputies. We do not expect Parliament to act upon all our programs, he said, and it would be a 'chimera' to believe that a revolutionary society can be created within a parliamentary and constitutional framework. It was necessary 'to proclaim loudly that we do not intend to limit ourselves to legal action'. In practice, however, Guesdists and their chief worked hard for social reform. Guesde did so on the national level and on behalf of his working-class constituents. In 1894 he fought for municipal pharmacies and for the enlargement of existing public services in Roubaix.[24]

Thus the acceptance of reformism by French Marxists was more than tacit. Without disowning violence they viewed the state as the representative of existing legality and tried to put it to the service of the working class. Lagardelle later called Guesde's own statism during these years 'incontestable'. The veteran socialist leader submitted legislation to the 1893–1898 Parliament calling for the creation of grievance machinery, for granting individual workers the right to vote for or against an intended strike, for the establishment and improvement of local labor councils, for a superior labor council – half the membership of which was to consist of workers elected by their unions – and for other agencies of industrial conciliation. Guesde fought for minimum salary levels, shop stewards, the national maternity fund previously referred to, a totally secret ballot and even free postage for the military. He was, Largardelle said, 'saturated' with democracy. That Guesde and Millerand then shared similar views on the usefulness of parliamentary programs was strikingly illustrated by the latter's attempts, as Minister of Commerce, to realize both by decree and legislation some of the schemes first proposed by Guesde. This 'legalization' of socialism accompanied, and issued from, an awareness that where the suffrage could be used, as in western Europe, workers had more to lose than their chains. Guesde made this clear when he said: 'If it is true that at the beginning of the nineteenth century the proletariat had no country, then democratic evolution has given it one.'[25]

With Vaillant, too, a newly elected deputy, revolutionary Blanquists also accepted and determined to work with parliamentary institutions. They called for reforms, entered into electoral coalitions and in particular supported the Ligue pour la Révision par le Peuple. The latter contained several deputies and municipal councillors and, according to its statement of objectives, sought to revise the constitution by a popularly elected assembly. 'Flexibility and freedom', proudly declaimed Millerand, 'best described the socialist party.' It no longer bound itself to 'narrow doctrine' but was rather the 'patient observer of reality'.[26]

The acceptance of reformism by Guesde, Vaillant and the majority of their followers had not taken place without criticism by a minority of dissenting militant socialists. In January 1896 the Parti ouvrier was accused of abandoning revolution and becoming obsessed with parliamentarianism, especially in the concern shown over the coming municipal elections. Critics allowed that the Socialist Union retained a revolutionary goal, but they found evolutionary means insufficient. These charges were discussed and repudiated by Dr. A. Delon, secretary of the Gard Federation. In defending reformism he predicted the tactic would bring victory to socialists in the coming elections and, reflecting the greater attachment to reform found in the provinces, unabashedly wrote: 'Long live good, warm soup, our best and most eloquent propagandist.'[27]

The debate drove home the need for a clarification of terms. In *La Petite République,* Deville asked for a working definition of a socialist, noting that some socialists were basing their objections to democratic forms on socialist theory itself. A minimum program for socialist candidates was becoming necessary. Guesde had again complained of Radicals calling themselves socialists in order to increase their working-class vote. Although it reminded him, he said, of the homage vice paid to virtue, it pointed to the need of a definition. He offered one for consideration: the 'real' socialist was the one 'cognizant of the necessary concentration of the means of production, and who sought to put that concentration into the hands of society'.[28]

Socialist candidates won many municipal elections on May 3 and 10, 1896. Socialist majorities were sent to Councils in Marseilles, Lille, Roubaix, Dijon, Toulon, Limoges, Calais and Vierzon; and minorities were won in Lyon, Bordeaux, Toulouse and elsewhere. The victory, howerver, pointed even more strongly to the need of a minimum program for the next general elections. If socialist candidates were to yield on the second vote to the one having a plurality on the first, they clearly had to know what constituted a socialist. There was a real danger, as several contemporaries put it, of socialism becoming a 'manner of hoping in common'.[29] On May 31, to honor Millerand's and Baudin's work in the Chamber, the Republican-Socialist Committee of the XIIth *arrondissement* scheduled a dinner. Millerand was the key speaker, and he used the occasion to set forth these criteria.

The diverse socialist factions were not universally represented; the syndicalist-oriented Allemanists refused to send delegates. The speakers' list, however, included the most prominent names in French socialism. The affair was held in the grand salon of the Porte-Dorée restaurant, 275 avenue Daumesnil, in the Saint-Mandé section of the *arrondissement.* Millerand's proposals exalted the reformist point of view and constituted a paen to universal suffrage; the word 'revolution', Daniel Hálevy noted, was not mentioned. But the program was accepted by all the socialist factions represented.[30]

Millerand stated his intention to suggest a minimum program for socialist candidates and, in the process, also hoped to state the aims and tactics of the party. The aims were those offered previously to the Collectivist Students group, and they reflected the integralist point of view formulated by Malon. Socialism was defined as 'the energetic will to assure to everyone in society the integral development of his personality'. This individualist ideal, however, could be reached only by society's readiness to appropriate and make available those things necessary to provide an individual with personal security and adequate means of development, that is, society's readiness to appropriate property. Liberty was a 'sonorous and empty word' unless based on, and guaranteed by, property. Collectivism, then, was set forth as the condition for individual fulfillment.

Socialism was a reaction to social injustice. It was also the scientifically determined and historically fashioned form that society must take. 'Neither the product of a dreamer's imagination nor the result of a philosopher's conception', it rather issued from capitalism and from the concentration of ownership created by capitalism. Millerand's analysis, simplified yet representative, was thus Marxist. He attributed industrial concentration to the 'rational application of technological improvement'. In driving out small ownership, however, concentration was creating a new kind of feudalism, which would 'necessarily and absolutely rule economic, political, and moral life', while subjecting the masses to 'that modern form of servitude called wage-earning'.

Collectivism proclaimed wage-earning as no more eternal than such earlier examples of human exploitation as slavery and serfdom. Thus capitalism had substituted for individual ownership the 'tyrannical monopoly of a minority'. As it had been necessary for the means of production and exchange to pass from individual to capitalist ownership, so would social ownership gradually be substituted for capitalist. And anyone not accepting this necessary and progressive substitution of social for capitalist ownership was not a socialist.

The method by which the transformation was to occur had been indicated. 'Successive incorporation' was to be used because 'no socialist dreamt of magically transforming capitalism, of building an entirely new society upon a *tabula rasa*'. Philosophers and ideologues built systems; collectivism constituted an ideal that never lost touch with reality. Still, ideals were not abandoned and criticism of Jaurès as a poet was 'beautiful and precious praise'. Not every political party could contain poets. Capable only of self-defense, capitalists could never stir the masses.

Socialism was to prevail because of the humaneness of its ideal and its freedom from dogma. Herein lay its distinctiveness from Christian socialism. The latter, Millerand said, was 'a pitiful counterfeit'. Far from being the agent of human emancipation, it served only as 'the instrument of domination of a hard-pressed theocracy'.

Reformism arose naturally from the Republic and its gift of universal suffrage and from the internationalism which constituted the very character of the movement. Patriotism and internationalism, however, were in no way incompatible. Socialists were Frenchmen and patriots at the same time they were internationalists. Those who fought the French Revolution had found little difficulty in reconciling the two.

The essential points, then, 'necessary and sufficient' to distinguish a socialist program were: 'State intervention in order to shift from the capitalist to the national domain the diverse categories of the means of production and exchange. The winning of public power by universal suffrage. International understanding among workers.' Millerand concluded by paying tribute to the socialist party as the best of instruments – irreducible in principles but tolerant of people and free of factions – to introduce little by little into a society prone to economic anarchy the peace and order of harmonious organization. It alone offered to the country a moral and intellectual ideal; and, to be invincible, it sufficed for socialists to remain united.

His remarks were conspicuous for what they omitted. Collectivism was reaffirmed, but there was no reference to violence; it was rather the inexorable result of unyielding forces, and small property owners, spokesmen for civil liberties and patriots had nothing to fear from a party subscribing to these teachings. The analysis was particularly appropriate for Millerand, based as it was on his experience and not on any sentiments. Hard work, discipline and organization had worked for him; they would work for socialism. Class organization and strikes were tools to be used in the process of emancipation; they were not intended as permanent means of insurrection. Accord, not division, was sought; and above the interests of the worker and the employer were placed the grandeur and prosperity of the nation.

The speech evoked a tremendous tresponse. *La Revue socialiste* correctly predicted it would become one of the more important historical documents of socialism. It would transform the Socialist Union into a conscious party possessing carefully laid-out programs and well-defined frontiers. His three criteria became the minimum program required by all who would enlist socialist support. Their adoption was necessary in order to enter the Comité d'entente socialiste that briefly united socialists in 1899, and they became the bases for selecting French delegates to the

Second International's Paris Congress in 1900. At least one uncommitted socialist deputy, Aimé Lavy, who had refused to join any socialist group, wrote to Millerand that he could support the Saint-Mandé program.[31] In so far as Millerand accepted collectivism, the program confirmed the dominant position reached by Marxism within French socialism and made the two synonymous.

After Millerand spoke, all present, in subsequent resolutions, approved the program set forth and so agreed on the necessity of maintaining the understanding reached. As the representative of Marxist socialism, Guesde toasted the Union as wholly socialist and anticipated it being called to public power. He avowed that there was no need of theoretical accord for the task of republican defense. But while accepting programmatic unity in order to attain immediate objectives, he rejected any structural or organic unity. This required changes in doctrine. Vaillant had fewer reservations and showered praise on Independent socialists. Millerand and his friends, he said, 'every day rendered incomparable services to socialism, because of their talent, their intelligence, and their popularity'. The Blanquist chief not only accepted reformists but refused to see any clearly-drawn frontier between socialists and anarchists and so favored a socialism open on its left as well as on its right. Guesde further qualified his support for the Saint-Mandé program by adding that revolutionary tactics would be restored if the bourgeoisie dared to interfere with the vote, the one means of emancipation available to the organized proletariat. His basic agreement, however, is a matter of record. He afterwards took pride in having 'thoroughly engaged' Millerand and Jaurès in Marxist collectivism. He anticipated an even better performance by socialists in the next election and estimated that he could 'leave the party in good hands'.[32]

Millerand's own analysis, penned forty years later, stressed his objective of formulating a minimum program able to find support from all socialists. 'If it carried a trace of some of the errors and illusions of Marxist doctrine', he wrote in a draft lecture in 1936, 'it sought to display the national character of the party and to underline the evolutionary nature of its propaganda.' For Millerand, the program's importance lay in the fact that it was read to the veterans of the party and that they did not reject it. He noted that if it had failed to win the support or the approval of other republicans, it had neither shocked nor offended them. For if it had, it would have been a dead letter. Hence Millerand revealed that his chief concern lay with fomenting socialist and republican unity.[33]

The opposition to his speech came from some Independent colleagues who found his program too restrictive. Mirman wrote the next day to say that he refused to be limited by any formulas, even those as broad in scope as the ones specified. The deputy Pierre Richard, returned in 1893 as a socialist-Boulangist, also found the speech 'too limiting' and 'continuing to call himself on Independent, implored Millerand not to subscribe to any 'dogma'. Millerand's future colleague, Raoul Persil, wrote that at the time, despite its repudiation of violence, the speech was found to possess 'revolutionary tones'.[34]

Some days later, after much discussion and by a twenty-seven to four vote with ten abstentions, the socialist group in the Chamber (consisting largely of Independents) formally adopted the program. Their resolution, however, promised not 'to restrict by any narrow formula the liberty of its members and the very development of socialism'.[35] One must conclude in observing the French socialist movement in the mid-1890s that the Saint-Mandé program found widespread acceptance; but of those who opposed it, most did so not because they found it too mild but, on the contrary, too restricted. Nothing pointed more directly to the parliamentarianism and reformism of French socialists at that time.

4. Millerand went to England late in July to attend his first international congress. The Second International had scheduled its fourth meeting in London, and placed at the top of its agenda was a discussion on tactics. Aware of its importance, Millerand had wanted a reporter to take a French transcript of the debate but was told that funds were insufficient. During his visit he inquired into the activities of his counterparts in the House of Commons and came back with an armload of documentation, like the draft bill then before the House on employers' liability in industrial accidents.[36] The bulk of his time, however, was spent on seeking a resolution of the conflict dividing the French delegation, that separating socialists and syndicalists.

In microcosm this was precisely the issue debated by the Congress. The Second International was all too aware of the great debate between the exponents of political and economic action, between Marxists and Bakuninists, that did so much to break up its predecessor. Anarchists had been fought successfully at the International's earlier meetings, the delegates to which had gone on record as expressing preference for political solutions. There was to be no place for those rejecting the Marxist emphasis on disciplined party behavior and scientific socialism. Arguments for the expulsion of anarchists were heard at the first Congress, in Paris in 1889; they were revived at Brussels two years later; and at Zurich, in 1893, it was decided to bar them from future congresses. Delegates not recognizing the necessity of political action – the model of German social democracy was paramount – were not to come. This decision, and its extension to syndicalists at London in 1896, was of major importance in the history of socialism. Although it did not mean, as anarchists rightly pointed out, that the International was committed to reformism rather than revolution, it tacitly recognized that in practice labor was to pursue its aims by legal and largely political means and that reformism had stamped international socialism with its imprint.

For British and German labor this constituted no problem; both movements, for different reasons and in different ways, were either integrated into their respective states or prepared to work within national political frameworks. However, French labor remained both outside of established society and unable to organize one of its own. The two-fold economy consisted of a large peasant-artisan class alongside a modern, but still decentralized and diminutive, industrial sector. French capitalism, in large part family-owned, small in size and unencumbered by the demands of labor, was among the most oppressive in western Europe and the French state among the most backward in social legislation. The fragmented structure of French capitalism best explains the persistent reliance on economic action by French labor. Syndicalism, the ideology that was to embrace and legitimize economic action, first emerged in the workshop and not in the factory. However, other and more historical reasons explain the continued popularity of economic over political action on the part of French workers. The anti-parliamentarianism taught by Proudhon was strengthened by the political 'betrayals' of 1848 and 1871 and reinforced by the attitude taken toward organized labor by the most dynamic faction within French socialism. Guesde's elemental Marxism persuaded the Parti ouvrier to place all emphasis on politics and reject economic alternatives. The Guesdist-controlled grouping of trade unions established in 1886, the Fédération nationale des syndicats, was viewed as a source of recruitment for the party and as a receptacle for its propaganda.

Thus hostility between unions – many of whose members regarded job grievances as more relevant than prescriptions for future society – and socialists early emerged as a factor in the history of French labor. To the former the growing commitment to moderation by the Parti ouvrier appeared as proof that politicians wanted the support of labor but would do little on its behalf. It appeared wiser to rely on the union, the *syndicat,* and on its ability to make use of the most effective weapon available to labor, the strike. Reliance on the strike, and on the great feelings of solidarity it could arouse, was built into a philosophy defending its use and upholding its importance, one later given theoretical expression by syndicalists like Georges Sorel. The strike was a revolutionary act; how much more revolutionary a general stoppage of work! It would sound the knell for the capitalist economy and force it to seek terms. Guesdists successfully fought off these ideas as irrational and romantic.

Faith in the trade union and its potential for economic activity received new impetus when the Paris Municipal Council set up the first Bourse du Travail in 1887. They proved fertile grounds for syndicalist thought. By 1892 ten such *bourses* founded a national organization, the Fédération des bourses du travail, and it soon rivaled the Guesdist federation of unions. Three years later the dedicated and deformed Fernand Pelloutier became its secretary. His intense efforts on its behalf and his ideas about its intended role assured the new federation's survival and endowed it with an ideology.

It was also in 1892 that the Marxists lost control of their own labor organization. Aristide Briand won approval of the general strike at the Marseilles Congress of the Fédération nationale des syndicats. The tactic had been denounced by Guesde and fought by the Parti ouvrier for two years. In 1894, however, the Marxists surrendered and withdrew; the Federation was reorganized the following year as the Confédération générale du travail. It was not wholly revolutionary; but, similar to the Fédération des bourses du travail, it was dedicated to working-class action. Thus events were turning French workers away from politics and back to economic organization as the means by which they were to defend their interests.

Anarchists, too, were changing tactics, and the new ones adopted brought them closer to syndicalists. In view of the effectiveness of government repression against anarchist terrorists both in France and abroad, Peter Kropotkin, Elisée Reclus and other theorists critical of total recourse to sporadic acts of terror, to 'propaganda by the deed', warned that continued reliance on them would isolate and destroy the movement. As an alternative, and as a means by which anarchism could find mass support and rely on something more than a series of ineffectual and isolated protests, they suggested the infiltration and control of the trade unions. Anarchism would then be brought directly to the workers, who in turn could become agents of revolutionary action.[37] By 1896 the process was well underway. Thus it was that anarchists like Jean Grave, editor of *La Révolte,* Emile Pouget of *Le Père Peinard,* Léon Parsons and Pelloutier came to London with trade-union credentials. Invitations had been sent to all political and union organizations; and socialists, who refused to relinquish their title as champions of the cause of labor, anticipated a struggle. The French delegation split over the question of syndicalist inclusion: Allemane and Vaillant called for their admission; Millerand, Jaurès and Guesde opposed.

The Guesdists posed the question neatly. Since socialists everywhere now recognized the need to win political power as an indispensable preface to social transformation, was it logical to admit those who on principle condemned political action? The French delegation, however, voted by the narrowest of margins, fifty-seven to fifty-six, to approve the union mandates. Socialists, even those like Jaurès who voiced sympathy for syndicalist élan and had avowed there were many roads to socialism, refused to accept the vote.[38] Socialists elected to office, deputies and councillors, insisted throughout they came with a special mandate, higher than that conferred by a trade union. They decided during an all-night meeting to seek recognition as a distinct group rather than participate with the syndicalists.

Accordingly, Millerand asked the General Assembly of the Congress for the right to form a second French section. He was cited not as condemning corporative action but participation with anarchists; and if the request was rejected, he threatened to leave with the minority. Although the Belgian socialist, Emile Vandervelde, seconded by Vaillant, feared the precedent of a double delegation, the Congress approved Millerand's proposal, voting by nation, fourteen to five. The vote completed the schism between socialism and syndicalism in France, and, with the presence of two French sections, the Congress proved one of the most agitated and chaotic so far held.[39]

Vandervelde recalled how other delegates heard through a door in Queen's Hall 'a deafening concert of savage outcries. It was', he said, 'the French delegation going about its work'. The unbelievable pandemonium prompted the British to label its meeting room 'the menagerie'. 'One exception, however [said Vandervelde] of which I have a refreshing impression. Among those furious people – and the word is not excessive – a man, a single man, calm and circumspect in his remarks, arguing with the quiet courtesy of a notary discussing the conditions of a contract... Millerand.'[40]

The Congress furthered the estrangement of syndicalism from parliamentary socialism. It had also revealed a falling-out among socialists themselves. There can be little doubt, however, that it was reformism that prevailed in international socialism. It had pervaded the work of three earlier congresses. That at London approved the demand for the eight-hour day and the right of free association for workers and repudiated the use of the general strike demanded by syndicalists. The decisions taken at these meetings demonstrated the degree to which the acquisition of public office had replaced the establishment of collectivist society on the ruins of the state as a socialist objective. But in excluding syndicalists, the delegates at London cut themselves off from those most critical of socialist opportunism; from those who warned most loudly against the socialist desire for ministerial posts.[41]

5. The enormous work-load and unending intensity was beginning to show its effects. A sketch made of Millerand in 1895 suggests slightly severe features. The square face, stern mouth and small eyeglasses impart, on the whole, an almost unfriendly feeling. His actions matched his appearance. He seldom displayed affection; he never *tutoied*. A colleague recalled Millerand receiving a visitor. He did not waste words or time; he usually had his back to the window while he surveyed his caller and, dispensing with useless preambles, let him know at once where he stood.[42]

Romain Rolland, observing Millerand in the Chamber of Deputies early in the new century, has left a superb critical portrait: 'Millerand had badly-cut gray hair, clean-shaven cheeks and chin, a small black mustache which looked out of place on the face of a lawyer; he wore eyeglasses, was dressed in a gray jacket, his head was lowered a little. When he listened he paid uncommonly close attention; he appeared fixed and hostile, never looked at the speaker, and took note after note. When he spoke his manner was harsh, retortive, pressing and aggressive. Without knowing why, I found him somewhat disquieting, sharp, deceptive, and dangerous. His speech was especially cutting; he was always armed himself and forever looking for the chink in the armor of his protagonist; he never struck at random. He must have been ill-tempered, for he scarcely smiled. That continual and hostile tension left an impression on me.'[43]

Millerand managed to spend considerable time with his legal practice. References to cases can be found regularly in *La Petite République*. The reason, it appears, was more than pecuniary. He loved the profession and appreciated the autonomy it granted him. 'I am still a lawyer', he told an interviewer in 1902. 'I want always to remain a lawyer for I wish above all to be independent.'[44] Not until after 1905 or 1906, however, did his practice provide any substantial income.

Given the need to build a clientele, it was assumed that the first few years of practice were not financially rewarding, even for the attorney who did not specialize in defending strikers and socialists. After leaving school the young lawyer was ignorant of the ways of the Palais de Justice; his training had been largely abstract. But he could get much valuable experience appearing in assize court. Well-established lawyers seldom appeared in smaller cities, and beginners made them something of a preserve.[45] Millerand spent many long days in provincial towns, regularly taking trains out of Paris.

He had received his *license en droit* in 1884 after his probation ended and was therefore entitled to appear in the Paris cour d'appel as an advocate. The Palais de Justice before the turn of the century was not the beehive of legal activity that it is now. Only about 700 lawyers then practiced compared to well over five times that number today. The pace was leisurely, and tradition followed. Dress was entirely in black; top hats were worn, and mustaches had recently become stylish. This world was fashionable, yet still old and calm.[46]

Millerand's most renowned case in these early years, and his most noted success, was his defense of the anti-military novel by Lucien Descaves, *Sous-off*. The author had previously published four or five novels. This one, appearing at the end of 1889, described the petty demands of non-commissioned officers, as well as other hardships that rendered life miserable for the recruit in the *caserne*. The tone was wholly in keeping with the intellectuals' disdain for military life in the early years of the Republic – and their efforts to reduce the length of required military service. The novel was sad and bitter but never licentious. Nor was it the first anti-military novel, but it was the first to be prosecuted. Boulangists especially denounced it; the earliest, loudest and most savage criticism appeared in Georges Laguerre's newspaper, *La Presse,* on December 6. The sparks caught; patriots defended the need for discipline, and the NCOs were defended by General Boulanger. The matter reached the attention of Freycinet, then Minister of War. Aware of possible repercussions, he with reluctance asked the Minister of Justice to prosecute. As he feared, it became a *cause célèbre*. On December 24 *Le Figaro* carried the petition of 154 writers denouncing the suit as an attack on the freedom of expression.[47]

The case was tried before the Cour d'assises of the Seine Department the following March 15. The writer was charged with breach of morals and with offenses against the army. Millerand and a lawyer named Tézenas composed the defense, and they argued that Descave's earlier works were stronger in tone than the one now put on trial. Tézenas pointed to the novel's usefulness in illuminating existing inadequacies and so prompting reform. Millerand focused on the scandals it depicted and asked if their exposure constituted a crime against society. An historian of the administration of justice under the Third Republic concluded that it was Millerand who secured an acquittal by seizing on the prosecutor's 'exaggerations'.[48]

More typical was Millerand's defenses of socialists or strikers, and they followed the pattern of those conducted at Montceau and Decazeville. The longest of these cases called for his repeated intervention on behalf of a collectivist agricultural union in Brittany. Something of a disciple of Malon, yet an indefatigable Guesdist propagandist and organizer in Nantes, the secretary of the area's socialist federation, Charles Brunellière, had founded the union. Landlords in the region tried to dispell it; the farmers fought back, and, at Malon's suggestion, Brunellière asked Millerand for help. However, the latter was unsuccessful in his efforts to defend the union in court in December 1893. Supported by the law, and by the Prefect who applied it, the landlords evicted those tenant-farmers who were members.

On Millerand's advice, Brunellière took a new tactic, one scarcely compatible with revolutionary theory. Millerand proposed fighting for legislation guaranteeing the union's right to exist. In June 1895 he put Brunellière in touch with the deputy from the area, who in turn brought him to the Minister of Agriculture. A bill favoring the farmers was submitted, and defended, by the government. It finally became law in early March 1898. The enormously impressed Brunellière loudly expressed his admiration for Millerand and, as we shall see, continued to do so after the latter became minister. Assured of its future, the union prospered, although one noted that it 'progressively lost its socialist character'.[49]

Millerand did not limit himself in the 1890s to defending individual liberties and labor interests. He was involved in a number of civil cases and in one of them defended the right of small businessmen to combine for legal purposes. The Affaire des canaux agricoles kept Millerand active in the Cour d'appel during January and February of 1895. On behalf of its shareholders, the Verdon Canal Company successfully sued its contractors for fraudulent manoeuvres and false claims. However, on appeal, many of the lower court's findings were reversed. The defendants and their bankers were amply represented in the Appeal Court by a battery of competent attorneys, including Waldeck-Rousseau. Millerand fought to have the lower court's judgment upheld. The case was lengthy and complex, and he was not entirely successful.

The defendants had objected to the right of the plaintiffs to group themselves rather than press litigation as individuals. In a *plaidoirie* that was ultimately published, Millerand defended their right to do so in order to retrieve their savings and fight fraud. They could not afford separate suits, and he asked whether French courts prohibited class action. One by one he recited the affirmative arguments of his adversaries and attempted to reply to them.[50]

His courtroom appearances were keeping him busy. The invitations of one enterprising hostess, Madame Marie Raffalovitch, whose salon attracted aspiring deputies, were turned down at least eight times in 1891 by Millerand because court appearances kept him from Paris. He defended clients in cities like Amiens and Limoges but did write to say that he would attend one *soirée* between trips to Reims. His rising notoriety both as lawyer and deputy opened more doors, however bourgeois. The noted *avoué,* Michel Milhaud, remembered Millerand as a guest in his home one night in 1895. He was the 'least acrimonious of those invited, and the ladies hardly recognized the eloquent socialist deputy or caustic editorialist of *La Petite République'* in the *bon garçon* who laughingly described his bicycle accidents or complained that his bourgeois days were much too short. Not only were the Raffalovitch and Milhaud doors open to him, but he received invitations from the Comtesse de Martel Mirabeau, known to her *intimes* as 'Gyp'. And the large dark hand-writing of the most prestigious of Third Republic hostesses, Mme. Ju-liette Adam, distinguishes his papers for these years. It was Madame George Renard who had introduced him, and the politically astute and wholly nationalist Juliette Adam was well aware that Millerand was one of Clemenceau's favorites. She wanted him to persuade his *patron* to continue his support for Boulanger but asked in vain.[51]

Millerand was hardly estranged from genteel society; he was much sought after, for professional reasons, within his own. There were several offers from newspapers, either for his fulltime services or for occasional articles.[52] It was law, however, and not journalism that preoccupied him and shaped his career. His legal practice had introduced him to the world of labor and socialism. It was to introduce him to the world of big business, although not until well after he had left the government would he represent corporate interests.

To begin with, the law shaped his conception of social questions. As with most of the other lawyer-politicians of the Third Republic, the Gambettas, Ferrys, Poincarés, Barthous, Waldeck-Rousseaus, Vivianis, de la Monzies and Berards, it was that of a jurist. This is precisely what Millerand has been reproached for: faith in the usefulness of legally formed conventions and contracts, discussions and arbitration; reliance on rational ways of conceiving, approaching and resolving problems; that is, faith in and reliance on the very postulates of civil law. The *plaidoirie* of the French lawyer is designed to convince a courtroom; it is minutely prepared and organized; nothing is left to chance; the parts are analyzed and regrouped in the best order. Usually the facts are recited; the pro-cedure is explained; the arguments of the adversary refuted and one's own presented. Millerand's speeches to the Chamber revealed this order and organization, and they invariably sought to make a case on behalf of a client. At the Faculté de droit Millerand learned that a judge was led to his decision by a demonstration of the reasons for it and that a jury could not escape the conclusion toward which the lawyer was moving. The Chamber of Deputies was seen as judge and jury.

Millerand's speeches, then, resembled his *plaidoiries*. They have been described by Lyon-Caen, his former teacher and later colleague: 'His eloquence is classic. It is classic because of the care taken in its composition; the clarity of the plan; the visibility of the divisions; the simplicity of the transitions; the slender and invisible threads relating the ideas to each other; the connections of the parts; the accuracy of their proportions. And [his eloquence] is modern because of the sobriety of its development, the absence of useless ornaments, the speed with which it rushes to its conclusion'.[53]

Lyon-Caen estimated that Millerand's art was adapted to the ends in mind. The training and discipline imposed in adolescence were put to use. Either directly or implictly, but invariably, he said: *Violà la question!* Courtroom mannerisms were also revealed in the Chamber. He never interrupted an adversary in the Palais de Justice and very seldom did so at the Palais Bourbon. As Rolland noted, he listened intently, all forces concentrated. An over-statement produced only a raised eyebrow, an error a quick look or frown. A rapid note written with evident satisfaction sufficed to inform the other of his blunder.

The juridical nature of his speeches generated a sense of coldness and distance. Thus in the emotion-ridden debate on the closing of the Paris Bourse du travail did Millerand open his speech attacking the government: 'I ask for the Chamber's permission to demonstrate, in a few words, and with facts, not metaphors, that in this instance the law has been broken not by the Bourse du travail, but by the government.' The brevity, factual tone and insistence on settling the question of legality were all present. If, in the midst of heated argument, a revolutionary colleague forgot his language, as on July 3, 1894, Millerand could icily interrupt the protests and expression of indignation: 'I would be grateful if someone could cite the constitutional law forbidding this means of expression.'

The advantages to a party of having its spokesman able to inject cutting reason into a discussion, and do so effectively, were many. The defects lay in Millerand's inability to free himself from reliance on texts and precedents. The concern for legality sometimes became oppressive and was often unnecessary. He searched for and found contradictions in the most irrelevant remarks of a minister. He could not prevent himself from analyzing the simple fact, and only with difficulty could he move from the specific to the general; and isolated facts always allowed for diverse interpretations. On February 16, 1893, he said: 'I do not question the motives of the government, but in politics only facts and results count.' But motives, especially for socialists, also counted. Millerand disliked rhetoric and cited the lessons of history only when his arguments were poor. He liked abstractions even less, and only infrequently did the Chamber hear him refer to 'the republican idea', or to 'the great and generous theme of fraternity'. Then he quickly came back to earth.

Millerand left questions of theory to Guesde and Jaurès. He was a tactician and less interested in ideas than in men and movements. He was concerned less with value than with number, less with doctrine than with parties. Consequently, he was concerned less with rebuilding than with repairing. He experienced no difficulty in, and revealed few moral deficiencies by, abandoning his demand for constitutional revision immediately after campaigning for it in 1889. For he continually strove for that part of his program that was likely to succeed; and the part likely to succeed was usually that which could best attract moderate support. Lawyers seek victories and are therefore tacticians; tacticians are opportunistic, and Millerand was all of these things, both as Radical and as socialist. He was to use the same tactics after his departure from the socialist party. In so far as he had always urged social legislation, he was sincere when he continued calling himself a socialist.

He seldom stressed ideology. His socialism was created by facts; it was, for him, inevitable; and his few doctrinal statements were all empirical. If socialism was the necessary secretion of capitalism, then it was logical to be a socialist. Accepting the inevitable, however, generated little enthusiasm. His socialism was not the kind that could permit inspiration to supplant precision, or rhetoric to take the place of logic. No hypocrisy or casuistry need be inferred when he maintained that socialism, rather than depriving individuals of their property, would work to consolidate their ownership of it. To charge the socialist party with wanting to suppress individual ownership, he told the assembled deputies April 30, 1894, was to slander it or distort its teachings. On the contrary, he said, 'what it seeks is the extension of individual ownership to the great mass of citizens'.

The loyalty of his constituency granted Millerand independence from his party; the love for, and ultimate revenue from, legal practice granted independence from politics itself. But it was also the law, at least as practiced in France, that granted him independence from clients, constituents and colleagues. For the French lawyer was not merely the agent of his client. He rather aided his client by speaking on his behalf and did so in his own name without necessarily identifying himself with all his client's demands. He has been described as something of a judge himself, who carried to court the results of his own examination. Thus the *plaidoirie* is an *exposé* and defense of the client's case but one stated and supported by the lawyer as he sees fit.[54] Millerand was intensely independent in politics in regard to both affiliation and style largely because he was a lawyer.

Practicing law enabled the politician to retain perspective; it also hindered him from distinguishing between a cause and a case. Unlike a Jaurès or a Guesde, even when wholly committed Millerand appeared detached and conveyed the impression of presenting a brief. He sought to win a victory for his client: at first, a striker, a worker, a wine-merchant; later, the army and the nation. In the courtroom, concrete result counted for more than rhetoric. By his intervention, France – or at least that part of it he was representing – gained something. Because he regarded his constituents as clients, he could all the more easily ignore the contradiction between his defense, as deputy, of the interests of the Bercy merchants after 1889 and his defense, as Senator from the Orne after 1925, of the *bouillours de cru.*

Perhaps another impact of his legal career on his socialist years was that it rooted him in society at large. In distinguishing between revolutionaries and revisionists in the ranks of German social democracy, the historian Peter Nettl noted that the latter were those who 'had in some way broken through the isolation from society in which most social democrats found themselves'. He found that among lawyers and journalists, many of those who actually practiced or published supported the revisionist cause; those who were disbarred, or whose socialist activities had hurt their practice, came out for the orthodox leadership.[55]

6. Millerand had left his parents' home in 1889 to move to an apartment at 234 boulevard Saint-Germain. He had few close friends, and they shared his professional and political interests, if not his views. Notwithstanding the difference in their outlooks – Poincaré had become a leading Progressive and served as Minister of Finance in 1894 – the two men retained much of the friendship dating from the Faculté de droit. A letter from Millerand acknowledged his friend's gratitude for some small favor. Millerand was pleased to have been of help and in warm tones hoped that Poincaré would call upon him again. Like Millerand he was more fond of the Palais de Justice than the Palais Bourbon. Both were cold and austere, and both would be made somewhat more tractable by their marriages.[56]

Common interests and activities also drew Millerand closer to Jaurès. Born the same year, both entered the 1885–1889 Chamber in by-elections and both evolved to socialism. The differences, however, were great. One was a philosopher and from the south: open, warm and receptive; the other was Paris bred, was serious and usually silent. An observation made by Georges Renard best pointed out the contrast. At lunch one day, outdoors in the Midi, Jaurès was holding forth, volubly. Millerand sat by, soundless, except to tell Jaurès at repeated intervals to recork the bottle of wine to prevent flies from settling. He finally did so himself. Millerand had remained a bachelor, and a possible reason may be drawn from a remark made on one occasion when M. and Mme. Jaurès and M. and Mme. Renard were exploring a monastery in the Tarn. Mme. Jaurès had waited behind, praying, her husband, bareheaded, at her side. Millerand looked at them and said, 'That is what would prevent me from marrying, if I wanted to'.[57]

He changed his mind, however, by the fall of 1898. In the archives of the Department of the Seine there is a certificate from the *mairie* of the XIXth *arrondissement* stating that on October 26, 1898, Etienne-Alexandre Millerand married Jeanne le Vayer. No mention of the fact was made in any newspaper. In a letter to Deville, Millerand reported that his wedding was small, with only the closest gathering, and he described himself as 'happy'.[58] He went into no detail in his *Mémoires* other than to say it was the same Mademoiselle le Vayer he first met at the Bouteillier home, but this time he had determined to make her his own.

Jeanne Victorine Julienne Marie le Vayer was born in Le Mans May 7, 1864. Although no longer wealthy, the family was once prosperous, and the elegance and confidence derived from an independent background was hers. The mother claimed as ancestors some Romanian royalty; the mode was aristocratic and the education refined. Her parents were divorced. Despite the persistence of rumors to the effect, there is no truth to the allegation made by Edouard Drumont, in *La Libre Parole* (July 11, 1899), that she was of Jewish descent.

Madame Millerand was Catholic but did not then practice, and the marriage was a civil one. The couple took an apartment on the rue de Saint Petersbourg near the Saint-Lazare sation. The first child, ean, was born in 1899, and a proud Millerand notified Deville of the event.[59] Alice, who most resembled her father, came three years later. Jacques, who would follow in his footsteps at the Faculté de droit, was born in 1904 and Marthe, the youngest, in 1909. None was baptized, although in later life all but Jacques chose to receive the sacrament.

Those who remember say that Millerand denied his children nothing. When reproached, he gently alluded to his own childhood and said that he wanted above all to see them *content*. Millerand insisted that his wife never wear black, not even at his mother's funeral.[60] He preferred her in grey, white or mauve. In contrast to the poise and eloquence displayed on the floor of the Chamber and at court, Millerand at home was clumsy, timid and often apparently shy. With company he seldom engaged in small talk, could not gossip; in fact, he hardly joined a conversation. He would not waste time, preferring to pick up some work, despite the presence of visitors. He was corrected by his wife for this breach of manners, but they apparently seldom disagreed. Those who came included Eugène Petit, a law partner, and his wife Sophie – the first woman to graduate from the Faculty of Law and practice; Joseph Caillaux, a young finance expert; Poincaré, Jaurès and, especially, René Viviani. Guesde and Briand, editor of the newspaper Millerand began to write for in 1897, never appeared; and a certain coolness soon displayed by Madame Millerand to her husband's radical friends did not encourage many visits.

Friends and relatives state that Millerand adored his wife; he thought of her constantly and frequently bought gifts. She was an attractive woman, although some found her cold; and contrasted with her refinement his own bluntness appeared all the more awkward. People who knew both insisted the wife exerted a strong, although indirect, influence on the husband. Her presence encouraged him to seek greater respect; it may well have been responsible for his beginning to entertain ministerial notions. Certainly the turmoil into which France was plunged during the Dreyfus affair provided the opportunity.

7. Prelude to schism

No one is more eaten up with envy than he who considers all men to be his equals.

GOETHE

Rien n'est funeste comme les sytsématiques qui prétendent imposer un plan tout fait aux événements et aux hommes.

JEAN JAURÈS, preface to *Discours parlementaires*

1. From the account of socialist activity given thus far, one might see only accord within the movement. That general agreement in fact existed was demonstrated by party-wide support of the Bourgeois ministry, the Franco-Russian alliance, the Saint-Mandé program and the countless proposals for social legislation. The personalities involved, however, were woven of complex emotions and desires. Understandings were not always complete, and when they were reached, the underlying motives were not always exalted. The files of the Sûreté Générale, the national police responsible to the Ministry of the Interior, and the Paris Prefecture of Police suggest that the acceptance by some former intransigents of a reformist outlook, and their later rejection of it, were in large part a reflection of political opportunism and private anxiety. A prime example was Jules Guesde.

Although they must be used with prudence, with fact separated from inference, the usefulness of police reports as a source for socialist activities cannot be underestimated. Despite their mounting representation in French legislatures, socialists were still viewed with suspicion as potential enemies of the state. Numerous agents were assigned to cover meetings, befriend party members, infiltrate higher councils and in every way inform prefects and the central government of their activities. The value of the material gathered and the insights acquired help to answer some of the historian's questions about the movement.[1]

The evidence filed suggests that in coming to reformism, Guesde, as distinct from Millerand, Jaurès and other Independent chiefs, could not easily distinguish between the defense of party interests and the strengthening and perpetuation of his position as its leader. If this were true only for the time that Millerand served as a member of the government, or

Jaurès as a vice-president of the Chamber, considerable doubt might be raised about the reliability of the archives. Because both men held some measure of power, it could be argued, they were treated favorably, and their opponents within the party discredited. The reports, however, are consistent: Guesde's stated motives were challenged when Millerand and Jaurès were only two of a number of socialist deputies and before the police had any reason to discriminate. Moreover, the two rival forces, the Paris Prefecture and the Sûreté Générale, working independently and often antagonistic, arrived at strikingly similar conclusions. Finally, the evidence contained in their files is frequently corroborated by other sources.

Reports to the Sûreté on the Parti ouvrier reveal, for example, that Guesde took pride in 'forcing' Millerand to commit himself to a collectivist view. 'He [Millerand] is... now outside of any possible ministerial combination until there appears a socialist ministry of which I am a part.' The thought, expressed in 1896, illustrated Guesde's foresight in regard to Millerand's future career in government. It also revealed his own ambitions within the socialist world.[2]

Some long available testimony supports the view that Guesde subscribed to reformist practices in part to make use of the Millerands and Jaurèses newly arrived in socialist ranks. Alexandre Zévaès, for many years his close assistant, recalled how Guesde 'cultivated' Millerand (and the Independent socialists), aiming to make use of his standing in the Chamber. The wish to annex Independents became Guesde's 'fixed policy'. He invited them to gatherings in the Nord and agreed with their principles at Saint-Mandé. Not that he was unimpressed with the potential of the new tactics; the socialist success in 1893 and his own victory convinced him of their value. But he viewed the 'respectable' Millerand and Jaurès as 'bridges over which the fearful and the timid would necessarily be led to socialism'. The Parti ouvrier could enlist directly the support of workers but only in a roundabout way that of artisans, small landowners and bourgeoisie. 'They still regard me as a bogey', Guesde admitted, 'I will therefore bring Millerand, Jaurès and Viviani, who are less frightening to the skeptics, to pave the way, and in the soil they will have broken, I will sow my good grains...'.[3]

Lafargue expressed similar sentiments. He had appreciated Millerand's aid in his defense after Fourmies and in subsequent campaigns. If Millerand, together with Jaurès, want to form a party of 'state socialists', he wrote to Engels late in February 1893, he needs the facilities that the POF can provide, just as we need him 'to reassure the timid'. In his reply, Engels feared that 'Millerand and Company' failed to appreciate the unique role of the Workers' party, a condition, he said, on which any alliance has to be built. On October 13 he told Lafargue that 'Millerand and Jaurès get more from you than you from them'. He acknowledged the possibility of cooperation, however, and in a letter to Laura Lafargue in December recognized that 'Millerand and Jaurès have taken the initiative against Dupuy and Casimir-Perier'. Laura Lafargue, in turn, wrote that Millerand was now getting support from workers who previously gave him 'a cold reception'. However, she said, 'he brings the petit bourgeois to us, [people] who regard Guesde and Paul as devils incarnate'. Writing about Jaurès the following March, Lafargue agreed: 'Jaurès won his popularity by himself; greatly respected, he gives socialism an air of respectability.'[4]

Material from the Paris Prefecture suggests that Guesde's reformism, whatever its origins, came to be resented by the revolutionary minority within his party. Although the POF presented a united front, some militant socialists privately assailed their leader. Shortly after the formation of the Socialist Union, Toussaint, Dejean and Avez made clear their disenchantment with evolutionary socialism. At an inner meeting they refused to accept Independents as true socialists and demanded an end to all affiliation with them. Zévaès' memoirs affirm this. He related that Guesdist deputies in 1895 were criticized for sacrificing principles to expedients in voting against repeal of the *lois scélérates,* and a gap widened between the party executive and the more moderate representatives in the Chamber. The account given to the Sûreté is similar and disclosed that the strongly Marxist Fédération de l'Est voiced its discontent with what it termed the Parti ouvrier's evolution toward 'state socialism'.[5]

It is notable that Guesde rejoined these dissidents only after the election of 1898, when he lost his seat to Eugène Motte, a prominent industrialist of Roubaix, a practicing Catholic and the antithesis of all Guesde stood for. The Marxist chief reentered the Chamber in 1906; until then he repeatedly voiced his disillusion with a capricious universal suffrage. 'With the end of the legislature of 1893–98', wrote Zévaès, 'there ended the reformist and legal period of Jules Guesde.'[6] He returned to his earlier revolutionary stand, and in the social legislation repudiated were several of his own proposals. There is sufficient evidence to suggest that by 1899 he was seeking an excuse to re-ally himself with the more intransigent elements within his party and that the opportunity was provided by Millerand's accession to a cabinet post.

2. An early sign of dissension appeared in 1897 within the administration of *La Petite République*. It resulted in a short period of Guesdist control of the newspaper and Millerand's departure from it. Revolu-

tionary elements had tried to increase their membership on the staff while Millerand was recuperating in Brittany from a bicycle fall in February 1896. In a letter to Fournière, he said that he had spoken with Guesde, Vaillant and others about the make-up of a list of political editors but had insisted that he remained 'sole master and consequently responsible – in the limits set by [his] view of the very interests of the paper and the party – for their choice'.[7]

A month or two before, a silent partner and one-time supporter of Malon, Simon, was replaced by Françisque Teillard. Reports sent to the Sûreté soon mentioned signs of estrangement between the new publisher and his editor-in-chief and evidence of the former's increasingly close affiliation with Guesde. By June, Teillard was asking Millerand to reshuffle his editors and to dismiss some of the older ones. Earlier letters, dating from January 1896, stressed the need to cut expenses; they cited the scarcity of resources and referred to printers' notes demanding payment of bills. Millerand resented this treatment and on several occasions threatened to resign. Each time Teillard implored him, for the sake of the party, to remain at his post. However, the editor's anger was mounting. A fragment of a draft letter he wrote stated that Teillard was chairman of the board and not manager. Millerand prepared a folder containing Teillard's notes, his own replies and Pellier's letter promising him full control over the political management of the newspaper. The animosity between the publisher and his editor spilled over into the Paris press in the late fall of 1896. *Le Figaro* published Teillard's letter of November 24 stating that he alone directed affairs. In the same issue, that of November 26, *Le Figaro* noted Millerand's declaration that he was running the newspaper. A Millerand draft letter to an unknown party in Lille placed full blame for the prolonged dispute on Teillard; he, Millerand, had tried for a reconciliation.[8]

Georges Renard, who had lost his job writing *feuilletons* for *La Petite République* and may not have been the most impartial witness, said that the Guesdists tried repeatedly to seize the paper. There were evenings, Renard recalled, when the printer received contradictory instructions and did not know who was in charge. On January 20, 1897, an 'exasperated' Millerand resigned his post and was replaced by Guesde, and the bitter Renard called it 'a triumph of Marxism in French socialism.'[9]

The larger issue was dissent between the socialist deputies in the Chamber, mainly Independent, and more militant socialists in party councils. The conflict between moderate deputies (many of whom comprised the staff of *La Petite République*) and party administrators over control of the movement was not, of course, limited to French socialism. It was a Frenchman, however, who noted that there was more in common be-

3. 'It is not too early to prepare for the elections of 1898, nor to get the socialist factions together again', Millerand wrote to Fournière in the early fall of 1896. The socialist chief was very much aware that despite the promise of the 1893 victory, his party had few positive achievements to boast of. The observant Scheurer-Kestner, from his vantage point in the Senate, wrote in 1896 that socialist legislative demands had 'no chance of success'. The parliamentary opposition was simply too great. Laissez-fairists like Paul Deschanel denounced any efforts at state intervention, preferring to await the progress that 'invariably' accompanied liberalism. No radical, Scheurer-Kestner admitted that he was 'amazed' by Deschanel's confidence. He noted the optimism of even the most ardent reformers, men like Albert de Mun, who unfailingly pointed to the likelihood of progress in present society and consequently denounced all extra-parliamentary action as unjustified. Scheurer-Kestner privately deplored the negligence revealed by French industrialists and their lack of concern for their workers and unfavorably contrasted the French record in social legislation to that carried out in Alsace by the Germans.[17]

The inability of French workers to organize effectively in defense of their interests reflected the decentralized status of industry and its uncompromising hostility to labor. At the dawn of the twentieth century the working movement in France lacked unity and sufficient solidarity to present itself as a large and effective force. It had clearly failed to provide adequate pressure for increased social legislation. A factory act of 1848 limited the worker's day to twelve hours, and in 1892 a ten-hour maximum was established for women and for children under sixteen, but administrative difficulties made it virtually unenforceable in mixed workshops of men, women and children. In 1896 the Minister of Commerce suspended its application. Trade unions received legal recognition in 1884, but employers found themselves responsible for labor accidents only in 1898. Such was the state of French social legislation at the end of the century. Progressists were not generally disturbed by labor's demands. They considered themselves 'moderates' – although not 'moderately republican' – and 'men of order', who, we have seen, with the increase in Radical and socialist strength in the 1890s, preferred to draw closer to Conservatives.

Still, structural explanations do not sufficiently reconcile the cohesion of the socialist delegation in the Chamber and its effectiveness in combating regimes found distasteful to the left after the elections of 1893, on the one hand, and the dearth of positive and social legislation and paralysis in face of the Progressist onslaught after 1896, on the other. If socialists were able to reverse Dupuy and Casimir-Perier, why were they helpless against Méline? In part the answer rests in the fact that in the late

1890s the economy had emerged from its long depression and began the great upward swing that would characterize it until after World War I. Real wages continued to rise, and, in a fashion similar to that of the 1920s, the problem in an apparently well-functioning economy was envisaged more as one of distributing growing profits than as politically tampering with the economic system itself.

A more immediate explanation for the French case, however, is one that has yet to be given adequate analysis. Despite the assurances made by reformists in the 1890s that evolutionary tactics would be employed, it is impossible to minimize the fear raised by the spectre of socialism and the ferocity of the bourgeois response to it. During the last decade of the century, more precisely between the municipal elections of 1892 and the legislative elections of 1898, the fear of socialism was one of the dominant characteristics of French political life. This movement of public opinion has not been studied but has been superbly documented by the French political sociologist, Pierre Sorlin.[18]

He demonstrated that workers suspect of socialist sympathies were hounded from their jobs; unions seen as hotbeds of revolutionary agitation were plagued by employers and government. Collective bargaining was rendered impossible, and 'yellow', or independent and conservative, unions were formed. Governments sympathetic to industry sent troops to contain strikes, closed the Paris Bourse du travail and made Fourmies a national symbol of repression. The advent of May Day sent a tremor through the respectable quarters of Paris, and the anarchist terror of the times only intensified growing panic. The established order was convinced that revolution was being revived in the form of organized socialism. It would collectivize everything and so destroy existing society. The middle classes were blind to demonstrations of reformism: Millerand's Saint-Mandé speech; Deville's analysis of Marxist principles (*Principes socialistes,* published in 1896); Jaurès' articles; and Guesde's pamphlets. They preferred to set up a caricature of socialism and hurl society's forces of repression at it.

It is in this context that support of the *ralliement* is best understood: as a defense of the established order. Although a minority of republicanized Catholics sought to aid the worker, most preferred to cooperate effectively with Moderates in a common defense of their mutual interests. Accordingly, they entered into electoral coalitions, reflecting in the words of a key Progressist, Eugène Spuller, a 'new spirit' and designed to defeat the common socialist enemy. A notorious example was Carmaux, where Catholics and Progressists joined forces against Jaurès. By the time of the 1898 campaign, the new majority was receiving additional support from anti-Semites, nationalists and even unrepentant monarchists. The danger now lay on the left, and there was much talk of a great anti-socialist party. Although never created, several republican *cercles* appeared as a first step toward meeting that objective. Merchants and industrialists in 1897 associated themselves with leading Progressists like Deschanel, Jules Siegfried, André Lebon, Poincaré and Waldeck-Rousseau in a Comité national républicain du commerce et de l'industrie. It worked to support the Méline ministry as the best guarantor of order and property and promised to campaign in the coming election. Unable to agree on long-term plans, the new allies accepted their lowest common denominator, that of preserving the status quo. Given a Moderate majority in both chambers, united by common fear and receiving widespread support from business, and given the weakness and factionalism of labor, the paucity of social legislation in France during the 1890s becomes more readily understood. And it was precisely this all-pervasive and irrational fear of socialism that prompted Millerand to provide reassurances and to publicize its teachings.

Millerand acknowledged that the left in the Chamber of 1893–1898 was going before the voters with empty hands. In a magazine article he credited socialists with having established for the first time a parliamentary force, with putting up a good fight and taking advantage of every opportunity to win reforms and advance propaganda. Socialist deputies, he pointed out, now went regularly to the scene of strikes, *ces tristes batailles économiques, dernier recours des travailleur aux abois.* He saw the coming elections as providing a further opportunity to disseminate socialist teachings. Stronger action, however, was ruled out: 'Socialism does not intend to submit an ignorant and hostile majority to the authority of a bold and valiant minority. On the contrary, it will bring around [that majority] to share freely in the ideas it believes just, and it is from that convinced and conscious majority that it seeks to win power. Its aim is to convince it. Its methods will be reason and persuasion. It will continually study, state its doctrines, provoke contradictions, seriously examine opposing views, and without anger dispell the fog of lies and slanders.'[19]

Millerand was aware that socialists and the left needed as much help as possible, and he tried to secure it wherever possible. When Brunellière asked his advice about which of two bourgeois candidates his socialist federation should endorse (it ran none of its own), Millerand's reply was swift and personal. He went to Nantes March 30 to rouse support for Jacques Escuyer, a local dairyman and author of legislation designed to establish a national retirement pension plan. 'He is a bourgeois', Millerand acknowledged, 'but a good bourgeois, an honorable man, a big industrialist who knows his business and does not starve those working for him.'[20]

Prior to the May election, government agents provided the Sûreté with a detailed report on socialist factions and their leaders. Although critical, the report underlined the reliance on reformist tactics. It described Guesdists as 'authoritarian' but whose aim was the parliamentary conquest of public power in order to apply their program. 'They have repudiated in large part all their previously violent methods, and the general tone of their speeches is moderate, of a sensible character.' To perform well at the polls, they have made alliances 'of a compromising nature' not only with Radicals but with *plebiscitaires* and anti-Semites. The writers estimated that 'in the real sense of the word they [were] no longer revolutionaries, but political jugglers, not without skill, but in any case having few scruples over the choice of means.' Blanquists were also seen as having evolved from authoritarian Jacobins to parliamentarians. Broussists, based in Paris, were of the least importance, while Allemanists, though few in number, comprised the most disciplined faction. Independents lacked real organization, and 'there is ill-feeling between them and Guesdists, although the two groups cooperate. Millerand is uncontestably the leader; Jaurès, the orator, and Rouanet, the business adviser.' Socialists, in whatever form, anticipated returning over 100 deputies to the Chamber.[21]

Subsequent reports filed during the pre-election period emphasized Guesde's fear of losing his seat. 'Guesde and Chauvin', opened one such report, 'want at any price not only union with socialists, but an alliance with Radical-Socialists and without conditions. They want to be reelected even at the expense of their party, convinced that once elected there will be time to rebuild.' Another stated that Guesde's anxiety had led him to suggest that a more likely choice run as socialist candidate in Roubaix and after the election cede his seat to the POF chief. According to yet another report, he secretly promised some parliamentary socialists not to run Parti ouvrier candidates against socialist deputies seeking reelection. He dared not mention this to the party executive but instead doctored the minutes of the last congress. It now appeared such deference would have to be made to the Socialist Union.[22]

Millerand's own parliamentary and ministerial ambitions did not pass unnoticed. However, emphasis was placed on his efforts to organize socialists for the coming election. 'The deputy of the XIIth *arrondissement* occupies himself not only with all socialist factions, but... he contracts, transacts, and negotiates with certain Radical groups, the press, and a number of other parliamentary groupings.'[23]

Millerand delivered a major campaign speech to his constituents February 12, listing as new and needed reforms the extension of prud'homme jurisdiction to cover all labor disputes, the secret ballot for rural workers – 'to eliminate Méline's tampering' – a two-year military service and, above all, old-age pensions. However, he refused to trace a general socialist program, arguing that the party was not a military regiment and that each candidate had to contract freely with his voters. The criteria set forth at Saint-Mandé served as a minimum and parliamentary action, in addition to trade union activity and propaganda, as a means. He did not speak to the great issue of the day, the Dreyfus affair, but reiterated the socialists' determination to oppose 'the Catholic church, Jewish banks, and Protestant financial interests'. Doubtless feeling the pressure of anti-Dreyfusard nationalists, Millerand again denied any inconsistency between the worker's concern with all mankind and his love of the French nation.[24]

A deputy, as his term in office lengthens, tends to become better known to his constituency than to his party's rank and file. At the same time, however, the 'services' rendered to his voters and the time spent in pursuit of local influence decreases. He often comes to show greater concern with national rather than with local symbols.[25] Millerand probably estimated that he had neglected the particular interests of his constituents. During the legislative session, moreover, there had been some conflict between him and socialists like Fournière and Vaillant, who were unable to appreciate the benefits of alcoholism and who endorsed a national beverage tax. Other socialists sought total abolition of the sale of alcoholic beverages and opposed home-brewing as well. Millerand suggested postponing the addition of any temperance plank to the party platform until a compensatory taxation plan could be worked out. Because of the socialist deputies' inability to agree on the issue, it became confused, and they took no action. Millerand's opposition to the *octrois* was less ambiguous. He denounced it as an internal barrier to trade and attributed its survival only to administrative lethargy. Paris alone paid 160 million francs a year, he said, and the national interest required its removal.[26]

Republican parties in general had tried to avoid the Dreyfus affair as an issue, and, in fact, the accompanying agitation aided the Nationalist and Conservative cause. The Progressist center suffered a slight check on the first vote, May 8, recovered somewhat on the second but did not substantially increase its plurality in the new legislature. Moderates numbered a little over 250, Radicals 178, but about eighty Conservatives and *rallies,* fifteen Nationalists and anti-Semites, including Drumont, now had a voice in the Chamber. Disappointed socialists returned fewer than fifty candidates.[27]

Millerand's fears over his own constituency had proved groundless.

His was a great personal victory, for he received over 8,700 votes of slightly over 9,900 cast. But only about twenty other socialists were elected on the first ballot, and both Jaurès and Guesde were defeated. Millerand asked for socialist discipline, and, although Gerault-Richard and Lavy lost on the *ballotage,* perhaps another thirty were elected. Since Méline's supporters had not appreciably increased in number, socialists could view the election as at least a moral victory.[28] But in contrast to the expectations raised after the breakthrough of 1893 – Guesde had predicted a socialist majority – the results were tragic. France, it was painfully apparent, was not about to vote socialist.

Miilerand put the best face on things. The defeats of Guesde and Jaurés were only temporary set-backs. Had not Guesde received more votes in 1898 than in 1893? Despite the loss of some of their finest orators, the socialists had after all increased both the size of their vote and their parliamentary delegation. As in the last legislature, the party would work incessantly to disseminate its principles. However, the chief effort of its *élus* would be to secure as many practical results as possible – retirement benefits, a two-year military service, fiscal reform – and could enjoy considerable success. This stress on results, he said, was dictated by the need for the party to demonstrate that it was capable not only of theoretical propaganda but of securing modest but real improvements for the workers who had shown confidence in it. He predicted that the socialist deputies would remain faithful to the promises made and the tactics followed the past five years.[29]

4. With Jaurès and Guesde defeated, the leadership of the socialist group in the Chamber unquestionably belonged to Millerand. At a meeting held June 1, the group entrusted him with its opening attack on the government.[30] The Méline cabinet still retained power, and the Progressist plurality asserted its strength when its candidate for the Presidency of the Chamber, Paul Deschanel, defeated the Radical, Henri Brisson.

Millerand took the floor less to challenge the ministry, for as André Daniel said, the country knew only too well of the running feud between Millerand and Méline, than to explain the socialists' intended role in the new Chamber. He described them as patient 'observers of reality' completely loyal to France. Referring to the Dreyfus affair, he said that the party defended all proletarians, including Jews, and attacked all capitalists, including Jews. He condemned Méline for accepting Conservative support; the Republic, for the first time since the crisis of May 16th, was threatened by a Catholic resurgence, and he accused the ministry of making an alliance with the right in a desperate effort to crush socialism.

Millerand listed the reforms considered essential by socialists and promised socialist support to any ministry that believed in their importance.[31]

Méline fought back; two members of his cabinet had failed to win reelection, his plurality had not increased and he was struggling for his political life. The socialists, he said, had not substantially increased their numbers. Millerand and other leaders were mere opportunists, and the government received the support of a wholly republican majority.   In reply to Millerand's query, did he intend to rely on the left or the right, Méline repeated the maxim that he would avoid all programs of reaction and revolution. The following day the ministry received a small vote of confidence, but only with the support of conservatives hostile to the Republic, and Méline resigned. Brisson formed a new government, and, while Millerand provided assurances of cooperation, he hoped it would not be 'too timid'.[32]

During the verification of mandates held by new deputies, Millerand questioned the tactics used by Guesde's successor and called for a committee of investigation. Using material supplied by Guesde, including affidavits and other testimony, he accused Motte of having exerted pressure on his workers and having his managers lead them in groups to the polls. He charged that prospective buyers had refused to purchase from Roubaix mills as long as Guesde represented the district, and that the ensuing unemployment contributed to the veteran's defeat.[33] To his surprise, the Chamber allowed Motte to take his seat. Guesde was again thwarted. He had found his electoral loss particularly crushing. After the euphoria of 1893, he had felt himself and his party on the eve of triumph. After a life of persecution and propaganda, exhaustion, sickness and impatience anticipating the final revolutionary crisis, he and several of his colleagues had been carried to public office on a wave of universal suffrage. He then envisaged victory as parliamentary, the sum total of the socialist deputies sure to be elected to the Chamber. The election shattered hopes of reaching an early majority. More devastatingly, it had rejected him; and in his place as head of the parliamentary legation of the party was a newly arrived bourgeois. A Sûreté report described Guesde as 'absolutely heartbroken' over his 'feeling of rejection' by socialists in the new Chamber. 'He believes there is a movement to 'force him from the party', noted the agent, 'and he refuses to attend the celebration scheduled at the Tivoli Vaux-hall.'[34]

The loss of revolutionary fervor and the reformism practiced by French socialists in the 1890s stemmed in large part, as we have seen, from the municipal and national election victories of 1892 and 1893. One characteristic of the 'deradicalization' process is the optimism that the successes initially won by recourse to moderate means must necessarily continue,

10

making disillusion all the greater when they do not.[35] A renewed response by the party's revolutionary left wing was to be anticipated.

On July 22, 1898, Millerand's name appeared as that of editor-in-chief of *La Lanterne*. No reason was given for the change except that Briand, who had suffered his third consecutive defeat in the past election, had asked him to accept the post 'in the interest of the party'. (Briand's biographer, however, pointed to a falling-out between the editor and his publisher.)[36] Millerand began to write a daily halfcolumn, under the sketch of a lantern, in which he commented on the news of the day and described what he considered particularly outrageous social injustices. As editor of *La Lanterne* Millerand found socialism no longer able to disinterest itself from the Dreyfus affair, now in its fourth year. The threat to the Republic posed by anti-Dreyfusards was to present his party with the opportunity to participate in power.

8. To power

On December 22, 1894, Alfred Dreyfus was found guilty of having transmitted military documents to Germany. Jean Jaurès, writing in *La Petite République* December 24, said that he should have been executed and surprised even socialists by hinting in the Chamber that the Council of War had received secret orders to save the rich officer.[1] Dreyfus never stopped proclaiming his innocence, and his family employed a young lawyer, Bernard Lazare, to prove it. By July 1897 Scheurer-Kestner was convinced and asked for revision. Fearing agitation, the Méline government refused to reopen the case, and Conservative and Nationalist newspapers vilified partisans of the traitor. To end the persistent unrest, the Army in January 1898 tried and acquitted the officer called guilty by the revisionists, Major Walsen-Esterhazy.

It was then that Emile Zola wrote his open letter to the President of the Republic. He accused Dreyfus' prosecutors of 'an abominable campaign to mislead opinion', and the case, despite attempts by nearly all politicians to avoid it, became an issue of primary political importance. When at the Zola trial Lieutenant Colonel Joseph Henry, an intelligence officer, revealed part of a secret dossier, a letter from the German military attaché to his Italian colleague, confirming Dreyfus' guilt, the Court hesitated no longer, and Zola was condemned. Revisionists refused to accept the new evidence, and with the eyes of the world upon her France separated into two opposed camps.

1. Millerand first took a neutral position and showed concern only with political and legal considerations. In December 1897, to the applause of the extreme left in the Chamber, he insisted that the government cease equivocating and reply firmly to demands for revision. But the socialist

leader was taking advantage of the opportunity to attack Méline and not defending Dreyfus. He rejected Méline's explanation that the question was strictly one of law and not the concern of the government or of parliament, neither of which, according to the Premier, was to question the rendered judgment *(la chose jugée)*. The government held that questioning juridicial decisions repudiated French tradition, and Méline's position was endorsed by General Billot, the Minister of War, who swore that Dreyfus had been justly condemned. Avoiding the issue, replied Millerand, would not stop Dreyfusards from striving to reopen the case; in such a serious matter the government had to take a stand. However, he made it clear that he was not asking for revision. The Chamber nevertheless passed a resolution 'respecting the authority of the rendered judgment' and denounced the 'odious campaign [to] trouble the public conscience'.[2]

If critical of Méline's handling of the case, then, Millerand was not speaking from a Dreyfusard point of view, and he voiced the opinion of many militant socialists when he suggested that the publicist and leading revisionist, Joseph Reinach, first rehabilitate those in his own family before attempting to rehabilitate 'a new Calas'. The reference was aimed at Baron de Reinach, involved in the Panama Scandal. The President of the Chamber admonished Millerand for his remark. Reinach sent his seconds the following day, and two shots were exchanged without result.[3]

At the outset of the revisionist campaign Millerand, like Guesde, had dissociated socialists from what he considered à bourgeois struggle. He no doubt estimated that socialist involvement would yield few practical results, especially from an electoral point of view. Still, he was preaching neutrality before the *Affaire* had aroused public passions and in so doing was following socialist tradition and precept. Millerand, Guesde and other socialist chiefs had rejected both Boulanger and his Opportunist opposition. Blanquists had issued a declaration of neutrality in 1888, though they ultimately became disenchanted with Boulanger and the following year ran a candidate against him. The policy statement issued by the Second International in 1891 constituted the orthodox socialist position. An American Jewish group had asked about the socialist response to anti-Semitism, and the resolution voted by the Brussels Congress clearly subordinated 'antagonism or struggle of race or nationality' to 'the class struggle between proletarians of all races and capitalists of all races'. It merely condemned anti-Semitic agitation as 'one of the manoeuvres by which the capitalist class and reactionary governments try to make the Socialist movement deviate and to divide the workers'.[4]

Millerand's stand drew criticism from both Dreyfusards and Nationalists. The latter upbraided him for not attacking the former, and Drumont accused Millerand of showing leniency to Jewish capitalists. (There were, however, no references to his ancestry, and presumably Drumont was ignorant of it.) Millerand placed himself as squarely opposed to anti-Semitism but contended that capitalist exploitation was immoral whether practiced by *habitués* of the synogogue or *familières* of the church. Dreyfusards, understandably enough, found Millerand's attitude, and that of organized socialism, scarcely compatible with revolutionary ideals of justice. As early as November 9, 1896 an indignant Lazare had written Millerand about a Zévaès article in *La Petite République*. He found its neutrality 'insulting' for a newspaper that professed to be revolutionary and wondered whether it were subsidized by anti-Dreyfusards.[5]

Two months later, thirty-three socialist deputies signed a manifesto calling upon party members to 'remain aloof' from bourgeois struggles. Although the proletariat was not insensible to justice, the manifesto stated, it refused to let itself be duped. Those now invoking the cause of human rights and individual dignity had stolen from workers all the guarantees claimed for Dreyfus. Among the signatures were those of Millerand, Jaurès and Guesde. The declaration followed the precedent set four years earlier when, in January 1893, *La Revue socialiste* had urged socialists to remain aloof from the Panama Scandal. In his history of the affair, and with the mellowness that often accompanies perspective, Joseph Reinach said that he understood the reasons given by the socialists and excused their attitude. They had fought bitterly against capitalist exploiters and were now asked to join them, while some revisionists were the same deputies and senators who had approved the *lois scélérates*.[6]

In another discussion of socialist neutrality, an observer estimated that the policy's two leading advocates, Guesde and Vaillant, probably underestimated the extent of their influence but attached some legitimacy to their claim that justice was impossible in an essentially unjust society. However, Daniel Halévy went on to distinguish the neutrality of a Guesde, who had said that 'the people do not have the right to bestow their pity', that is, a neutrality based on doctrinal reasons, from that of an undoctrinare Millerand, who felt it would be bad politics. The latter predicted that agitation resulting from socialist support of Dreyfus would only profit the cause defended – and the campaigns fought – by militarists and anti-Semites.[7]

Millerand persisted in his refusal to take sides and, we have seen, made no mention of the case in his electoral platform of 1898. The socialist chief also feared that his party's involvement would compromise the fragile and precarious unity so recently achieved. Thus it was that in the spring and summer of 1898 he immersed himself in the safe, it not insignificant, study of a workers' pension plan.[8] On July 8, Brisson's Minister of War, Godefroy Cavaignac, revealed part of an alleged confession by Dreyfus – which the revisionist intelligence office Picquart called a forgery, getting himself arrested for his accusation. Millerand wrote the next day in *La Lanterne* that the speech 'relieved the public conscience', and 'until the day these documents are proved irrefutably to be forgeries our duty is to observe silence'. Then he called once more for the policy of noninvolvement first urged before the elections.

Millerand's refusal to support the revisionist cause increasingly disturbed the Dreyfusards, and in particular Joseph Reinach. The latter's hostility to Millerand and to socialists was of long duration. In the early 1890s Reinach accused socialist deputies of base hypocrisy. They owned property, in some cases substantial amounts, he charged, but during election campaigns 'thundered against capitalism'.[9] Millerand's stand angered as well the young socialist destined for literary fame. Charles Péguy, a staunch Dreyfusard and spokesman for sympathetic students at the École Normale, resented socialist neutrality and especially that of Millerand in as much as it emanated from the virtual head of the party.

Péguy sent a steady stream of letters of protest to newspapers and to prominent socialists.[10] Expressing the sentiments of his fellow *Normaliens*, he labelled *La Lanterne* anti-Dreyfusard and implored its editorial staff to follow the example now being set by Jaurès. The Socialist party, he cried, could play the role of a great arbiter, but it too has its 'general staff' and as one of its chiefs, the 'great technician, Alexandre Millerand. This renowned inventor of the so-called Socialist Union cleverly pleads in desperation, writes confusedly, though interestingly. ... We will never be like him'. Péguy resented Millerand's contributions to *L'Éclair*, then anti-Dreyfusard, and threatened that younger socialists would attack him unless he 'mended his ways'. He wrote to Georges Renard, now editor-in-chief of *La Revue socialiste,* on July 10, 1898; Péguy accused Millerand of failing to have *La Lanterne* either safeguard socialism from Rochefort and the 'new Boulangists' or defend justice against the General Staff, and he was 'painfully surprised' to hear of Renard's collaboration. The disturbed Renard accordingly urged that the party 'keep in touch with the younger generation', something, he said, Jaurès was insisting on.[11]

In the summer of 1898 Guesdists and Blanquists joined with Millerand in asking that socialists take a neutralist stand. In his *Mémoires* Millerand described the dilemma on which French socialism then found itself. On the one hand, he asked, was it not the duty of the party, as Jaurès so eloquently began to plead, to participate in the struggle for justice? On the other, how could it desert the long combat against capitalism only to join forces with the bourgeoisie in defense of a wealthy army officer condemned by his peers? He later wrote: 'On my part, after much mature reflection, I felt that our party could share in that agitation only on the day proof of juridical errors was clearly demonstrated.' That Millerand agonized over his decision was revealed in a letter to Renard: 'I am not unaware of the difficulties of my situation. They are apparent at first glance. I will strive to overcome them by dint of clarity, sincerity and composure. Conciliatory, anxious to gather and understand every conviction, I take a stand and remain unshakeable once my mind is made up. This is how I try to be. It would be wholly impossible for me to act any differently. My shortcomings and faults do not escape me. Some new ones may very well be revealed. Perhaps the epoch through which we are passing will improve my style and means of expression, hardly my leading qualities.' Accordingly, he did not prevent Renard from defending a Dreyfusard point of view in the pages of *La Lanterne*. In a subsequent note, Millerand expressed his inability to understand Jaurès, who, he said was 'gripped by a veritable frenzy, and it was useless to try to reason with him'. He agreed with Léon Blum, who, until his own conversion, feared that Jaurès would make socialism unpopular by 'irritating public opinion', and who tried to dissuade him.[12]

The great voice opposing neutrality was now that of Jean Jaurès. Defeated in the 1898 election, he threw himself into editorial work on *La Petite République*. Once convinced of Dreyfus' innocence he viewed the affair not as a simple struggle over the guilt of an officer but one between progressive elements in the Republic and the organized forces of reaction. During the summer of 1898 he wrote a series of articles, *Les Preuves,* to demonstrate the innocence of Dreyfus. A number of Possibilists and Allemanists converted as well, the former to defend the Republic, the latter to conform with their anti-militaristic and anti-clerical views. The remaining socialists, like Millerand, continued to stand aside.

2. All was changed by the confession of Colonel Henry. Cavaignac was forced to compare samples of Dreyfus' handwriting with that of the alleged confession and, after close examination of the letter reportedly sent by the German military attaché, accepted the possibility of forgery. Arrested at the end of August 1898, Henry left a confession and committed suicide. General Boisdeffre, the Chief of Staff, then resigned and the affair seemed at an end. The entire republican press accepted the need for revision. Most socialists, including Millerand, abandoned their neutrality. 'On that day', he recalled, 'I became an all-out revisionist, with no reservations.' Reinach spoke of the confession creating 'thousands of instantaneous conversions'. On that day, he quoted the critic, Jules

Lemaître, 'we all accepted revision'. Henry' confession converted, among others, Pelletan and Caillaux.[13]

Jaurès' popularity reached new heights. Incredibly, on the very morning of Henry's confession, he demonstrated in *La Petite République* that the dossier had to be a forgery. His renown equalled that of Zola; he displaced both Guesde and Millerand as leader of the party, and his name became synonomous with socialism in the mind of the public. As a socialist deputy, Gabriel Mermiex, suggested, the widespread acclaim for Jaurès may well have paved the way for a socialist in the government. Gerault-Richard reportedly drank a toast to 'the socialist minister who will inaugurate the next century'.[14] Jaurès himself had implicitly predicted executive involvement the previous November: 'I believe', he had written at the end of an article in *La Revue socialiste,* 'that the next characteristic of the socialist movement will consist of more direct and extensive particpation on the part of the working class in day-to-day political and social action.'[15]

Millerand wrote in *La Lanterne* on September 2 that 'revision imposes itself'. On September 5 he said that he had been a fool. Two years later during a Chamber debate over amnesty for those involved, Méline reminded Millerand of his remarks to Reinach. Millerand acknowledged them, admitting that his revisionism began only after the disclosure of the Henry forgery and that Jaurès had been 'more perspicacious and clairvoyant than I'. He then wrote to Reinach to say that it had given him great pleasure to apologize publicly as 'a reparation due you for the heavy injustice I had involuntarily committed'.[16] Despite, or because of, these expressions of self-recrimination, Millerand showed most concern with bringing the affair to a speedy conclusion. Political agitation had temporarily shelved social reform, and he wished, he said, to return to it as soon as possible. On September 21 he wrote in *La Lanterne* of the need to end political 'diversions' and resume the work of social legislation.

In addition, Millerand warned that republican reaction to anti-Dreyfusards, in a misplaced excess of zeal, might jeopardize the very liberties the Republic had pledged itself to protect. In November 1898 a Radical-Socialist deputy of the Seine, Levraud, submitted legislation designed to prohibit teaching on the part of all religious orders. Initially presented to the 1885–1889 legislature, the bill was now reintroduced in the wake of resentment directed at anti-republican army officers whose education had been predominantly religious. The Bonapartist deputy and former Boulangist, Paul de Cassagnac, denounced the measure as an attack on the liberty of conscience. Millerand's remarks paralled those made in opposition to vengeful anti-Boulangists ten years before. Clericalism, he said, constituted a threat. Even so, the regime was to be defended by measures of principle conforming to true republican doctrine, like separation of Church and State, and not by facile remedies borrowed from the techniques of its enemies.[17] The Levraud proposal was ultimately shelved, but when Millerand was to take a similar stand against Combes he found himself isolated from the Radical and socialist majority.

The affair, however, was far from over. To the astonishment of Dreyfusards, anti-revisionists regarded both confession and suicide as acts of courage. They accepted the version of conservative and nationalist newspapers which insisted that Henry's patriotism had prevented him from revealing the true documents – for their disclosure implicated the Kaiser himself and would probably lead to war. *La Libre Parole* showed its esteem for the hero by organizing a fund for his widow.

Nevertheless, the Brisson ministry began the slow work leading to revision. It announced its decision to send the case to the Cour de cassation, which in turn would decide upon the question of revision. Unlike a court of appeals in the English or American sense, this highest French court could not decide definitively on the merits of a case. If it 'broke' the decision of a lower court, however, the case must be retried. This would mean a new court-martial. Then two new blows aimed at Dreyfusards followed in quick succession. General Chanoine, Brisson's new Minister of War, betrayed the Cabinet with the news that he shared the anti-revisionist views of his predecessors and resigned. The ministry fell October 25. President Félix Faure called on Charles Dupuy, who formed his third government on November 3, 1898. Moreover, the President of the Court's Civil Chamber, Quesnay de Beaurepaire, questioned the competency of the Criminal Chamber which was to decide upon the need for revision. No reason was specified, but Dreyfusards were quick to point out that its President was a Jew and that the section was noted for its liberal views. De Beaurepaire wished to see legislation enacted to transfer the case to the Court setting as a whole.

3. The turmoil created by the Dreyfus affair and, consequently, the danger confronting the Republic precipitated a renewal of emphasis on socialist unity. After the general election of May 1898, Jaurès gave an important speech calling for immediate structural unification. At the time it received only half-hearted support. Vaillant at once made known his reservations; the separate factions provided the force behind French socialism and hasty fusion might create disorder and disunity. Millerand then agreed; unity presupposed the existence of a united will in favor of it. Because the socialist party owed victory to its 'independent elements', they were not to be sacrificed in vain.[18]

The initial reaction on the part of Vaillant and Millerand to Jaurès' proposal was one of considered caution; Guesde's was absolute hostility. A report in the files of the Paris Prefecture of Police, dated June 30, 1898, quoted the opinion of his lieutenant, Gabriel Farjat: the scheme was a 'bauble of Jaurès'. No socialist faction supported it with the exception of the 'feeble Broussists'. Jaurès had taken the initiative in urging unification; he unfortunately had also said that 'the old parties no longer can justify their existence'. The remark visibly upset Guesde and Vaillant. The former made known his resentment of 'newcomers giving lessons to old *militants,* to already tried and tested parties'. Two observers – and subsequent biographers of Jaurès – attributed the hostility of the veterans to the fact that '[he] had tried to go over the heads of the old chiefs who wished to keep their identities'.[19] The police report referred to above concurred. Guesde, Allemane and Vaillant, it said, rejected unity 'at any price', fearing 'the loss of their personal power, their abdication' and 'the pure sacrifice of twenty years of past efforts to organize their respective factions'. Convinced the unification attempts could only profit 'newcomers' to socialism, they hoped they would prove futile.

The movement towards unity got underway when most socialists became convinced that the threat to the Republic's existence was real. The young rightist, Charles Maurras, justified Henry's suicide as an act of supreme patriotism. Paul Déroulède revived the old League of Patriots, an aggressive organization that seemed to take special delight in disrupting meetings of the Dreyfusard League for the Defense of the Rights of Man and the Citizen. A series of strikes swept through France in the fall of 1898. The government despatched troops to Paris, by early October almost an entire army corps. Soldiers occupied railway stations throughout the country. There were rumors of *coups* by disgruntled army chiefs, rumors easily believed by the anti-militarist socialists. Daniel Halévy has written of the period: 'The officers were fidgeting... Who would silence them?... The country, leaderless, drifts, with sails slack, like a boat abandoned to the winds.' He said further that the right hoped to profit from the disorder, judging the time ripe for a *coup*. Guesde and Vaillant also appreciated the seriousness of the situation, and many Frenchmen anticipated a reactionary effort to bring down the regime.[20]

Socialists began to come to its support. Years of parliamentary participation and the countless appeals to achieve goals by legal means now bore fruit. They identified themselves with republican institutions and rallied to preserve them. Independents led the way; the socialist group in the Chamber issued a declaration of protest against the concentration of troops in the Paris area. Parti ouvrier members at their Montluçon

Congress in September then pressed the attack for socialist unity when they demanded the formation of a permanent central organ. They contended it would unite socialists on the basis of the minimum requirements set forth at Saint-Mandé and so coordinate their efforts at republican defense.[21] On October 16, at the Salle Vantier on the avenue de Clichy, during a meeting convoked by the party's National Council and representing all socialist factions – Millerand and Jaurès attending as delegates of the socialist press, the *ad hoc* Comité permanent de vigilence was created. In grouping the leading French socialists – Vaillant, Brousse, Guesde, Allemane, Fournière, Jaurès, Briand, Millerand and Viviani – it carried the germ of future unity. The resolutions formulated on October 16 expressed the intent of the delegates to bring together all revolutionary forces. They would direct their appeal to the proletariat in its entirety, both to protest any infringement of working-class liberties and to help defend the Republic.[22]

These objectives, however, could not be met by an organization whose role was limited to the dissemination of information. By December its members recognized the need for a more effective organ. They created a successor Comité d'Entente socialiste, which began to function the following month. It was designed to examine all questions of interest to socialism, but, lacking any right to interfere in the internal operations of its member organizations, its authority was also limited. Still, the organization created was to survive until the end of 1899, when it was replaced by the first Congress of Socialist Organizations. With its hierarchy of section, federation and administrative council, the commitee's structure resembled that of the Parti ouvrier and foreshadowed that of the unified party founded in 1905. Political control was vested in a national congress meeting annually; in the interval between congresses an executive council, composed of an interfederal committee and the socialist deputies in the Chamber, was to act as administrative organ.[23]

Membership on the Comité d'Entente posed a problem for Independents. They now appeared for the first time as a coherent national grouping but one not yet organized as a party, only as more or less associated committees. The point, as Léon Blum later observed, was that for Independents, as for all other socialists, no meaningful unitary structure was created; the Comité d'Entente functioned only 'an administrative wheel, without life and without its own power to conciliate or to sanction'. Nothing had changed, for its members could commit their respective organizations only in the degree to which they were authorized to do so at any given time. The point, too, is that any major question, like the participation of a socialist in the government, could be approved or rejected only by an annual congress.[24]

The bright prospect of unity, however, pushed these considerations to the background. Millerand and *La Lanterne* could not restrain their delight and pride in the latest series of events. In spite of the faults of the bourgeoisie, Millerand wrote, it could rely on workers to safeguard the regime. Although nowhere explicitly suggested, it was probably now that he envisaged an even more effective method of winning socialist support for the Republic and, at the same time, demonstrating labor's maturity and sense of responsibility: direct governmental participation. Once again, however, reports flowing into the Sûreté described the troubled waters beneath the surface. On the Comité d'Entente, Guesde was depicted as complaining bitterly of what he regarded as failure to appreciate his sacrifices on behalf of socialism and lack of respect.[25]

4. Millerand plunged into the revisionist controversy as if to atone for lost time. The Army was determined to try Picquart for his accusation of forgery, and Dupuy said the government lacked the right to intervene in a purely military affair. On October 28 Millerand tried to prove to the Chamber that the ministry could legally postpone the trial until the question of revision was decided on. He asked deputies to imagine the consequence of Picquart's condemnation if the Court later found Dreyfus innocent and decided to reopen the case. But his resolution to have the Minister of War ask for postponement was rejected. As in his speech of the proceding December, Millerand intervened as a jurist, dismayed at the twists given to the law. His remarks, however, were seen by nationalists as irresponsible and as leading to 'judicial anarchy', their author a fullfledged revisionist.[26]

To Millerand's surprise he received unexpected support from some Progressists. In the Senate Waldeck-Rousseau also sought to have the Picquart court-martial postponed – and with the same results. Millerand admitted later to having long admired Waldeck-Rousseau as Minister of Interior in the Ferry cabinet for his role in the battle to legalize trade unions. (He could scarcely admit to having admired his insistence on repressing the Parisian desire for greater autonomy.) In addition to the political differences separating them – Waldeck-Rousseau had returned from five years of retirement as an anti-socialist Senator of the Loire, the coldness of the latter and the natural shyness of the former had long prevented a meeting. Common friends now brought the socialist deputy and the Progressist Senator together, and Millerand took the opportunity to congratulate Waldeck-Rousseau on his speech.[27]

Millerand intervened once again on December 19 when the Minister of War, Freycinet, announced the appearance of 'new evidence'. Because its disclosure would 'jeopardize' national security, he promised to show it to the Chamber only on condition that it remain classified. Millerand rejected the demand for secrecy. Let all be known, he told his fellow deputies, and if there are to be any conditions, the Court must determine them.[28] Anti-revisionists centered their campaign on the proposed *loi de dessaisissement,* the legislation designed to transfer the case from the Criminal Chamber to the Court sitting as a whole. Millerand, like all revisionists, denounced the plan.[29]

Despite fierce opposition, the appropriate parliamentary committee brought the bill before the Chamber on February 10, 1899, and thus forced all deputies to take sides. Millerand tried to demonstrate that the Criminal Chamber, contrary to the claim set forth by authors of the intended legislation, did not hold any predetermined opinion on the affair. He asked whether the government was unaware that spearheading the attacks on its competency were the anti-revisionists. If they managed to discredit the Criminal Chamber, what was there to prevent them from next discrediting the entire Court? Dupuy denied any ulterior motive, insisting that his sole reason for wanting the Court enlarged was to give its decision the force of a decree and so make it invincible. The Chamber passed the bill.[30]

The discussion of this law and its approval marked a political turning point in the Dreyfus affair. On February 9, seventy-one deputies representing all parties, including Progressists like Barthou and Poincaré, had signed a manifesto rejecting it. On the day following its enactment many of the same names appeared on a declaration of protest. It described the anti-revisionist campaign as the third great assault against the Republic, following *le seize mai* in 1877 and Boulangism at the end of the 1880s.[31]

In the February 11 issue of *La Lanterne,* that carrying the text of the declaration of protest, Millerand asked for full socialist support of the regime. The Republic, he said, appealed to all her defenders, and socialists must respond. In joining with other republicans during the emergency, their independence would not be sacrificed. In any event, the Republic, the necessary instrument of social reform, was now threatened, and everything else became secondary. The message for Millerand marked no new departure; the language, however, was among the most emotional ever used. 'Before the common peril', he wrote, 'we ask everyone to help, be he moderate, radical, or socialist. You are republican; that is enough. Give us your hand, comrade, and forward for the Republic.' By February 1899, then, Millerand wanted socialists to rally to the defense of the beleaguered Third Republic.

5.   Revisionists won an important victory after the death of Félix Faure. Emile Loubet, the candidate of the left, defeated Méline for the Presidency on February 19. Millerand had supported the candidacy of Brisson but preferred the much less conservative Loubet to Méline and predicted 'veritable civil war' if the latter were elected. 'He would never resign as did Casimir-Perier.'[32] An attempted nationalist *coup* by Déroulède failed pitifully during the funeral on February 25. On March 5 Millerand lauded Waldeck-Rousseau for his speech in the Senate against the *loi de dessaisissement*, calling it 'marvelous... with impeccable form and force of irony, but with high views and worthy ideas'.[33]

The High Court meanwhile discussed the case. Millerand followed its daily progress and could not conceal his delight in hearing the court reporter refer to Dreyfus as innocent. Then the Court announced its decision; it annulled the condemnation of Dreyfus and asked for a new court-martial. 'Justice Triumphs', ran the headline in *La Lanterne* on June 5, and Millerand, in view of the decision, viewed the new trial as 'a simple formality'.

Were plans made to overthrow the Republic? Daniel Halévy, we have seen, was convinced of it, and certainly many of his contemporaries agreed. On March 31, at his trial before an assizes court, Déroulède brazenly told the jury to acquit him 'if you want me to try again'. He was acquitted unanimously and carried in triumph from the court-room.[34] Clemenceau spoke of 'civil war' in the June 2 issue of *L'Aurore*. Jaurès wrote that 'reaction triumphs' in *La Petite République* the same day. Colonel Marchand, back from Fashoda, attended a reception in his honor given by nationalists, and the popular soldier used the opportunity to condemn the government.[35] The day following the Court's announcement President Loubet was assaulted at the Auteuil racetrack by an anti-Dreyfusard. Millerand and Viviani questioned the ministry on its failure to take adequate precautions for his safety, and the Comité d'Entente called on Parisians to demonstrate at the neighboring track, Longchamp, the following week.

While these events were unfolding, Millerand continued to turn out the series of articles in *La Lanterne* showing his movement toward the position that only a government of republican defense could stave off a nationalist attack. On February 11, in language similar to that of the *Petite République* declaration of 1893 imploring republican socialists to vote for its candidates, he had called on every republican to rally to the regime. By June 4 he was saying that the Republic's best defense was to strike at its oppressors. On June 8 union was again seen as necessary and the Socialist party was realizing wherein lay its supreme interest. On the 10th and 11th the situation was described as perilous and rappro-

chement among republic factions vital. He admitted that he had previously opposed republican concentration as unnecessary; now the need
was urgent. Everything was to be subordinated to the only legitimate
preoccupation for a republican: safeguarding the regime and its democratic institutions.

On June 12 a Vaillant interpellation held the Dupuy ministry responsible for acts of police brutality committed at Longchamp. The split in
Progressist ranks had so widened that the party could no longer give
Dupuy undivided support, and he lost his majority. *La Lanterne* noted
that the 'debt owed since 1893' had been 'repaid'. Loubet asked Poincaré to form a new government, and in his editorial comment, Millerand
hoped it would 'reflect the common concerns of all and not lend itself
to any one point of view'.

In *L'Éclair* the same day he denounced as slander the view that socialists must be excluded from the next cabinet as foes of the Republic.
Since their entry into public life, they had consecrated all their force and
energy to its support. To call them potential traitors ten years after
Boulangism revealed the greatest possible ingratitude. A union of all
republicans was necessary, and socialist voters were among the most ardent among them.

We always claimed, continued Millerand the following day in *La Lanterne,* that the premier-designate must exercise complete liberty in his
choice of colleagues. Let him choose the most worthy, no matter from
which quarter they may come. On the 16th Millerand wrote that no republican would quibble over the choices of the statesmen to take power.
He acknowledged rumors naming Viviani as a possible minister and noted the intense feeling in some quarters that the appearance of Viviani
and Poincaré in a cabinet would constitute 'an abomination'. Millerand
professed surprise in as much as both names were found on the February
manifestos.

The rumors, as Poincaré later disclosed, were well-founded; Millerand
had not only described but had helped to create them. On June 16th he
privately visited Poincaré and told him that in view of the gravity of the
crisis he and his socialist friends wished to help. Because it seemed necessary in forming a cabinet to appeal to all republican forces, he suggested Vivani.[36] In his *Mémoires* Millerand justified his action by pointing out that because socialists already had committed themselves by
sending representatives to republican defense groups in the Chamber, he
had not hesitated to go to Poincaré on Viviani's behalf.

Poincaré, however, rejected Millerand's advice. He did not estimate
in 1899 – nor would he thereafter – that the interests of socialists and republicans were in any way similar, and he would not combine two such

divergent parties in the same ministry. Perhaps, as a biographer stated, he feared that the accession of socialists to power jeopardized the role he envisaged for himself as a Tory reformer. Reinach, on the other hand, suggested that Poincaré drew back at the prospect of reformist socialism in power, finding it easier to combat revolutionaries – although he dared not say so. Poincaré himself, at the time of the publication of some Waldeck-Rousseau papers by *Le Matin* in 1911, said in a letter to the newspaper: 'I refused Millerand because behind him there were revolutionaries. Since then Millerand and Viviani have proven themselves statesmen, but only in the degree to which they separated themselves from the collectivist party.'[37]

Some observers noted Viviani's total unawareness of the attempt made on his behalf. Given his youth and former intemperateness, they insisted that his candidacy could hardly have been considered seriously by Poincaré. Millerand, therefore, had in reality proposed himself and had hoped the hint would be taken. Militant socialists later labelled the act unauthorized as well, for he failed to consult with the party's Comité d'Entente before visiting Poincaré. We have seen, however, that in view of its loose structure only a national congress held the authority to approve or reject such action. Millerand's supporters later maintained that the administrative council of the Comité d'Entente had in fact been notified, thus giving Millerand full liberty to act, and that most socialists accepted the eventual participation of one of their own in the government. One political reporter commented that because Millerand's own local political organization never adhered to the Comité he was not formally required to consult with it. The issued was to be debated extensively in the future, but in June of 1899 few expected any cabinet to survive, and principles were not then discussed.[38]

In any case, Poincaré placed his party first and so failed to win approval of his ministry. Radicals objected particularly to the presence of his friend, Louis Barthou, who had opposed them as minister in the Méline Cabinet. Partially on the advice of Poincaré, Loubet now turned to René Waldeck-Rousseau as the man with the best chance to end a ministerial crisis already six days old.[39]

The choice was not entirely unexpected, for on the day of Dupuy's resignation many considered him a possible successor. Although as late as the spring of 1898 Waldeck was seeking to head a vast conservative coalition uniting all moderates and even elements of the right, a year later he was accepting the aid of Radicals and socialists to defeat his former allies. Why this change of heart? Simply because he was convinced that a reactionary threat constituted the greatest danger confronting the nation. Millerand had found him an especially desirable candidate and the very night of Dupuy's fall sent a special delivery letter to the Senator's secretary and factotum, Ulrich, requesting that his employer return to Paris. The fact that only a year before the two had campaigned against each other at Roubaix, with Waldeck-Rousseau supporting Motte and Millerand Guesde, neither deterred Millerand from approaching Waldeck nor Waldeck from ultimately offering Millerand a portfolio. If Waldeck disdained socialist politicians, he was nevertheless convinced that a 'domesticated revolutionary' would become an agent of good order. He was also very much aware that Millerand's presence in a cabinet would ensure the support of at least the Independent socialists and perhaps bring about the neutrality of others. And Millerand, notwithstanding occasional collectivist oratory, was in many ways closer to another bourgeois lawyer like Waldeck-Rousseau than to militant socialists like Guesde and Vaillant.[40]

An examination of the Waldeck-Rousseau papers permits us to trace the steps taken by the premier-designate after he received the mandate to form a ministry. His scribbled notes reveal recognition of the need to 'represent all factions' and to 'end agitation and impose respect for the Constitution'. His papers also contain some of the letters and telegrams of encouragement that he received. One from Senator Bernard assured him of Radical support and then suggested: 'Millerand will not be out of place in a ministry of republican action to liquidate the Affair... despite possible repercussions.'[41] Evidently Waldeck-Rousseau first concerned himself with the controversial Ministry of War. Two generals, Zurlinden and Chanoine, had accepted and had then resigned from the post. A civilian appeared more reliable, and Waldeck thought of himself and Casimir-Perier as possibilities. However, an early draft of new cabinet members contained the names of Generals Galliffet and Brugère. Further along on this draft, among candidates for other positions, Millerand's name also appears but with a line drawn through it.[42]

Waldeck's chief concern lay with safeguarding the Republic. In a self-memo, he wrote that 'above any disagreements [ministers] must place a common ideal, the republican idea, [as] the highest raison d'être'. The premier-designate was an admirer of Galliffet, the General who led the last cavalry charge at the battle of Sedan, who ruthlessly crushed the Paris Commune and who together with Waldeck had been in Gambetta's *entourage*. The two men had kept in touch, and Waldeck was aware that a bored Galliffet would regard the offer as a challenge.[43] After the General's name he wrote that there was 'no stricter observer of discipline' and 'no one with more respect for the Constitution'. Yet, Waldeck noted that he would 'have to speak with him about 1877', about the readiness of another General, MacMahon, to override parliamentary interference in order to achieve his objectives. The concern shown with the Ministry of War suggests that Waldeck thought first of filling this post and then of balancing his choice of Galliffet and of securing leftwing support by selecting Millerand.

This analysis squarely contradicts the account of Waldeck-Rousseau's Finance Minister, Joseph Caillaux. The latter wrote that Millerand was decided on before Galliffet and that Galliffet was seen by Waldeck as a counter-weight to Millerand. Caillaux also maintained that Millerand, 'the socialist', unctuously approved the choice of Galliffet.[44] An explanation for this account, unsupported and unrealistic, may rest on the animosity felt for Millerand by Caillaux at the time that the latter was writing his memoirs because of Millerand's repeated attacks on his pacifism during World War I.

His letters to Joseph Reinach indicate that if Waldeck thought of including a socialist, he momentarily dropped the idea in view of the hostility to it shown by Poincaré and other Progressists. Waldeck reconsidered after deciding upon Galliffet. He did not regard the presence of a representative of the extreme left either as creating difficulties for the cabinet or as furthering the socialist cause. He later wrote that the strength or weakness of a party did not issue from the presence or absence of one of its members in a ministry, a lesson Millerand was to apply in forming his own cabinet in 1920.[45] Waldeck saw only advantages in Millerand's participation, particularly the socialist support he expected it to bring. He doubtless recalled the precedent set by the Freycinet ministry in 1886, which had required Radical support in order to survive. To win it, the Premier had selected Radicals like Granet and Lockroy to serve respectively as Ministers of Posts and Telegraph and of Commerce.

According to Joseph Reinach, who helped advise him, once Waldeck was convinced of the need to form a ministry of republican defense and to appeal to every political grouping, Millerand, leader of the parliamentary socialists, appeared as the logical choice to represent 'the most advanced opinion'. He recognized Millerand's talent as organizer and his avowal as early as 1898 that the socialists were again ready to support any ministry willing to undertake reforms. Moreover, from the standpoint of Waldeck-Rousseau, an 'intelligent conservative' but nonetheless a conservative, Millerand's reformist socialism was the least disturbing variety.

Why Millerand rather than Jaurès? As Reinach recalled, 'Whatever the oratory merits and the political intelligence of Millerand, they would not, however, have sufficed to justify his becoming minister if he had been only a brilliant exception in his party. On the contrary, he was the most representative type, when at that precise moment of socialist evolution, the bulk of the party had become political and practical, not yet renouncing the impossible, which is the source and motive power of all progress, but attaching itself to the possible and the preferred'.[46] Admittedly, Jaurès had been one of the leading promoters of that evolution. However, Millerand's role, as observed by Reinach and Waldeck-Rousseau, was even more important in shaping opinion, and he seemed the better choice. Governments may use philosophers in formulating the ends to which they aspire, but politicians are usually preferred to carry them out. And as Reinach pointed out, Jaurès, during the Dreyfus affair, 'both in conviction and in timing had preceded the proletariat; Millerand had marched in step with it'.

Waldeck-Rousseau, meanwhile, experienced difficulty from Progressists demanding more representation in the new cabinet. Discouraged, he complained to Arthur Ranc and Valentin Simond, two Parisian newspaper editors and friends, that he found his former Radical and socialist enemies more cooperative than his colleagues. He refused in disgust 'to remake the Dupuy Cabinet' and returned to Galliffet's property at Clairefontaine 'to go fishing'.[47]

On Wednesday afternoon, June 21, a group headed by Millerand and including Jean Dupuy, editor of the mass daily, *Le Petit Parisien,* Simond, and Ulrich, visited Waldeck-Rousseau. Millerand insisted that he try once more and told him no one else was 'capable of saving the Republic'. Waldeck thought him under an illusion but agreed to return to Paris and make a second attempt. In his *Mémoires* Millerand said that he visited the premier-designate at Simond's request but took credit for persuading Waldeck to renew his efforts. At the time, he brought to his attention the finance expert, Caillaux, with whose talent he was much impressed.[48]

This time it took but a few hours for Waldeck-Rousseau to draw up a proposed cabinet for Loubet. The speed with which this was done suggests that Waldeck's earlier refusal had been a feint. He gave himself the Ministry of the Interior and that of War to Galliffet. The difficulty lay in finding a post for Millerand. As he explained in his note to Reinach, Waldeck decided against the Ministry of Justice because with it went the vice-presidency of the Council. Appointment as Minister of Education might provoke demonstrations in the schools, as Minister of Public Works, strikes and disturbances. The Ministry of Commerce appeared most suitable; it administered the post, telegraph and telephone (PTT) 'where the functionaries can remain indifferent'.[49]

The rest of the cabinet reflected its moderate republican nature. Delcassé retained the post of Foreign Affairs, while Education went to Georges Leygues. For the remaining posts Waldeck-Rousseau chose members of parliament whom he felt that he could easily dominate. The moderate republican, Monis, an admirer of and associated with Waldeck since the end of 1898, was a good jurist, a mediocre orator and totally faithful. Dupuy, the director of *Le Petit Parisien* and the new Minister of Agriculture, according to the testimony of his son, was 'delighted with the honor'. Decrais, a colorless deputy of the Gironde, had not hoped for his promotion to the Ministry for the Colonies. Pierre Baudin and Caillaux, named respectively Ministers of Public Works and Finance, both under forty and deputies for only a short time, were respectful and grateful. De Lannessan, who earlier had been named executive governor of Indochina and whose career was seemingly at an end because of his involvement in a financial scandal there, appreciated his new chance as Minister of the Navy. Waldeck-Rousseau was very much aware of his vastly superior position. The best government, he said, was that which the premier is able to dominate.[50]

6.   In the interim, rumors flew among socialists about the possible entry of Millerand into the cabinet being formed, but the prospect aroused no indignation. Independents welcomed the reports 'with pleasure and surprise' and regarded the alleged accession as having 'very good effects' and as promising 'the best results'. The official Guesdist organ, *Le Socialiste,* did not discuss the likelihood of Millerand's participation. It had shown no anxiety, however, over Waldeck-Rousseau's early intention to include Casimir-Perier in his ministry and so, we may assume, thought predominantly in terms of republican defense. The newspaper merely acknowledged that socialists were once again called upon to support the regime.[51]

Blanquists, like Independents, were prepared to accept Millerand's entry. At a meeting of the Comité revolutionnaire central only one member, Zimmer, objected in principle to the appearance of a socialist in a bourgeois government. Breton, Landrin and Dubreuilh spoke in favor of the move and pointed to the exceptional political situation requiring a protective coalition. They claimed Millerand's position at the socialist right would permit him to act more easily without compromising the party, and they hailed the work which as minister he could accomplish for socialism. With that single exception all present endorsed ministerial participation.[52]

A further indication that socialists were aware of Millerand's possible inclusion in the new ministry came in a story by Etienne Rognon, a Parti ouvrier member, in *La Dépêche de Lyon* and subsequently reprinted in *Le Socialiste.* He reported a conversation with Briand in which the latter told how Millerand informed Jaurès, Viviani, Briand himself and one or two others of the proposals made to him and asked their advice. Briand urged him to refuse in view of the possible complications created for the party by his acceptance. Jaurès, who eighteen months earlier had warned socialists against accepting 'a parcel of power', backed by Viviani now took a contrary view: never was a more favorable situation offered to the proletariat; it was an historical moment, and he urged acceptance as 'absolutely necessary'. Millerand, encouraged by these words, said that he would probably receive the Ministry of Justice. There was no mention of Galliffet.[53]

Once informed by Millerand of Waldeck-Rousseau's interest, Jaurès reported the news to his colleagues on *La Petite République*. Included were the Blanquist, Dubreuilh and the Guesdist, Gabriel Farjat. Shortly after, Reinach, acting as intermediary between Waldeck-Rousseau and Jaurès, told the latter of the inclusion of General de Galliffet. He would act not only as a counterweight to Millerand but was perhaps the one minister with sufficient authority to instill respect for the Republic within the officer class.[54]

Jaurès now hesitated. Galliffet had played a leading role in the destruction of the Paris Commune and was still regarded with horror by the left. The presence of a socialist in the same cabinet as the 'butcher of the Commune' would be anathema to the party leaders who had suffered at his hands.

The influence exerted on Jaurès by Lucien Herr, the socialist librarian of the École Normale, was vital in the determination of the former's acceptance of the Waldeck-Rousseau, Millerand, Galliffet ministry. Herr had previously persuaded him that Dreyfus was innocent; he now insisted that the matter of most pressing concern was republican victory. If in order to achieve it this cabinet had been found necessary, then one had no choice but to accept the *fait accompli*. His view in fact corresponded to Jaurès' underlying concept of the vital role projected for socialism in the ideal republic and to his elevation of unity, first socialist and then republican, as the desired end to which all else was subordinate. If Jaurès continued to blame Millerand in his innermost heart, it is a matter of record that he became the champion of participation and remained the latter's faithful defender in the stormy years that followed.[55]

Party leaders in Parliament, although aware of the rumored invitation extended to Millerand, had not convened as a group even to discuss the ministerial crisis. Jaurès expressed his surprise at their failure to meet and determine collectively a course of action. Accordingly, Eugène Fournière, then secretary of the group, convoked a session for June 21 at which Millerand was to clarify his supposed ministerial status. The chief source for an account of this gathering is a series of letters sent by Vaillant and Jaurès to a new socialist review, *Le Mouvement Socialiste*, in 1901.[56]

Millerand told his colleagues that he had received an offer to join a ministry early in the crisis. The attempt, however, had not succeeded and negotiations were broken off. Throughout he had acted on his own responsibility without engaging that of other socialists. The question, therefore, as Vaillant emphasized in telling the story, was entirely academic and was so regarded by those present. Vaillant insisted as well on having refused at the time to show sympathy towards negotiations of this kind but admitted that he had declared himself satisfied with Millerand's conduct. Recognizing the possible reopening of negotiations, he stipulated that any future acceptance by Millerand would in no way bind the party. To this condition Millerand assented.[57]

The potential presence in the cabinet of Galliffet was not imagined, much less discussed. 'No one present', wrote Vaillant, 'neither Millerand nor any member of the Socialist group, pronounced the name of Galliffet or spoke of a ministry in which he might participate.' The implication is plain, and it has been accepted by the most prolific historians of the French socialist movement, Alexandre Zévaès and Paul Louis; Millerand must have known of Galliffet's inclusion but, preferring to present his colleagues with a *fait accompli,* decided not to mention it.[58] Only the following day did Vaillant learn that a government had been formed containing both men. He immediately sent a special delivery letter to Millerand in which he first expressed his disbelief at the news but, if the news were accurate, begged Millerand to reconsider. He stated that the participation of Galliffet would invalidate his earlier decision to let Millerand act on his own responsibility. And following publication of the official ministerial list the next morning, Vaillant took steps to separate his Blanquists from the parliamentary union of socialists.[59]

Despite his initial annoyance, therefore, at Millerand's independent action, Vaillant had made no objections to his possible entry into a ministry – had, in fact, laid down the condition under which it could be done – until he learned of Galliffet's inclusion. Vaillant's biographer admitted as much: 'What provided the indignation, even the revolt of the revolutionary socialists was not the ministerial parcipation of Millerand, but the fact that he sat at the side of Galliffet. For Vaillant, this constituted the most important reason for his opposition.'[60]

In his reply to Vaillant's letter to *Le Mouvement Socialiste* – which Jaurès said he felt 'stirred to write' – he made three points. First, the socialists present at the June 21 meeting showed no surprise at Millerand's possible participation. Second, that originally, when the question first came before the party, no difficulty of principle, no objection drawn from the concept of the class struggle had been made, no reproach for deviation or compromise had been formulated. Third, although freeing the party from responsibility, Vaillant had shown neither anger nor repulsion towards a combination which called a socialist to power. It was not a matter of principle but the 'very natural and legitimate emotion produced by the accession of Galliffet that determined Vaillant's reaction'.

Otherwise, said Jaurès, there would have been no objection to the individual entry of a socialist into the government. For 'to thrust into power an avant-garde force while retaining entire liberty of revolutionary action was completely compatible with Blanquist tactics'. But the name of Galliffet rendered Vaillant incapable of maintaining a detached attitude, and only later were there invoked the general formulas 'class struggle' and 'impersonal dictatorship of the proletariat' in order 'to found in principle a condemnation which originated in fact from causes wholly accidental'. The best proof lay in Vaillant's own letter to Millerand, for nowhere does he accuse him of abandoning principles. He placed all emphasis on Galliffet with the implication that were the General eliminated the cabinet would then be acceptable to all.[61]

In reply to a request by the German reformist socialist, Georg von Vollmar, in 1901, Millerand described his entry into the cabinet. He agreed with Jaurès that Vaillant's version 'did not hold water'. On an enclosed copy of the latter's special delivery letter sent to him almost two years earlier, Millerand underlined in red what was in his opinion the key sentence – the one referring to the possibility of Galliffet's participation: 'That would invalidate what was said yesterday to the Socialist group.' Clearly, concluded Millerand, the sentence would have been impossible if the group had condemned the idea of my entry.[62]

With regard to the charge of complicity raised against Millerand, Jaurès insisted on having informed the *militants* – notably Dubreuilh – that there existed the possibility of calling Galliffet to the ministry. In his own account Reinach practically absolved Millerand from withholding any news. He stated that at the departure of the June 21 meeting of socialists he confronted Millerand for the first time since their duel and only then gave him the communication from Waldeck-Rousseau telling of the decision to include Galliffet. If true, Millerand cannot be accused of failing to inform the socialists; he may have suspected it but simply had not known and naturally enough refused to speculate in their presence. Reinach described – and accounted for – Millerand's reaction; he would prefer to be minister without Galliffet but was to accept anyway 'because he was not frightened by responsibility and also because he felt himself ripe for power and tired of sterile opposition...'.[63]

7. The country received news of the new ministry, according to Daniel, 'first with incredulity, then with surprise, and generally with disfavor'. It had united an aristocratic general responsible for the bloody suppres-

sion of the Commune with a socialist deputy of Paris, both under the tutelage of a statesman who only recently had used all his eloquence to combat collectivists and radicals. Some quarters hailed it as a 'ministry of all talents', others as a 'ministry of all contradictions'. The shocked Pelletan wrote in *L'Éclair* June 24 that it was 'an inconceivable and dismal fantasy... a joke'. *La Républic française,* Méline's organ, called attention to the presence of socialism in power and mournfully predicted the extension of its control over the country. Arthur Ranc later recalled that 'the name of Millerand was like a kick in an anthill, in a beehive'. Moderate Progressists like Charles Jonnart, a friend of Waldeck, regretted that the new Premier was forced to base his support on radical parties. The most vehement opposition came from the Nationalists. *L'Intransigeant* addressed its editorial of June 24 'to the sons of the 35,000 shot in 1871' and cited Millerand as collaborator of 'the executioner of 1871'.[64]

Clemenceau, on the other hand, writing in *L'Aurore* June 23, hailed the cabinet as *coup de théatre.* He recognized the strangeness of the combination but said that only the most extraordinary circumstances could have justified it. It is all to Millerand's honor, he added, to accept responsibility. Doubtless within the socialist party 'there will be fools to accuse him of personal ambition, but it is he who will have served his country... a beautiful act of faith... worthy of the merit of the Republic'. Despite future differences between the two men, Millerand could not forget Clemenceau's confidence in him at the time. Viviani, who had replaced Millerand as editor-in-chief of *La Lanterne,* took exception to Galliffet but also pointed to the necessity of the coalition (June 24). In a personal letter, Poincaré told his friend that he disapproved of his decision.[65]

With his acceptance, *le cas Millerand* and an 'era of schisms' opened for French socialism. When the Chamber reconvened June 25 Vaillant and the small group of Blanquist deputies seemingly agreed to leave the parliamentary union of socialists and together with members of the Alliance Communiste révolutionnaire founded the autonomous Groupe Socialiste révolutionnaire. Although their declaration referred to Galliffet as executioner of Communards, it offered no clear reason for the formation of the new group. Moreover, some of the deputies whose names appeared below the manifesto of autonomy denied ever having been consulted with by party leaders. Apparently the authors of the declaration issued it without their consent.[66]

Jaurès, other Independent socialists and Possibilists applauded the act. In the June 24 issue of *La Petite République,* Jaurès justified participation as recognizing the need for socialists to share in the defense of the besieged Republic. Brousse, writing in the same newspaper August 7, asserted that the safety of the country was the supreme law and vindicated all measures of defense. Younger Independents like Albert Thomas and Paul-Boncour also defended Millerand for joining the cabinet. Thomas felt the time was ripe for a socialist to play a role in government; he described the advantages it could bring to workers and dismissed opposition to it as motivated on grounds other than principle. Millerand's personality, he acknowledged, did not help matters; he was not popular, he had quit his friends. Thomas agreed with Léon Blum, who attributed the criticism to a 'mixture of various doses of vanity, suspicion, and ambition, a failing inherent in the French psyche'.[67]

The reaction on the part of Marxists, like that of Blanquists, revealed a divergence between the views of party leaders and those in the rank and file. The same day as the Blanquist departure from the Socialist Union, Guesdist deputies issued a manifesto marked by ambiguities and contradiction. They found themselves 'unable to approve of a ministry headed by Waldeck-Rousseau, a man of big business and high finance, and including Galliffet, the butcher of republican and social Paris in 1871'. Still, 'to safeguard the Republic, the necessary instrument of social transformation, against militarist and clerical attack', they promised support of 'energetic republican policies directed against conspiracies of seditious generals, Jesuits, and all reactionaries'.[68]

Guesdist deputies thus promised conditional support of the ministry. However, 'the manifesto', Aaron Noland wrote, 'did not meet with the approval of Guesde, Lafargue, and other party leaders, and before long these deputies were directed to take a new line'.[69] On June 25 the National Council of the Parti ouvrier approved a resolution stating that the Guesdist deputies had 'nothing in common' with the ministry and ordered them to withdraw at once from the Socialist Union and form their own parliamentary group.

On June 26, in one of the noisiest and most ill-mannered sessions ever witnessed, the ministry appeared before the Chamber. Clemenceau described the ensuing sound as 'a long howling of hyenas'. Waldeck-Rousseau said, 'I had the sensation of being in a cage of wild beasts'.[70] The presentation of Galliffet caused the demonstration by the extreme left which we have already observed. In the face of repeated interruptions the Premier-designate tried again to complete the reading of his ministerial declaration. But if its head was momentarily unnerved, the cabinet was never really threatened. Although pretending indifference to the forthcoming vote, Waldeck had lined up the support he needed. He knew that the Radicals would in all likelihood approve; he could count on the support of moderate socialists and hope for the abstention of others. The outcome would depend on the way in which his own party would go. He needed, and was to obtain, eighty of their votes and accordingly had spent time in parliamentary vestibules to win promises of support from about a third of the Progressists. He was aware that the long ministerial crisis had limited considerably their choice of alternatives.[71]

Despite their denunciation of the ministry, a majority of Blanquists and Guesdists abstained rather than join forces with 'reactionaries' to oppose it. Their abstention, together with the approval of the ministerial socialists, provided the margin of difference and made possible the acceptance of the new government by twenty-five votes.[72]

Now began the attempt by the party leaders to denounce Millerand's participation from the point of view of doctrine. On June 27 his decision to join the ministry was called – for the first time – socialist defection.[73] On July 14 Guesdists, Blanquists and the Alliance Communiste issued the joint manifesto presenting the reasons for their refusal to support Waldeck–Rousseau. It took the form of an appeal to 'working and socialist France', and there were invoked the declarations of principles previously lacking.

The chief assertion set forth was that 'the Socialist party, party of class, cannot be or become, except under penalty of suicide, a ministerial party'. The signers separated themselves from those supporting ministerialism in order to end the 'so-called socialist policy previously followed', full of 'compromise and deviation', and to substitute for it a class, revolutionary policy. The contradiction between the two had clearly been demonstrated by the entry of a socialist into the government 'hand in hand with the fusilier of May'. 'There cannot be any accord between those who have compromised the honor and interests of socialism and those in charge of defending them... We cannot be a ministerial party. Party of opposition we are and must remain.'[74]

But the great majority of socialists rejected the Manifesto. The Marxist and Blanquist rank and file, including five Guesdist deputies, as well as Independents took exception not only to the content but to what they regarded as the brutal manner of expression. They were unable to identify themselves with the position taken by party leaders. Local groups also stated their disappointment or openly offered their support to Millerand.[75] There may be found in the Jules Guesde Archives in Amsterdam *cahiers* with pages of press clippings describing favorable and unfavorable responses to the Manifesto. The latter contains approximately three times the number of pages as the former.[76] One particularly hostile response was that of the Bordeaux veteran organizer, Raymond Lavigne. In a letter to Guesde he assailed his chief for 'brutally unleashing a war against Jaurès and Millerand'. The writer subsequently dissociated himself from Guesde, Vaillant and their followers, declaring they were all possessed with '*l'idée fixe de faire du mal*' to the ministerialists.[77]

A well-documented set of reactions on the part of one provincial Guesdist was that of Brunellière in Nantes. He wrote to Millerand on June 24 admitting his surprise at seeing him in the government but relaying the approval of the farmers and stating that his presence there demonstrated the power enjoyed by socialism and pointed to subsequent electoral victories. Aware of the forthcoming hostile Parti ouvrier declaration, Brunellière wrote Millerand on July 13, this time to express his indignation at seeing his name on the Manifesto. Apparently Guesde had placed it there without his knowledge or consent. Brunellière protested to Guesde that as Secretary of the Nantaise Socialist Federation he must be consulted, and he threatened to have the Federation take up the matter at its next meeting. 'You cannot use my name without asking me', he told the Parti ouvrier chief. We feel that Millerand has acted on his own responsibility, and while our only regret is the inclusion of Galliffet, we expect great services from the Minister of Commerce. Brunellière followed his letter with a visit; he implored Guesde not to widen the schism in French socialism. In a letter to a friend dated August 14, he enthusiastically approved of Millerand's first decrees and revealed his hopes for POF unity at the party's forthcoming Epernay Congress.[78]

The reasons for the hostility earlier shown by the party leaders to Millerand's entry offered by Blum, Thomas and Paul-Boncour agreed with those advanced in both Paris Prefecture and Sûreté reports. A communiqué to the latter noted that the formation of the cabinet provided the excuse long sought by militant leaders to restore their own diminishing power within the movement. A report to the Prefecture stated bluntly: 'Galliffet is only a pretext. ... The real motive is the envy aroused by the talent of Jaurès on the part of Vaillant and Guesde.' Another communication to the Sûreté added that 'if Jules Guesde has led the POF and the National Council to fight the Waldeck-Rousseau ministry, it is not so much because of General Galliffet as it is to diminish the present influence of Jaurès, whom he considers a serious rival'.[79]

In a bitterly worded attack on Guesde in the September 14 issue of the *Revue Blanche,* Péguy offered a similar analysis. He accused him of being 'ignorant of socialism' and of opposing the cabinet because of his hostility toward Jaurès. Three days earlier, a second court-martial held at Rennes had found Dreyfus guilty. Péguy's criticism of Guesde, who had continued his opposition to the government during the trial, became more intense. 'Because he did not work for bourgeois justice', wrote Péguy, '[Guesde] has commited military injustice... Things reached the

point where to some socialists Dreyfus was simply the man who has become a nuisance to Guesde.'[80]

Two anti-Guesdist articles in a centrist newspaper, *Le Petit Blue,* published on July 24 and 27, criticized the Marxist chief at length. It traced
the history of his reformism to 1891, when universal suffrage freed Paul
Lafargue, and to Guesde's own electoral victory in 1893, as a result of
which Roubaix became a 'holy city', and French Marxism entered its
parliamentary phase. During the Dreyfus affair, Guesde and Vaillant
slipped to 'second rank' within the movement. Guesde had particularly
felt his authority ebb when he traveled incognito to the German Social
Democratic party's Stuttgart Congress and realized he was no longer
considered the official representative of French socialism. He longed to
regain status, and the inclusion of Millerand in the Waldeck-Rousseau
Ministry together with Galliffet provided a 'wonderful' opportunity.

None of these analyses is incompatible with the official explanation
offered in the joint manifesto or in subsequent declarations and speeches
displaying Guesdist and Blanquist hostility to Millerand. Participation
signified a new tactic, jeopardized the class struggle concept and was
incompatible with the effort to establish socialist unity on strong theoretical foundations. Still, their similarity, regardless of their diverse origins,
and their readiness to distinguish the position taken by the party chiefs
from that held by deputies and the rank and file suggests that both the
appearance and the intensity of the doctrinal explanations were inded
prompted by other, more private, considerations. This does not prove
that Guesde was guilty of duplicity; it suggests he was no longer able to
distinguish between personal and party needs.

The ministerial socialists who gathered about Jaurès in defense of
Millerand's participation included Independents like Viviani, Briand,
André Lefèvre, Gerault-Richard and Rouanet, as well as the Possibilists,
Brousse, Lavy and Heppenheimer. Their reply to the July 14 Manifesto
appeared in various newspapers and magazine articles. Jaurès maintained
that participation was the logical outcome of the policy to win public
power, a policy receiving the support of all socialists in the 1893–1898
Chamber. In an important article, Rouanet demonstrated how the signers of the Manifesto were guilty of the same defections of which they
now accused Millerand. Since 1893, he wrote, socialist thought was one;
Guesde and other militants had on numerous occasions cooperated fully
with the orthodox political parties in the Chamber. Now, after initially
ascribing exclusive guilt to Millerand, they extended their censure to
include the entire parliamentary union. Rouanet, too, denied that it was
a question of principles; it rather 'revolves around groups and persons

which tended to disguise themselves behind theoretical difficulties in order to justify them'.[81]

Independent socialists shared Jaurès' indignation at the violent terms of the manifesto 'excommunicating' Millerand and at the 'bitter, brutal, offensive condemnation of the struggle which we have been waging for the past fifteen months'. Rejecting doctrinal distinctions, they agreed with Jaurès who wrote in *La Petite République* on July 15: 'The Galliffet incident is only an occasion and a pretext. Those who condemn us are massively opposed to socialist unity.' Some, like Deville, detected the stale animosities dating from the struggles for *La Petite République*. Rejecting any legitimate doctrinal difference, they saw the Parti ouvrier as the 'eternal source of division of the socialist movement'.[82] Guesdist federations and groupings holding such views included those of Nantes, Lyons, the Pyrénées-Orientales, the Vaucluse, some groups in Paris, the Gard, Roanne, the Bouches-du-Rhone, Limoges, Bordeaux and the Gironde. Members of the last unanimously sent to Millerand a statement of their support and expressed confidence that 'during his tenure as minister he would amass the greatest possible profit for the socialist movement'. Claude Willard has written that even the Guesdist 'bastions' in the Nord were shaken; the Lille section voted its approval of Millerand's entry while that of Roubaix denounced the Manifesto. Numerous other groups came out for Millerand and criticized the Parti ouvrier leadership. Even spokesmen approving the Manifesto's content, like those from the Isère Federation and its section in Grenoble, 'energetically rejected its more ambiguous passages'.

The POF leadership stood fast before this outpouring of discontent. Guesde went to the Nord and to the center of the country. Lafargue began to buttress the Manifesto with doctrinal considerations equating the invitation to Millerand with the bourgeois tactics of 1848, which, he said, successfully 'quieted' Louis Blanc and 'domesticated' the movement. Both experiences pointed out the need for socialists to unite on clearly defined theoretical bases.[83] Jaurès had suggested the holding of a general congress of socialist groups to decide definitively on the question of ministerial participation. Such a congress was necessary for, as we have seen, Millerand's entry could be neither conciliated nor sanctioned by the Comité d'Entente. The idea took hold, and all planned to attend a proposed meeting in December. Guesdist, Blanquist and Alliance chieftains included themselves as well, for, in Noland's words, 'refusal to arbitrate the Millerand case might well have been construed by the rank and file of these factions as added proof that their leaders were indifferent or hostile to the common desire for socialist unity...'.[84]

By way of preparation the POF in August debated the issue at its own

Epernay congress. In four days (August 13–16) of secret sessions – from which even the SPD's *Vorwärts* reporter was barred – the idea of participation found 'many defenders'.[85] One motion from the floor asked that the executive committee be censured for affiliating the party with its Manifesto. Guesde gave up the attempt to secure unqualified support of his antiministerialist position, and, in view of the clearly hostile declaration of July 14, it must be taken as the strongest indication of the differences separating a majority of the rank and file from the leadership. In turning to the work that could be accomplished by a socialist minister, Millerand received support from ministerialist Guesdists. Several POF newspapers reproduced his speeches and covered his work in detail. When the Minister of Commerce was invited officially to speak at Lille, the chief Guesdist citadel, early in October, it seemed a spectacular disavowal of the July Manifesto. The following month the collectivist municipal councillors of Limoges gave him an 'enthusiastic' reception.[86] The party leadership, however, never ceased its opposition to the ministry, and the 'case' would be settled only in 1904 when, at the end of what Fournière called a 'crisis of impatience', the French socialist movement fell under the temporary control of its more militant policymakers.

8.   The rest of the socialist world followed events in France intently. The particular reaction to them reflected and extended the attitude toward tactics previously adopted. Thus in England pragmatic Fabians at once applauded the entry of a socialist into the government. More surprising was the approval granted by the Marxist Social Democratic Federation. Henry Hyndman, who professed to follow French affairs 'closely', wrote that it was the 'duty of every French socialist' to support the Waldeck-Rousseau ministry against a 'clerico-military reaction' and a 'threat to liberty'. In Hyndman's opinion, the Parti ouvrier's July denunciation was dictated by Guesde's own antagonism.[87]

The Millerand case put German theoreticians to work. Revisionists like Bernstein and Vollmar approved; we have seen that the latter sent messages of support to the Minister of Commerce. In the center, Karl Kautsky, the SPD's leading and official doctrinarian, at first displayed ambivalent feelings. Although largely opposed to participation, he doubted that violence was necessary for the socialist conquest of the state, and, by implication, sanctioned Millerand's entry. On the other hand, the issue under consideration was less than vital, and a socialist in power might create an illusion of force; socialists had still to remember they constituted a minority. Radicals like Karl Liebknecht went further than Guesde and Vaillant in opposing participation. Even Jaurès' Dreyfusard views were not spared; indeed they were seen as having contributed to the present imbroglio. Likewise, for Rosa Luxemburg the importance of the case could not be minimized: 'It was a question of the whole sum of political and economic problems, of principles and tactics which represent the very heart of the socialist struggle.' She acknowledged that participation was the logical consequence of socialist infiltration of power. If socialism, however, were to be introduced only after the destruction of capitalism, and if socialists aimed at hastening its downfall, then participation was selfdefeating. Socialists can sit in a parliament, she said, but not in a government, for the latter only executes laws and cannot introduce principles. The socialist in government, if an enemy of the present order, must either be in constant opposition to his colleagues – an untenable position – or he must fulfill his functions, that is, not act as a socialist, at least not within the limits of government action. The experience, she concluded, appears as one which can only prejudice the principle of the class struggle. August Bebel disapproved on the grounds that Millerand had not been named by his party, and he predicted the 'tragic dissolution' of union among French socialists. Emile Vandervelde, speaking for Belgian socialism, held similar reservations; aside from 'exceptional cases', he opposed participation because the disadvantages outweighed the advantages and because it was better to give unconditional support to Radicals than to compromise oneself by sharing power.[88]

To further evaluate world socialist opinion, Jaurès and Gerault-Richard used *La Petite République* to organize an 'international consultation' on the question of the Dreyfus affair and ministerial participation. They addressed twenty-nine leading figures in the socialist world, from Victor Adler to Emile Vandervelde. To the first question – 'Can the socialist proletariat, without jettisoning the principles of the class struggle, intervene in the conflicts of the diverse bourgeois factions, either to defend political liberty, or, as in the Dreyfus Affair, for the sake of humanity?' – twenty-seven respondents said 'yes' without adding qualifications. The second question – 'To what degree can the socialist proletariat participate in bourgeois power; and is the principle of the class struggle absolutely and in every case opposed to the taking of partial possession of ministerial power by the socialist party?' – revealed greater controversy. Twelve replies were for the most part affirmative; seventeen were largely negative. Of the seventeen, eleven acknowledged the eventuality and approved of it in very exceptional cases but specifically excluded the one under consideration. The most adamant rejections, it was to be observed, came from those areas where the likelihood of a socialist winning power was remote and even difficult to contemplate.[89]

The impact of *le cas Millerand* on French and international socialism, and their ultimate repudiation of ministerial participation, was enormous. At the risk of oversimplification we may say that it was to inspire a renewed reliance on revolutionary tactics and, in so doing, alienate the reformists who refused to agree. One's attitude toward ministerialism came to serve as a test of his commitment to socialism, and that attitude had to be negative. Lenin regarded 'Millerandism' as the chief threat to socialist success, and he rejected the comparison made by Plekhanov between Millerand's participation in a cabinet with Galliffet and the participation of Louis-Eugène Varlin, a French worker and *militant* in the First International, in the executive committee of the Paris Commune. For Lenin, Varlin participated in a 'revolutionary government with petty bourgeois democrats who defended and safeguarded the Republic', while Millerand participated with Galliffet in an epoch 'immediately preceding the revolution' and by so doing resisted it. The one took place in a democratic revolution; the other thwarted a socialist revolution; and the two cases were not to be confused. Lenin later denounced those socialists who joined governments during World War I as guilty of deliberate treason, and he was to make antiministerialism a test of eligibility for the Third International.[90] For French socialism the Millerand case was to guarantee that there would be no government participation – aside from temporary inclusion in *Union sacrée* cabinets during the early years of World War I – by socialists until Léon Blum formed a ministry in 1936.

Alexandre Millerand, probably when a law student

Jean-François Millerand, Alexandre Millerand's father

Amélie Millerand, Alexandre Millerand's mother

Raffaelli's painting (1885) of Clemenceau speaking. Millerand is in the Third sow,
Hird from the left

Mensonges in extremis

Il est temps que la période électorale finisse. M. Péchin devient fou.

Deux jours de plus et il accuserait le citoyen Millerand et M. Waldeck-Rousseau d'être les auteurs de la catastrophe de la Martinique.

Aujourd'hui, il n'en est encore qu'à les accuser d'avoir puisé dans le coffre-fort vide de Mme Humbert, des millions pour leurs besoins électoraux, tout comme la Patrie Française a pour sa campagne électorale, extrait des millions des coffres-forts pleins *des Congrégations et des nobles Dames de France*.

Quand M. PECHIN ne divague pas il ment.

En bon élève des Jésuites cet Escobar attend l'heure où il juge qu'on ne pourra plus lui répondre pour accuser le citoyen MILLERAND de s'être marié civilement à Paris, mais religieusement à Florence.

C'est un Mensonge!

Le citoyen MILLERAND s'est marié civilement au 9ᵉ arrondissement à Paris; il ne s'est marié religieusement nulle part pas plus à Florence qu'ailleurs.

Si l'assertion de M. Péchin était exacte, ses amis les curés n'auraient pas manqué de lui fournir l'extrait de l'acte qui constaterait ce prétendu mariage religieux.

Il n'a pu le faire, pour cette excellente raison qu'il n'y a jamais eu de mariage religieux.

Voilà Citoyens, par quelles inventions et quels mensonges *in extremis* aussi grotesques que répugnants, M. PÉCHIN espère escroquer un mandat de Député.

Vous répondrez à cette infamie en votant tous pour le Citoyen

MILLERAND
Le Candidat de la République

LE COMITÉ :

Le Président	Les Vice-Présidents	Le Secrétaire	Le Trésorier
L. LACHAMBEAUDIE	J. ALLARD, BOISON	J. ROUX	Eug. DUCROUX

Campaigning in the XIIth Arrondissement (1902)

Alexandre
Millerand
as Minister
of Commerce

Jean Jaurès

Waldeck-Rousseau

Galliffet

Emile Combes

9. The socialist minister

Je peux vous apporter cette affirmation; née de
l'expérience, qu'en trois ans de pouvoir j'ai plus
fait pour mes idées et pour mon pays qu'il ne
m'avait été donné de faire en dix-huit ans de parlement.

MILLERAND, at Vierzon, April, 1903

1. Shortly after it invested the new ministry, Parliament adjourned for
the summer holidays. Waldeck-Rousseau was consequently granted
nearly four months of relative freedom to put into effect those measures
he considered necessary to carry out measures of republican defense. He
had twenty-three prominent nationalist agitators arrested, including Déroulède, André Buffet, agent of the Orléanist pretender, and Jules Guérin,
chief of the Anti-Semitic League. (All but the above-named three were
to be acquitted by the Senate sitting as a High Court the following November.) Galliffet, meanwhile, made attempts to reassert the authority
of the Minister of War. He forced Pellieux, Zurlinden and Roget, the
most outspoken of the anti-republican generals, to resign; three members
of the Council of War retired; and promotions were distributed on a
more equitable scale.

Guérin, however, had first taken refuge with some followers in League
headquarters on the rue de Chabrol. Constrained by Waldeck-Rousseau,
the Prefect of Police, Louis Lépine, was allowed only to cut off the gas
and water supply and lay siege to the house. For thirty-eight days the
outlaws resisted, fed by the bread, ham and wine thrown from the upper
deck of passing buses, and the affair took on the dimensions of a farce.
But the Premier had a horror of force and bloodshed, and, according to
Lépine, 'all his ministers, with the exception of Millerand, shared Waldeck-Rousseau's opinion'.[1]

The incident reveals the initial difference between the two men, for
Millerand, if no revolutionary, was still progressive and impulsive. Where
possible he replied positively to those radicals who sought his help in
getting government employment. His private papers, however, as well as
those from the Ministry of Commerce, reveal surprisingly few requests

12

for jobs. In August 1899 Jaurès and Georges Sorel intervened on behalf of the sick Pelloutier, who was to die in three years. Millerand was able to appoint him an investigator in his ministry's Labor Office. Delegates to the subsequent Congress of the Fédération des Bourses du travail initially denounced Pelloutier for accepting but finally acquiesced. Millerand also received an anxious request from both M. and Mme. Jaurès to speed the promotion of a needy Toulouse railroad worker. After hearing from Brunellière in a less offical capacity, Millerand had a member of his staff, Maurice Violette, defend two small land owners in court. The archives of the Ministry of Justice reveal that the new minister took the initiative in interceding on behalf of at least one fellow socialist.[2]

The siege of 'Fort Chabrol' indicates as well the nature of their future relationship, for Waldeck-Rousseau exerted a great moderating force upon Millerand and perhaps more than anyone else completed his political education. He was the only man Millerand ever acknowledged as *maître,* and Millerand's loyalty to his chief was such as to have him defend the principles of the ministry in succeeding legislatures. Waldeck's photograph occupied a central spot in Millerand's home. Count Carlo Sforza, beginning his long diplomatic career, was then attached to the Italian Embassy in Paris. He got to know Millerand and attested that the latter learned much from Waldeck-Rousseau. Although finding it 'a rare thing in politics', Sforza 'was convinced that the young minister, Millerand, coming straight to power from the furthest benches of the Socialist party, deeply experienced, if not the imprint, at least the attraction of a man like Waldeck-Rousseau'.[3]

Their association turned into something resembling friendship – or so at least Millerand thought. Occasional invitations from M. and Mme. Waldeck-Rousseau undoubtedly flattered the Millerands, and the minister must have been especially pleased to see his wife accorded what to him was her rightful place in society. Madame Waldeck-Rousseau congratulated Madame Millerand on the birth of her second son, Jacques, and in her letter spoke admiringly of the Minister of Commerce. News of the birth came when Millerand was with the Waldeck-Rousseaus, who at once toasted the new arrival. Millerand's gratitude, we shall see, may have led him to exaggerate the extent of Waldeck-Rousseau's liberalism and the importance of his role in regard to the social legislation initiated by the government. His loyalty to his chief never wavered. Running for reelection in a closely contested campaign in 1902 and denounced by the socialist opposition as obsessed with power, he did not hesitate to identify himself with Waldeck-Rousseau. A poster read: 'It will be the honor of my life to have been called to the side of the statesman of whom the republican party is so justly proud, to have shared in the work of republican defense and action which, since June 25, 1899, constitutes the history of his country.' Millerand's letters to Waldeck were among the warmest he wrote. In one undated draft he congratulated the Premier for his Toulouse speech setting forth the cabinet's religious program: 'I join in the ovation prepared for you by the Republican party. I am very proud of having had the great honor for the past sixteen months of witnessing and, as little value as it may have, assisting in your work.' One of the last letters written by the dying Waldeck-Rousseau in 1904 went to Millerand to thank him for defending the ministry in the Chamber, and the latter was instrumental in founding the Waldeck-Rousseau monument, which stands today in the Tuilleries Gardens. Millerand also wrote the preface to an early biography of Waldeck-Rousseau.[4]

But if two men seemed created not to understand each other, scarcely to communicate, it was the President of the Council and his socialist minister. Both were shy and quiet behind a facade of apparent coldness, and each, despite his parliamentary eloquence, could have toured the world in relative silence. One had headed the socialist deputies in parliament, the other had served as the lawyer of high finance, the defender of Eiffel, and had taken the initiative in organizing business interests against the threat of socialism.

Still, despite different political backgrounds, some basic similarities emerged. Like Millerand, Waldeck-Rousseau recognized a need for social reform, perhaps following the path indicated by his father, who had pressed for it in the revolutionary government of 1848. Although insistent on individual failings rather than social evils, Waldeck *père* felt that employers and workers must associate and that it was the task of government to provide such necessary machinery as joint conciliation bodies. He defended professional association as the means to increase efficiency and morale, although as a delegate to the Constituent Assembly in 1848 he pointed to the impossibility of social legislation until the instruments of production were once more fully operative.[5] Like Millerand, Waldeck-Rousseau's famous timidity stemmed from a lack of worldly ease; it gave rise to apparent aloofness in society and to an utter simplicity of style in the court room. An observer described his briefs and arguments as 'simple to the point of nudity', with few metaphors, exclamations or apostrophes. His air of disdain was doubtless reinforced by experience and success, as was to be the case with Millerand. No lightweight, Poincaré remarked when appearing against Waldeck-Rousseau in an early case: 'I had the feeling I was a poodle barking at a statue.'[6]

If Millerand, moreover, shied away from ideology, Waldeck detested it. His biographer stated that it was even impossible to define any *a priori* ideas he may have had and that 'events dictated his acts'. He was an opportunist like Gambetta, although like Gambetta, he strongly subscribed to the *scrutin de liste* as the key to the problems faced by the Republic.[7] Both by precept and example, Waldeck-Rousseau was to reinforce the opportunism already present in Millerand's nature, and the latter's association with him was to isolate Millerand from socialism.

2. Millerand brought to the Ministry of Commerce his accustomed ability for thoroughness and hard work. Georges Renard recalled the remark of a subordinate in 1901: 'We worked as much in eighteen months with him as in the preceding ten years.' From the ministerial archives comes the following example of exactitude. Soon after taking office Millerand asked colonial officials – in this case the Governor-General of Algeria – to determine the extent to which existing labor legislation, particularly the voluntary arbitration law of 1892, had been applied. (The answer, a detailed report, was for the most part negative.)[8]

The new minister gathered a loyal and competent staff. It contained Raul Persil, an administrative aid who became *chef de cabinet* and was to remain Millerand's chief assistant; Aimé Lavy, who had represented the Union of French Secondary School Teachers at congresses of the Second International and whose pride in his long association and friendship with the family reached the extent that he resented newcomers; Joseph Sarraute, who practiced law in Paris and was to obtain a doctorate of law in 1910, a man who was absent-minded and brilliant and would become a friend of Millerand; Eugène Petit, who handled legal questions and who, with his wife, Sophie, was always welcome at Millerand's home; Maurice Violette, the undersecretary, who previously had acted as Millerand's secretary and had offered his services in the event that Millerand again needed him. Yet another lawyer, he was interested in labor associations and had written on the subject. Others, listed in the *Mémoires,* included Jacques Bompard; Arthur Fontaine, Director of Labor; Gabriel Chandeze; Alfred Picard; and Emmanual Rousseau. In addition to Persil, Rousseau, Bompard and Petit were to continue their political or legal association with Millerand well into the 1920s. Millerand credited them with being totally devoted to the public interest and having 'only the faults of their virtues'. Apparently their 'scrupulousness' and 'exaggerated formality' occasionally delayed and annoyed the fast-moving minister.[9]

Perhaps the most significant member of the staff was Arthur Fontaine. An engineer in the Corps des Mines, his interests were varied; he was absorbed by letters as well as technology, and he had left the ranks of big business for what he felt was his 'social vocation'. Described as 'one of the most noble figures of French social life of the epoch', he was to be the mentor of Albert Thomas at the International Labor Office. One observer held him as responsible for no less than 'all the labor legislation [enacted] during the first quarter of the twentieth century'. Thomas' biographer maintained that much of 'Millerand's work was the fruit of Fontaine's labors'. Since 1891 the Ministry of Commerce contained an Office of Labor, charged, among other duties, with collecting statistics and holding factory inspections. Millerand enlarged it to a Department of Labor, put Fontaine in charge and kept him there. It is difficult to separate the work of the two men; the one certainty is that the initiatives taken during Millerand's tenure were more numerous than those that came before or after.[10]

The staff, although hard pressed, put in no less effort than Millerand himself. The legendary power of work is recalled by every acquaintance. He carried his briefcase and documents with him at all times and could busy himself with them anywhere. There were few inspirations; his ideas derived rather from the application of order, logic and method. According to Persil, Millerand held a cabinet meeting every Friday during which he expected each divisional head to acquaint him with projects completed the preceding week. He listened to their reports, insisted on concise presentations of their opinions on suggested courses of action, weighed them and then gave his decisions rapidly and clearly.[11]

Millerand's health remained excellent. He walked at least an hour a day, beginning his day promptly at six *A.M.* Conferences and appointments began no later than nine.[12] His sense of precision and organizational abilities had only increased with time. If invited in September to make a visit the following spring, either in France or abroad, Millerand could open a notebook, consult a time table and announce the date and time of his arrival. And he was usually able to keep his word. Despite his heavy schedule even the least important letter was answered completely and promptly – although he now required the aid of half a dozen secretaries.

Almost twelve years earlier, during Chamber debate on a penitentiary budget, he had voiced his opinion on the general role of a minister. Millerand deemphasized special technical prowess; it could be acquired on the job. A minister was rather 'a manager of managers' who provided his ministry with initiative. His role was that of organizer, administrator and instigator. In a letter to Joseph Reinach, Millerand also called attention to similarities between his methods as deputy and as minister. As the former he had tried always to put himself in the place of the average citizen. Now in power, with enlarged responsibilities, he said that he worked all the more to retain this procedure.[13]

A guiding principle derived from his wish to instill within workers the

conviction that the instrument of their social emancipation was association and that the individual left to his own devices was rendered useless.
Hence the emphasis placed on trade unions. Tactics, too, in no way differed from those advocated in the past and to a large extent reflected the
story of Millerand's own rise to power. 'I do not believe in miracles', he
said, 'no matter from where they may come, not any more from below
than from above. I have faith only in rational and organized human
effort. It seems to me that after having specified the goal which we seek,
the first step in our approach is the determination of the method – that
the very conditions under which we live imposes on our action.'[14]

He saw his country as provided with the benefits of democracy. The
ultimate emancipation of her people, or her workers, was only the coronation of the work of centuries, a process in which the French Revolution
had marked a decisive phase. Under the Republic revolution became
not only absurd but dangerous. Millerand noted with irony that those
who appealed to it showed remarkable discretion with regard to tactics.
To be revolutionary permitted one, under the pretext of awaiting the
unknown day of total change, not to act and to criticize those who did
and who took responsibility for their actions.

3.   Millerand soon found that the Ministry of Commerce provided a terrain broad enough to offer numerous opportunities to meet working-
class demands. He was determined to take advantage of as many as
possible, for, as he later admitted, he was 'haunted' by the concern that
the arrival of a socialist in power must mean tangible improvement in
the status of labor.[15]

During the summer of 1899 a series of administrative decrees began
to stream from the ministry's offices on the rue de Grenelle. This is not
the place to examine or evaluate them in detail; they offer a preliminary
insight, however, into the relative roles played by the Premier and the
Minister of Commerce in matters of industrial and welfare legislation.
On August 1 (completed by the decree of October 10) he reorganized and
renamed the Labor Office. As the Department of Labor it received full
rights of inspection in mines and factories in order to maintain minimum
standards of hygiene and safety, and it was authorized to collect and
publish statistics relevant to working conditions. Another decree created
a Department of Insurance and Social Welfare (Direction de l'insurance
et de la prévoyance sociale) with responsibility to apply the recently
enacted workers' compensation law. Both departments ultimately became part of the Ministry of Labor founded by Clemenceau in 1906.[16]

The decrees which followed on August 10 were viewed as 'an epoch in
French social legislation'. Known as *les décrets Millerand,* they described

the minimum working conditions required for state public works contracts. Reflecting an old Broussist demand, Millerand had long insisted on the need for the state to set standards and so provide an example to private industry.[17] Because, however, they were decrees and not laws, no court could penalize employers failing to comply. The government could take punitive action only by refusing to associate itself with the offending firms. He based state contracts on those already called for in existing trade union contracts. In the absence of a union, joint associations of employers and workers would be created to determine standards – including minimum wages. That unions consequently received considerably more power and influence was wholly in keeping with Millerand's view of their importance to the economy. And with its appearance in state contracts, the principle of salary minimums was established on a national scale.

Millerand got the idea when on the Paris Municipal Council. In 1882 some of its members attempted to give the city 'the right to fix a minimum wage and maximum hours for all city contracts'. The precedent was set in May 1888, when Edouard Vaillant introduced a minimum-wage provision in public contracts. Although at first annulled by the Ministry of Interior, by the late 1890s it had become accepted practice in Paris and in several large towns. These ordinances, however, had never been sanctioned by law, and several deputies sought clarifying legislation.[18] Socialists in the Chamber were prepared to set bases for salaries and limits on hours. Others saw these proposals as preludes to collectivization. Without mincing his words, Waldeck told Millerand that 'ministerial Progressists would not accept a minimum salary or a reduction in the length of the working day'. The cabinet was caught on a dilemma; it required the support of both ministerial socialists and ministerial Progressists, and so could neither drop the question nor insist on a debate. Hence the recourse to decrees. Millerand, then, had wanted to satisfy the left. However, he was limited by Waldeck-Rousseau, who, at the outset, revealed his concern with political imperatives. We shall see that regardless of his need to retain leftwing support, and despite the presence of a socialist in his government, he was to take few initiatives in matters of social legislation and would do so only when considered absolutely necessary to ensure its survival.[19]

Millerand's acquiescence in the decision to issue decrees issued from his overriding concern with results and revealed his own awareness of the need to retain Progressist support. He tried to reassure the Chamber that its initiative was in no way endangered. The forthcoming decrees, he pointed out, were based on precedent, were not illegal because they made no mention of sanctions and in any case required final approval by the

Conseil d'Etat, a further check on the government's decree-making power. The unaccustomed display of activity at the Ministry of Commerce, however, reminded moderates that at its head was an avowed collectivist and left them fretful. André Daniel also implied that Millerand insisted on, and 'rushed through', the decrees solely to enhance his own prestige. Members of the socialist rank and file, on the other hand, praised his work and again took the opportunity to congratulate themselves on his presence in the government.[20]

4. Renewed concern with the Dreyfus Affair interrupted any work of social reform. Shortly after the investiture of the cabinet, Millerand suggested that Galliffet give orders for Dreyfus' release. However the Minister of War had refused on the grounds that it would constitute improper procedure and had insisted on holding the second court-martial. The ministry was divided on the issue. The one convinced Dreyfusard willing to base his acts on his beliefs was Millerand. For Waldeck-Rousseau the objective was to keep order at almost any price and to prevent new attacks against the regime. De Lannessan and Decrais estimated Dreyfus was innocent but did not display their feelings. Caillaux and Dupuy were also reticent. Monis, Baudin and Leygues agreed with President Loubet on the deplorably irregular procedings without pronouncing on the question of guilt. Delcassé was preoccupied with foreign affairs and hesitated to alarm France's anti-Dreyfusard Russian allies. Galliffet showed himself ambivalent. Despite his defense of Picquart he wished to end the affair as quickly as possible in order to calm the military. His conviction that Dreyfus would be acquitted persuaded him to reject Waldeck-Rousseau's request to drop the case.[21]

To the indignation of the Dreyfusards, the Rennes court-martial found Dreyfus again guilty of treason – though with 'extenuating circumstances', and sentenced him on September 11 to ten year's imprisonment. The agitated cabinet met the next day and decided to ask for a presidential pardon. But Mathieu Dreyfus refused on the grounds that it would not erase the verdict. With the support of revisionists who wanted to carry the fight to a finish, he was determined to appeal the decision.

It was then that Millerand, according to Reinach's account, 'with his facility for legal affairs suddenly discovered a most unexpected obstacle'. An appeal, he told the Dreyfusard leadership, would probably be of no avail. The Rennes judges, 'in their disturbed state', had neglected to add to the verdict the statement prescribed by the Code in regard to the need for continued police surveillance following expiration of the penalty. If the High Court again quashed the verdict, a third court-martial, in view of this technicality, would be wholly justified in limiting itself to an additional opinion on the need for such surveillance. And because it was a purely procedural question, there would be no need to hear testimony. The decision of the judges would be unanimous, and the advantage now gained from a split decision would be lost. Millerand strongly urged that Dreyfus renounce the right of appeal and accept a pardon. After much reflection, including consideration of his brother's shattered health, Mathieu, and finally the hostile Jaurès and Clemenceau, acquiesced. When Clemenceau asked about the certainty of a presidential pardon, Millerand swore that he would resign if one was not forthcoming. And when Loubet delayed for a week to await a more propitious moment, Millerand, backed by Waldeck-Rousseau who threatened similar action, submitted his resignation on September 19. Loubet signed the pardon, and the case, except for formalities, was over.[22] Millerand's intervention and plea to have the right of appeal renounced may have been based on legal considerations; it also reflected the government's fervent wish to end the affair as soon as possible.

There was, however, an unpleasant aftermath. On October 10, 1900, the Chamber voted against reopening the case and on December 18 approved an amnesty for all concerned parties. The Senate acted similarly a few days later. Revisionists learned with dismay that anti-Dreyfusards could no longer be prosecuted. Clemenceau was especially irate. He denounced Waldeck-Rousseau and Millerand as 'degenerate sons of the Revolution' and as worthy successors of Méline who saved 'the criminal chiefs of the great Jesuitary'. Within a month of the amnesty vote he founded the newspaper, *Le Bloc,* in order to continue criticizing the cabinet. The first issue accused the Premier and Millerand of having 'gone back on their word' in supporting the bill. Subsequent issues were no less caustic; Clemenceau condemned the cabinet for its 'opportunism' and its 'socialisme embourgeoisé'.[23]

Within Millerand's party socialists were divided between intellectuals and nearly all the departmental federations, on the one hand, and, on the other, the executive council of the Comité d'Entente. The party chiefs who largely comprised the latter were simply disinterested. Their attitude was revealed by Vaillant, who, according to Daniel Halévy, had 'nothing better to say' than: 'We must only concern ourselves with the interests of the Dreyfusards or anti-Dreyfusards who are in the party.'[24]

5. Once returned to the rue Grenelle, Millerand ran into the opposition of his Premier. The Minister of Commerce was to make numerous trips during his three years in office, ostensibly presiding at public functions, like the dedication of a post office, but often outlining future projects in his speeches. Before departing on one such trip, Millerand sent Waldeck

a draft of remarks scheduled for delivery at Limoges on October 1. He intended to propose a larger role for the state in the nation's economy and planned to denounce clericalism as the 'eternal enemy' while affirming the need to preserve absolute liberty of association. He would also urge the suppression of courts-martial in peacetime. Waldeck-Rousseau found the speech entirely too radical and in any event resented a minister making general policy statements; he told Millerand not to speak in the name of the government. He reminded him of the conditions under which the cabinet was formed and of the need and duty of the socialist party and its representative in the government to support the union they had voluntarily entered. Army reform in particular was not to be stressed. Urging moderation, he asked Millerand to speak instead of the need to maintain republican unity by focusing on the continued threat to the country. Waldeck-Rousseau agreed on the need to curb the religious orders hostile to the government, was in fact planning appropriate legislation, but insisted on the right to announce it. He was wholly unable to support Millerand's reference to increased state intervention.[25]

The Limoges speech was thus comparatively mild. Millerand warned of attacks against the regime and once more upheld conventional means of change to achieve social objectives. Even so, the conservative deputy, Denys Cochin, wrote that, because of Waldeck-Rousseau and his socialist minister, it was parliamentary liberty and not the Republic that was endangered. He pointed to Millerand as 'the real President of the Council' and called on loyal Frenchmen to resist it.[26]

Millerand delivered a more radical and collectivist speech at Lille two weeks later. He may have felt it was appropriate in the aftermath of the Creusot strike. In September 1899 the workers of this great metals and armaments works went on strike after rejection of demands that their union be recognized as sole bargaining agent. As a means of dramatizing their plight and 'appealing to the public powers', they decided to walk *en masse* to Paris. Both sides despaired of negotiation and were prepared to accept state arbitration. An apprehensive government had contemplated the prospect of 10,000 workers marching across France, and a grateful Waldeck-Rousseau welcomed the opportunity to act as intermediary. On October 9 the Premier rendered an ambiguous decison allowing both labor and ownership to claim victory, but one which nevertheless maintained the 'open shop'. One writer has suggested that the repercussions in the socialist party were such as to force Millerand to reaffirm collectivism at Lille.[27]

The Minister of Commerce went to Lille officially to dedicate a vocational school and was warmly received by Delroy, the Guesdist mayor, by the town's socialist council and by crowds of workers. A revolutionary general councillor reminded him not to lose sight of the social revolution, while a delegate of the Belgian Socialist Party praised his moderate stand. Millerand tried to show the usefulness of the Republic for workers and in so doing said: 'The collectivist mandate, as I pointed out at Saint-Mandé, is not only a legitimate and fruitful hypothesis but is every day verified by facts.' The reformist approach to the winning of public power was defended as meaning 'a little more liberty, a little more justice, a little more well-being'. Jaurès applauded the speech and once more pointed out that Millerand's language matched that used when a deputy.[28] The blunt confirmation of collectivism, on the other hand, disturbed not only moderate opinion but the head of the government. Although not to set forth any precise program before autumn, Waldeck was determined to retain and strengthen his support. He wanted to set an example of national solidarity and so calm his distraught countrymen. Accordingly, at a cabinet meeting later in the month he reprimanded Millerand for those remarks at Lille stressing the importance of a socialist in the government. 'Everything concerning the cabinet's policy is up to the President of the Council and up to him alone', he maintained, and his ministers were henceforth required to submit copies of all speeches in advance.[29]

When the Chamber reopened in November the conservative deputy Eugène Motte compared Millerand's speech with one delivered by Waldeck-Rousseau only a year before, in which the latter had said that 'collectivism leads to servitude along roads of hatred and anger'. He then asked the Premier to define his position. Privately critical with his ministers, Waldeck rose to their defense in public. He replied that none need sacrifice his opinions 'on the altar of the cruel goddess of power'. He, personally, had not abandoned his anti-collectivist sentiments but asked that his ministry be judged on its acts, not on the individual pronouncements of its members. The Chamber approved the work accomplished during the summer and voted its confidence in the government.[30]

6. Millerand credited the Creusot strike with redirecting his attention to the necessity of strengthening trade unions as a means of easing relations between employers and workers and 'substituting peaceful and legal methods for violent strikes'.[31] Together with other strikes it also turned Waldeck-Rousseau to the trade union as the instrument by which France's labor problems might be solved.

That French workers were growing increasingly dissatisfied with their lot and expressing themselves in the one way available to them was readily apparent. Beginning in the summer of 1899 and extending over the next two years, successive waves of strikes swept over France. From only

397 in the period between January 1898 and July 1899, the number of strikes between January 1899 and August 1900 jumped to 953. Not all, of course, were of equal size and duration, and a more useful indicator of labor unrest is the number of individual working days lost. These figures are even more revealing. After the strife-ridden year of 1893, the number had fallen to 600,000 in 1895 and again in 1896 but rose to 800,000 the following year. In 1898, largely because of turmoil in the building trades, it increased, but only to 1,200,000. But in 1899 lost working days exceeded 3,550,000 and in 1900, 3,760,000. The country had never experienced such widespread working-class discontent.[32]

Economic reasons, while paramount, do not fully explain either the multitude of strikes beginning in 1899 or their intensity. A desire to change societal forms, as well as to exert pressure on their employers, persuaded many workers to walk off their jobs. We have seen that small-scale and decentralized industry had generated a limited and largely ineffective trade-union movement. The membership of the average union numbered only about 140 workers in 1890 and only about 200 in 1911. Their small size and scattered locations explain the importance attached by unions to regional federations and national organizations. Their poverty, which limited their ability to wage long strikes, as well as the enduring influence of anarchist sentiment, in large part accounted for the syndicalist solutions resorted to by French labor. Workers suspected socialists in Parliament, most of whom came from the middle classes, and found reliance on economic action entirely justified. Unconvinced of the efficacy of legal means and finding armed insurrection useless in the face of a powerful state, but confronted by employers willing to sacrifice their economic interests in order to maintain appearances of authority, numerous advocates of economic change continued to depend upon the strike. Their message was disseminated, especially in the cities, by the influential Bourses du travail.[33]

If prompted by questions of salary and working conditions, the great strikes of 1899–1901 often broke out before the formulation of specific claims. The situation at Creusot, an industrial complex resembling a vast and isolated feudal patrimony, with factories, homes, stores, schools and local government either belonging to or controlled by the Schneider family, was not unique. The weavers of Giromagny (in the territory of Belfort) objected to continual surveillance while on the job; the miners at Montceau resented company control over virtually all aspects of their lives. The Loire miners demanded above all else recognition of their union, and this was also true for the Belfort metals workers and the Morez (Jura) watchmakers. The union would serve not only as bargaining agent, it became clear, but would further their sense of self-respect. The strikes at Le Havre originated in protests directed against the attitude of the officers of the Compagnie Générale Transatlantique *vis à vis* their employees. The increase in the number of strikes, the differences separating the two sides and growing resistance on the part of some employers, who supported 'yellow' unions, led to demonstrations and clashes. In two instances, the results were to prove tragic. In June 1900 at a strike at Chalon-sur-Saône, police fired on and killed three demonstrators, the most serious incident since Fourmies. In February of that year, soldiers had killed nine agricultural workers during a strike at Martinique, but this event received far less coverage in the press. It was this movement of strikes that forced Waldeck-Rousseau, who had largely anticipated political action for his government, to concern himself with labor legislation.[34]

A number of Conservatives and Progressists insisted that the sudden increase in industrial conflict and the presence of a socialist minister was more than coincidental. They saw everywhere the hidden hand of Millerand. Agitation began in 1899 with the arrival of a socialist in the government. In exchange for socialist votes, they reasoned, the government was prepared to tolerate, and even encourage, strikes. The writers on *L'Intransigeant, Le Gaulois, Le Journal des débats* and *La Libre Parole* went further: Millerand and his socialist henchmen actively promoted disorder.[35]

Put this way the interpretation was patently absurd. It contradicted Millerand's entire past reliance on the use of legal machinery to correct social injustices and presupposed a close relationship between him and syndicalists who relied on extra-parliamentary action. In fact, the socialists with whom he was affiliated never ceased to preach moderation. Those on the staffs of *La Petite République* and *La Lanterne* worked to maintain the Waldeck-Rousseau ministry in power and sought to avoid making difficulties for it. Jaurès, Viviani and Briand offered their services as mediators. Marxists, we have seen, dismissed the general strike as romantic and contradictory to political action. Socialists of all persuasions suspected trade-union activity as hasty and immature; unions still served best, in their view, as recruiting grounds for socialism.[36] That the unions returned these feelings in kind was to be demonstrated by their boycott of the first Congress of Socialist Organizations held at the end of 1899 and of its successor the following year,

Yet the explanation offered by the right was not without foundation. Millerand's accession to power, and the willingness of French labor to see the government as sympathetic to its demands, reinforced by the Premier's intervention in the Creusot strike, helped to account for the growth of the strike movement. If trade-union leaders held reservations and feared that reformism might convince workers there was a place for them within the capitalist system, the cabinet and the presence of a socialist in it enormously encouraged the rank and file. Petitions and letters to Millerand poured in from groups of workers, as well as from socialists. They naïvely requested assistance of all kinds. A Social Studies Circle in Vitry-le-François wanted support for its library. The Bourse du travail of Villeneuve-sur-Lot complained of workers being forced from their jobs. Others wanted financial aid in order to send a delegate to a fair. Some appealed for rulings on local disputes; to put 'yellow' unions 'on the right path'; to subsidize vocational courses; to preside over social gatherings sponsored by relief committees. One Paris workers' group asked for legal advice; others wanted the government to transmit their grievances to employers or to provide arbitration. The Creusot workers were the first to request, and to receive, arbitration at the hands of this government. Millerand, Baudin and Waldeck-Rousseau received similar requests from strikers in Saint-Etienne; miners in Perrecy-les-Forges, Montceau, Carmaux and Saint-Elroy; tailors and coachmen in Paris; weavers in Saint-Quentin and Giromagny; construction workers in Angers; and dock workers in Marseilles. They asked that a member of the government intercede on their behalf or merely open negotiations with their employers. These requests all pointed to working-class confidence in the government and hope for its support. For once, it was felt, the authorities sided with labor. That these sentiments were not entirely justified and that the strikes issued from more profound causes in no way altered the fact that those who made them felt encouraged by the government in power and did not fear a harsh reaction from it.[37]

One other causal relationship between Millerand's entry into the government and the outbreak of strikes is worthy of mention. There is evidence to show that in a small number of cases strikes were incited solely and deliberately by opponents of the ministry, both militant socialists and nationalists, to embarrass Millerand. De Seilhac pointed specifically to one in Montceau as an example of political strike formented by antiministerial socialists. The Nationalists of *La Libre Parole* and *L'Intransigeant* also worked to create industrial unrest. The Minister of Justice received reports that the dockers' strike in Marseilles in December 1901, the one which subsequently paralyzed the city, was provoked and, in part, initially subsidized by Rochefort.[38] The dismay with which Millerand regarded these activities probably contributed to greater feelings of uncertainty about militant socialists and the usefulness of any continued relationship with them.

Waldeck-Rousseau's attitude toward workers evolved but remained ambivalent. At first unsympathetic and ready to identify labor unrest as the work of 'agitators', he soon came to regard their demands as legitimate. This position was reinforced by the systematic hostility shown by employers and their refusal even to negotiate. The successful outcome of his arbitration of the Cruesot strike persuaded him that some government efforts were justified. But when confronted with specific demands, like that of a miners' delegation for a minimum salary in 1901, he reverted to form and refused to intervene. He limited himself to offering advice and, remaining attached to the strict liberalism taught at the Faculté de droit, rejected what he called excessive intervention on the part of the state. Any sympathy shown for workers' organizations issued from an empirically based conviction that they were indeed seeking conciliation and that it was their employers who refused concessions. Waldeck-Rousseau's social ideas, in the opinion of his biographer, had not basically changed. He never ceased to regard the task of government as that of safe-guarding the right to work as well as that to strike. In an undated letter to his Minister of Commerce, he reproached Millerand for making what he called a concession to a group of striking workers. He wrote again to condemn state intervention 'riding roughshod over the free consent of the interested parties'.[39] He only urged that steps be taken to limit existing unrest; it was the extent and severity of that unrest that persuaded him to join with Millerand in seeking means both to prevent and to alleviate industrial conflict.

7. Impressed by the willingness of organized labor to negotiate, and displeased with unyielding industrialists, Waldeck-Rousseau approved of and actively supported Millerand's efforts to strengthen trade unions. The two men introduced, but were not to see enacted, a government bill on November 14 designed to 'complete' the legislation enacted in 1884 establishing their legality. It would endow them with a legal personality distinct from that of any of their members. Not only would this ease collective conventions with management, but, in receiving the right to possess property, unions might undertake profit-making activities 'in order to increase their resources'.[40]

Millerand did not conceal the fact that the bill reflected a longstanding wish to see workers professionally associated. He told the Chamber that the growth of trade unions and labor exchanges formed the *idée maîtresse* of his administration. At a dinner sponsored by the Associations cooperatives de production he described the government's role as that of doing everything possible to further unity among working men, and at the opening of a dental school in Paris he said: 'I am an incorrigible, impenitent partisan of unions.' In allowing unions to name factory inspectors, the August decrees had given them new rights of inspection and enlarged their responsiblities. Subsequent decrees provided for union representatives to serve on Labor Councils and even for certain government subsidies to union treasuries.[41] In December 1899 he had the state set an example by permitting 100,000 PTT workers to unionize. The bill extending their legal capacity must therefore be viewed in this larger context of doing everything possible to further trade-union growth. Millerand estimated that unionized workers would not be as prone to hold sporadic and violent demonstrations. It was this consideration that had prompted Lockroy to submit the bill calling for their legalization in 1876 and Waldeck-Rousseau, we have seen, to help secure its passage in 1884. That some unions rejected the law precisely reflected their fear of integration into the capitalist state.

Millerand's efforts to further union growth bore fruit but fell far short of the goals envisioned. Still, in terms of increased membership, the previous four-year period, 1895–1899, has been described by Georges Weill as a 'period of stagnation', and that after 1900 as one of 'continuous growth'. On January 1, 1899, there were in all of France only 2,361 trade unions with a total membership of 419,761. By January 1, 1901, the figures had risen to 3,287 unions with 588,832 members and in 1902, to 614,173 union members, an increase of forty-seven percent. Weill credited Millerand with providing the necessary impetus. But historians of the French labor movement correctly point to its relative inability to keep pace with industrial growth. In the half-decade before World War I, of some five million eligible workers in industry, only one million belonged to unions. The reason may be found in the decentralized status of industry as well as in a variety of other causes which we cannot examine here.[42] It may also be attributed to the resistance shown both by employers and workers.

The hostility to working-class organizations and to social legislation on the part of French management has already been commented on and, if short-sighted, requires no further explanation. That enormous opposition also came from workers, socialists and syndicalists is logically relevant to our subject and calls for elaboration. Briefly put, they feared that the extension of union powers would destroy the class consciousness of workers. Guesde asked socialists to reject the bill as 'a trap' intended to immobilize unions and squander their means. Pelloutier objected on the grounds that the bill would shift the initiative from militant minorities to majorities concerned only with increasing their union's resources. He said that for each *militant* there were nine egoists; and, once possessed of property and the taste of ownership, unions would hesitate to jeopardize themselves financially by calling strikes.[43]

Despite Millerand's efforts the bill never reached the Chamber floor for debate during his term of office. Waldeck-Rousseau helped to advance it – according to his biographer his sole personal initiative in the realm of social and labor legislation – but attached so little importance to the idea that he never insisted on debate. To keep the measure alive, Millerand reintroduced it as a private bill in 1902 and again in 1906. He called for its passage in lectures and articles and asked both employers and workers to recognize the legal and necessary role of unions in industrial society. Not until 1920, when Millerand headed his own government, did the substance of the bill became law.[44]

It was also in November 1899 that Millerand announced the opening of negotiations for an international congress to abolish night work for women and told the Chamber of his intention to revise the ten-hour law of 1892. We have seen that the ten-hour maximum established for women and children under sixteen was virtually unenforceable in mixed workshops of men, women and children and that in 1896 André Lebon, the Minister of Commerce, suspended its application. Guesde and Lafargue then took the initiative in calling for a unified-hours law, one setting a maximum of hours for all workers in mixed establishements. Their bill was buried in parliamentary committee.[45]

Millerand first attempted to enforce the existing legislation by creating regional commissions – composed of delegates from both employers' associations and trade unions – to oversee its application. In a circular letter to the prefects of France, he spoke of the government's 'determination' to enforce the law. (Subsequent letters insisted on the enforcement of other existing regulations, especially an 1893 decree prohibiting manual labor to those under eighteen and limiting the hours worked by apprentices.) However, Millerand finally acknowledged the need for a new unified law and sponsored a version of the bill originally suggested by Guesde in 1896. It would first impose an eleven-hour day on all workers in mixed establishments and gradually reduce that maximum to ten hours. The principle of progressive reduction was prompted by Senate opposition to the earlier bill. The socialist deputy Colliard now suggested that the ten-hour limit be arrived at in stages over a four-year period, and the revised legislation carried the names of both men.[46]

Legitimate criticism came from those who pointed out that establishments hiring only men, as well as agricultural, commercial and professional occupations were left untouched. Industrialists complained that France would be placed at an economic disadvantage *vis-à-vis* other European nations lacking this legislation. Syndicalists and socialists seized on that part of the law which temporarily increased to eleven the ten-hour maximum called for in 1892 – although the latter had been found unenforceable. Guesde took the opportunity to sound the cry of treason. Vaillant and Rouanet initially urged application of the 1892 law.[47]

For an historian of French socialism during these years, however, it was the 'tenacious obstruction' of Guesde and Vaillant that postponed passage of the bill. 'Once again', said Jacques Pinset, 'the reforming work of Millerand was shackled', and labor legislation remained retarded in France.[48] The newly formed General Committee of the Congress of Socialist Organizations discussed the proposed law in a tumultuous session January 15, 1900. Jaurès stated his support: for the first time since 1848, he said, workers were to have their hours reduced. But a Guesde-Vaillant resolution condemned the bill in its entirety; the Committee produced a tie vote and could not endorse it. The tide began to turn when in the next few weeks a growing number of trade unions declared themselves favorable. According to a Sûreté report, Guesde, Vaillant and their associates were 'very much disturbed' *(très affectées)* when the Federation of Transport Workers decided to support the measure. 'Until the last moment', reported the agent, 'Guesdists and Blanquists worked for its defeat and hoped thereby to profit at the expense of the Minister of Commerce.' Now they were forced to be more circumspect and to 'conceal their annoyance...'.[49]

The Chamber approved the Bill; Waldeck-Rousseau defended it in the Senate; and it became law March 30, 1900. It reduced from twelve to ten hours the working day of 1.2 million men and from eleven to ten hours that of 600,000 women. It also made then ten-hour day a reality for 433,000 children. Jaurès congratulated the Chamber for enacting 'one of the greatest reforms in the past half century' and attributed the silence of revolutionary socialists to their inability to deny reduced hours to workers.[50]

8. During the parliamentary session of 1900–1901 Millerand submitted two controversial bills. Neither was accepted at the time. In vastly attenuated form they became law only after years of persistent effort by their author. One was a highly complicated proposal designed to settle strikes by applying new and compulsory arbitration machinery. The other was intended to provide workers with old-age benefits. Neither received much support from management or labor. The former saw compulsory arbitration legislation as unwarranted interference with the right of an individual to dispose freely of his property, the latter, as an infringement on the right to strike. Similarly, important segments of both sides resented the contributions expected of them to a national retirement-benefits plan. The treatment accorded these proposals reveals the extent of the difficulties experienced by Millerand as minister and also sheds light on the evolution of his relationship to his party.

Millerand first attempted to improve industrial relations by strengthening and enlarging the functions of existing conseils des prud'hommes. These local arbitration councils had been created by Napoleon I, but their origins can be traced to the thirteenth century. Convoked by local authorities, they concerned themselves with resolving individual, not collective, disputes between employers and workers. The minister wished to extend their competence and make appeal to them compulsory in all cases involving the state. Legislation to this end was approved by the Chamber in February 1901 but rejected two years later by the Senate – although some provisions, excluding the principle of compulsion, became law in 1905 and 1907. Millerand was able to create eight new councils and enlarge 170 others. However, local and purely advisory arbitration councils provided few solutions to the problems of an increasingly industrial society.[51]

In 1864 the Chamber discussed a bill allowing workers to form coalitions in order to bargain or strike. Its spokesman, Emile Olivier, asked why no one had designed legislation to ward off outbreaks of industrial conflict. In 1886, Lockroy, then Minister of Commerce, sponsored an arbitration bill, but it never reached the Chamber floor. Legislation enacted in 1892, based on the Lockroy bill, provided for government-established permanent arbitration councils, but on a wholly voluntary basis and with no provision for sanctions other than adverse publicity for the side rejecting arbitration procedings or the decision of the arbiter. The inadequacy of the law was clearly demonstrated the following year: in a strike in the Pas-de-Calais the companies involved simply refused to submit the dispute to arbitration. Between 1893 and 1920 the machinery it provided was used only in 18% of the strikes in France and, when used, was rarely successful. Voluntary recourse to justices of the peace and to local civil tribunals was clearly inadequate in an age of nationwide strikes.[52]

The contingent of socialists that entered the Chamber in 1893 showed concern both with the establishment of what today is called 'grievance machinery' and with the need for improved arbitration procedures. On February 8, 1894, Jules Guesde submitted legislation 'organizing the right to strike'. It constituted one of the sources of the bill Millerand was to submit almost seven years later, and in 1900 Millerand repeated the words first used by Guesde in the latter's *exposé de motifs*. It deplored the state of anarchy prevalent in strikes and stated that the ballot, 'the normal mode of action in political society, must become that of economic society'. The collective right to strike had long been abandoned to special usage, and the Parti ouvrier chief found it necessary to apply democratic precepts to the labor movement. Collectivization, he said, showed deference to a higher law, to majority rule, and only within the latter could order prevail. Accordingly, Guesde proposed that workers be given the right to vote on the calling of a strike and to vote at stated intervals for its continuation. However, his bill was shelved by the Moderate majority in the Chamber. Yet another source of the legislation proposed by Millerand was Waldeck-Rousseau's successful arbitration of the Creusot strike. It provided for a committee of shop stewards to meet regularly with its counterpart in management. There is also evidence to suggest that the compulsory arbitration scheme adopted by New Zealand in 1894 received close scrutiny at the Ministry of Commerce.[53]

Millerand mentioned his intended arbitration proposals when opening the Creusot pavilion at the Paris Exposition and referred to them in other speeches delivered during the summer of 1900. In brief, he found the legislation enacted in 1892 woefully insufficient. It had been applied only thirty-three times, in the seven years since it became effective, to a mere six and one-half percent of the strikes that had taken place. More damaging, it failed to offer any preventive measures. Waldeck-Rousseau welcomed the principle of joint labor-management committees, suggested the title and some minor improvements and encouraged Millerand to work for its passage. The author would thus appear to be the Minister of Commerce.[54] Use of the Premier's name as co-sponsor would disarm parliamentary critics less likely to reject it if sanctioned by the markedly bourgeois chief of government.

Accordingly, the bill relating to the 'Amicable Settlement of Disputes Relative to Labor Conditions' was submitted by the two men November 15, 1900. It is useful to note the original provisions, for Millerand's willingness to modify them not only demonstrated his well-developed sense of realities but led to a first falling-out with Jaurès. Application of the law was compulsory only in contracts involving the state. In sum it provided for shop stewards elected by workers to present grievances to management at regularly scheduled meetings. (As in the case of the Schneiders, management had occasionally provoked strikes by insisting on hearing workers only on an individual basis.) The industrial conciliation these meetings might provide was seen as vital; production would remain uninterrupted by strikes only if the interests of both parties were respected. In cases of unresolved dispute, each side was to designate arbiters, rather than resort to strikes or lockouts. In the event that management refused either to name an arbiter or abide by the arbitration arrived at, a strike was declared in effect. If workers rejected arbitration, they were free to strike. The right to strike, then, was upheld, but only after conciliation attempts had failed. However, it required approval by a majority of the stewards in a secret vote, representing at least a third of the workers in the establishment, and, if decided on, was made mandatory for all. This vote had to be renewed every seventh day of the strike. Meanwhile, arbiters from the local labor council would be designated, and their decision was to be followed for at least six months. Failure to do so meant that the offending party would be forbidden for three years to elect union administrators, delegates, prud'homme councillors or members of chambers of commerce or labor councils.[55]

Millerand's immediate aim, then, was to reduce the number and duration of strikes by establishing grievance machinery and by insisting on recourse to arbitration. Workers were given the opportunity to decide whether they would be bound by the law. Trade unions, he maintained, would not be hamstrung but rather have their growth facilitated by accustoming workers to collective bargaining procedures and discussion of common corporate interests. Specifically, only union members could elect stewards and vote whether to strike. The arbiters would come from the very labor councils in which unions were already represented. Millerand said he was unable to understand how such rules, in his view the same principles and conditions of free government, would lose their character and virtue when carried from the body politic to the workshop. He wanted the bill 'to substitute for the unexpected explosion of a conflict the regulated and normal exercise of a right'.[56]

Several of these provisions had been inserted only a few weeks before Millerand submitted his proposal. Aware of criticism that its scope was too broad and its coverage too great, and willing to compromise to further its chances of passage, the minister agreed to have the law apply only to establishments containing more than ten workers – in the final draft, more than fifty – and in contracts not involving the state only when both workers and management agreed in advance to accept the plan. These limitations gave rise to a disagreement between Millerand and Jaurès, one terribly revealing of their respective characters. Millerand had informed Jaurès of the proposed changes, and the latter replied on November 3. He regretted them, could not help but express his feeling that they weakened the bill enormously and said that if Millerand had acted because of pressure placed on him by the cabinet, he ought to consider resigning.[57]

Millerand was shaken and responded at length. In an undated letter he acknowledged the warmth and generosity of Jaurès' support. It reflected their participation in a 'common cause'. It was in the name of that cause that Millerand asked him 'to coldly reexamine the situation, to judge it and me with it, free of all extraneous influence, and from the sole point of view of the republican and socialist interests to which I, like you, subscribe'. The minister pointed out that the basic provisions of the bill remained intact: the permanent creation of shop stewards, the obligation to strike if decided upon by a majority, compulsory arbitration and legal sanctions. If the revised bill were restricted to those establishments in which workers and employers agreed to accept the plan, those were precisely the ones containing strong unions, with workers sufficiently aware of their rights to impose them. He then wrote: 'And in cold blood, do you believe it is better for me to resign than to submit such a bill? I swear to you I can sign a bill like this with the same serenity, the same certainty of conscience, as with the [Ten] Hour Law. In both cases I advance by stages. In both cases I appeal to the proletariat to organize itself, to become conscious of its interests and its ability to use the weapons of legality I place in its hands. Best, and most important, in both cases I have remained a loyal, and I believe a useful servant of our cause. Let us speak clearly and get to the point! Is it desirable to make this reconstruction of my bill a pretext for my resignation? That is the question! ... I will follow your advice. I will desert both the socialist and republican cause. I accepted a post of combat. I will remain there as long as I am permitted to serve socialism and the Republic. I see that the bill I am about to introduce draws fire from both sides. One does not serve his ideas and his party, and who knows this better than you, without being misjudged. But in doing this for you, it will be a new and very cruel heartbreak for me. Believe me, my dear friend, if I have ambition, it is too great to be satisfied with the title of minister. I have, I dare say, the same ambition as you; to serve totally and usefully the cause which you defend.'

Millerand then said he wanted to see Jaurès; the latter replied by special delivery letter and presumably was persuaded to approve Millerand's revised legislation.

Accordingly, Jaurès and the Independent socialists declared themselves favorable. The former compared the measure with that previously submitted by Guesde and pointed out the similarities. In a subsequent article he said that compulsory arbitration would not jeopardize the right to strike because experience showed that it was usually the workers who requested it. Jaurès was convinced that such arbitration was the way to equate the economic bargaining power held by labor with that held by employers; it was equivalent, he said, to the role played by universal suffrage in furthering labor's political power.[58]

Opposition came, not only as Millerand had expected, from business elements, syndicalists and militant socialists, but initially from within the government itself. Caillaux described the cabinet as 'amazed' at the clause making the decision to strike binding on all workers in the event that a majority accepted it. Together with Dupuy and Leygues, he deplored the absence of individual choice and resented Millerand's exposing the government, given its precarious position, to a parliamentary reversal. He said that he and his colleagues tried to persuade the Minister of Commerce either to further modify or to withdraw the bill. However, the latter 'stubbornly refused and fought for each item'.[59]

For French syndicalists the strike was a form of warfare, not to be settled by negotiation. Editorials in the CGT newspaper, *La Voix du peuple,* denounced the measure as aiming to deprive workers of their rights and as destroying the ideal of the general strike. Revolutionary movements, it was held, were usually the work of small minorities. Many women and other non-professional workers were far from militant, and so their power to vote would only neutralize the efforts of those seeking change. Militant unions refused even to consider debate. One delegate to the Nice Congress of the Fédération des Bourses du travail (September 1901) was to say: 'We will never discuss the law, because that would be to acknowledge it.' On the same occasion, Jean Grave said that 'to accept discussion with one's exploiters is to acknowledge their right to exploit' and that revolutionary action is decided on by a 'militant elite', by 'a conscientious and bold minority'. Another delegate, Georges Yvetot, told the Congress that the Millerand bill set delays on implementing strikes in order 'to crush the initiative of the minority'. In a similar fashion, the socialist executive committee, created at the first Congress of Socialist Organizations late in 1900, voted on May 3, 1901, to reject the bill as 'contrary to union organization and to the objectives and interests of workers'.[60]

Jaurès chided syndicalists and hostile socialists for their fears. With respect to the neutralization of 'revolutionary minorities', workers would be described as truly organized only when they were grouped to make decisions affecting their welfare. He stated flatly in *La Revue socialiste* that the proposed legislation was 'a government realization of Guesde's former bill and an important date in the history of the proletariat'. He defended the measure as a logical extension of the collective bargaining concept, and asked that it at least be studied as such. The powerful German Social Democratic party joined with the many French working-class organizations favoring the bill. Spokesmen for the SPD found it revolutionary in nature and admired its democratic base and the right of participation it granted to workers. The syndicalist-oriented Lagardelle admitted that generally workers had sought arbitration and employers had consistently refused to obey the 1892 law. In reply to Jaurès' article, moreover, he wrote that 'while there is nothing in common between the Socialist party and Millerand', his position as minister had powerfully aided the development of trade unions (although he went on to say that it was the government's intention to transform unions into political organizations designed to serve as state auxillaries, and hence, as detrimental to socialism.)[61]

Various chambers of commerce opposed the compulsory aspect of the strike. The bill provided that if a majority of the stewards representing at least a third of the total number of workers voted to strike, all must strike. Therefore, as the Rouen Chamber pointed out, 101 workers in 300 could force 199 to strike. Opponents renamed it 'the compulsory strike law'. Industrialists were of one mind in complaining that they would lose control over their own factories. Specifically, they denounced the proposed creation of shop stewards, prefering to deal with individuals, and they rejected the government's obvious desire to have trade unions accepted as representative of labor. They criticized the favoritism shown by the bill to organized workers, who alone delegated representatives and decided whether to strike. Millerand saw these provisions as constituting a 'veritable, peaceful evolution', one marking 'for the first time the legally acknowledged right of workers to intervene in factory administration'. This was precisely what management denounced. It complained that while work was stopped in the event that the employer refused arbitration, consequently disarming him, the union possessed reserve possibilities. Hence while many workers' organizations and independent socialists favored the bill, most industrialists were hostile; Pelloutier and the Bourses opposed; and the cabinet itself was divided.[62]

This opposition was too great; the text never reached parliamentary committee. As with his proposal to extend the civil capacity of unions, Millerand resubmitted the measure as a private bill in subsequent legislatures. He spoke for it before such varied audiences as the Paris Chamber of Commerce, the Cercle Voltaire of Bordeaux, and the Société des études professionelles. He did not preclude the possibility of further revision. Still, as the years passed, Millerand came to stress the benefits the measure would bring to national unity and to insist that domestic tranquility necessarily preceded efforts on behalf of international peace.[63]

As Minister of Public Works in the first Briand cabinet he co-sponsored a compulsory arbitration bill for railroad workers and also introduced legislation creating a permanent representative body for labor. As Premier in 1920, together with his Minister of Labor, Paul Jourdain, Millerand again sponsored provisions of the bill. He hoped to profit from the wartime experience of joint employers and workers committees, and the new proposal called for compulsory conciliation attempts and arbitration only in utilities involving the public welfare. Once rendered, however, the arbiter's decision was not compulsory. As a *project de loi,* a version of the measure, the Loucheur bill, passed both chambers in 1929. It provided for compulsory recourse in certain areas to labor councils but left arbitration on a voluntary basis. The question was taken up by a Popular Front government, when Premier Camille Chautemps invoked these precedents, and again after World War II.[64]

During Millerand's socialist years this measure, like others submitted, never received full party support. A sympathetic colleague concluded: 'Such was the bitterness of the internecine war of divided socialism, that when [Millerand] proposed, after Guesde, the instrument of compulsory arbitration, Guesde's colleagues used the bill as a weapon against Millerand and his friends, and even among the latter he could not obtain a majority.'[65]

9. Late in July, 1901, in a speech to the Associations cooperatives de production, Millerand summarized the work thus far accomplished and pointed to some guiding principles. He had accepted power because it appeared to be 'the real means of applying my principles and beginning the reforms I judge useful to my country'. In the nineteenth century, progress was furthered by the bourgeoisie; in the twentieth, the task would be that of the workers. Society had to assist and could provide no better point of departure than by convincing them that the peaceful conquest of political power now constituted the most reliable method. But victory depended on labor's ability to organize. And only through association could it be made aware that power implied responsibility. Government had every reason, then, to favor trade union growth.[66]

The minister further tried to implement his ideas by assigning trade unions greater representation in the reorganized Superior Labor Council and in newly created regional labor councils. Composed of appointed representatives of labor, management and government, the former had been established in 1891 as a central advisory body to suggest necessary labor legislation. However, it was largely ignored by all three and also held suspect by labor. Millerand estimated that its membership did not adequately reflect working-class interests. In a decree dated September 1, 1899, he provided that one third, or twenty-two members, be workers elected by unions and that every member of the Council receive a salary. Representation in government by economic profession and not merely by political affiliation was an idea well established in French socialist thought. Malon, for example, had favored a bicameral legislature, one chamber standing for political interests, the other, economic; and he predicted the second would become more powerful.[67]

Millerand found it logical to establish as well a system of regional consultative bodies. Patterned on a Belgian model, they were designed to advise departmental and municipal officials, determine averages for wages earned and hours worked in a geographic area and in every way cooperate with the Superior Council. Participation in these councils would accustom workers to meeting regularly with employers and so help to harmonize relations between them, perhaps the government's most important objective. Accordingly, a decree issued December 17, 1900 (completed the following January), created the conseils du travail. Composed of delegates representing labor and management, they were also intended to furnish advice in the drafting of labor contracts and competent mediation in cases of dispute.[68] Nearly everyone resisted the decrees. Like those of August 1899, they were condemned by legislators for granting to private organizations rights generally associated with public power and for violating principles of universal suffrage in as much as trade unions, rather than individual workers, elected representatives.

An historian of the European socialist movement, Carl Landauer, viewed the labor councils as decidedly compatible with socialism because, (1) only organized labor was represented, and (2) they extended state jurisdiction to the regulation of wages and working conditions. Indeed, the provision granting unions the sole right to determine working-class representation was the one attacked most bitterly by employers. They correctly pointed out that the great majority of French workers was not organized and obviously did not appreciate Millerand's precise intention to promote the growth of trade unions by endowing them with special privileges. Thus the decree was taken as additional proof of what might be expected from a socialist minister. When told in the Chamber that the Law of 1884 made no such distinction between union and non-union workers, Millerand replied that the strength of a union rested on its authority to speak for all the workers in a given industrial establishment. But in November 1902, despite his opposition and that of his successor at the Ministry of Commerce, Georges Trouillot, the Berenger Law granted all workers, organized or not, the right to choose representatives. The regional Conseils du travail never took root, and their importance remained largely theoretical. The experience, however, served as a precedent to the 'politique de la presence', to the participation in joint labor-management committees that the CGT, in part converted by experience, in part constrained by events, began to practice in August 1914.[69]

By encouraging occupational grouping in government, Millerand was conceivably moving into the broad current of French corporatist tradition. Deeply rooted, long-lived and highly appealing, it carried sympathizers like Albert de Mun and the Marquis de La Tour du Pin and reached to the corporative sub-parliament favored by the Mouvement populaire républicain after World War II and to De Gaulle's ideas on the 'participation' of capital and labor in industrial enterprise. These men all saw as the final aim of association workers sharing directly in the profits generated by their labor and so becoming labor-capitalists. Because of the corporative element implicit in Millerand's proposals, some Christian democrats approved of his legislation and began giving him their support. Most, however, felt uncomfortable with what they regarded as unjustifiably extreme proposals. They favored, for example, regionally grouped professional organizations and were willing to entrust them with the administration of a national retirement-benefits system. However, they estimated that Millerand's insistence on compulsory contributions was entirely too radical.[70]

To further encourage union growth and responsibility, a circular letter stipulated that assistant labor inspectors were to be recruited from retired workers and that all labor inspectors were to get in touch with working-class organizations for information on local employment conditions. Unions were thus treated as auxillaries of power. Inspectors were specifically enjoined to visit union headquarters, ask for complaints and in every way cooperate with union officials.[71] Eleven years earlier, during Millerand's first term as deputy, he had supported the Bovier-Lapierre bill designed to punish employers interfering either with the establishment of trade unions or with their development. His work as minister differed only in the extent and scope of his assistance to organized labor.

Although the contribution made by the regional councils was to be minimal, the reorganized Superior Labor Council exerted considerable influence in the years to come. In his account of welfare legislation in the late nineteenth and early twentieth centuries, Charles W. Pipkin credited it with providing 'at the critical time of French social legislation a leadership in social investigation', one that drew the attention of the government to its work of social welfare. There was no important bill which had not first been studied and discussed by the Council before it reached the Chamber floor. The government either submitted intended legislation for its opinion or heard its suggestions on needed laws. In 1926, for example, the minimum age for children employed in factories was raised on the Council's recommendation, and it played a leading role in preparing the social insurance legislation of 1928.[72]

To ensure that trade unions were properly representative of working-class interests, Millerand refused to sanction a rival labor exchange established by 'yellow' unions after their expulsion from the Paris Bourse du travail. He also issued a decree reorganizing the Labor Exchange and placing it entirely in the hands of its member unions. In assuring their autonomy by granting them the right to name their own administrative officers, hitherto designated by the Prefect of the Seine, Millerand doubtless recalled his association with autonomists on the Municipal Council. Reporting on this decree, the conservative *Journal des Débats* accused the minister of preparing an 'upheaval of society'.[73] It was not, however, social conservatives, as formidable as their oppostion was, who most effectively obstructed his work. Militant socialists managed to regroup their forces and, aided by those ministerial activities least compatible with collectivism, reasserted their authority, even over their representatives in parliament.

10. The Millerand case

L'histoire du socialisme en France est l'histoire
d'épurations successives, dont finalement le mouvement sort appauvri en hommes et en idées. Ra-
res sont les moments où ont pu se réaliser des
synthèses hardies tentant de répondre à tous les
aspects d'un monde mouvement...

GEORGES LEFRANC, *Le Mouvement socialiste sous
la troisième république*

1. Thanks in large part to the strenuous efforts of Jaurès, the socialist
factions had agreed to hold a general congress in December 1899. Placed
high on the agenda were the questions of ministerial participation and
party unity. The persistence and scope of antiministerialist criticism
cannot be exaggerated. From the moment the Waldeck-Rousseau government took power, revolutionary leaders condemned it relentlessly. As
early as July 30, Lafargue denounced the Saint-Mandé Program as well
as the entire Socialist Union. He said that at the time he had considered
the speech 'vague' but chose to avoid criticism for fear of alienating possible bourgeois support. During a debate between Jaurès and Guesde,
held in anticipation of the forthcoming congress, the former reminded
his audience that Lafargue had at first welcomed Millerand's entry into
the ministry as 'a decisive symptom' of socialism's growing force. Approval of his participation in no way accounted for, or denoted approval
of, Galliffet's sins; examples of the bourgeois capacity for wrong-doing
were to be avoided only be eliminating capitalism itself. In reply, Guesde
denied that the Republic was endangered in 1899 and reminded Jaurès
of Millerand's many efforts during the Dreyfus affair to preserve party
neutrality.[1]

Resentment on the part of the Guesdist and Blanquist leadership at
seeing Jaurès and Independent initiative succeed in bringing about a
renewed effort at socialist unity, and their anger at the latter's suggestion
that the 'old parties' no longer had a role to play, had not abated. Lafargue was to vent this hostility when he sarcastically told the Congress:
'We, the old *militants,* are crotchety, irrational, and incapable of understanding the new, enlarged, and embellished integral socialism.' Newcomers, he charged, came to the party because of its strength; they did

nothing to organize it; they wanted only to exploit it. And the anger of the *militants* mounted as the government took action similar to that taken by previous governments. The cabinet, Millerand included, had approved Waldeck-Rousseau's decision to postpone immediate suppression of the Budget des cultes. The report to the Sûreté which followed spoke of 'the hatred of Guesde, Vaillant, and their followers for Millerand', their retention of the 'heavy grudge' *(sourde rancune)* caused by his and Galliffet's presence in the ministry and their determination to make every effort to force the former to resign.[2]

We have seen that the Parti ouvrier at its Epernay Congress condemned the present example of ministerial participation but had refused to bar it in principle. On the evening of December 2, the day before the scheduled opening of the all-Socialist Congress, Guesde held a reception to welcome POF delegates from the provinces. The party executive described it as providing an opportunity to decide on common tactics. According to a Prefecture report, it was largely an attempt to impose discipline. The rank and file had made it known that it viewed the reestablishment of socialist unity as primary and, tired of incessant factional disputes, that it believed the Millerand case could be rationally and amicably resolved. Some delegates thus resented pressure 'that agreement be reached with Blanquists... so that Millerand's government would be rejected by a majority of the socialist party', objecting that imposed unanimity might deprive them of their independence or contradict their mandates. Still, a majority acknowledged the need for discipline.[3]

The First General Congress of French Socialist Organizations convened December 3 to discuss both the Millerand case and party unity. For two days speaker followed speaker, one approving of Millerand's entry, another rejecting it. Jaurès recalled the remarks of speakers at the Parti ouvrier's Epernay Congress who said they had expected the arrival of a socialist in power. He described socialist participation in national government as the natural consequence of socialist participation in Parliament and municipal chambers and said that responsibility in the latter was not essentially different from that of a socialist minister. The invitation had stemmed from the need to defend the Republic, the most valuable tool possessed by workers and one which had to be retained. Moreover, because socialists could never determine exactly when collectivist society would fully replace capitalism, the date of the revolution very much uncertain, they must continue to work for reforms in order to prepare for that day, and with what better instrument than a socialist minister.

Vaillant, on the other hand, stressed the nature of the class struggle and the necessity of distinguishing a tactic from a principle. Was the party to remain revolutionary or become semi-bourgeois? A socialist minister by the very nature of his position was forced to cooperate with the government in power, and the latter represented bourgeois interests. A clear example of this predicament would occur when the ministery of which he was a member ordered troops to the scene of a strike. Workers would thereupon lose all confidence in socialism. Lafargue again discountenanced ministerial participation as a socialist victory. He saw it rather as a 'bourgeois trick', similar to that played by admitting Louis Blanc to the Provisional Government in 1848. In both cases the middle class had sought to neutralize socialist forces. Zévaès rejected the analogy between socialists in the Chamber and socialists in the government; the former, because it reflected the will of the people, was permissible; the latter reflected only the decision of a premier-designate seeking a wider basis of support.

When Guesde finally rose on the evening of the second day, he said that the ministerial participation of a socialist would destroy the international solidarity of the proletariat. The leaders of international socialism were right in opposing it. For there would appear, in addition to a French Millerand, an English, Italian and German Millerand, whose presence in their respective governments would bind socialists to the ruling bourgeoisie – even to the extent of supporting war policies – and in so doing bring an end to internationalism. Not mentioning Millerand by name, he said that the socialist minister had so far been unable to bring any socialist principle to fruition. In reply, Briand pointed to the near unanimity of socialist opinion in the 1890s, and hence almost everyone in the movement contributed to the arrival of a socialist in power. If the party, as a consequence, was going downhill, Guesde and Lafargue helped lubricate the slope.

Millerand made one visit to the Congress. He came about 10 A.M. on Wednesday, December 5, and was greeted with cries of 'à bas Galliffet'. He was booed, unable to speak and, according to the police informant present, 'chased from the hall'.[4]

The resolution finally approved (by an 1140 to 240 vote) matched that of Epernay in terms of ambiguity. It neither approved nor repudiated ministerial participation, stating only that when 'exceptional circumstances' arose, the question would be fully examined. Socialists, meanwhile, were to work both for revolution and election to public office. To prevent a possible departure by Marxists and Blanquists, before voting this text it first accepted Guesde's amendment – that the class struggle prohibited the entry of a socialist into a bourgeois cabinet – to go on record as opposed to the principle of participation. This vote went 818 to 634. The outcome supports Halévy's contention that the Millerand case, at that time and for most socialists, was viewed as accidental and, because there had been no unified party to judge and few expected that a similar situation could soon reappear, as 'water over the dam'. Primary consideration was to be given to party unity.[5]

The thorny choice lay between federation and fusion of the various factions. Guesde contended that total unity would mean total conflict, and it was decided to form the newly established party, the Parti socialiste français, as a federation of the varied factions based on the principles of Saint-Mandé. Each faction was to retain its identity and name its own candidates on the first ballot. Following SPD and Guesdist organizational procedure, the directing voice was to be an annual congress; in the interim an executive committee, staffed by delegates from the various organizations and proportional to their strength, was to manage affairs. Guesde had made the price of his support clear: the party and its committee would reign supreme. 'There would no longer be any independent socialist press', he said, and 'the independence of our socialist *élus* must disappear, for the same reason and in the same conditions.' The deputies will no longer be their own masters, nor even be responsible to their constituents; they must answer to the French proletariat; and, as in Germany, the party will control its parliamentary division, limiting it to a single vote on every issue. On hearing these conditions, Halévy reported, the moderates in the hall were 'overwhelmed, fell silent, and felt a wind of steel passing over them'. These stipulations were intended to preserve the dominant position of the established leadership as well as heighten the effectiveness of the party.[6]

The ground swell for unity carried everything before it, although it could not conceal the differences of opinion still separating the rank and file from its leadership, particularly their conflicting attitudes toward Millerand. If not favorable to a socialist minister, the average delegate clearly was not hostile. Yet everything was subordinated to the realization that an alliance had been sealed, that there were no longer Guesdists, Broussists, Blanquists or Allemanists but only socialists. As the strife of the past five days was drowned out by the lively Carmagnole, and then the more solemn Internationale, everyone present, from aged Communards to the newest recruit, was affected.

However, the preceptive François de Pressensé wrote in *L'Aurore* on December 17 that the fundamental dilemma of democratic socialism had not been resolved. 'Once in an election', he said, 'one had to be a reformer, if not a reformist.' On the other hand, he was quick to point out, if socialism became another, albeit more progressive, version of the Radical party, it lost its *raison d'être*. Whether an effort by the veterans to prevent the jettisoning of the party's revolutionary equipage; whether their natural disillusion with reformism after the disappointing results of the 1898 election; whether an identity crisis they were experiencing; or whether a combination of all these things can never be determined with accuracy. What remains clear is their turn to the left and their determination to use the executive committee of the newly formed Parti socialiste français to pattern socialist tactics on those followed before 1892–1893.

The committee insisted, in the name of unity, on controling the contingent of socialist deputies and the socialist press, both largely Independent and moderate. The actions and proposals of the socialist minister, whom they could not control, were opposed and repudiated. Among the latter were the ten-hour bill, the compulsory arbitration bill and, we shall see, a national retirement-benefits plan. Sûreté reports described these divisions and accurately predicted continued dissent. 'If union was acknowledged', read one not atypical statement, 'it was done so by the delegates and not by their leaders. ... Guesde and Vaillant do not in any way desire the rapprochement just achieved, and while amply preaching the benefits of union, do not believe in its realization.' The agent writing this report expressed his opinion that if unity ever came, the 'old leaders' would necessarily first have disappeared.[7] Events proved him wrong. They did not disappear and got a unified party on almost their own terms.

2. Opponents of the ministry nearly overturned it in the aftermath of the strike at Chalon-sur-Saône. We have seen that in a clash with police on June 2, 1900, three workers were killed. The tragedy appeared to bear out Vaillant's warning, and militant socialists stepped up their attacks on the government. Guesdists resolved to make use of the shooting in every way; one proposal called for the erection of a monument to the Chalon dead with the inscription: 'Victims felled by the shots of a ministry containing a socialist.' With Blanquist cooperation they planned to hold a public meeting in Paris with the aim of winning Nationalist support. Nationalists, on their part, wished to gain the allegiance of dissatisfied socialists, and the Sûreté, for one, estimated they had reached accord on tactics.[8]

In the months that followed, reports coming to the Sûreté repeatedly described how the 'still irreducible adversaries of the ministry' persisted in attempts to have Millerand ousted from the party. Guesde was seen as 'working to create a hostile current' and as 'complaining bitterly' about the proposed Ten-Hour law. 'Never, not even against Méline', stated yet another report, 'have there been so many outbursts by Guesdists and Blanquists against a ministry.' Guesde appeared to have made some concessions at the all-Socialist Congress but used the time gained to prepare for battle. That he indeed regarded these concessions as temporary was revealed in at least two of his letters to Karl Liebknecht.[9]

A plan designed to embarrass Millerand was described by a member of the party executive to a Sûreté agent. French socialists made an annual pilgrimage to the 'mur des fédérés' in the Père Lachaise cemetery, and, overcoming the opposition of the few Independents on the committee, the Guesdist Chauvin proposed that the wreath to be placed carry the inscription: 'To the victims of Galliffet.' The proposal was seen as in no way isolated, and the agent compared the Guesdists to reactionaries in their opposition to the government. Earlier the committee had moved that 'governments in a bourgeois regime can never be anything but an expression and instrument of the bourgeois class', and the resolution fell one vote short of unanimous acceptance. The larger conflict remained that between the party executive and the parliamentary socialists who refused to submit to its control and even contested its authority. The committee denounced the 'political preoccupations' of the deputies, accused them of neglecting the 'higher interests' of socialism and threatened to bring the issue to the attention of the next congress. In these skirmishes Guesdists and Blanquists were joined by syndicalists, delegates of autonomous federations and, on occasion, by some Broussists and Independents.[10]

The Parti ouvrier took the offensive in its stronghold in the Nord; the Federal Congress of Caudry on August 5 voted a resolution correctly interpreted as a veritable declaration of war: 'Never have the workers been so deceived, condemned, cut down, shot, and massacred. ... Never has war against the working class been waged as relentlessly as under the Waldeck-Rousseau–Millerand ministry. ... The so-called government of republican defense has been a capitalist government. ... All its members, with no exceptions, from the former socialist Millerand to the lawyer of the Panamists, Waldeck-Rousseau, merit the curses of the entire proletariat.' The Paris-based federation of the Parti ouvrier a month later resolved 'to discard from the Parti socialiste français all the non-revolutionary elements who cooperate and compromise with the bourgeoisie'. Its proposal to base a united party on clearly revolutionary principles, together with the resolution of the Caudry Congress, was adopted at the POF's Ivry Congress in September.[11]

Although at opposite ends of the political spectrum, the most determined opponents of the ministry found it convenient to join forces against it. We have seen that during the Boulanger craze a precedent for socialist cooperation with Nationalists had been set. The Dreyfus affair provided an opportunity for a renewal of this compact, and, according to Zévaès, then a high-ranking Guesdist, this understanding was strengthened at the turn of the century.[12]   Reports filed at the Sûreté also affirm that by early 1900 Guesde had entered into an 'alliance' with Nationalist opponents of the ministry, who in return stepped up their attacks on Independent socialists and praised the revolutionaries in the party.[13]   Socialist delegates from regional federations were complaining that private interests dominated the party executive, and, like Zévaès, the police concluded that Guesde, Drumont and Rochefort were indeed cooperating in efforts to upset the government and limit the effectiveness of the largely Independent group of deputies.   The division between the latter and the militant party chiefs became acute, and, by the summer of 1900, the unity reached only a year before appeared to have come to an end.

Whether the hostility displayed by revolutionary socialists toward the government can more properly be explained in psychological than in ideological and political terms cannot be precisely determined.   Still, moderate socialists everywhere estimated that the militant leadership was most concerned with what it viewed as its loss of status within the movement.   In his memoirs, though as terse and impersonal as their author intended, Millerand managed to convey his disappointment at 'the total lack of understanding' and the 'passive inertia if not open enmity' by the working as well as the business classes.   He said that he 'hurled himself again and again' at their resistance but received pitifully small response.[14]

3.   A respite from legislative difficulties came with the Paris Exposition of April-November 1900.   Long and intensively planned, and entrusted to well-trained administrators rather than transient politicians, it resembled earlier French fairs that had invariably served political purposes.   The Exposition, according to its historian, in 1899 served as a rallying point for anti-Dreyfusard patriots.   In 1900 it 'acted as a tranquilizer' and 'helped to refurbish a tarnished French image'.   Having taken no part in its planning, Millerand's role was limited to supervising, signing papers and making speeches.   He momentarily disturbed promoters when he ordered prefects to provide reduced fares for visiting workers' delegations, but this decision, too, had been taken by his predecessors.

The minister had intervened more directly the previous fall when the Schneiders informed him that the strike then underway would prevent Creusot from participating.   Millerand said that he was appealing 'on behalf of the country' when he asked the firm to reconsider and promised certain government concessions: chiefly, extended time for preparation and loans of military machinery.   It was the Minister of Commerce who inaugurated the great Creusot pavilion on the Seine near the Eiffel Tower, and the location and notoriety given to the exhibit prompted critics

14*

to regard the Exposition as 'consecrated to the glory of Creusot'. Millerand took pride in this demonstration of French industrial might but also applauded the institutionalization of shop stewards provided by the arbitration ending the strike.[15]

Millerand's official presence aroused feelings of satisfaction not unmixed with pride on some parts of the French left. Even so critical an observer as Charles Andler described how 'no one has forgotten the powerful effect produced during the Universal Exposition when a socialist minister presided over the great industrial fête, where, for the first time, the workers were not forgotten'.

Still, the proceedings provided an irresistible opportunity for opponents of the ministry. Newspapers on both the right and left reminded their readers of the socialist emphasis on economic equality and in adjacent columns printed menus of the elaborate dinners given for visiting dignitaries at the Ministry of Commerce. Millerand, like Jaurès, was on one occasion accused by an austere polemicist of the period as indulging in too much *homard à la Lucullus*. Millerand ignored the charge. (Nor had Jaurès defended himself; his reply, 'We are not ascetics', helped stamp him with his character and passed into Jaurèssian legend.) The minister was criticized by militant socialists for traveling luxuriously, on one occasion requisitioning a railway car. Even those sympathetic to his participation in the government could not help but react to such unnatural phenomena as President Loubet taking the arm of Madame Millerand. Madame Georges Renard, whose criticism may have been aroused by other instincts, 'regretfully' noted 'it was the end of a legend'. Bruneillière wrote to a friend that he now doubted the wisdom of participating in a bourgeois administration. The most widespread indignation, however, followed the presentation to the minister of medals and honorary titles by the Austrian and Russian governments, and 'Baron' Millerand became an object of reproach. It promoted at least one comparison between Millerand's socialism and the type espoused by that advocate of expositions, Louis Napoleon.[16]

A related cause for alarm had been the Paquin affair. In early spring, as candidate for knighthood in the Legion of Honor, Millerand sponsored the Parisian couturier Isidor Jacob, alias Monsieur Paquin. He was criticized for his choice in the Chamber on the grounds that Paquin disregarded labor legislation in his workshops. The minister's reply was weak: the entire Council of the Legion had already approved, and others besides Paquin disregarded the laws. Some sixty years later Millerand's *chef de cabinet,* Persil, absolved him from responsibility and used the incident to illustrate his patron's loyalty to his staff. Apparently Waldeck-Rousseau assigned the task to Millerand – another observer called the latter's unquestioning acceptance an example of the discipline of his ministers – who in turn delegated it to Persil. Millerand did not know Paquin but took full responsibility for the choice. More significant was the aftermath. Zévaès revived an old socialist resolution, originally put forth by Millerand himself, together with Guesde and Jaurès, forbidding Legion decorations to employers disrespectful of labor legislation. But as one of Waldeck's ministers, Millerand found the measure excessive, and it was defeated.[17]

The summer, nevertheless, was a happy one. The Minister of Commerce no doubt relished his busy schedule. Together with the President of the Republic and the Commissioner-General of the Fair, he seemed to be everywhere, continually officiating and orating. He could feel some sense of accomplishment because of the Exposition, taking advantage, for example, of the presence of the many foreign visitors to help create an International Association for the Legal Protection of Workers and serving as President of its French section after its establishment in 1902. The Association asked that each member nation adopt similar social legislation in order to prevent the use of higher labor costs as an argument against reform within any one of them. It sought international adoption of a retirement-benefits plan based on that applied in Germany and of the systems of compulsory arbitration practiced in Australia and New Zealand. Millerand also asked Delcassé to arrange for a European congress to take the necessary measures for the abolition of night work for women.[18]

In the Paquin affair, the left had succeeded in embarrassing Millerand for his irresolution. The right continued to condemn him for his socialism. In a general critique of the government, Denys Cochin accused the Minister of Commerce of wishing to make the Exposition 'the triumph of collectivism'. Méline agreed; he said that it was the chief of the socialist party who sat in the cabinet and that his influence on it was 'preponderant'. The government, he contended, attacked other associations but spared the socialist party's executive committee.[19]

Galliffet also accused Millerand of subverting the cabinet and, partly because of this, in May 1900 resigned his post at the Ministry of War. He had threatened similar action several times before. Now he told his friend Princess Radziwell that Waldeck-Rousseau, in order to preserve his majority, was more deeply than ever under the influence of Millerand and compelled to move toward 'socialism and anarchism'. Nothing else, he said, could account for the Premier's insinuation that army officers backed a new plot to overthrow the Republic – the immediate cause of Galliffet's resignation.[20]

Galliffet's hostility was in no way personal; he admired Millerand as 'remarkably intelligent' and in his inimitable style had informed a news-paperman that 'except for Waldeck-Rousseau, who is first rate, and Millerand, I am with pigs and imbeciles'. The General respected socialist discipline and fervor. He told the young Paul-Boncour, then an assistant to Waldeck-Rousseau, that if he were starting again he might very well be a socialist – although any commitment on his part to egalitarian-based ideologies became clouded when he added that some were born to command and 'idiots' to obey. Galliffet could appreciate Millerand's refusal to disclaim his socialist identity in official circles and in drawing rooms. One evening, according to Paul-Boncour, at the Waldeck-Rousseau's, Millerand turned to a guest maligning the Commune, gave him a rare smile and said: 'Forgive me for not agreeing. I cannot forget that without the Commune I would not be here.'[21] The sustained presence of Galliffet in the ministry repelled socialists. In branding Millerand an enemy like Galliffet, one overwrought *militant* had threatened the minister with bodily harm. The latter doubtless experienced relief when news of the resignation arrived. More socialists showed confidence in the cabinet, although revolutionaries continued their opposition.[22]

4.   As a Radical deputy Millerand came to believe in the need for state intervention to safeguard the rights of the old-aged. He never regarded private philanthropy as anything but inadequate, and his platform of 1898 called on society to 'pay its debt' to former workers by approving a national retirement-benefits plan. As minister he drew upon numerous precedents and earlier proposals to formulate an appropriate bill.[23] It was to be his last major proposal as Minister of Commerce.

He presented the measure to the Chamber on June 13, 1901. On the same day a well-timed article by André Lefèvre in *La Petite République* reminded workers they still lacked retirement protection and that those who insisted on a perfect law would do well to realize it. Millerand credited the deputy Jacques Escuyer with championing the plan designed to finance the program. The bill provided for retirement benefits for all salaried workers, save domestics, earning less than 4000 francs a year. They would receive payments after sixty-five years of age, or earlier if disabled. Funds would be provided by the equal and compulsory contributions of workers and employers; the state, as administrator of the funds, was to pay three percent interest. Provisions were made for workers well along in years to enter the program but to draw correspondingly smaller benefits on retirement. Local pension programs and mutual-aid societies would be left untouched and were seen as supplementing the national plan.[24]

To win approval of the principle of old-age benefits, Millerand referred the Chamber to Barrère's remarks made in the National Convention about the right of every citizen in a democtatic society to be raised above the necessities of physical existence. State participation was seen as economically justified by anticipated increases in productivity and, consequently, in national income. Private organizations, commended for admirable poineer work and estimated as still useful, were plainly inadequate both from the point of view of coverage and size of payment rendered. The minister regarded compulsion as 'legal, necessary, and just'; as in the areas of education, military service and taxation, it was imposed on society in the interests of its members. The plan, he said, would be compulsory, or else it would not be. The protesting employer must learn to regard his contribution as an investment in his workers.

Compared to its underlying principles, Millerand acknowledged, the bill was far from ideal. But he doubted that the Chamber, 'because it could not do everything, would prefer to do nothing'. When on June 20 the socialist deputy, Mirman, sought to increase its coverage, Millerand was to resist the attempt to send the bill back to committee. The proposed change required four to five hundred millions in new taxes, a responsibility no finance minister could take. Anticipating another potential objection, Millerand argued that old-age security, far from weakening, would strengthen the moral fiber of a nation. He identified 'misery' as the first 'germ of corruption in a great people' and hence the 'most dangerous enemy of liberty and decency'. Thanks to Millerand's perseverence, counterproposals, like that submitted by Vaillant, were defeated. Of twenty-six proposals to amend, nine were rejected, twelve reserved for later articles and three withdrawn; the two adopted were technical in nature.

After fourteen sessions of debate, the Chamber on July 1 voted the first paragraph of the first article establishing in principle the right of the state to administer a national pension program. However, the proposal to continue the discussion received only a thirty-five vote majority. Mirman's proposal to extend its scope lost by only twenty votes and revealed that an alliance had been formed between deputies wanting a better bill .and those opposed to any. Opponents of the measure then succeeded in winning approval of a Nationalist deputy's resolution asking that the government gather sample opinions from all interested parties. Marking the strength of the opposition, the Premier decided not to contest the resolution. Millerand had protested that all interested parties were consulted, but in vain. Without government support the resolution returning the legislation to committee was passed by seventy votes, effectively burying it. Aside from a handful of Independents, socialists either supported the motion to shelve, or abstained. Waldeck-Rousseau, it was clear, permitted Millerand to issue decrees and supported his efforts to encourage union growth and introduce industrial arbitration. A retirement-benefits plan was not of sufficient importance to be made a question of confidence. For one historian of the French labor movement, 'it was plain that the heart of the Premier was not in these economic reforms'.[25]

The opposition was indeed enormous. The bill was condemned by industry as socialist, by syndicalists as weakening class consciousness and by militant socialists, as for example those at the Parti ouvrier's 1901 Congress, as a 'vast swindle'. The earlier declaration of the POF's National Council described it as 'an electoral manoeuver to atone for killings at Chalon' and called it 'knavery' for workers to supply the capitalist state with funds. As if in an afterthought, however, the Council added that if a pension plan were to be established, workers ought not pay at all. The Council asked all party members to organize opposition movements within trade unions. The bill, during that legislature, never emerged from the Chamber.[26]

Millerand was to resubmit the measure as private legislation in 1902. As President of the Chamber's Committee of Insurance and Social Welfare – a committee created by him as minister – he won a promise of support from the Combes ministry. When Combes resisted debate, as we shall see, Millerand challenged the government in 1904. Throughout 1905 he repeatedly raised the question. One occasion was especially noteworthy. Paul Grunebaum-Ballin, the future Councillor of State and at the time Briand's associate, recalled the latter's 'masterful' speech of July 3, 1905, defending separation of church and state. He described it as 'one of the rare sessions in the assemblies of the Third Republic... an hour of national grandeur'. After Briand descended from the tribune, the Chamber voted to post the speech. The hour was 10 P.M. and the deputies were exhausted. Nonetheless, Millerand rose to ask for immediate discussion of workers' pension legislation. He spoke on its behalf on Ferbuary 22, 1906, and the following day the impressed Chamber passed the bill. For an historian of French social legislation, 'it was due to Millerand that old-age pensions became in 1905 an active legislative question', and he could write in his memoirs: 'I was able to look at the road travelled with a certain satisfaction.'[27]

In 1909 Millerand said that the bill, now before the Senate, contained the germ of a no less desirable type of insurance, that of unemployment. The following year, a considerably watered-down version became law. Viviani nevertheless saw it as Millerand's greatest achievement.[28]

As High Commissioner to Alsace-Lorraine in 1919, Millerand studied the application of German social insurance in the two provinces; as

Premier the following year, he recommended that the system remain in force after their reintegration into France. He appointed Paul Jourdain, an Alsatian administrator, as his Minister of Labor, and both men were determined to have the country benefit from the 'Alsatian experience'. As President of France, Millerand sponsored a government social security bill in 1924. Given the time necessary to secure social legislation in the French parliament and the need to restore fiscal health after World War I, it was approved by the National Assembly (now with trade-union support) only in 1928 and went into effect two years later. Insurance was provided for accident, disability, old age and death, and a provision for family allowances was made. This legislation was to endure until vastly enlarged after World War II. A French economist credited Millerand with having laid down 'the basis of our code of social insurance'. In his discussion of the Act, Charles W. Pipkin said, 'the work which was begun in the legislative session of 1898–1902... was for the time done'.[29]

It was Edouard Vaillant, however, as a member of the Paris Municipal Council, who had introduced not only the principle of the minimum wage but also that of social insurance. That Vaillant joined in the struggle urged by socialists to defeat the proposal provided striking testimony of the change in tactics adopted by them.

5. The French delegation to the Socialist International, meeting in Paris in September 1900, split along anticipated lines. Independents, Possibilists, Allemanists and most autonomous federations numbered among the defenders of ministerialism; anti-ministerialists included Guesdists, Blanquists and the Alliance communiste. Nor could the world's leading socialists take a definite stand. The resolution of Enrico Ferri prohibiting ministerial participation and supported by Guesde and Vaillant was rejected. The Congress approved instead the compromise of Karl Kautsky ambiguously condemning in principle the participation of a single socialist in a bourgeois government but acknowledging its usefulness in times of exceptional circumstances. Because the question was one of tactics, it was held that only individual socialist parties could make the appropriate decision.[30]

Later that month the Second General Congress of French Socialist Organizations opened its doors. Able to exert greater influence at home, Guesde and Vaillant at once made known their hostility to anything resembling the moderation shown by the International. The latter's biographer wrote: 'Vaillant was more intransigent, more immovable, more intractable then ever.' At the International's meeting, in the midst of 'indescribable tumult', he had publicly branded socialist deputies as 'accomplices' to the Chalon shootings.[31]

As the Congress nevertheless showed signs of seeking a compromise, bitterness mounted on the part of revolutionaries. When it moved to vote by delegates rather than mandates, so ensuring a ministerialist majority, Parti ouvrier delegates refused to accept the decision and, at the first pretext, marched out of the hall. The real reason for their departure was their minority position and inability to impose their views. Jaurès and Briand again defended Millerand's conduct. Although Briand found his proposed arbitration legislation incompatible with the idealism of the general strike, he argued that Millerand's work as minister more than fulfilled the goals set forth as deputy. Vaillant directed the attack on *ministériellisme,* but every resolution denouncing it or asking for the censure of assenting deputies was voted down. Then the ministerialist majority, preponderant after the Guesdist departure, fully absolved these deputies for supporting the government in the Chalon debate. Because of this vote ministerial deputies could believe there would be no criticism from their party if they continued to cooperate with other leftwing republican groups in the Chamber.[32]

Guesdists, meanwhile, organized themselves as a new party based on the class struggle concept. Blanquists were sympathetic but, hopeful of the Marxists' return, did not follow their example. Thus at the Third Congress of Socialist Organizations, boycotted by Guesdists (though Delroy attended and was subsequently expelled from the POF) and held at Lyons in May 1901, Blanquists revived the Millerand case. The Congress overwhelmingly rejected a Vaillant-backed resolution stating that Millerand, by entering the government, had placed himself 'outside of the party', and Blanquists and members of the Alliance communiste walked out to complete the schism opened at the Paris Congress. They now joined with Guesdists to form the revolutionary Parti socialiste de France, and the unity proclaimed in 1899 formally came to an end. Containing disciplined Guesdists and Blanquists (and, while repudiating ministerialism, incorporating into its platform the three Saint-Mandé principles), the new party was strongly structured. Although ministerialists defended reformist socialism and anti-ministerialists, the revolutionary variety, the struggle between them centered on the socialist minister. He took on ever greater symbolic dimensions, the attacks directed against him becoming more virulent.[33]

After the Paris and Lyons withdrawals, more young socialists wondered whether a more profound cause of the revolutionaries' opposition rested on the unspoken but real fear of the 'old guard' that it was losing much of its authority. In her reply to the *Petite République* enquiry in 1899, Rosa Luxemburg, no friend of ministerialism, pointed to *le cas* as a sociological rather than an isolated phenomenon. Every great spontaneous class movement of the proletariat, she said, does not respect the individual identities of the different organizations and threatens to sweep them away.[34]

The ministry continued to survive, and the gulf between militant socialists and Millerand widened. In 1901 leftwing dissidents in the Parti socialiste français also withdrew. They had accepted as an expedient socialist cooperation with progressive bourgeois parties and became dismayed by what they saw as the party's steady drift to the right. During the summer the impending visit of Tsar Nicholas II was announced. That revolutionary socialists would abandon the policy of cool reserve but courteous welcome given the Russian squadron in 1893 was a foregone conclusion. That the ministerialist party's executive committee would also ask socialists to refrain from welcoming the hated autocrat was less predictable. Millerand, as minister and adhering to the 1893 policy, found himself unable to comply, and the autonomous Loire-et-Cher Federation on October 9 asked for his expulsion. The move was easily defeated, but by the following January Allemanists and four autonomous federations withdrew from the party and completed the division in socialist ranks.[35]

Threats to expel Millerand had intensified, and Brunellière, to take an example of one important provincial socialist, revealed his irritation on hearing of them. Commenting on the objections to Millerand's presence in the official reception given the Tsar and Tsarina, he told two dissident Allemanists that he was 'tired of sterile cases', and told Hubert Lagardelle that he found the Millerand case 'unnecessarily complicated'. Millerand's representation in the party of a moderate and evolutionary element greatly diminished the inconvenience of his presence in the ministry. 'Our party cannot escape the common law of possessing a left, a center, and a right; and Millerand is part of the right.' Insisting only on a clear distinction between the party and Millerand, the Nantaise concluded that 'if Jules Guesde, Vaillant, or Allemane were ministers in his place, the question would be much more serious because socialist doctrine, the very essence of our party, would be destroyed. This is not the case here'.[36]

Brunellière might have spared himself the effort; revolutionary syndicalists, militants and now dissident socialists did not ease their attacks on the minister. As we have seen, they fought his every proposal. In announcing the visit of Nicholas II, *La Figaro* noted that Millerand had been denounced within his own party's higher councils and commented that he could not serve two masters: the party and the government it detested. Millerand underlined the comment and saved the clipping.[37]

That the left stepped up its attacks on Millerand scarcely deterred the right from continuing its own condemnation, and the minister provided it with additional opportunities. Perhaps in part to reestablish his social-ist credentials in time for the congresses of December 1900, he reasserted collectivist doctrine while speaking in Lens. The city was a leading coal-mining center in the Pas-de-Calais, with adjoining metals industries and textile manufacturing. Its working force supported Millerand, and dur-ing his visit on October 7 the streets took on a holiday-like air. Crowds gathered to hear speeches during the day; fireworks and dancing took place in the evening; and these demonstrations revealed the widespread popularity that a socialist minister enjoyed in the provinces. In his pre-pared remarks Millerand once more proclaimed the existence of the working class as transient. As at Lille a year earlier, he paid homage to the Saint-Mandé principles and specifically called for the peaceful social-ization of the means of production.[38]

For Jaurès, the speech offered further proof of Millerand's moderate yet still essentially Marxist socialism. Similar comments came from the other side of the political spectrum; Daniel heard it as 'a eulogy of col-lectivism', while Louis Barthou, already an important Progressist deputy and former minister, depicted Millerand as wholly faithful to socialist doctrine and hence still a dangerous protagonist. Barthou urged Waldeck-Rousseau to disavow his colleague, and the latter paused long enough in his Toulouse speech of October 28 – that previewing his anticlerical program and intended Associations Act – to state that 'the transfer by the state of private to collective ownership is not part of our program'.[39] When the Chamber reconvened the following month, Ribot accused Waldeck of contradictory behavior, Millerand of inconsistency and both men of wishing to impose socialism on the government. Millerand re-jected the charge, pointing to fundamental similarities between his Lens speech and one delivered as a candidate in 1889.[40] The cabinet withstood the attack, and the ambiguity with which it was charged must rather be ascribed to the right. On the one hand, it voted with anti-ministerialist socialists who accused Millerand of drifting from socialism; on the other, it denounced him for subscribing to collectivism. At Firminy, in January 1902, Millerand reaffirmed his commitment to 'the social ownership of economic power'.[41]

However, he remained faithful to the reformist outlook, invoking the need 'to guarantee the security of the house that shelters, together with tomorrow's ideal, today's reality', and calling on his party to define its position on foreign and colonial issues. He wanted it to assume the re-sponsibility befitting a great republican reformist party. Practical contin-gencies had to be tackled, for, in order to change the world, one began by modifying the *milieu*. If Daniel nevertheless continued to regard Mil-lerand as a revolutionary, the minister, in point of fact, was concerned with stabilizing the nation's governing institutions by having his party play an evermore responsible role within them. Notes taken in early December 1901 reveal that he was already thinking of strengthening the Presidency of the Republic and enlarging the electoral college for that office.[42]

The Tours Congress of the reformist Parti socialiste français, meeting in early March 1902, agreed with Millerand on his socialist status. This Congress, ignored by Guesdists and Blanquists and no longer attended by leftwing dissidents, was held in relative calm and hence at last able to establish some semblance of structure. Unlike the highly centralized Parti socialiste de France, it proclaimed the autonomy of the departmental federations, reserving to them the responsibility of enforcing party discipline, and this decision made Millerand accountable to his Seine Federation. In the program ultimately approved, the delegates took a decidedly reformist stand. Nowhere disclaiming revolution, they declared that it would be 'fatal to neglect in its name the great forces of legal action which in a democracy are at the disposal of the consciously organized proletariat'. The dictum that socialism was essentially republican prefaced a long list of reforms. At the same time the Congress appeased what remained of its left wing by deciding against future ministerial participation unless first approved by the party. Thus Millerand was neither applauded nor condemned, and for revolutionaries this constituted further proof of the embourgeoisement of the PSF.[43] But if repudiated by militant socialists, by the end of his tenure of office Millerand was very much a member of the reformist socialist party in France.

6. Only the briefest of summaries can describe the most significant of Millerand's remaining accomplishments at the Ministry of Commerce. Insofar as he concerned himself with implementing specific improvements in existing procedures, it was difficult for revolutionary socialists and syndicalists to vent their opposition. In a decree issued on August 24, 1899, Millerand extended workmen's compensation rights to cover all profit-making establishments. And in February 1901 he persuaded the Chamber to expand from fifteen to thirty days the time available to a worker to file his claim. In 1901 Millerand codified all laws, regulations and decrees relative to labor accidents and in a circular letter to the prefects asked that the benefit of any doubt be granted to workers. Then he made accident insurance more easily available to employers. The ministry also began the laborious task of codifying all existing labor legislation and decrees in order to arrive at a definitive text.[44]

Hygiene legislation was improved and extended to include sufficient heat, cleanliness, and time and facilities for workers' rest periods. De-

crees issued on May 3, 1900, prohibited women and children from working in surroundings specified as unhealthy. A magnificent example of
Millerand's thoroughness may be found in one of his circular letters to
labor inspectors. He instructed them to enforce an earlier decree calling
for a sufficient number of chairs for female employees of retail establishments. The minister defined 'sufficient' as meaning the same number
of chairs as the total number of women in each room, excluding those
intended for customers, and he required that notice to that effect be
clearly posted.[45]

Millerand himself become a model employer. In the part of the ministry concerned with the post, telegraph and telephone, he carried to
fruition some of the reforms proposed as reporter for the PTT budget
in 1891. He at once tried to eliminate the risk of saturnine poisoning on
the part of communications workers by requiring that all insultors be
made with leadless glaze. Before becoming minister in 1899, Millerand
had brushed aside the official retort of the Dupuy cabinet to a postal
strike then in progress; to the argument that the government must keep
public services operating, he replied that postmen asked only for a living
wage. We have seen that he had the state set an example in furthering
workers' rights to organize by establishing the Syndicat des ouvriers des
PTT, with a provision for creating shop stewards. Mailmen were also
organized, and a decree issued on March 2, 1900, granted PTT workers
a minimum salary and set a limit on hours worked. The minister also
improved the free medical services to which they were already entitled.[46]

However, his efforts on behalf of PTT workers could be denounced by
syndicalists. The young Léon Jouhaux feared that the Minister of Commerce was trying to seduce labor and integrate it into the state. 'Millerandism', he said, 'was a dangerous deviation' insofar as it made civil servants, and then ministerial agents, of some of the most active *militants*.
'Subordinating the actions of working movements to ministerial authority', he feared, 'would make the postal workers organization no more
than a tool in the hands of the government.'[47]

In November 1900 Millerand submitted legislation to establish free
state employment offices. As both Radical and socialist he had opposed
private agencies because they charged excessive fees for the services rendered. He estimated that an 'annual tribute' of seven million francs was
deducted from salaries paid to Parisian workers alone.[48] Like his Ten–
Hour Law, Millerand's bill provided for a transition period; it granted
municipalities of over 100,000 inhabitants five years in which to establish
free agencies and suppress private ones without indemnification. The
Chamber voted the measure, or versions of it, four times in the next three
years; on each occasion the Senate either rejected or transformed it

radically. In 1903, after Millerand ceded on the question of indemnity, the Chamber approved the measure by an enormous 500 to 16 majority. On February 3, 1904, after its supporters in the Senate capitulated on the compulsory suppression of private agencies, it became law, and France was ultimately provided with a network of state employment offices. In addition, and later that same year, Millerand submitted legislation calling on the state to subsidize the unemployment benefits administered by trade unions.[49]

More than a decade earlier, Millerand had called for improvements in water transportation, particularly in the merchant marine. As minister in October 1901, he again questioned the usefulness of basing government subsidies to private shipping on distances traveled, charging that this procedure encouraged and continued the construction of outdated sailing vessels.[50] Within two months the Chamber enacted legislation requiring that vessels maintain a minimum average speed in order to qualify for state aid. A provision providing for the state to defray the costs of installing armament on merchant ships revealed how Millerand was thinking in terms of national security. To an ever larger degree social legislation was justified, among other reasons, by its ability to produce a strong and united France.

As minister Millerand defended the Méline tariff of 1892 and held as necessary the subordination of special interests to the national interest. Greater importance was attached to France's export trade. In 1901 he told the Alliance syndical du commerce et de l'industrie that tariff stability constituted an indispensable condition to industrial development. As additional efforts 'to maximize the productive forces of the country', he submitted legislation designed to improve port facilities and inland waterways.[51]

The wish to increase national strength in part explained the impulsion given by Millerand to technical and vocational education. Vocational school reforms, reorganization of the National Conservatory of Arts and Trades and its endowment with property-owning rights, greater decentralization in general education and additional facilities for adult education were all regarded as falling under the purview of the Ministry of Commerce. They were provided for in a series of decrees beginning with that of October 11, 1899.[52] These decrees served as antecedents for the cabinet post of Undersecretary for Vocational Education created by Millerand in 1920.

There is even evidence pointing to Millerand's specific intervention in the area of foreign affairs. We find Delcassé wiring Constans, the French ambassador in Turkey, on June 21, 1901. The Minister of Foreign Affairs reported that his colleague at the Ministry of Commerce had learned of the German government's efforts to accompany its proposed railroad from Konya to Bagdad with a telegraph line. Millerand had told Delcassé that France would benefit from a similar line and even provided him with an estimate of the costs. Delcassé instructed his ambassador to look into the possibility of France receiving the same privilege from the Turkish government. We also find the French ambassador to Italy, Barrère, once in April and again in December 1901, expressing his surprise to Delcassé over Millerand's concern with promoting Franco-Italian industrial relations. It was at the end of the year that the Minister of Commerce approved the negotiation of a cooperative agreement between an Italian firm and Le Creusot. He said that he found it preferable for Italy to establish business ties with France, not Germany.[53]

7. The general legislative elections were scheduled for April 27 and May 11, 1902, and Moderates seemed more determined to limit the socialist vote than to enlarge their own. *Le Temps* called for a coalition with Radicals to 'free' the ministry from its dependence on collectivists, while Méline warned of the 'army of revolution' outfitted by the Minister of Commerce and asked whether Waldeck-Rousseau was blind to it.[54] Millerand anticipated a difficult personal campaign. That it proved the most arduous he fought and the closest he came to defeat was due to opposition from the left as well as from the right.

Aware that ministerial concerns with national issues might have irritated his constituents, he turned to local matters in the few weeks before the elections. And criticisms of the 'deputy from Bercy' in a Montpellier newspaper suggested that he was defending the interests of his wine merchants, albeit at the 'expense of national viticulture'. Millerand pointed to the benefits that workers in the XIIth *arrondissement* could anticipate from such enacted legislation as the Ten-Hour law, from a general increase in union growth and from such proposed legislation as a national retirement-benefits plan, progressive income tax, two-year military service and return to the *scrutin de liste*. Otherwise, he had to fall back on the work previously accomplished.[55]

Regardless of rampant industrial strife, issues like labor legislation and tax reform played a small part in the election. The major question was laicism; candidates addressed themselves to the government's recently enacted Associations Act. The right mobilized to defend what it called religious liberty, the left to assault clericalism. The outcome was by no means predictable, especially in Paris, where Nationalists had won a surprising victory in the municipal elections of 1900. Millerand faced the opposition of a highly placed Guesdist, René Chauvin; an Independent socialist, Alphonse Moutiez; a Nationalist, Doctor Pechin; and ten lesser candidates. Fourteen in all fought each other on the first ballot, and revolutionary socialists and Nationalists worked harder to unseat Millerand than to have one of their own elected. Guesdists campaigned intensively, estimating that the railway workers in the constituency would not forgive Millerand's 'betrayal' and that liberals had tired of his granting decorations to the 'reactionary bosses' on the rue Faubourg Saint-Antoine. Even the minister's friends predicted that he could not win a majority on the first ballot.[56]

Millerand expected some obstacles; he learned how widespread they were on appearing at his first campaign rally April 13. It was held in a local school, and according to newspaper estimates there were perhaps 2000 people within the building. Those who had arrived too late to enter remained outside in crowds. Most were hostile, and the uproar was tremendous. Millerand spoke only when he got relative quiet, coldly and without gestures. Guesdists berated the voters of the *arrondissement* for their earlier support of the minister, accusing him of duplicity and responsibility for the Chalon and Martinique dead. Millerand won the endorsement of the postal workers union, however; its poster said; 'He gave us the right to associate.'[57] A sympathetic local newspaper, *La Frende,* on April 27 reminded its readers that Millerand had his ministry for the first time admit women as clerks, that there were twenty working in the building on rue de Grenelle and that it was also during his tenure of office that the first woman was appointed to the Superior Labor Council.

Millerand fell short of winning a majority on the first ballot by some 700 votes.[58] Apart from that of 1889, the election was the first he failed to win at the outset since campaigning in the constituency. The runoff vote, he was all too aware, would enable his opponents to join forces against him in support of the runner-up, the Nationalist candidate.

Millerand stepped up his campaign, delivering a speech almost every day. Between April 27 and the vote of May 11, his Republican-Socialist Committee spent more than 7000 francs, of which the candidate's contribution amounted to at least 1000 francs.[59] A handful of major chords were struck and repeated. Millerand took pride in the accomplishments of what he called the Ministry of Republican Defense and at having been a republican-socialist since 1889. He equated his present positions on non-violence and the Russian alliance with those taken almost a decade before. Unlike the speeches, however, his posters and circulars became acrimonious. Millerand rightly attributed their increasingly strident message to the gutter campaign waged by the Nationalists; afterward he called it the 'most bitter, violent, and perfidious our constituency ever experienced'.

15

His campaign received an enormous lift, and victory was made possible, when local Guesdists announced they could not support Pechin and asked their voters to stay at home. Their newspaper in the district, *Le Courier du loi* in its issue of May 8–9 thereupon predicted a Millerand victory. Success was assured when the Independent Moutiez asked his supporters 'to defeat reaction' by voting for Millerand. Moutiez was subsequently assaulted on the boulevard de la Bastille, and he accused Pechin's hirelings of the act. In a final speech Millerand told his audience that its choice lay between a Nationalist and a Republican majority. The former, in defending teaching by the religious orders, threatened to revive old racist and religious wars. It threatened as well to interrupt André's republicanization of the Army. And in coming to the aid of company unions, it revealed its opposition to social reform, including the proposed establishment of a national railroad workers union. Given his newly won support, Millerand defeated his Nationalist opponent by 335 votes. Paschal Grousset experienced considerably less difficulty winning in the second constituency of the *arrondissement*. Other socialists did not fare as well: Viviani and Allemane lost to Nationalists; Guesde was once again defeated; but Jaurès was reelected. Brunellière warmly congratulated Millerand and found new praise for reformist tactics.[60]

Republican discipline managed to overcome an inconclusive first vote, which meant a victory for the forces supporting the government. Put simply, 339 ministerialists confronted 255 anti-ministerialists in the new Chamber.[61] Léon Bourgeois easily defeated Paul Deschanel for its presidency, pointing to its leftwing complexion. While Radicals needed socialist support and called for a return to the old policy of 'no enemies on the left', we shall see that the alliance established was directed not against social injustice but clericalism. The struggle against what Millerand called the 'economic congregations' would be largely neglected by victorious Dreyfusards.

On June 3, before the new Chamber could convene, Waldeck-Rousseau suddenly announced his resignation. His official letter to President Loubet gave ill-health as the reason and announced the Premier's intention to return to a lesser role in the Senate.[62]

The explanation offered was not wholly false; no doubt the cancer that was to take his life in 1904 had already appeared. However, as his papers revealed, particularly his private correspondence to Loubet, copies of which were sent to his ministers, Waldeck believed that the cabinet, in view of the election results 'no longer correspond[ed] to the exigencies of the present situation. It found its *raison d'être* in the disturbances of 1899'. The Premier reviewed the defection at that time of his fellow Progressists and admitted that his need to look to the extreme left in order to form a majority explained the presence in the cabinet of 'the most advanced opinions'. Although then a wise move and successful in staving off a threat to the regime, the situation had changed, and he refused 'to transform a necessary and happy expedient into a technique of government and permanent doctrine'. Today, Waldeck said, because of the Radical victory 'it was necessary to stop, if not retreat'. To demonstrate his concern over a large leftwing majority, the Premier sent Loubet a copy of the list of injunctions he had drafted during the campaign, guidelines intended for moderate candidates facing 'socialist-collectivist' opponents.[63]

Because it was vital that the cabinet hold its ground, it had encouraged the enactment of much social legislation. Waldeck could not have expressed himself, or revealed his opportunism, more clearly. 'We have been condemned to adopt as the higher rule', he confessed, 'placing above everything else the need to survive. ... We have had to make concessions in principle while striving to prevent their enactment. ... One day, to avoid defeat, we had to submit an income tax bill'; on another, 'it was necessary for us to take part in the debate on workers pensions'. Waldeck said that a more radical Chamber required a more radical government and predicted that his own would not last six months. To avoid debate and political repercussions, he would give poor health as the reason for his departure.

Loubet agreed that too many 'concessions' to extremists had been made and, reluctantly, accepted Waldeck's resignation. The occasion was the first on which a ministry voluntarily stepped down without having experienced a loss of confidence. According to Loubet, Bourgeois and Brisson preferred not to attempt to form a new one. Partly on the suggestion of the outgoing Premier, Emile Combes, a Radical Senator and former Minister of Education in the Bourgeois cabinet, was given the mandate. It was to be perhaps Waldeck's poorest choice.[64] Millerand's replacement in the Combes ministry was Georges Trouillot, a Radical deputy from the Jura and the reporter of the Senate 'Associations' committee that Combes had presided over. Millerand returned to socialist ranks as a deputy.

8. Most historians of the French socialist and labor movements have not described Millerand's work as minister. If his contemporary, they feared to generate the impression of taking sides; if writing well after the event, they withheld comment because Millerand's ultimate evolution discredited him. Yet, as Fournière said, he undeniably made the Ministry of Commerce, until then subordinate, a significant cabinet post. By themselves his accomplishments, using any standard of measurement, were

considerable, but as important was the impetus given to future social legislation. In evaluating the work of the ministry, Wallace Pipkin said that it 'ended an old period and began a new one, an opportunity opened for a fresh attack on old problems. ... The new century began in France with organized labor possessing a power it had not had before, and the government was committed to a policy of intervention in the industrial system'.[65]

Paul-Boncour, who was temporarily to leave the Socialist party because of its continued opposition to ministerial participation said that Millerand made more progress as Minister of Commerce 'than years of parliamentary discussion would have allowed'. He credited Millerand with making the Waldeck-Rousseau government the first openly to encourage independent trade unionism. Ironically, it was to be the future chief of the unified socialist party, Léon Blum, who completed part of the work begun by that ministry. Blum's collective bargaining act of June 24, 1936, guaranteed the right of unions to organize freely and, by providing for active government intervention in promoting the negotiation of contracts, ensured their right to speak on behalf of their members. In so far as the act spurred union growth and destroyed forever the absolutism of industry, it fulfilled objectives long-stated by Millerand.[66]

Regardless of the government's small but compact majority, few of Millerand's bills were enacted with any degree of promptness. The Senate was invariably hostile, and deputies showed themselves as hesitant in matters of social legislation. Their desire to economize was coupled with a fear of increasing taxes. Economic reform, Joseph Reinach observed, is always slower than political reform because 'interests offer more resistance than principles'.[67] Even when favorably disposed, legislators encountered slow-moving parliamentary machinery: the Workman's Compensation Act of 1898 had required eighteen years for passage.

The cabinet, furthermore, lived in the shadow of the Dreyfus affair; not until after 1905 did the nation turn with any deliberation to the work of social reform.[68] Waldeck-Rousseau, and Combes after him, subordinated welfare legislation to what they considered the logical conclusion to the work of republican defense; curbing the anti-republican religious orders. We have seen that Waldeck's inherent conservatism in matters of social reform led him constantly to urge moderation on Millerand. Most responsible for the delay, however, was the enormous opposition from both right and left.

Business saw in Millerand's work the seeds of collectivism. It accused him of denying labor the right to work and of attempting to subvert the economy. Even Poincaré, a defender of the ministry and still close enough to Millerand to *tutois* him, complained that the government followed socialist policy. The far left accused him of betraying the revolution. Anti-ministerial socialists and syndicalists repudiated the reformism that had marked the labor movement in the 1890s. They condemned and fought almost every bill proposed and every decree issued by the Ministry of Commerce. Reviewing their arguments and surveying labor's experience with a socialist minister, Georges Sorel wrote in 1911 that the movement had gained little by Millerand's participation. He estimated that Waldeck-Rousseau aimed at transforming syndicalism into a political organization designed to serve as an auxilliary to a democratic government, although in the process some palliatives would be accorded workers. Hubert Lagardelle said the ideals implicit in labor councils and in arbitration machinery constituted the government's only valid achievements.[69]

The opposition of Guesdists and Blanquists was particularly bitter – and discouraging. Usually the party leaders showed more hostility than did the rank and file, and their criticism, often unjust, had to be endured. Their uncompromising opposition may well have stemmed, as numerous witnesses have suggested, from feelings of resentment and fear over their loss of status within French socialism. Still, within each criticism there was a core of legitimate complaint. The Ten-Hour Act temporarily raised the number of children's working hours; retirement benefits were incompatible with the sending of troops to Chalon – Lafargue called it 'the pension of the dead'; and compulsory arbitration required workers to rely on the good offices of the government. Moreover, anti-ministerialist socialists assumed that increased attempts at social legislation worked to reduce the class-consciousness of the proletariat. French workers, regardless of their political enfranchisement, were denied basic economic rights until after World War II. Employers either refused to recognize trade unions or sought their destruction, thus rendering them unstable and instilling within them the need to preserve militancy in order to survive. In this context it can be argued that Millerand's efforts to integrate French workers into society without fundamental concessions having first been wrung from management may have been faulty. Perhaps both Millerand and Waldeck-Rousseau, as Pipkin observed, placed 'too much confidence in the machinery of state control and in the ability of trade and professional organizations at that period in France to meet the responsibility placed upon them. ...'[70] Regardless of the validity and ultimate justification of many of these observations, the abandonment of reformism begun near the turn of the century and intensified by Millerand's participation marked a radical departure from the emphasis placed on social legislation by nearly all socialists after their electoral successes in 1892 and 1893.

A single and illuminating example of the turn back to revolution was found in the review of Lavy's book, in the anti-ministerialist *Le Petit Sou,* on the work of Millerand. The writer stated that while the minister's efforts could not be entirely ignored, they were tantamount to 'draining a bottomless pit'. The implication was clear; once more socialists were to strive for revolution as the means by which society could fundamentally be transformed. Concurrent with the abandonment of pacific tactics by militant socialists was the rise of revolutionary syndicalism. We have seen that as early as 1901, at its Lyons Congress, the CGT repudiated political action. It was to take an even stronger stand at Amiens in 1906. The combined opposition of revolutionary socialists and syndicalists led one partisan to say of Millerand's work that given such intransigent resistance, the wonder is he did so much.[71]

The argument advanced by anti-ministerialists that Millerand had discarded his socialist trappings on becoming minister will not stand up. His position as minister required the observance of certain formalities: the presentation of elaborate dinners, the acceptance of medals and the decoration of powerful industrialists. These provided additional opportunities for attack. Admittedly the pomp and ceremony were not forced upon an unwilling Millerand. If he personally maintained a realtively simple regimen – preferring to walk and use the new Metro – he undoubtedly took pride in proving himself to his cultivated wife and providing his children with the comforts lacking in his own childhood. Tendencies toward orderliness and authority were strengthened, and a taste for executive power was implanted. Doctrinally, however, he remained what he had been. Jaurès wrote that Millerand as minister was as much of a gradualist as he had been as a deputy. 'What is true', he added, 'is that Marxism itself has increasingly turned workers from old revolutionary methods, and advised them to rely on the legal and gradual conquest of power by means of universal suffrage.' The conclusion of Georges Lefranc is correct: 'When Millerand left the Ministry of Commerce one can admit without hesitation that he remained faithful to his previous conception of socialism. He had never believed that working class emancipation would arise from a *coup de surprise* or from a *coup de force,* from a miracle or from the dictatorship of a man or of a party. He never believed in insurrection or in violence.'[72]

Whose was the greater initiative in the social legislation sought, enacted and decreed during the ministry? The answer of some contemporaries that most credit must go to the Premier clearly stands in need of revision. Despite the presence of nearly fifty socialists in the Chamber since 1893 no appreciable amount of social reform was achieved until Waldeck came to power. Still, the establishment of his government also marked the first appearance of a socialist minister. The evidence rather supports the conclusion that aside from those measures extending trade-union rights, Waldeck-Rousseau exerted more of an obstructive than a creative force.

With the exception of Delcassé, Millerand and his colleagues had seen their careers either promoted or regenerated by appointment to a cabinet post. Like the unknowns of Gambetta's 'Great Ministry', they helped to create a legend of Waldeck's prowess by paying unceasing tribute to him. Millerand credited him with much of the social reform accomplished. He endowed the Premier with a social concern that he said emanated from his father and described his Associations Acr as completing the work begun with the legal recognition of the trade unions. In continuing to display their respect and loyalty, the Waldeck-Rousseau ministers experienced a sense of solidarity forged in admiration of their self-appointed mentor. As he advanced in years, Millerand's own estimation and gratitude mounted. His readiness to identify himself with the ministry in the 1902 election campaign, although it could scarcely further his chances, has already been noted. After the death of her husband he remained devoted to Madame Waldeck-Rousseau. Almost four decades later a Popular Front government advanced some proposals and traced their antecedents to the Waldeck-Rousseau cabinet. In criticizing them in the Senate as excessive, Millerand took advantage of the opportunity to pay homage. While praising Waldeck's social work, he reminded his collegaues of what he identified as the former's primary teaching: that no social reform was possible without accompanying economic prosperity and that reform was to be justified by seeking class solidarity and attained by relying on gradual and progressive legislation.[73]

By 1902 the cooperation of the Premier in efforts to apply arbitration, enact a retirement law and reform the *octroi* were applauded by *La Revue socialiste* as 'serving the cause of social reform'. Observers pointed to closer ties between the Premier and his socialist minister. Daniel portrayed them as 'intimate collaborators', and Paul Strauss, a Radical and future spokesman for the Pension bill in the Senate, wrote of 'complete harmony' between the two.[74] In the preface to his *L' Œuvre de Millerand,* Lavy spoke of their 'warm support'.

Waldeck became something of an idol for Millerand, and the latter unconsciously began to imitate him. He grew even more silent and less prone to making metaphors. He placed an ever-higher premium on political independence, on material success, and may even have become skeptical of – though never hostile to – democratic processes. Moreover, Millerand never deviated from one principle held by Waldeck-Rousseau: to broaden the base of his support and avoid all issues calculated to divide a heterogeneous cabinet and its majority. Even so, it would be a distortion of fact to say, as did Barthou, that Millerand fell wholly under his influence and yielded to his very doctrines, methods and politics.[75] What is known of Millerand's earlier career militates against this interpretation. His work as minister continued and built on his work as deputy. And because he brought working-class support to the government, his position in it was necessarily one of strength.

The evidence, much of it in the Waldeck-Rousseau papers, suggests that in large measure the Premier regarded the social legislation defended as little more than happy expedients designed to ensure the continued support of leftwing deputies in the larger task of defending republican institutions, and, that task once accomplished, he refused to maintain his alliance with the left. In Pierre Sorlin's comprehensive and exhaustive analysis of his career, the Premier emerges as an opportunist with little conception of social problems and only a superficial knowledge of socialism. Never an idealist, he became a Dreyfusard because of the danger he saw confronting the Republic. Although one of the first politicians to envision social problems in nonpolitical terms, his solutions remained those conceived in the middle of the century, in provincial Rennes where large-scale industry had hardly begun and private charity still sufficed. His social ideas scarcely changed since his youth. He dreamed of conciliating workers and their employers and envisioned trade unions as a bridge between them, but much of his sympathy for the former was created by the uncompromising hostility of the latter. In other areas ripe for reform Waldeck remained prudent. Miners seeking an eight-hour day and an increase in retirement benefits were advised to show patience and to demand reform only when all interested parties agreed on the need for it. He rejected the principle of a minimum salary because he opposed state intervention in economic affairs; he refused to substitute the state, he told Millerand, for the free consent of concerned parties. On his deathbed he appealed to his long-time friend and Prefect of Police, Louis Lépine: 'You will say, won't you, that I have never been either a socialist or a Radical.'[76]

The various proposals for social legislation supported by the ministry were done so reluctantly and held as necessary to ensure its survival. The Premier regarded them as 'concessions in principle', and, we have seen, sought to 'impede their realization'. When Millerand asked for authority to set limits on night work for women and children, Waldeck replied that there were 'other, more pressing dangers'. By inclination and necessity, he preferred political to social questions. He let Millerand improve administrative agencies already functioning but refused to let him innovate. The latter's August decrees for the most part enlarged the responsibilities of the Bureau de travail. The Premier devoted himself to keeping his government alive: in three years the ministry replied to over 350 questions and interpellations, and Waldeck personally responded to 191 of them.[77] That he did so with repeated success constitutes his great contribution to the history of his country, that of republican defense.

The evidence reveals, however, that in the area of social legislation he remained essentially conservative. He never discarded his fear of socialism, indeed, never overcame a suspicion of abstractions. The Premier's testimony here, and the behavior that reinforced it, demonstrate that much of the legislation proposed and enacted between 1899 and 1902 belonged to Millerand. It was Joseph Reinach's estimate of Waldeck-Rousseau, not Millerand's, that was correct: he was a conservative, although an intelligent one.

11. Expulsion

Change with a party, however inconsistent, is at
least defended by the power of numbers. To remain constant when a party changes is to excite
invidious comparison.

WINSTON CHURCHILL, *Thoughts and Adventures*

Conception et méthode sont solidaires. On ne
peut être révolutionnaire en théorie et réformiste
en action.

MILLERAND, open letter to Jean Jaurès, in
La Petite République, March 15, 1903.

Waldeck-Rousseau may be held responsible for at least the opening phase
of the anticlerical campaign fought in the aftermath of the Dreyfus affair. We have seen the priority placed on his struggle against the religious
orders. Largely to implement the policy of republican defense, in part to
satisfy his leftwing supporters and possibly to shield the Army from further Dreyfusard attacks by raising an alternate target the Premier tried
to neutralize the church by striking at its educational and political power.
Direct action sufficed against the most belligerent of the antirepublican
orders, the Assumptionist Fathers and its newspaper *La Croix.* An
assault on other orders, or *congrégations,* required the enactment of additional legislation. However, the law finally passed by Parliament differed from that conceived by Waldeck-Rousseau; and the one applied
by his successor, Emile Combes, was in some ways antagonistic to it.
These distinctions must be insisted on; for Millerand and other Waldeck-
Rousseau ministers remained loyal to the program officially set forth
by their chief and with him denounced what they viewed as successive
perversions of it.

What was that program? According to the notes he made of his last
conversation with Loubet, Waldeck had informed the President of the
policy he thought best for the country, and they may be regarded as his
testament politique.[1] He urged the President to try to preserve the Concordat and, accordingly, retain budgetary provisions for religious expen-
ditures. The Premier said that he had fought not for the suppression of
the religious orders but rather for their control and regulation by the
government. The bill sent to the Chamber in 1900 – and previously approved by the cabinet – had required associations not seeking special

privileges from the state merely to supply a declaration of aims and a list of officials in order to receive authorization. Special permission, however, was needed if a group also sought legal status, which meant the right to receive legacies. Associations w th foreign affiliation, and this included the great bulk of the *congrégations,* would require state authorization in the form of a decree issued by the Conseil d'Etat. It was expected that orders considered undesirable by the government would be refused.

In his Toulouse speech of October 1900, Waldeck pointed out the need to regulate the wealth and widespread extent of religious teaching, considerations, he said, that had long rendered the orders threats to republican security. He rejected the charge that the bill aimed at destroying them; it only followed the example set by the Old Regime and the Ferry ministry in prohibiting the most dangerous. In 1902 he told Loubet that requests for authorization submitted by charitable and other 'socially useful' *congrégations* should be supported but that, in any case, each petition must be decided on its individual merits. The French embassy at the Vatican would thus be retained and continue to serve as an instrument of foreign policy. The Premier went so far as to regret the competition between Catholics and conservatives in the 1902 election; it had allowed Radicals to defeat many 'level-headed' republicans. He admitted to having kept the government neutral in those constituencies fielding a candidate who accepted a 'minimum' policy, that is, support of the Concordat. This resolute defense of the Concordat on the part of Waldeck-Rousseau was wholly in keeping with his view that hostility between church and state was largely an administrative problem and that priests were essentially functionaires who should abide by the rules set for all civil servants.[2]

The character of the Associations bill was radically altered by anti-clericals in the Chamber. Predominant in the Bloc des gauches, they first rendered the existence of the orders more precarious by requiring not a simple decree of authorization but a law – and the parliamentary debate it required. As a result of committee deliberation, it was also proposed that members of nonauthorized *congrégations* be denied the right to teach. Waldeck-Rousseau witnessed the marked transformation of his bill but, sensing the shift in sentiment, probably estimated that a misshapen act was better than no act at all. His repeated references to the necessity of applying principles of common law at all times revealed that he attached chief importance to its execution.

The Senate accepted the version of the bill received from the Chamber. However, the committee reporting on it, chaired by Combes, reduced to three months the period allowed the *congrégations* to apply for authorization. On July 2, 1901, the Associations Act became a law. Its impact would depend on the use made of it and that, in turn, depended on the attitude of the new Chamber and the new government. We have seen that the elections of 1902 considerably strengthened Radical representation in Parliament. Traditionally anticlerical, the party, along with its socialist allies, held church influence responsible for Dreyfus' condemnation. Seeing in the church a perpetual threat to republican stability, it eagerly took steps to disarm the clergy and republicanize the Army. Radicals also anticipated taking vengeance on the moderates who had long denied them power. And precisely because he reflected the more radical complexion of the new Chamber, Emile Combes became Premier.

The Bloc des gauches had substantially influenced, but had never dominated, a government headed by the energetic and respected Waldeck-Rousseau. Reinforced by the election and finding itself under a government headed by Combes, it could exert more direct influence. The new Premier, according to a student of the French executive branch of government, 'no longer offered to the powers of the parliamentary elements the passive resistance and haughtiness of his predecessor'. The 'délégation des gauches', formed by the various groups of the left, decided on tactics and proposed solutions, and, while it assured the ministry of a stable majority, it also assured the majority the continued cooperation of the ministry.[3]

Combes' resolve to enforce strict application of the new law coincided with the pressures exerted by the anticlerical majority in Parliament.[4] He struck first at nonauthorized establishments of legally recognized *congrégations*. Three thousand schools, in operation before passage of the law, failed to apply for authorization. All were required to close in eight days except those in areas having no corresponding lay establishment. To Vatican objections, the government replied that it would tolerate no papal interference; to the demonstrations that broke out in some communes, it reacted by enforcing the decision within the time allotted.[5]

When the Chamber voted penalties, including prison sentences, for infractions of the Associations Law, the government found itself armed and able to change significantly the procedure established to grant or deny authorizations. Whereas the law required the successive votes of both chambers to decide on a petition, the vote of only one was now considered sufficient. Hence a refusal by either to discuss a request meant unequivocal denial. Moreover, fifty-three male orders were not evaluated on their individual merits, as the former government had wished, but lumped together and collectively refused authorization.

Eighty-one women's *congrégations* were similarly disposed of.[6] In its unaccustomed enthusiasm the Chamber of Deputies found itself with little time to spare for social legislation.

To all these changes Waldeck-Rousseau objected strenuously in the Senate and was seconded, both privately and in public, by his former ministers. When Combes attempted to organize a 'délégation des gauches' in the Senate, the resistance organized by Waldeck was chiefly responsible for its failure. When the latter delcared that Combes had perverted the law of 1901, the impatient Premier offered to let his predecessor retake the government. However, Waldeck continued to insist that the cabinet reflect the composition of the Chamber – although he preferred to see at its head a Radical of the Léon Bourgeois variety. By the spring of 1904 the Chamber was discussing legislation to prohibit religious orders from teaching of any kind and was ultimately to decide on the dissolution in five years of teaching congregations already authorized. This was the direction taken by the government and the Chamber, unfortunately, from Millerand's point of view, at the expense of social reform and particularly his own bills. This situation was eventually to arouse his opposition and bring about his departure from organized socialism.

1. After leaving the ministry, Millerand moved his family into a residence in the suburb of Chateny Malabry, near Sceaux. Here his daughter Alice was born. He then rented the modest but comfortable house at 10 rue Mansard, a quiet street in Versailles. He ultimately purchased the house, generally lived in it during the summer holidays and was to die there. To maintain a residence and office for his law practice in Paris, Millerand occupied two apartments at 2 avenue de Villars, in the VIIth *arrondissement,* not far from the Eiffel Tower. With scattered exceptions he would remain at this address until 1935 when he moved permanently to Versailles. Living quarters were on the fifth floor, Millerand's office and working space, on the ground floor. The office was well furnished, with chandelier, bookcases and work table piled high with papers, brochures and books.[7] Through the many windows of the upper-story apartment, one could see the Invalides, Champ de Mars, Montmartre and the wooded hills across the Seine.

Photographs taken at the time accentuated Millerand's earlier distinguishing characteristics. His face and shoulders appear more massive, his hair, although still cropped, thicker and whiter, his back a trifle round. The general impression generated was one of relative health and well-being. A photograph, in possession of his eldest daughter, shows him almost smiling, rare for Millerand, and in evidence only when with his family. Still, it was Péguy's description that is best remembered: 'With his square head, those square shoulders, square forehead, that square will, square judgment, seated at a heavy oak table, that almost violent energy... .'[8]

Three of his four children were born by 1904, and all who remember agree that Millerand was 'very much of a family man'. He had numerous photographs taken of his family, many from the noted photographers of that period, Felix and Paul Nadar. He was no disciplinarian; the mother and children apparently made the decisions. He insisted that he only wanted them *content*. Even with his sons his modesty was excessive. He never conversed intimately with them, never appeared before them until fully dressed and was too shy to reveal his feelings. The picture is that of the bourgeois father, cautious, conservative, but entirely faithful.[9]

The passion for work had not diminished, and responsible for long periods of sustained energy was his great vitality and persistence. His papers give evidence of the reading accomplished and array of reports prepared. Serious and determined, he was described by Viviani as a 'cannonball with glasses, always moving towards his target, who acted as if there were no time to lose' but 'a good friend, faithful if severe'. According to Madame Petit, wife of the former staff member and colleague and friend of the family, visitors to rue Villars still included Caillaux, friendly until the bitterness which estranged them before and during World War I; Poincaré; the well-liked Viviani; and, at least until 1903, Jaurès. Stephan Pichon, his colleague on *La Justice* also came. But Sunday teas were reserved for other and different intimates – a countess, a duchess, a Catholic banker, all friends of Madame Millerand.[10]

As minister, Millerand was first exposed to wealth and a more elegant life style, and the dinners and the *soirées* of the ministry reminded him of his awkwardness. His position opened to another world. For example, Anatole France asked him to have Leygues, his colleague at the Ministry of Education, exert influence to have Madame Moreno play Daphne at the Odéon, and Anatole France thanked him afterwards for his 'concern with the arts'. Charles Jonnart sought Millerand's advice and support for his candidacy as Resident Minister in Algiers and became a close and valued friend.[11] But although a lawyer for twenty years, his practice had never provided him with meaningful income. He had little money of his own and none from his wife. Not until he became minister was Millerand able to afford life insurance. Now his growing family and his desire to have Jeanne compete on equal terms with the wives of his colleagues prompted a different set of concerns. Madame Waldeck-Rousseau, Madame Caillaux and other cabinet wives were cultivated, well-groomed women. Millerand was proud of Jeanne, who was attractive and possessed an aristocratic style, in their presence.[12]

His general health, as always, was excellent. Millerand retired early, did not smoke and preferred water, and his meals were for the most part frugal. For distractions there were parlor games and occasionally billiards, at which he was nearly always beaten. There were no sports or hobbies. He read little that was not official or legal, and what he did read was light. There was little music and no art, the chief recreation consisting of country walks. Together with his family he left Paris as early as possible in the summer and, thanks to the long parliamentary vacation, was able to return late in the fall. They did not always remain at Versailles but might be found at Karlsbad or Provence and above all in Switzerland, where he loved to walk, not climb, in the mountains.

In both his legislative and legal work, his ability to provide compromises and find common denominators had only increased. Georges Renard wrote admiringly: 'I have seen big businessmen, Social Catholics, and trade union delegates amazed at finding themselves in unanimity over a text which presented and explained by him, appears acceptable even to such diverse opinions. As little sectarian as possible, he welcomes and unites interests from wherever they may come, and asks only that they prove their sincerity by concrete acts.'[13] His faults consisted in pushing these virtues to an extreme. They included a lack of casualness, a chilling surface coldness and a tendency to speak his mind which sometimes isolated him from his colleagues.

2. In an age still foreign to expense accounts, Millerand found that he had spent nearly everything he had earned as minister. Possessing perhaps 1,000 francs in savings, he now faced the problem of supporting a family and in a style previously unknown to him. It was a foregone conclusion that he would return to the profession he revered, and with one or two gaps his law practice provided him with a substantial income for the next several years. Associated with Joseph Sarraute and Eugène Petit, Millerand plunged into law after 1902 and soon had one of the more important firms in Paris, able to charge fees of up to 20,000 francs. His cases were largely civil, and consequently he entered more fully into the world of finance and industry.

In the half-decade following the resignation of the ministry, however, Millerand involved himself chiefly with religious corporate interests and not financial ones. With a handful of other lawyers, most notably Charles Lyon-Caen, Millerand acted on behalf of several *congrégations* in the forced liquidation of their property and was heavily criticized for the income allegedly derived. The terms of the Associations Law of 1901 left no alternative but for lawyers to be charged with the liquidation of the goods and property of dissolved orders, a situation bound to lead to scandals and profiteering. Only in 1910 were receivership procedures put into the hands of government administrators. Moreover, nothing in the laws of the Third Republic prevented an elected official from continuing his private business, unless and until he became a cabinet member, an omission that encouraged hordes of astute lawyer-politicians to run for public office.

Millerand recognized that acceptance of any case with political overtones, certainly one having its origins in the government in which he had served, meant exposure to criticism. He nevertheless agreed to do so, and the explanation lies largely in his close identification with Waldeck-Rousseau. Millerand argued that the Associations Law presented a series of complex and delicate problems whose solutions depended on the way in which the law was executed. Receivers would establish principles of jurisprudence because the issues involved were totally new. Although some attorneys refused to involve themselves, either on grounds of principle or for fear of possible reprisals, Millerand estimated that his three years' collaboration with Waldeck 'demanded' it, and he was doubtless strengthened in his resolve by Combes' execution of the law.[14] During the course of the next few years he defended the interests of Augustins, Benedictines, Marianists, Franciscans, Jesuits and other orders and in the process made considerable sums of money. But he was accused of earning much more than he did, and his defense of the *congrégations* generated more political damage than financial gain.

He repeatedly denied receiving the hundreds of thousands of francs claimed by critics, and what evidence there is bears him out.[15] The figures found in his papers were generally in the hundreds of francs for only one case, and there does not seem to have been more than two or three a month. And, apparently, he did not take all he was entitled to. François Delasalle, a jurist acting as liaison between the receivers and the attorneys representing the *congrégations,* wrote to Millerand and other lawyers in the fall of 1903 in an effort to settle fees for the past year. He noted that Millerand had received payments only for his defense of the Augustins but had represented at least five other orders, and Delasalle asked Millerand to name his fee. The latter replied the next day that he had been sufficiently recompensed for most of the period and would leave the rest to the other's discretion. Delasalle reported this reply to a M. Menage, one of the receivers, and added: 'We know that he is not a man of money. Here is new proof of it. He is pushing disinterest too far. If you have remunerated him well in terminating the liquidation of the Augustins, should he not be paid for the thirty other defenses under your jurisdiction and the three before Duez [another receiver]? To ask the question is to answer it.' Menage's answer on the 22nd agreed but argued that it was not up to him to insist that Millerand be paid in full. Apparently he was not.[16]

3. In acknowledgment of his work as minister, Millerand was chosen to preside over the Chamber's Committee of Insurance and Social Welfare. With Jean-Baptiste Bienvenu-Martin, the Radical deputy for the Yonne and future Minister of Labor, he worked on new social legislation and on the projects earlier proposed, particularly the Pension bill. Committee work, rather than participation in Chamber debates, now stamped Millerand's parliamentary activity. Until the spring of 1904 he was virtually silent in the Chamber; a minister after 1899 and replaced by Jaurès in 1902, he would never again, as after 1898, speak for the socialist deputies. Trouillot appointed him President of a new extra-parliamentary Merchant Marine committee. Authorized 'to examine the situation of the maritime industries', it led to considerable correspondence between shipbuilders seeking government aid and an increasingly sympathetic Millerand.[17]

However, he devoted himself to securing additional social legislation. His social welfare committee soon discovered that because the powerful Bloc des gauches had turned the attention of the Chamber to the government's anticlerical policies, its struggle was to be long and arduous. To generate outside support, Millerand spoke before dozens of businessmen's and workers' groups to explain and defend the proposed retirement-benefits and arbitration plans. These speeches stressed the advantages accruing to the nation in the event of enactment. Mention was also made of the need for national prosperity to finance reform and of the indispensability of great public works programs to develop national resources and communications networks.[18]

Millerand's concern with the national interest and his refusal to distinguish it from socialist internationalism, though of long duration, had grown during his years at the Ministry of Commerce. As editor of *La Petite République* he detected a kindred spirit in Eugène Fournière, and, we have seen, wrote more candidly to him than to any other associate. As minister, he occasionally revealed his plans to, and congratulated Fournière on, the latter's various publications. In an important letter dated August 4, 1902, he praised his article on nationalism published in *La Revue socialiste*. A summary of the article's leading points thus sheds light on Millerand's thinking here.[19]

Fournière rejected the nationalism of writers like Barrès and Paul

Bourget as hostile to Jews, Protestants, Freemasons and nonconformists. He contrasted it with that of a Jules Lemaître, freed of clerical overtones and compatible with the Declaration of the Rights of Man. Accordingly, Fournière asked for the return of Alsace-Lorraine not in the name of some incomprehensible mystique 'in the manner of a Brunetière', but, to use a later expression, as a right of national self-determination. He granted that had Alsatians agreed to incorporation into Germany, Frenchmen would have had no alternative but to accept. This kind of nationalism, he argued, created no obstacle to international order and, in fact, formed a precondition for it. Accordingly, the writer hailed the French Revolutionary wars of liberation and regretted their transformation into wars of conquest. He traced the growth of aggressive nationalism through the nineteenth century, concluding that the willingness to resort to wars fought in its name would be brought to an end only by the establishment of an internationalist socialist order.

In a remarkably acute analysis, Fournière viewed Boulangism not as a conservative movement but as an early essay in nationalism and as such, natural, spontaneous and popular. Conservatives had profited because of the 'gross and stupid chauvinism' displayed. Responsible were French educators like Paul Bert, the physician-politician and Gambetta's Minister of Education, who 'stressed obedience and sacrifice'. An illustration of its growth was the degeneration of the Ligue des patriotes. Déroulède began as a Gambettist but reverted to a plebicistary. Fournière denounced as retrograde the conversion of a patriotism founded on the rights of nationalities to one based on force. A French annexation of the Palatinate, in the event of a successful war with Germany, would be as detestable as was the seizure of Alsace-Lorraine. The writer condemned both positivism and Catholicism as antirevolutionary and as having led, although for different reasons, to widespread support for the anti-Dreyfusard position. He also criticized socialism for its narrow doctrine, materialist metaphysics and stated willingness to use violence.

Millerand reported that one passage 'gave me special pleasure' and that meditation on it 'would profit many of our friends'. The question of Alsace-Lorraine had to be taken up, he said, or 'we must prepare for fearful misunderstandings and risk deplorable consequences. In my view you have admirably pointed out the question, as we must formulate it, of defining revenge as the defense of popular legitimacy. We have neither the possibility nor the right of renouncing that revenge. ... What you say of socialism and its errors is only too true. ... You have paid for your fidelity to the truth with your seat. I am sure that you will not wait too long for the revenge that is due you and us'.

Millerand published his views on the Alsatian question in his preface to a book on the subject appearing in 1903. He described the loss of the two provinces in terms of 'violence and injustice' and defended Frenchmen anticipating their return. Still, he specifically denounced reliance on force to repossess them, preferring arbitration and expressing his confidence that justice would prevail. Millerand compared the socialist position on the issue to that of the Radicals in the 1880s; it would most adequately be resolved by a program of social justice at home.[20]

There is evidence, then, of national pride and disenchantment with organized socialism after Millerand's departure from the Ministry of Commerce. He clipped and saved an article published in January 1902 that singularly reconciled collectivism and patriotism and which found antecedents for so doing in the Revolution of 1848 and in the Paris Commune. Nations were viewed as indispensable and as reflecting the need for European administrative units. In the face of 'hostile English lords and a hostile German kaiser' the French nation could not disarm; it could only strive for universal disarmament. The writer referred to the debt owed by civilization to France and found entirely credible the prospect of Paris serving as the capital of world socialism. German socialism was regarded as narrow and dry; a more humanistic variety was desirable, one conceivably couched in the very appropriate language of the French revolution.[21]

Millerand revealed his own dismay at what he called the 'aridity' of French socialism during the 1903 Berne Congress of the Association for the Legal Protection of Workers. In attendance were delegates from business, labor and government. The former French minister told the German representative, Alfred von Bülow, brother of the Chancellor, to try to control his bureaucrats, presumably balking at the prospect of international regulatory agreements. 'They are more doctrinaire and impractical', he said, 'than even our most stupid socialist dreamers. After all, industry must progress.'[22] Concern with French national interests and reliance on reform were not new for Millerand. Now he found the Chamber obsessed with anticlericalism and, exasperated, began to rethink certain socialist tenets.

4. Millerand's committee attempted to secure further social legislation. The Combes government lay stress on anticlerical measures, and the two were heading for a clash. In a rare remark to the Chamber (June 12, 1903), Millerand staved off a proposal to shelve old-age insurance as prohibitive in cost. Two years later he was still asking reluctant deputies for constructive criticism rather than intransigent opposition. He had promised, at the celebration of Jaurès' election and 'as a socialist', to

press for enactment of the Pension bill and had implored the well-wishers not to let the glow of victory blind them to still-needed social legislation.[23]

At a delayed celebration of his own victory held on December 2, 1902, Millerand spoke in the XIIth *arrondissement* and indicated the direction he thought his party must take. Centering on the implications of operating within the republican framework, his remarks constituted a mature and, as such, important exposition of reformist socialism. Millerand still considered democracy as the instrumentality of socialism and the Republic as the regime within which it was to evolve and which it must incarnate. 'The Republic', he said, 'is the political formula of socialism, as socialism is the economic and social expression of the Republic.' Since their entry into party politics, socialists had identified themselves with it and must therefore accept the responsibilities as well as the benefits of this identification. And that implied that while retaining their own characteristics and ideals, socialists would enter into relations with other democratic parties in order 'to take their part in the administration of the general interests of the country'.

He referred to the work of his friend, Joseph Sarraute, *Socialisme d'opposition, Socialisme de gouvernement,* as the best theoretical summation of the reformist position. It condemned the concept of the class struggle as wrong and dangerous under the republican regime and pointed to the necessity of seeing things from a French point of view. Labor could not remain indifferent to the troubles 'tearing apart the country' but had to participate if for no other reason than self-interest; history demonstrated that workers usually constituted the chief victims of civil discord. 'If socialism [Millerand said] has the right of awaiting its triumph only by the means put at its disposal by democracy, it has the duty of not neglecting any one of them... no evasion of responsibility, no weakness bordering on treason. ... Its duty is increasingly to become an organized governmental party, and, by peaceful means, under republican law, to transform socialist doctrine from sterile formula to living reality.' Specifically, parliamentary socialists could no longer ignore good management of public finances because reforms had to be paid for. While they must remain vigilant during financial debates, he concluded, it would be childish for them either to reject the budget or abstain from approving it under the pretext of orthodoxy.[24]

These remarks offered nothing very new; even the proposed modification of tactics could be taken as a logical extension of the views held by socialists since the turn to reformism in the early 1890s. Millerand's attitude and some of his words strikingly resembled that shown on the Paris Municipal Council in 1884. However, the suggestion that socialists approve the budget, as he had asked Radical councillors to do, represented a departure from previous party practice. Millerand defended his proposal by insisting that the party must display the courage of its convictions. If it chose to remain marginal, refusing its obligations, it should say so. If, on the contrary, it accepted responsibility and did not wish to limit itself to the role of critic and adviser, it should begin acting accordingly. The choice was to be made definitively at the PSF's next congress, at Bordeaux, and Millerand expressed confidence that reformism would triumph.

He also rejected the military metaphors favored by Guesdists. Logical and literal-minded, Millerand found them inconsistent with the acceptance of normal political action. This vocabulary, he said, might have its uses, but to talk at the same time about parliamentary methods was in effect to admit that the state of war was an image not to be taken seriously by any socialist. 'To storm a ridge by votes', a student of the movement noted in agreement, 'could hardly have sounded like the initial phase of a bloody insurrection.'[25]

This proposed 'politique de réalités' drew both criticism and applause. The revolutionary journalist Charles Rappoport accused Millerand of seeking counterrevolutionary reforms and of envisioning the revolution merely as a series of palliatives. These socialists, he said, 'view capitalist society as a frivolous woman who, after making repeated concessions, fully surrenders'. A moderate provincial newspaper pointed to similarities between Millerand's proposals and the tactics adopted by Gambetta. The 'great tribune' had acknowledged his failure to push through the Belleville Program at once and decided on a gradual approach. He called himself a 'man of government' and contended that 'a year of power was more fruitful than ten years of opposition', although shrewdly retaining a quasi-revolutionary vocabulary to ask for change. He looked askance at doctrine and shrank from panaceas, arguing instead that 'every day there is some progress to be made'.[26] There is much to be said for the comparison. As a Gambetta protégé, Waldeck-Rousseau was doubtless influenced by this attitude. In so far as his own influence on Millerand was immense, lines of continuity in the Third Republic were strikingly lengthened. Millerand's evolution, moreover, could not help but win the approval of old Gambettists like Joseph Reinach, sealing the reconciliation between the two men begun during the last stages of the Dreyfus affair.

Millerand, then, had proposed that his party modify its behavior in the new legislature by placing greater emphasis on the need of socialism to participate fully in republican politics. It may be taken as the tactical counterpart to his strengthened concern with reforms and with French national interests, but as little more than an extension along theoretical and tactical lines of the view of socialism generally held since 1893. In the bitter struggles over his own participation in government, however, militant socialists had already repudiated that point of view. When a majority of parliamentary socialists also chose to repudiate it, Millerand was to find himself outside of socialist ranks, although his direction had scarcely changed since his entry into the movement.

5. The former minister put these ideas into practice by voting for several controversial bills during the following months. On January 21, 1903, he approved the 'secret funds' clause in the budget of the Ministry of Interior, monies used in part for religious purposes. He explained that considering himself as having been part of a 'concordatory government' for three years, he could no longer join in 'empty demonstrations'. His colleagues in the parliamentary socialist group either voted against the budget, or, like Jaurès, abstained. Two days later, of all the socialists in the Chamber, only Millerand supported the decision of the Minister of War to have the government prosecute trade-union leaders at the Paris Bourse du travail for publishing an anti-militarist pamphlet, the *Manual du soldat,* encouraging recruits to desert. That syndicalism, and now militant socialism, were becoming increasingly antipatriotic was to be demonstrated in a survey of labor leaders taken by Lagardelle in 1905. All but one admitted to sharing antipatriotic and anti-militarist sentiments.[27]

On January 26 Millerand voted against a resolution submitted by the socialist Jules Breton calling for abolition of the *budget des Cultes,* and on the 29th he opposed another socialist motion to abolish the French embassy at the Vatican. Both his votes ran counter to prevailing party opinion – although most socialists acknowledged the futility of their action, and at least one, Sembat, could not take them seriously. Both votes also reflected the position held by the Waldeck-Rousseau ministry and, we have seen, were wholly compatible with the former Premier's last program. Delcassé in particular had urged that the Vatican post be retained for diplomatic reasons. It was becoming evident that the gulf separating Millerand and revolutionary socialists now extended between Millerand and Independents. Jean Louguet was to refer to his votes as 'especially scabrous'.[28] Early in March, in a series of newspaper articles and letters, there appeared open signs of dissent between Millerand and Jaurès.

At the beginning of the month, the former published a slim volume of speeches accompanied by a lengthy preface and entitled *Le Socialisme réformiste français.* In a review article in *La Petite République* on March 7, Jaurès called it 'a strong and beautiful work' and stated that Millerand was the same man as when he had first entered the party, a moderate socialist always advising his associates to avoid frightening the public.

However, Jaurès criticized what he regarded as the excessive emphasis placed on reformism and evolution.[29] Perhaps, he said, consideration should be given to other tendencies within the Socialist party. 'It is possible that the accession of the proletariat will be accomplished one day by extralegal means. None of us holds in the palm of his hand the secret of the socialist world.' Although far from substituting revolution for evolution, he went on, we must proclaim that the social order is not a mere extension of the capitalist order. It is our ideal that gives us strength. Jaurès admitted that democracy made possible political and economic organization and so freed the proletariat from resorting to 'hazardous force which never produces any real change in society'. Then he said: 'I would like to show Millerand by some examples that the very method which he advises, and that which he is right in advising, that of continual, legal and progressive action, risks being distorted or abated if the essential revolutionary virtue of social thought was no longer present in us and explicitly recognized by us.'

In an article published in the newspaper three days later, Jaurès affirmed that Millerand remained a collectivist. Proof, he said, lay in the latter's desire to achieve the 'transformation and enlargement' of private ownership and in acknowledgement in the preface of *Le Socialisme réformiste français* of the reality of class antagonism. However, Jaurès pointed to the absence of any program describing how this transformation was to be carried out. The basic fault in Millerand's position, he said, was his exculsive attachment to that which enlightened, fortified and organized the proletariat in today's society without sufficiently previewing the formation of a new one. On March 12 Jaurès again praised Millerand's work as minister and admitted that additional responsibility necessarily accompanied additional power. Still, the Republic was no longer endangered, and labor should agree to further participation only if the government allowed more socialist action in its program.

However valid Jaurès' criticism, he embodied the contradiction between idea and act that parliamentary socialists were unable to explain away. Moderate socialists like Millerand could argue that if, as Jaurès maintained, republican defense was no longer a pressing issue and should permit additional social reform, was not the obvious answer deemphasis of the struggle against the religious orders and work for such social legislation ready for enactment as the Pension bill? Jaurès was reluctant to do this because he was convinced, and with cause, that social and intellectual freedom would not be secure in France until the political influence of the church had been destroyed. The Associations Act had limited its power; only separation from the state would render the church politically impotent. That Jaurès was also very much concerned with party unity, and willing to compromise in order to obtain it, is a consideration to which we shall return.

Millerand's votes, particularly his refusal to abolish the *budget des Cultes,* had so disturbed the socialist world that on March 12 he was called to defend them before his own Seine Federation.[30] The Federation was debating a resolution to expel him, and, although its records no longer exist, the gist of Millerand's defense appeared in his Vierzon speech of March 14 and in an open letter to Jaurès on the 16th.

Millerand had already suggested that the party would do well to forego empty gestures. The Concordat between church and state, he said, was still a fact – thus necessitating state subsidies – and separation was to be brought about by legislation not by suppressing funds. Jaurès, however, found rejection of the budget not only helpful, but in need of affirmation by, and the sole means at the disposal of, the extreme left to remind the government of the goal in sight. He agreed that legislation was infinitely more desirable than withholding money to bring about the desired separation, provided that the Chamber and the government were committed to it. That they were in fact so committed, Jaurès found himself unable to acknowledge.

To reply publicly to criticism of his parliamentary conduct, Millerand spoke at Vierzon, a Blanquist stronghold, two days after his appearance before the executive committee of the Seine Federation. He was accompanied by Breton, Persil and Henri Sellier, a future General Councillor of the Seine Department. According to a witness there were almost 3,000 people in the audience and only one interruption, described as something of a record for the city.[31]

Millerand predicted the emergence of a classless society containing only associated producers, enjoying the same rights, possessing common ownership of the means of labor and receiving the integral product of their labor. The way to accomplish all this lay in ever-greater association on the part of labor and the steady application of social legislation. Consequently, further delay in the passage of the bills already presented to Parliament was impermissible. In a manner not unlike that of present-day democratic socialist thinking, he no longer showed concern solely with the redistribution of wealth but also with its total increase and so found that he could not separate production from labor. The proletariat would further its cause in a wealthy country. The socialist party, therefore, was no longer to identify itself exclusively with working-class interests but would best serve them by performing as a great national party. For this reason, although resolved partisans of peace, socialists would commit the worst of errors if France were in any way weakened as a result of their activity. Hence his vote against the authors of the anti-militarist pamphlet urging recruits to desert. That was anarchism, not socialism.

With respect to separation of church and state, Millerand declared himself no less a partisan than in previous years but as one who was unable to understand how it would be accomplished by rejecting a budget. Such tactics had been useful when the party was opposed by a government friendly to the church, clearly not one headed by Combes. On the contrary, its avowed anticlericalism created a new situation, which in turn called for new tactics. Suppressing funds, if voted, would only upset the first ministry really interested in limiting the church's power.[32] Millerand elaborated upon these remarks in an open letter to Jaurès published March 16 in *La Petite République*. While we both want separation, he said, Jaurès relies on traditional tactics. I believe mine are more appropriate. Socialists opposed the budget only because they knew their opposition would be futile, and the average deputy would most certainly have changed his vote if it had threatened, even momentarily, the life of the cabinet. Thus the party displays two attitudes – one when in power, the other when out. It must begin to take itself seriously, give itself integrity, and only by so doing win the continued support of the country.

Both speech and letter had concluded with a restatement of the reformist position. Millerand agreed with Jaurès that it was misleading to describe socialism as an extension or prolongation of capitalism. But he found it equally misleading to disengage and abstract certain characteristics of present society and offer them as its complete image in order to present socialism as radically opposed in order to justify revolution. Reality, wrote Millerand, is more complex and difficult. Present-day society cannot be considered as a whole, to be retained or rejected in its entirety. The most diverse elements constitute it, and some of them, like equal rights and universal suffrage, should be secured and developed by future society. Hence the usefulness of reformism, which Millerand said he was determined to defend at the forthcoming Congress of the Parti socialiste français.

The Seine Federation rejected the resolution to expel Millerand by a seventy-two to fifty-one vote. Those supporting exclusion had also wished to have socialist deputies held responsible to the party rather than to their consituents, as was the case with Guesdists and Blanquists in the Chamber. But they found themselves outnumbered by unsympathetic Independents and Broussists – the latter relatively numerous in and around Paris. Parliamentary socialists showed dissatisfaction with Millerand's conduct but preferred to let others take punitive action in as much as they shared an uncomfortable amount of the guilt. If able to prevent his expulsion, however, Millerand's supporters could not turn aside a vote of censure.[33] Both sides resolved to continue the struggle at Bordeaux; reformists wanted to see him absolved; militant socialists vowed to work for his exclusion.

In the interim, opposition to Millerand within the Parti socialiste français continued to mount. Two leftwing militant socialists, Gustave Hervé and Pierre Renaudel, reviewed his votes, one by one, in *La Petite République*. They concluded that Millerand had already cut himself off from other socialist deputies and, because of his preeminent position within the party, had inflicted serious damage on it. Because this dissent could only generate incoherence and threatened to substitute individual for collective action, they stated their intention to press charges at the Bordeaux Congress.

6.   The PSF's Fifth Annual Congress opened at Bordeaux on April 13, 1903.[34] The opposition to Millerand had based its plan of action on the reorganization procedures adopted at Tours the preceding year, particularly the stipulation in Article X of the party's constitution that local federations incurred responsibility for having members respect party programs and principles. The Seine Federation could be accused of violating this article and compelled to take action.

In separate speeches Renaudel and Hervé stressed as fundamental socialist doctrine the concept of the class struggle and, after examining Millerand's votes, found them wholly incompatible with it. He intended, they said, not limited collaboration but permanent alliance with the bourgeoisie, and they suggested as his possible motive the craving for personal power. They called for Millerand's expulsion from the PSF and for the repudiation of reformism as socialist strategy on the grounds that it tended to diminish class consciousness.

Joseph Sarraute, speaking as chief theoretician of the reformist view, referred to the dispute in terms of democratic versus revolutionary socialism and sought to demonstrate how democracy, becoming characteristic of Western European society, required fundamental rethinking of the class struggle concept. With political power no longer exclusively in the hands of property owners but rather invested in the majority of the people – capable of acting in its own interests – democratic socialism necessarily replaced the revolutionary variety. The 'revolution' had already occurred, and Millerand's conduct in the Chamber was only its logical and inevitable consequence. The Congress, therefore, was to judge not an individual but a philosophy of socialism.

Jaurès took a position between that of the irreducible opposition and the absolute defense. Placing party unity first, he spoke brilliantly to effect a great compromise. He insisted that Renaudel and Hervé were in error by refusing to recognize the democratic potential of French society. Sarraute was also at fault for overly emphasizing the impact of universal suffrage at the present time. Government was still very much influenced by economic power, and the proletariat must necessarily achieve economic equality before being able to operate freely in the political sphere. On the one hand, he said, it was a mistake to regard – as did Guesde and his followers – the state as only the tool of the class in power. On the other, if socialists must concern themselves with national interests, as Millerand had urged, they had to do so from the point of view of the proletariat. Jaurès acknowledged the complexities of the problem. Millerand's behavior, then, warranted criticism, for the difference between progressive bourgeois elements and socialism must clearly be delineated. Exclusion, however, was condemned as 'brutal, unjust and impolitic'. Self-criticism needed no justification, and socialism had to admit diverse interpretations.

A committee composed of one representative for each federation nevertheless submitted a resolution calling for Millerand's expulsion 'on the grounds of his anti-socialist votes'. That the Congress rejected it was due to Jaurès' last-ditch fight. The impassioned leader beseeched the party to admit the right of free thought. Millerand, he insisted, was already censured by implication, and his exclusion might easily lead to similar purges within the local federations. A number of newly convinced delegates then declared that their mandates were not binding. On condition that Millerand engage himself to respect future party decisions, they gave the Jaurès counter-resolution a small majority. The congress closed with Millerand still an accredited member of the Parti socialiste français.[35]

No longer in the government and therefore able to participate in party gatherings, Millerand had spoken on his own behalf. He once more attempted to demonstrate how each of his votes had been consistent with reformism and then told the assembled delegates: 'If you stand for revolution, exclude me. I cannot share that idea, contradictory to my conduct and to yours for the past ten years.' He called himself a socialist-republican, maintained that he had never separated the two and would continue to serve both causes. After Jaurès had implored the delegates to forego expulsion, Millerand promised to be 'a disciplined soldier of his party' in as much as he was in accord with it on the issue of ministerial participation. Consequently, he could conceive of no difficulty to prevent him from obeying its decisions and walking 'hand in hand' with other socialist deputies. He would retain the right of initiative, however, to propagate his reformist views. Millerand's defense, then, had rested largely on his long-standing repudiation of violence. However, he had spoken of class solidarity as well as class struggle, maintaining that both were facts and identifying the ultimate objective of socialism with the former. He had also argued that there were no longer grounds on which to distinguish national interests from those of the proletariat; and the Congress, by retaining Millerand as a member of the party, implicitly accepted these conditions.

In his bimonthly *chronique,* Lagardelle admitted that Bordeaux signified a triumph for the evolutionists, and he held Jaurès responsible. The Congress, he said, definitely consecrated Millerand's theories and practices in so far as none of the delegates had protested when he claimed that all of them were in accord on fundamental reformist principles. Another observer agreed – and could not help but note that Jaurès had shown himself more arduous in Millerand's defense than had Millerand himself. But although *Millerandisme* won at Bordeaux, the Yonne Federation, Hervé's own grouping, refused to submit and withdrew from the PSF. The revolutionary Somme Federation withdrew later in the summer. These departures may well have persuaded Jaurèssists that the more militant elements among them could never accept the emphasis placed by Millerand on readily attainable objectives and made them aware of the need to seek firmer ground.[36] At the very least, we may conclude that regardless of the decision to absolve Millerand, and by implication to leave room for reformism, the Parti socialiste français was far from united. It was, in fact, returning to the revolutionary stand already taken by Guesdists and Blanquists.

7. Within a month of the Bordeaux Congress Millerand had his committee prepare a modified version of the Pension bill to present to the Chamber. He defended his Trade Union and Arbitration bills at the Université populaire of the Faubourg Saint-Antoine on May 16 and scored a success when the Chamber, before adjourning for the summer holidays, enacted into law his decree forbidding the use of lead in industrial paint. But it took no action on the national retirement-benefits plan. On June 15, visibly disturbed, Millerand asked for its speedy passage. He forced the issue: did or did not Parliament want old-age insurance 'to fulfill the promise made by the Revolution, to grant the right of life to the aged?'[37]

The Combes government provided little or no executive pressure; it continued to preoccupy itself with the religious associations and was now drafting legislation to outlaw all teaching orders. On the 27th Millerand sent a letter to the Premier, restrained in tone but reminding Combes that the committee awaited the government's decision whether to support pending retirement benefits.[38] Turot wrote the same day in *La Petite République* that the ministry must seize the opportunity to prove it was not hypnotized by the *congrégations* and could carry out a democratic program. Old-age insurance had been promised and a refusal to comply was tantamount to treason; a government could not rely on a wholly negative program.

Signs of dissatisfaction with Combes' anticlerical programs were shown by Waldeck-Rousseau. Socialist complaints were registered as early as 1902. Two months after the formation of the Cabinet, a writer in *Le Mouvement socialiste* questioned the legality of Combes' decrees and commented that 'exaggerated anticlericalism has not always prevailed within the socialist party'. He found it 'regrettable that socialism must be delayed by useless violations of individual sensibilities' and concluded that the party 'truly has better things to do than endorse the ministry's anticlericalism'.[39]

Nonetheless, by the spring of 1904 Radicals and socialists in the Chamber were considering the legislation to prohibit religious orders from teaching – and ultimately decided on the dissolution in five years of teaching *congrégations* already authorized. When Waldeck-Rousseau denounced Combes on the floor of the Senate June 29, 1903, parliamentary socialists called him to task for it. Only adversaries of the Associations Act appreciated the speech, they charged, and Waldeck ought to take seriously the work he himself began.[40] Writing in *La Petite République* July 7, Jaurès admitted the absence of reform but avowed that Parliament would not be duped by those wanting to use the social question to make it renounce or even ease the struggle against the political power of the church. The republican majority, he promised, would persevere until the job was done.

Millerand seemed particularly distressed by Waldeck-Rousseau's condemnation of Combes. He wrote to Brunellière urging him to read Waldeck's speech and, we may assume, urged others to read it too. The former minister was as critical of Combes' style as he was of his politics; ministers, he said, ought to be more 'cold-blooded' and less 'nervous'. Brunellière agreed but feared that an early reversal of the ministry would lead to 'insurmountable difficulties' and, like Jaurès, argued that it was necessary to complete the struggle against the church. It would be far worse, he said, to have a government afraid of it.[41]

French socialists were diverted from these questions when, during the summer, they learned that at its Dresden Congress the German Social Democratic party passed a resolution reaffirming the orthodox conception of the class struggle – and its consequent emphasis on revolutionary tactics – to defeat decisively the revisionist movement within its ranks. Conservatives in France anticipated seeing socialists everywhere forced to shed their gradualist trappings. According to *La Petite République*, militant socialists were 'now obliged to consider reformists as heretics, schismatics, and second class citizens'. Jaurès promised that French socialists who hoped to profit from the Dresden Resolution would be disappointed. Although strong and united, he declared, German socialists lived under an empire while those in France benefitted from a democracy.[42]

When the Chamber reconvened in the fall and took up the budget of the Ministry of Interior, Millerand kept the promise made at Bordeaux. Rather than approve, he abstained from voting on the resolution to suppress the secret funds provided therein. A number of other parliamentary socialists also refused either to support or reject this budget.[43]

However, he found himself unable to agree with other socialists during discussion in November of the budget of the Foreign Affairs ministry. The socialist deputy, Hubbard, had asked the government to propose an international agreement on the limitation of arms. Speaking for the ministry, Delcassé said that if proposed by another nation France would willingly follow suit. However, it seemed wholly inappropriate for the defeated nation to take the initiative in questions of disarmament. The Hubbard resolution received only sixty-one votes, but Millerand was the only socialist to vote with the great majority supporting Delcassé. He had again implanted himself in what he regarded as grounds of principle and as a result had again broken with his party, even with those in it most sympathetic to him. Brunellière wrote to a colleague at the beginning of January 1904 that Millerand was wrong to reject revolutionary socialists as anarchists. They constituted a force able to balance 'state socialism'. Ever hopeful of unity, the Nantaise maintained that it was necessary to retain two wings in the party, provided that each could endure the other.[44]

The Seine Federation met at the beginning of January to debate Millerand's vote on the Hubbard resolution. Like others in France, this Paris-based federation resented the independence displayed by socialist deputies. Its membership, now under leftwing control, had already censured Millerand prior to the Bordeaux Congress, agreeing with Renaudel's position. It customarily met on the premises of a 'people's university', 'La Fraternelle', on the rue de Saintonge, and, remaining faithful to its militant stand, was ultimately to join the Communist International. The Federation expelled Millerand from its ranks and, consequently, from the Parti socialiste français. The relevant resolution stated that 'despite his promise to walk hand in hand', Millerand's 'disastrous individualistic policy' violated socialist doctrine. Especially denounced was the vote of

November 23, 'where of the entire parliamentary socialist group, he alone voted with the reactionaries'.[45]

The reaction from his former colleagues on *La Petite République* was swift and unequivocal. In coming to Millerand's defense, the editor-in-chief, Gerault-Richard, wrote that the move 'knocked out one of the most useful, most creditable and sincere *militants* of our party...'. The reasons offered were fraudulent because Millerand was not remiss on any point in either program or doctrine. When the socialist party called for international peace and simultaneous disarmament, it never stipulated that France could not take the initiative. 'But it was necessary to lash out. Our party suffers from religious atavism. It periodically feels the irresistable need to establish dogma, to excommunicate heretics. It does not judge facts in themselves, but only after contingencies.'[46]

Turot agreed the next day that Millerand's vote in no way betrayed the party, and he asked whether socialists intended to deny freedom of expression within it. In a later article he recalled the occasion when Millerand, as editor-in-chief and although reluctantly, printed a strong article in favor of the general strike and then replied to it. Jaurès remained silent; he did not want to add to the argument and further divide the party. According to his biographer, he was also 'strangely confused' and caught on the horns of a dilemma. He had favored reformism while recognizing the virtues of revolution but had begun to wonder about the costs of collaboration with the Bloc des gauches: Millerand's expulsion, his party's antisocialist votes, 'the easy confusion between reformist socialists and Radical-Socialists, and above all the discontent of the party's rank and file'.[47]

His own Comité socialiste in Carmaux, however, regretted the expulsion and let the former minister know of its views. Other declarations of support came in letters and telegrams from diverse sources: a group of socialist deputies, the association of postal workers, some masonic lodges, a socialist group in the XIVth *arrondissement,* which subsequently withdrew from the Seine Federation, various sections of other federations, the Montmartre section of the Vigilance Committee, mutual aid organizations, general councils and government administrators. Millerand saved thirty-seven such communications from private individuals and over fifty from assorted groups.[48]

In some cases he received testimony of the devotion of the socialist rank and file. *Le Mouvement socialiste* published the good wishes and letters of encouragement from the socialist committee of the XIIth, and also from the XIIIth, XIVth, XVth, XVIIIth and XIXth *arrondissements*. Whatever their form of expression, they all identified Millerand with socialism.[49] This evidence is doubtless impressionistic and fragmentary.

Still, it suggests that Millerand continued to receive support from the rank and file in and outside of Paris. There was no question but that he retained the support of a majority of his constituents. He continued to profit immeasurably from the *scrutin d'arrondissement* which enabled him, like countless others in the Third Republic, to remain active in politics regardless of the lack of any party support. That Millerand nevertheless persisted in his long-standing opposition to this voting system and was to campaign even more strongly for a return to departmental-wide constituencies was not the least paradoxical aspect of his career.

The reactions of other prominent socialists followed anticipated lines. The Blanquist Louis Debreuilh, now secretary of the revolutionary Parti socialiste de France, predicted that Millerand's expulsion would lead to the dislocation of the rival reformist party. He pointed out that Millerand was first denounced by militant socialists four years earlier but admitted: 'We were never able to accuse him of ambiguity, although the same could not be said for Jaurès.' The militant Longuet exulted and saw chances for a united revolutionary party as very much improved. But Georges Renard continued to question the distinctions that socialists insisted on making between the conduct of municipal and general councillors, mayors and deputies, on the one hand, and ministers on the other. He also failed to appreciate the procedures of deputies who reported on parts of the budget, even voted for sections of it, but had to reject the final product. Brunellière apparently overcame his earlier bewilderment over Millerand's votes. He disapproved of the Seine Federation's act, 'which is in general badly seen here'. He vowed that he would not attack what he called Jaurèssian socialism, promising that if his name were again used by those who did he would disclaim the action. He assured Millerand that he was and should remain the leader of a reformist socialist party and that he continued to hold working-class support.[50]

Writing in *La Petite République* January 17, one of Millerand's defenders in the Seine Federation, Heppenheimer, stated flatly that the expulsion was not a political act but the simple revenge of a hostile minority. The diverse factions within the Federation had supported the move only because many of them now saw the sacrifice of Millerand as the only means by which peace and unity for the party could be assured. Thus reinforced, the minority which three times in the past had failed to drive Millerand out of the party was now able to do so.

The reaction of the bourgeois press was understandably sympathetic. If *Le Temps* may be cited as our example, the great republican daily reminded its readers of Millerand's speech of June 10, 1895, rejecting Hanotaux's decision to send a naval squadron to Kiel as incompatible with French dignity. He had then received the support of socialist deputies. The newspaper wondered why after 'five years of power' – three with Waldeck-Rousseau and two with Combes – socialists had not reinforced the position taken in 1895. They instead opposed the policies every government must take, and *Le Temps* warned Frenchmen to take the lesson to heart. If this was the treatment accorded a socialist who refused to submit 'body and soul', it said, imagine that planned for the bourgeoisie.[51]

The response of Millerand's first political mentor was conspicuous for the number of contradictions it contained. Clemenceau wrote in *L'Aurore* January 7 that Millerand could not be taken as even a Radical-Socialist: he had failed to oppose the use of troops at the scene of a strike. Although he had somehow managed as minister to retain his personal honor, Millerand was woefully deficient in the discipline expected of socialists. Responsible for changing his views in the past few years was the influence exerted by Waldeck-Rousseau. Yet in professional politics the beginning of wisdom lay in one's ability to make concessions and acquire a spirit of conservation.

Although enjoying the right to do so, Millerand decided not to appeal the decision. In an exclusive interview granted to *Le Temps,* he said that after three years with Waldeck-Rousseau he had felt the need to defend himself at Bordeaux. The Congress approved, and he chose 'not to begin over again'. One detects in the words a trace of the frustration doubtless influencing his decision. He said that he intended to remain a socialist, if not within the party, then as an Independent. A more complete, but essentially similar, explanation is revealed in his private correspondence. Edgar Milhaud wrote to Millerand on January 7 to report the view of the *Vorwärts* correspondent, Kreitchewsky. The latter had written that Millerand was ousted, while others in the parliamentary group shared his views. Milhaud urged Millerand to appeal. In his draft reply, however, Millerand viewed the incident as 'inevitable' and as the 'fatal result of the party's ambiguity' – it could not flirt with revolution and reform at the same time. He wrote: 'In these conditions I am not disposed to reopen the struggle fought out at the Bordeaux Congress: I do not see how it would be useful. I remain scrupulously faithful to the program I always defended in the ranks of the socialist party. My adversaries, in striking out at me, are the first to admit it. It is, therefore, the policy, much more than the man, that is being attacked. If one feels that his program is right, he must have the courage to defend it, regardless of the consequences, to the end.'[52]

Resentful of other socialists for insisting on his expulsion rather than his proposed legislation, Millerand conveyed an impression of relief, or at least indifference. Dubreuilh estimated that he viewed his departure as a positive benefit; he would no longer be encumbered by his party. Given Millerand's taste for independence and the extent of the rupture between him and other socialists, the interpretation may be sound. Or, Millerand may have been putting the best possible face on things. At any rate, three days after his expulsion he was speaking at the College des Hautes Etudes sociales on the need for improvements in vocational education.[53]

Some contemporaries and at least one historian of French socialism believed that Millerand's expulsion was in no way foreordained. Charles Andler wrote that 'his ultimate evolution would without doubt have been different if the French socialist party could have overcome its envy of the *élus* whom, following public opinion, it had accredited. Its hostility, however, was such as to make it impossible for them to do the work the party had prepared them for'. In his history of the socialist movement, Georges Lefranc wrote that Millerand 'had suffered criticisms, sometimes unjust, often wounding'. Could he have recouped his popularity? Albert Thomas, noted Lefranc, fell from grace within the SFIO during the 1918–1920 period. However he regained sufficient prestige, thanks to his work in the International Labor Office, to become once more a leader of the party. Millerand lacked any such vehicle for redemption, and he was soon caught up again in political manoeuvering. Paul-Boncour put his finger on the 'drama of all the dissidents, especially those in Parliament', when he wrote: 'A socialist in government can hardly remain a socialist if socialism is not there to support him.' And he added that 'socialism in power was the only kind that mattered unless a revolution was going on'.[54]

It will be recalled that the vote leading to Millerand's expulsion – his refusal to have France take the initiative in proposing general European disarmament – matched in content and language the position taken in his 1893 speech celebrating Sembat's election.[55] No other single exhibit demonstrates so well the basic consistency of Millerand's conduct. If he no longer found himself in accord with his colleagues, it stemmed from a shift to the left by French socialism, first revolutionaries inspired by Guesde and Vaillant, then a majority of reformists. However, the breach between Millerand and other socialists was made irreparable by his momentous decision to attack the Combes ministry.

8. Together with other republicans in the Bloc des gauches, socialists remained preoccupied with the ministry's anticlerical legislation. On March 3, 1904, Jaurès spoke in favor of suppressing the teaching orders. Combes defended the proposed legislation on March 6, and within a few days the Chamber began discussing it. By the middle of the month *La*

Petite République noted that no time seemed available for retirement benefits. A contemporary put it more bluntly: social reform had ground to a halt, and employers enjoyed a respite from government interference on behalf of their workers.[56]

As early as July 1902 some concerned Blanquists stated their intention to inform Parliament that the anticlerical struggle as then pursued constituted a digression, turned aside the proletariat from agitation and made it await with patience 'the reforms promised and anticipated for thirty years'. A month later *Le Mouvement socialiste* acknowledged that 'the struggle against clericalism monopolizes socialist energies'. In its November and December issues of that year the periodical printed replies to an inquiry it had initiated on 'anticlericalism and socialism' and found that Europe's leading socialists shared this opinion. Emile Vandervelde recognized the historical roots of anticlericalism in France but wondered whether it did not constitute 'an excessive expenditure of force and energy, better consecrated to more essential tasks'. Karl Kautsky agreed that 'to engage the proletariat side by side with the bourgeoisie in a new *Kulturkampf* [was] to misdirect its revolutionary impetus, to dissipate without profit its revolutionary force'.[57] More than a year later *L'Humanité* said it had to admit that the reforms promised by Combes had not been carried out. Millerand's sympathizers found this reprimand exceedingly mild and pointed out that the militant socialists who reproached the Waldeck-Rousseau ministry with having emphasized anticlericalism at the expense of social reform made few such criticisms of Combes. Moreover, as one Independent newspaper protested, Millerand's successor at the Ministry of Commerce had not continued along the lines laid down; Trouillot was also charged with failing to consolidate the work accomplished.[58]

We have seen that Millerand, on at least three occasions, publicly vowed to work for enactment of the Pension bill: at Carmaux in October 1902; in his constituency on December 3 of that year; and at Vierzon in March 1903. He had successfully fought against returning it to committee and fought in vain against returning it for further study, the act effectively burying the measure. Throughout early March 1904 the Chamber debated the proposed law on the teaching orders. During one such debate, late in the afternoon of March 17, the presiding officer of the Chamber interrupted a speaker and announced to the startled deputies that Millerand wished to question the government on its intentions about the retirement-benefits plan. Combes agreed to hear him at once, and Millerand walked to the tribune in the midst of a great silence.[59]

The deputies were very much aware that up to this point Millerand had avoided all debates on current policy and had consistently supported the cabinet – as the socialists had so carefully observed. They knew that he had confined himself to committee work and had made intense efforts on behalf of his unfinished legislation. They were less aware of the extent of his dissatisfaction at watching Combes apply the Associations Act in a manner which, for Millerand, was incompatible with the intentions of its author. Rather than used as the instrument designed by Waldeck-Rousseau to suppress the most belligerent *congrégations* and to achieve understanding between the Republic and other religious orders, it was wielded, he wrote in his *Mémoires,* as the 'propitious weapon' òf militant anticlericalism.[60] Millerand had approved, but silently, Waldeck's futile attempts at protest.

He now told the Chamber that the comittee finished its study of a modified pension plan as long ago as January 1903, sending the text to the Premier and copies to his Ministers of Finance and Commerce. Only on July 1 had Combes replied. Although approving the bill in principle, the latter revealed his plan to present it to the legislature only at the end of its mandate; suppression of the orders necessarily took precedence. Rouvier, the Finance Minister, refused even to reply to letters from the committee asking him to consult with it. Millerand questioned Combes' attitude, for it contradicted the promises made at the time he assumed office to work for the enactment of pending social legislation. A government, Millerand warned, must not limit its horizons and ambitions in the struggle against the *congrégations.* He credited Waldeck-Rousseau with never sacrificing reform, indeed, never distinguishing social action from republican defense.

The moment for old-age insurance, moreover, was never more appropriate. Parliament recently passed legislation granting assistance to the infirmed and in so doing again advanced the principle of a national retirement-benefits plan. And refusal by the government to take action was benefitting the right. The previous month, he pointed out, the upper house approved legislation establishing state employment offices, but the compromise making it possible was offered by a conservative. A royalist in the Senate recently asked that prud'homme jurisdiction be extended. Absorbed by the struggle against the orders, the government and its Radical majority had abandoned reform to others and, by allowing conservatives to regain the initiative, imperiled progressive elements within the country. He assured Combes that he was in full agreement on 'the necessity of pursuing the laic work of the Revolution' but warned that the ministry would lack both the means and the force to do it if at the same time it did not carry out a program of social reform.

Combes acknowledged Millerand's cooperation in the conflict with the *congrégations* and only regretted that the latter had seen fit to interrupt it at its most critical moment. He attempted to prove that the ministry, far from being absorbed by religious matters, still concerned itself with social legislation and cited numerous bills and plans for military and fiscal, as well as religious, reform. In regard to retirement benefits, various proposals had been placed before the National Assembly since at least 1892, and he said that he failed to understand why the present government was reproached with dereliction when that containing the questioner himself had been unable to see its own plan realized. The challenge, concluded Combes, fooled no one. Its promoter hoped to divert the Chamber in its campaign against the orders. Millerand denied it was a question of personalities or that the Pension bill was a diversion. He submitted a resolution affirming the will of the Chamber to enact, with required ministerial assistance, the necessary legislation.

The proposal was warmly received by the right, long hostile to the Radical-dominated and socialist-supported government. If it also received the support of a sufficient number of other deputies who had tired of Combes' anticlericalism and believed that he had indeed neglected social reform, the cabinet might well have been reversed. That it was not was due to the fervent defense of Jean Jaurès.

Jaurès had always considered the religious orders as the primary threat and was to regard separation of church and state as 'the greatest reform which has been attempted in our country since the French Revolution'. In his first overt opposition to Millerand, he said that he had defended the latter out of friendship and in view of the legitimacy of reformist socialism – which had kept the movement within its republican context. Socialists had supported Waldeck-Rousseau as well as Combes, and Millerand's criticism had been given repeatedly for the past five years, even during the time he was minister. To return to power, Millerand was now ready to upset the government, and the country could not afford it. If it were necessary, Jaurès asked, to have social and laic programs, was it not equally necessary to have a majority to carry them out? If, with the aid of the right, the Chamber managed to overthrow the present ministry, how would it form a new one? The reversal would only shatter the instrument of laic policy.

The resolution expressing confidence in the ministry obtained priority over Millerand's – and so saved it – by only ten votes, including those of seven ministers. *Le Temps* pointed out that the government triumphed by three votes and owed its survival to the socialist party – which the newspaper again accused of dictating its policies.[61]

With this interpellation, Millerand's separation from organized socialism was made final. More so than with his controversial votes in 1903, he had confronted every shade of socialist opinion in the most dramatic

way possible and had openly pitted himself against Jaurès. The support
he now received came largely from the center and the right. Some letters
of encouragement came from friends, or were anonymous, and many
came from outside of Paris. Others revealed the extent to which even the
moderate socialist groups rejected his act. The socialist-republican circle
of Albi offered its congratulations to Jaurès and sent Millerand a copy.
A Perpignan socialist group was 'happy that Jaurès taught you a lesson'
and accused Millerand of 'betraying independent socialism'. Its Montpellier equivalent was more brutal. A Marseille republican-socialist
group branded him 'a traitor' and advised him to form a cabinet with
France's leading reactionaries. Millerand was addressed as the 'former
minister', 'the ex-socialist', 'ex-republican', who 'passed bag and bag-
gage to the reactionary camp'. Besançon republican socialists censured
his policy of 'bidding for votes' and his 'ministerial ambition'.[62]
Independent socialists – and former colleagues – were bewildered.
Writing in *L'Humanité* in June, Jaurès implored him not to ignore the
appeals of his friends. Viviani, in the same newspaper, summed up prevailing resentment – and perplexity – over his break with socialism. 'To
possess the strength that comes with maturity, so much ardor for work
and persistence of will, and to sacrifice all that to suggestions born of self-
love and an ambition which time alone would have satisfied... . After
having saddened the heart, it confounds the mind. One does not understand.'[63] These reactions all presaged the debate over Millerand's motives
in attacking Combes.

9.   Critics argued that Millerand was part of a carefully devised plot to
overthrow the cabinet and that the Pension bill served only as a pretext.
They noted that the Committee of Insurance and Social Welfare, scheduled to meet earlier the same day, had never really convened and that
the benches on the right were 'miraculously' filled, while the left and
center had the usual rate of absenteeism. Combes called it a conspiracy
long in the making, uniting opportunists in the center, dissidents on the
left, the former Waldeck-Rousseau ministers and the conservative right.
That Millerand's challenge was certainly not spontaneous is supported by
other evidence. He had written a draft of his remarks, although it is
impossible to say how far in advance. His notes and supporting documentation, particularly that proving the government's breach of promise,
reveal that he prepared his speech as thoroughly as for any case in court.
Sûreté reports filed before March 17 described preparations taken by
Millerand as 'manoeuvres' designed 'to embarrass' the government and
linking his name with those of Doumer and Ribot. Reports commenting
on the interpellation, while acknowledging Millerand's authentic dis-

content over the delay in enacting old-age benefits and the failure to win support from Vaillant, who had fought for them for many years, affirmed that it was a well-kept secret.[64] That a 'plot' was carried out, then, cannot be denied. What can be questioned were the motives behind it.

That the right wanted to reverse a Radical ministry may be taken for granted. That Millerand may well have despaired of seeing significant social reform undertaken by a cabinet consumed by anticlericalism is entirely tenable. His career demonstrated that he thought more of the goal in sight than affiliation with any particular group. We have seen that he separated himself from his more uncompromising Radical colleagues on the Paris Council. He left the Radicals in the Chamber, yet held back from joining the socialists because both parties continued to seek vengeance on Boulangists at the expense of social legislation. At the time of the Dreyfus affair Millerand urged neutrality because he was afraid socialists would lose votes. He also wanted the party to pursue clearly identifiable working-class interests – already associated with national interests – and as minister worked to end the affair and so return to them as speedily as possible. Seen in perspective, there is nothing inconsistent about Millerand breaking with his party to secure desired ends; it was the ends, and the realization that power was necessary to attain them, that remained constant.

In defense of his interpellation, Millerand pointed to the support he had given to the ministry since its formation in 1902. He condemned Combes' subordination of social to anticlerical legislation. The battle against clericalism would in any case be won by keeping the support of the uncommitted center. Replying to the charge that he had jeopardized the vote outlawing teaching orders, Millerand denied that legislation was necessary. The government could achieve its objective by a 'simple decree' issued under its own responsibility. Consequently, it required deputies to expend time and energy that could be used in more profitable work. Millerand cited his committee's promise to support the ministry in its struggle against the orders, an admittedly indispensable preface to reform. But if Combes refused to turn to social reforms until clericalism was laid low, then in a country impregnated with Catholicism he would put them off 'until doomsday'.[65]

Still, the critics were right in denying that the retirement-benefits plan was Millerand's sole source of concern. They failed to appreciate the extent of the loyalty accorded Waldeck-Rousseau by his former ministers, particularly Millerand. Loubet's secretary at the Elysée Palace, Abel Combarieu, related that Waldeck kept his cabinet fully informed and showed confidence in its members. When it decided in 1901 not to make the forthcoming Associations Act retroactive, each felt that he had shared in the taking of the decision. When Combes later made part of the act retroactive, few felt more resentful than the former ministers and associates.[66] Pierre Baudin, Leygues, Caillaux, De Lannessan, Jonnart and Millerand took personal offense at what they viewed as Combes' misrepresentation of Waldeck's religious program, and their common resentment brought them more closely together. It helps to account for their hostility towards the man accused by Waldeck himself of perverting the work of the ministry.

In 1904 Waldeck-Rousseau was dying. He wrote to Millerand from the Cap d'Ail two days after the latter's interpellation, thanking him for defending the ministry. He said that it had nothing in common with the 'monomonia' displayed by the current government, for 'anticlericalism is a manner of being, expressed by extemporaneous acts; it is not a government program'.[67] In so far as they appeared to sanctify an independent political posture, these words can only have heightened Millerand's disregard for established parties and strengthened his determination not to let them dictate his course of action. The letter doubtless reinforced his conviction that he was right to have attacked Combes and thus dispelled any doubts that might have arisen at finding himself totally out of touch with prevailing leftwing opinion. In a self-memo written shortly after, he referred to the Senate's March 1 vote to increase state aid to pauper children and added Waldeck's words: 'Anticlericalism is not a government program.'[68]

The ties linking Millerand to Waldeck-Rousseau, never really extensive, were reinforced in the years following the latter's death. Much of the responsibility belongs to the widow. Madame Waldeck-Rousseau wrote frequently to the Millerands thanking them for their concern during her husband's last days, requesting legal and personal favors in the years after and appreciating their efforts in carrying them out. One letter, sent within a month of Waldeck's death, expressed her gratitude for Millerand's 'delicate intervention' in some matter and stated that her husband was 'right in thinking and speaking so highly of you'. Her letters to other former associates of her husband rekindled their loyalty to the Waldeck-Rousseau cabinet and its program. She told Millerand of Waldeck's fear that if state and church were separated, Rome would send reactionary bishops to 'manipulate [the nation's] priests'. She consulted with Millerand about plans to publish some of her husband's papers, in order 'to correct' those who believed that Combes was in fact carrying out Waldeck's intentions. In 1908 the widow asked Millerand to review a biography of her husband, evoking Waldeck's affection for him. Her subsequent letter of appreciation further strengthened Millerand's conviction that his ex-chief had thought more highly of him than he had revealed.[69]

Some friends of Waldeck decided to hold a yearly dinner in his honor, and Millerand presided over the first. He was instrumental in raising funds to erect a bust of Waldeck-Rousseau in the Tuileries Gardens and eulogized him at its dedication in 1910.[70] Thus it was that the myth of friendship and shared objectives was created; it helped to account for Millerand's condemnation of the government he saw as betraying its predecessor.

If Madame Waldeck longed to see Millerand replace Combes and told him so, her husband had harbored no such sentiment. In his last letter to Loubet (March 24, 1904), Waldeck-Rousseau recognized Combes' weakness after his near-reversal and noted that if dignity were a condition of its existence, the cabinet would already be defunct. He advised Loubet to consider the likelihood of Georges Leygues, the Minister of Education, forming a new government. The former Premier then weighed the possibility of a cabinet headed by Millerand. He admitted to holding his former Minister of Commerce 'in esteem' but was unable to see him designated at the present time. After his 'courageous intervention', he would refuse anything that looked like a reward. Loubet agreed; he appreciated Millerand's 'intelligence, talent, and courage' but considered his political and social doctrines as 'dangerous' and still regretted the necessity of his entry into the government.[71]

Millerand's denunciation of Combes made it certain that the split between him and socialism was decisive. Neither Jaurès nor Herr ever forgave him for having weakened the very difficult position in which they had placed themselves in 1899. The socialist *Le Cri du XIIe arrondissement,* in its issue of March 26, extensively described Millerand's betrayal and specifically attacked his plan to finance retirement benefits by relying on a state fund as 'robbing workers'. Brunellière regretted that Millerand was lost to socialism and predicted that the 'clericals' would soon make overtures to him. Millerand was misled; Guesde may have been right after all; and in any event it was time for socialists to return to the class struggle.[72] In the next national election, that of May 1906, Millerand was running against the official party candidate, Paul Lafargue.

Paradoxically the very act which isolated Millerand from the left was his attack on the government for preferring anticlerical to social legislation, for Guesde himself had never regarded either anticlericalism or antimilitarism as legitimate socialist objectives.[73] After Combes' resignation in January 1905, and with the advent of a unified party, the pursuit of an anticlerical program was formally down-graded. Socialist deputies, dismayed at the prospect of running in the following year's election with empty hands, framed a resolution for the new (Rouvier) government. Its author, Sembat, recalled there had been no social legislation to speak of for three years. Although he would not want to be thought of as renouncing separation of church and state, he said that because they were essential for workers, socialists placed retirement benefits in 'the first rank of their concerns'. By 1906, at the unified party's Limoges Congress, Guesde was to say that the struggle waged against priests had not led socialism anywhere and that antimilitarism was irrelevant in class war. Both, he maintained, were polemical and vulgar and constituted part of the old Radical program.[74] Thus it was that Millerand's interpellation of Combes was ratified by the party had disowned him. But in 1904 no help came from socialists, revolutionary or otherwise, and he found himself, in his attempt to enact social legislation, allied with the right.

Equally paradoxical was the fact that Millerand, as a socialist leader, fell not only because of the leftist groundswell but because of his violation of the reformist policy of cooperating with the Radical party – a policy he had long and ardently defended. Moreover, despite their long – and justifiable – hostility to the church, it is not particularly plausible that French workers cared more about the measures directed against the religious orders than about old-age pensions and other welfare proposals. Conceivably, the struggle could have been carried to working-class constituencies. There is no sign that Millerand even considered the likelihood. Given the coldness of his political style, it would have been impossible for him to have done so. Millerand was condemned for his ambition, and the accusation is well-founded. As an explanation for his attack on Combes, it is not particularly helpful. The immediate result was the loss of any political base. Not until 1912, when he served as Poincaré's Minister of War, was the right to look upon him with favor. The charge, moreover, was inadequate; Camille Pelletan refused to support Waldeck-Rousseau, yet was not accused of ambition.

As its ultimate consequence, Millerand's interpellation helped persuade Jaurès to disavow the reformism that he had so long defended. The latter was to accept the decision taken by the Second International later in 1904 to condemn ministerial participation and return to a revolutionary basis for a newly unified French party. If incompatible with his own judgment, he found that he could no longer defend reformism and still hope for party unity. Acceptance, on the other hand, would permit rapprochement with revolutionaries like Guesde and Vaillant, whose militancy had taken on new luster, and so make unity possible. By rejecting

Combes, Millerand helped to make possible the socialist unity for which he had fought so energetically in the 1890s.[75]

10. The issue raised by the 'Millerand Case', that of ministerial partici-pation, was finally resolved by the Sixth International Socialist Congress held at Amsterdam in August 1904. In accepting the Dresden Resolution voted by this Congress and basing the tactics of their new party on it, French socialism formally abandoned the legalist, reformist approach that it had come to rely on.

Delegates to Amsterdam had insisted on the unification of socialism in France. One bourgeoisie, they said, called for only one socialist party. The Parti socialiste français and the Parti socialiste de France thereupon established a joint unification committee, the *sine qua non* of which was the withdrawal of the former from the Bloc des gauches. Parliamentary socialists were to revert to a policy of intransigent opposition and limit their activites to the defense of working-class interests. The new party was to be distinctly revolutionary, although some measures of social melioration might be pursued. The goal envisaged was the total collec-tivization of society and was to be attained by irreducible opposition to the established bourgeois order and to the state representing it. Socialists were to reject every means of maintaining the government, including mil-itary credits, secret funds and the budget itself. The unity realized, then, was of an entirely different order than that called for at Saint-Mandé. Now stressed were the international organization of the proletariat and class action; the basic texts omitted references to the nation and to the legal conquest of power.[76]

For the sake of unity, Jaurès and a majority within the PSF agreed to these terms at the Party's Rouen Congress in March 1905. At the Globe Congress in Paris the following month the unified Socialist party (Sec-tion français de l'Internationale ouvrière) was born. However, many Independents, in a manner similar to that of the minority of the SFIO which fifteen years later was to reject the conditions imposed by commun-ists for membership in the Third International, turned down unity on these terms. Briand summed up the general resentment of this minority by regarding the conditions set forth at Amsterdam as the triumph of German Marxism over the democratic traditions of French socialism and as the definitive victory of revolutionaries over reformists. Eugene Fournière reproached Jaurès with seeking to achieve unity at any price, including disavowal of the ideas defended since 1893.[77]

J. L. Breton was especially bitter; he said that 'the reformist tactic was sacrificed on the altar of unity' and that the 'policy of sectarianism' and 'verbal intransigence' was followed to the bitter end. It marked the divorce of socialism from the republican party. Like Fournière, he was particularly resentful of Jaurès for renouncing the program he had supported so ardently and for defending with equal passion the opposing point of view. In the face of this 'desertion', reformists struggled in vain, unable to resist the 'irrational impulse to unity'. Socialists would henceforth participate in debates on the budget and then vote against it. Jaurès gave in, concluded Breton, because of the way the Millerand case developed. Millerand had pleaded reform at Bordeaux but had spoken in terms of class solidarity. His language was that of national socialism, no longer the same as that of Jaurès, and, in discrediting reformism, he turned the great tribune to German orthodoxy.[78]

The turn to the left by French socialism, begun my militants before the turn of the century, was now complete. Jaurès got his unity, but in the opinion of most dissidents the price was too high. They regarded him and his followers as acting too hastily, and Fournière described the entire movement as passing through a 'crisis of impatience'.[79] Reformists could not have easily anticipated that the return to revolution would prove incomplete and that tacit acceptance of reformist practices would soon re-emerge. French socialist deputies, for example, were to accommodate a number of ministries before 1914 without making disarmament or the abandonment of colonial holdings a condition of their support.[80] But in its ebb back to revolutionary Marxism after the turn of the century, Millerand remained behind. The next reformist wave, when it came in, did not pick him up – for he was well on the way to nationalism, then irreconcilable with socialism.

Epilogue

You say that I have become a conservative?
I have remained what I was all my life.

IBSEN, to my friend the revolutionary orator

A man may wish well to all peoples of the earth,
but he can really do good only for his own country.
Your Committee, convinced of this truth, has limited its view of the world to the French people.

SAINT-JUST, to the National Convention

Le socialisme national est la négation du socialisme.

ADRIEN PRESSEMANE, chief of the socialist
Fédération de la Haute-Vienne

1. In the months following the interpellation of March 17, 1904, Miller-
and continued his opposition to the government. Whereas he had initially sought to reverse it for showing relative indifference to social legislation and exaggerating the anticlerical program of its predecessor, he
also resented what he saw now as Combes' determination to create a
police state in France.

An interrogation of the Minister of Justice on June 10 – by a Radical
deputy on the question of excessive legal fees – provided Millerand with
another opportunity to denounce the cabinet. He first objected to the
attempt of Vallé, Combes' Minister of Justice, to shift the blame for
authorizing a general increase in court expenses to his predecessor but
then began to criticize the government as a whole for placing undue
emphasis on its work of laicization at the expense of social reform. What
began as a minor act of solidarity with the Waldeck-Rousseau cabinet
became, for Millerand, an extension of his March 17 attack on the government's general program. He said the ministry was unable to achieve
or administer and dissociated the Republic from what he called its faults.
In the process, he let drop the remark that he could not even be assured
of the honesty of Edgard Combes, the son of the Premier and the Secretary-General of the Ministry of Interior. According to Combes' biographer, Edgard had acquired a taste for luxuries, had amassed gam-
bling debts and was rumored to be trafficking in favors. The Catholic
newspaper, *La Petit Dauphinois,* long a defender of the Carthusian

monks, wrote that the order was refused authorization for having resisted the attempt of Combes *fils* to make it pay the 1,000,000 francs he demanded. This was the order located at the famous La Grande Chartreuse near Grenoble and more renowned for the quality of its liquor than its monastic piety.

In his reply, the Premier again defended the accomplishments of the ministry, particularly its suppression of the religious orders. When he added that if 'obsessed' by clerical legislation, he had not enriched himself with the spoils, an unidentified voice evoked the alleged attempt at graft.

Combes admitted his son was offered a bribe but had not proposed sanctioning the Carthusians. At this disclosure many deputies were on their feet demanding to know the names of those involved. The Premier said that he could not identify the parties but had to remain silent, 'for the sake of higher political interests'. He then intimated that the Chartreux intermediaries were known to Millerand, and this only added to the turmoil. The concern with graft eclipsed the original debate, and the the angry and puzzled deputies, to avoid another Panama scandal, at once voted to set up a committee of inquiry to hear all relevant testimony.[1]

Even the most loyal of Millerand's former colleagues could not conceal their perplexity at his latest attack. The next day, Viviani asked what was becoming of him. The issue of legal fees served only as a pretext to launch another assault at the ministry, and, in a 'fit of impatience, anguish, and fear', he was 'throwing away years of work'. Jaurès wondered whether Millerand knew what he was doing and said that in an effort to secure the power he so highly prized, he was becoming 'the tool of the counterrevolutionaries' and 'chaining himself to the clericalism of de Mun and the nationalism of Doumer'.[2] Paul Doumer, a leading Radical-Socialist, had served as Minister of Finance in the Bourgeois cabinet and then as Governor-General of Indochina. He had recently returned to France and as champion of the income tax and a national retirement-benefits plan led the dissident Radical opposition to Combes.

The Committee of Inquiry asked suspected intermediaries between the monks and their expensive protectors, as well as other interested parties, to testify but found it difficult to disentangle the complexities of the affair.[3] It appeared that Edgard Combes had been approached by a minor official working at the Ministry of Commerce, a M. Lagrave, who had served under Millerand as well as Trouillot. He represented the interests of an industrialist named Chabert, who was also a member of Comité républicain du Commerce, de l'Industrie et de l'agriculture, better known as the Mascuraud Committee. This was a liberal group representing small businessmen, established in 1898 to subsidize the election campaigns of less affluent republican candidates. Spokesmen for the committee identified Millerand as the cabinet member most concerned with it in the elections of 1902. He had asked Combes, for the sake of 'higher republican interests', not to reveal the extent of its contribution to helping Radicals win the elections. This proved to be the nature of Combes' reference on the floor of the Chamber, a matter implicating Chabert but wholly irrelevant to the Chartreux.

At one hearing, Combes' Attorney-General, Cottignies, disclosed the contents of some letters discovered at Chabert's home and tried to demonstrate how they incriminated Millerand. The most damaging of them, he said, was written to Chabert by a business acquaintance, a M. Bonnet, on January 2, 1903. It contained the sentence: 'On receipt of this letter do not forget to telephone your friend Millerand. Tell him to keep his eyes open so that in L[agrave]'s absence what has been set aside does not disappear.'

A member of the Committee of Inquiry, the conservative Catholic deputy, Denys Cochin, although politically opposed to Millerand, insisted that the latter be given the opportunity to testify and defend himself. The former minister proved that he had nominated Bonnet for the Legion of Honor as a reward for services rendered on behalf of French industry. However, the government resigned before the nomination could be acted on, and Millerand asked his successor to honor it. Trouillot replied that in view of the many requests for decorations, he could comply only if another cabinet official with an unused nomination made his available. Millerand asked his former assistant Lagrave, whom he knew was on good terms with Edgard Combes, to intervene at the Ministry of the Interior, and Bonnet ultimately received the decoration. The letter, then, referred not to any attempt at bribery on behalf of the Chartreux monks but to Bonnet's fear that the honor reserved for him might yet fall through.

Millerand concluded his testimony by regretting the government's manner of persecution, not so much for himself, as for the country. He was guilty, he said, only of excessive independence and asked anyone doubting it to investigate his financial holdings. He had entered the Ministry of Commerce with only a few thousand francs saved and had left with less than he had entered. At this moment, he could leave his family only his untarnished name but that he was determined to defend. According to an observer, Millerand, on finishing his testimony, looked 'pale as a sheet' but was speaking coldly and in full control of his nerves. The members of the committee, even those opposed to him, applauded when he finished and ultimately viewed the attempt to inculpate him as char-

18

acter assassination. They took umbrage at the government, suspecting that Combes was responsible for Cottignies' actions and on June 29, by almost a two to one majority, approved a resolution expressing indignation at Combes' methods and censuring his Attorney-General.[4]

Two days later, on July 1, Georges Leygues questioned the ministry on its intentions regarding Cottignies; his real motive, however, was to give Millerand the opportunity to defend himself on the Chamber floor. The latter condemned a ministry that defended its programs by trying to ruin the reputation of its adversaries. He could protect himself; someone less fortunate might not be able to, and it was necessary to reject this system of government. Millerand received an ovation, including the applause of many in the Radical majority. Caillaux and Clemenceau passed to the opposition, and, in the opinion of one newspaper, this widespread criticism of Combes marked the beginning of the disintegration of the Bloc's support for the ministry.[5]

Millerand had said that a government resorting to slander failed to guarantee individual security. His resentment and fear of Combes' tactics was strengthened by the disclosure that the Ministry of War was selecting for promotion only those officers holding anticlerical convictions. The indignation of the nationalist opposition knew no bounds. What was new, of course, was the source of the information and not the practice, but the coalition of dissidents and conservatives had been unable to reverse the ministry by attacking its anticlerical policies. It had failed to overthrow the government after Combes broke off diplomatic relations with the Vatican and achieved more success in attacking the ministries of Navy and War. Pelletan was accused of letting the former fall into disarray in his efforts to republicanize it and liberalize its promotion policies. General André was interrogated on October 28, and following a stormy session the cabinet survived by only four votes. It had, in fact, lost its majority.

On November 4 Millerand, Leygues and Ribot censured the cabinet on its tactics. Millerand said that he could not distinguish between the present government's wish to promote anticlerical officers and that of previous regimes to promote only practicing Catholics. A republican army could not be created by adopting the disreputable techniques of the enemy, and he envisaged a similar system spreading to civilian life in which each would denounce his neighbor and every commune would have its official informant. Again the cabinet was saved by a handful of votes, and Millerand's speech again received greatest applause from the right.[6]

André resigned on November 15, but Combes showed no sign of discontinuing the practices that brought down his Minister of War. He tried instead to extend them when on November 18 he ordered prefects and under-prefects to inform the government about all civil servants and candidates for civil service positions or promotions. Four days later the Premier asked that in conservative districts a *délegué* chosen by the prefect, defined as a 'noteworthy citizen invested with the confidence of republicans', submit his opinion on the qualifications of those eligible for promotion, 'especially from a republican point of view'. These orders resulted in a flurry of requests to interpellate the government, but Combes managed to postpone them.[7]

Numerous observers have left testimony about other devices resorted to by the head of the government. In an attempt to elicit votes from opposing deputies he apparently promised them to have changes made in the *Journal officiel* for the sake of appearance. His distribution of patronage was enormous, and there appeared an 'unparalleled' number of *chefs, adjointes, sous-chefs* and *attachés,* all of whom comprised a huge entourage. The names and voting records of friendly – and unfriendly – deputies were carefully noted for future rewards. An attempt was also made to press primary school teachers into service as *délegués*.[8]

In reply, Combes pointed to his tenacious opposition and the right of every government to defend itself. He justified taking the advice of *délegués* in those districts whose deputies questioned the very legitimacy of the Republic. He threatened that the fall of his ministry implied the end of republican-oriented projects in as much as dissidents on the left could reverse him only with the support of the right. But the political atmosphere grew increasingly unbearable, and at least one conservative deputy solicited the aid of the left in defending 'integrity and honor'.[9]

On December 8, Millerand and Leygues interpellated the ministry. The former called the establishment of the *délegués* an 'anonymous and official espionage'. No minister of the Empire would have dared to stoop to such abject practices. Only the Chamber could liberate the country from 'the most abject and repugnant domination', and from this speech was derived the epithet of the Combes ministry – *'le régime abject'*.[10]

Because of its patronage the government managed to retain its precarious majority. The following month, however, Doumer's victory over Brisson, the Bloc's candidate for the Presidency of the Chamber, portended its fall. The cabinet resigned January 19 without having formally been put into a minority position. Combes accused Millerand of having secured the collaboration of the right to oust him from office. Still, when the new Rouvier cabinet was outlining its program, Millerand said that he would press for early debate on the workers retirement-benefits plan.[11]

2. We have observed the birth in April 1905 of the unified Socialist party and the refusal of a number of reformists to acquiesce in what they considered a return to revolutionary Marxism. In the election of 1906 twenty-four of these dissidents, including Briand and Zévaès – the latter had gradually assumed a reformist position, were sent to the Chamber. With the cooperation of some local groupings also preferring to remain independent, they reestablished the old Parti socialiste français at a Lyon congress in 1907. The delegates agreed to follow the principles laid down at Saint-Mandé, namely, to operate through political channels while disavowing any direct action like the general strike and to work for international cooperation among workers, but with the right of national self-defense clearly reserved.[12]

Viviani, who had resigned from the SFIO shortly after its founding, and Millerand, who was also reelected in 1906, identified themselves with the revived party, although Millerand did not formally become a member. Unlike their counterparts who before 1905 had refused to choose among the several factions in French socialism, but had kept the friendships made in one or another of the various sects, those who now regarded themselves as 'Independents' came from all socialist groups and were united only in their rejection of the decisions taken at Amsterdam. With the appearance of the many foreign crises of the first decade of the twentieth century, the Parti socialiste français took an increasingly patriotic stand, was generally not considered socialist at all and was not allowed to attend the Second International's Stuttgart Congress in 1907.[13]

After the 1910 election thirty deputies, returned to the Chamber either as Republican-Socialists, as was Millerand, as Radical-Socialists or simply as Republicans, formed a Republican-Socialist group. It called for collectivism only in heavily concentrated industries and in public utilities. Included were former Independents like Millerand, Viviani, Gerault-Richard and Fournière and newcomers like Paul-Boncour and Paul Painlevé. At Toulouse in 1911 the group took the shape of a party. It pledged to work for completion of the Pension Act of 1901 by adding sickness and unemployment insurance, as well as for an income tax and various administrative reforms. Two conditions, however, were expressly set forth as prerequisites to all reforms and revealed a distinct conservative bias: the need to increase national production and to maintain public order.[14]

The Parti Républicain-socialiste was less a party than a collection of individuals united only on the most common denominators. It underwent a severe schism over Poincaré's election to the Elysée in 1913 and the issue of the three-year military service. Convinced by 1912 that the threat from Germany took precedence over all other concerns, Millerand supported both Poincaré, in whose cabinet he was serving as Minister of War, and the extended service. The year may be taken to mark his ideological passage into the nationalist camp. Survivors of the party changed its name in 1917 to the Parti socialiste national to distinguish themselves from internationalists seeking a negotiated peace.[15] Millerand continued to lay stress on national unity after the war and used the theme as the basis for a new coalition he helped to organize in 1919, the Bloc national.

3.   The Marxist triumph in 1904–05, though to shape the destiny of the movement, by no means proved absolute. French socialism accepted the revolutionary contours insisted on by the Second International, and 'neo-Guesdist' leadership prevailed. Even so, as early as the half-decade preceding the War gradualist tactics were once again pursued, and this justified many of the concessions made by Jaurès. Responsible were Jaurès' own personal superiority and the lack of unity among militant socialists. Their disagreements, with the issue of participation finally removed, soon resurfaced. Indeed, militant syndicalists and socialists sympathetic to syndicalism saw the SFIO as a reformist party scarcely different from the progressive bourgeois elements with which it was once more willing to collaborate.[16] Even the socialist leadership acted sufficiently reformist to discount any reference to the 1890s as an aberration in the history of French socialism. The veterans Guesde and Vaillant, the one pursuing the dictates of his rigid orthodoxy, the other continuing to demonstrate his concern for the workingman and revealing an ever-growing political pragmatism, began to respond as they had a decade before. They were predominant in their respective federations in the Nord and the Seine, the two most powerful socialist groups in France. They were, in turn, followed by younger party chiefs like the militant Jean Longuet and Pierre Renaudel, as well as the more moderate Albert Milhaud and Albert Thomas.[17]

At Limoges in 1906 Guesde condemned the revolutionary stand taken by the CGT at Amiens and startled newspapermen when he warned of the 'dangers of exaggerated internationalism' and spoke in terms of 'national duty'. At the SFIO's Nancy Congress the following year, he denounced any recourse to the general strike in the event of war. If carried out, the winning power would be the nation with the fewest socialists, and those in France necessarily had to support their country.[18] Vaillant overcame the opposition of Hervé and the uncompromising advocates of insurrection at the Saint-Étienne congress in 1909, and socialists once again agreed to support Radicals on the *ballotage* vote. At Nimes in 1910 the party granted additional local autonomy to its member federations; they could use their judgment in deciding whether to enter into alliances with bourgeois groupings in order to promote reform, extend civil liberties and defend democratic institutions. A counter-proposal prohibiting such alliances was easily defeated. The following year these federations were specifically empowered to support republican candidates on the second ballot.[19] The socialists tried to stave off impending war. When it came, the great majority, like all its western counterparts, resolutely supported the government. That most socialists became understandably disenchanted as the war dragged on, and sufficiently impressed with Bolshevik successes to join the Third International in 1920, constitutes the exception in the history of the movement rather than the rule. The rump SFIO and those who joined it in a massive rebuilding effort in the early 1920s remained only theoretically faithful to their revolutionary traditions. Unlike its communist rival, the SFIO was very much a government party. It supported the Radicals in the election of 1924 and in those that followed, even choosing to 'exercise power' in 1936 and again in 1945 and 1956. Those who despaired of the return to 'orthodox' Marxism in 1904–05, and accordingly rejected the unified party, could scarcely have predicted these developments.

The new nationalism that preceded the onslaught of World War I was supported by munitions-makers and ship-builders. It nevertheless differed from that which had marked anti-Dreyfusards. It was not anti-Semitic and offensive but determined in what it regarded as its duty to the country. Its chiefs included Poincaré, Delcassé, Briand and Millerand. Like Péguy, the latter was profoundly affected by the attempted *coup de Tangier* and had admitted his allegiance to the new cause as early as 1905. A revolutionary orator reproached him with having rejected yet another resolution calling on France to take the initiative in disarmament. He had replied: 'If it is to be a nationalist to believe that at the present time it would be a crime and folly to disarm, yes, I am a nationalist, and you who seek to brand me with that epithet, if you do not agree, you can keep your votes. I do not want them.'[20] As Minister of War in 1912, Millerand demonstrated his new sense of priorities by fighting to establish a three-year military service and to reorganize the army's high command and by laying the foundations for an air force and encouraging Poincaré to announce his candidacy for the Presidency of the Republic.[21]

Other militant elements in the French labor movement were also effectively abandoning revolution. Reformist forces under August Keufer, secretary of the book-workers' union, Eugene Guérard, of the railwaymen, and Victor Renard, of the textile workers, had never accepted the revolution preached by the CGT leadership. In 1909 Léon Jouhaux became Secretary-General of the Confederation; he tempered his militancy with pragmatism and ultimately proved acceptable to the reformists. Organized labor supported the war effort in 1914. In 1912 the erratic Hervé was converted to the cause of national self-defense, and was embarking on the road that would lead to collaboration with the Germans in World War II. Lafargue's suicide in 1911 removed still another link between Guesde and his internationalist past. At the end of the first month of fighting in 1914 Guesde, Sembat and soon Vaillant joined Jules Méline and Denys Cochin in a 'sacred union' coalition government. The SFIO had granted its permission, and Jules Guesde became a minister.

4. That socialism came to the support of the Republic was in part the consequence of Millerand's work, for together with Jaurès he had never ceased to equate the two. To be sure, the shift in tactics stemmed from the growth of liberal and democratic institutions, especially the right of association and extension of the suffrage, and reformist leaders rather articulated than originated this change. Even so, a decision taken by socialists in 1899 made possible the formation of a republican defense coalition ministry. Had they refused to cooperate, said Roger Soltau, the forces of the right could have formed another coalition 'which might have made a successful appeal to a still uncertain public opinion'.[22] But the die had already been cast; the party was no longer one of intransigent opposition but was ready to take its place among other parliamentary groups. Years of effort by Millerand and Jaurès to achieve working-class unity and have it advance in democratic and parliamentary channels had proven effective. Both men viewed the Republic as a means to a more equitable society. However, it had been Millerand who, rightly or wrongly, judged that the former socialist policy of absolute antagonism was selfdefeating and that action without power was impossible.

Millerand was not the first to lay stress on the socialist conquest of public power. Possibilists called for a piecemeal approach even before he became a party member. Still, they differed from reformists in at least one marked respect. The followers of Brousse, said Gabriel Mermeix, had been only a *gagne-petit*, 'smearing the cockade with pale colors to pick up some votes from the petit-bourgeois and send a few representatives to the Paris Municipal Council'.[23]

Millerand's emphasis and not his approach changed during his socialist years. His collectivism and idea of the class struggle, never strong to begin with, gradually diminished to the point where expropriation was advocated only in utilities and in highly concentrated areas of production. In a fashion similar to that of present-day social democrats, he came to believe that it monopolies had to exist it was probably better for the state to exercise them. His participation in the government only reinforced those tendencies making for moderation. Millerand did not repudiate social and economic concerns; he ultimately subordinated them to national imperatives. Like Maurice Barrès, with whom he was to collaborate in 1919 in fashioning the Bloc national, he said that he aimed not at destroying the ownership of property but at giving the worker his rightful share of it and so developing his sense of responsibility.

Unable to accommodate himself to requirements of party discipline, Millerand was to remain an independent in politics. Labels meant little and ideology even less. Like the mature Gambetta, whom he came to admire greatly, he envisioned the task of government as isolating and then solving, in as empirical a manner as possible, the various problems confronting the nation. And if the party with which he was affiliated failed to agree with his priorities or his solutions, he withdrew from it. He twice parted company with his fellow Radicals; he delayed joining his new socialist friends and later brought about his expulsion from the party by flagrantly violating its policies. He was to quit the Briand and Poincaré cabinets in 1910 and 1913, respectively and to be forced from the Ministry of War in 1915 and from the Presidency of the Republic in 1924. Perhaps no greater tribute can be paid to the Third Republic than by recognizing that its institutions somehow permitted so heterodox a politician to climb so high.

As a socialist minister Millerand set on a firm foundation the principle of state involvement in the economy. The stimulation and aid to union growth was described by the economist Leroy-Beaulieu as 'revolutionary'. In writing of the reformist direction taken by French socialism, Daniel Halévy noted that far from unleashing any class war, socialism had 'happily transformed it. Once unfeeling, it made it responsive; once instinctive, it made it deliberative'. He reviewed the largly futile working-class insurrections of the nineteenth century and contrasted them to workers now 'organizing themselves and seeking in their congresses the principles of a just society'. No one, he said, has ever seen anything like it. 'This entry into action by the working masses is one of history's outstanding developments, perhaps the most important.'[24] That Millerand helped persuade his party to accept and enlarge its commitment, and that of labor, to the Republic may provde a more appropriate comment on his socialism than would his expulsion from it. The party no longer had room for people like him, and no doubt the party had grounds for so thinking. An account of Millerand's socialist years nevertheless illustrates the early efforts of socialism itself seeking to adapt to modern industrial society.

Notes

NOTES TO PREFACE

1. Jules Delafosse, *Portraits d'hier et d'aujourd'hui* (1912), pp. 13–14; Henri de Roland, *Galliffet* (1945), p. 176; and Joseph Caillaux, *Mémoires, Vol. I; Ma jeunesse orgueilleuse, 1863–1869* (1942), p. 123.
2. JOC, June 22, 1899; cited in Roland, p. 176.
3. Carl Landauer, 'The Origin of Socialist Reformism in France', *International Review of Social History*, XII (1967), Part I, p. 96. I am aware of the methodological criticisms this definition may generate. Compère-Morel, in his *Grand Diction-*

---

* Unless otherwise indicated the place of publication is Paris.

naire socialiste du mouvement politique et économique national et international (1924) and G. D. H. Cole, *Labour in the Commonwealth* (New York, 1919), among others, have argued that the reformist is concerned only with the immediate effects of the reform proposed on the particular problem being tackled; that he has no complete or coherent social philosophy; that he seeks fast remedies to cure a past abuse and is not concerned with a fundamental change in the social system. I have, however, viewed reformism chiefly as a question of tactics because of three reasons: (1) Most socialists always sought as their objective basic changes in the status of the economically under-privileged and in expanding public direction over productive property; (2) What socialists did is at least as important as what socialists said; and (3) I am less concerned with the 'correctness' of reformism, from a theoretical point of view, than with Millerand's position *vis-à-vis* that of the socialist party at any given time.

4. Philip M. Williams called Millerand 'the pioneer on the well-travelled road to fame and power which winds its tortuous way from Left to Right'; *Wars, Plots and Scandals in Post-War France* (Cambridge, 1970), p. 24. See also Richard Barron, *Parties and Politics in Modern France* (Washington, 1959), p. 93; Julius Braunthal, *History of the International, 1864–1914* (London, 1966), p. 257; and John Marcus, *French Socialism in the Crisis Years* (New York, 1958), p. 93 for examples of similar views.

NOTES TO CHAPTER 1: THE ORIGINS

1. A sister, Victoire, married a farmer in Roche, J. B. Garnery, and remained there. When he was President of the Republic some attempts were made to trace Millerand's ancestors to the fifteenth century and give them a noble status. Marcelet and Malson, *La Famille Millerand de Roche. Etude monograph à vue d'archives* (Saint Dizier, 1923), p. 5.

2. Archives of the Department of the Seine. A folder on Alexandre Millerand contains birth and baptismal certificates, 75GH/91.

3. MP–JM. The unpublished *Mémoires* of Alexandre Millerand were written in Versailles in 1943, shortly before his death, and are in possession of his younger son, M. Jacques Millerand. Hereafter referred to as *Mémoires;* p. 4.

4. *Mémoires,* p. 5.

5. Georges Wormser, *Georges Mandel, l'homme politique* (1967), pp. 14–15. Social scientists of a behavioral persuasion have pointed to the importance of the family, particularly the middle-class family which calls for high levels of achievement, in shaping the demands made by an individual on himself. They have also stressed the role of the mother in supplying the necessary motivation and resolution. Bernard Barber, *Social Stratification: A Comparative Analysis of Structure and Process* (New York, 1957), pp. 321–359; Harold Lasswell, *Power and Personality* (New York, 1948), pp. 43, 47, 49. Still, this in no way precludes the likelihood of other early factors (e.g., teachers, peers) playing an equally important part. Nor does it reject the assumption that personality is not definitively 'set' in childhood but continues to undergo modification in adult life. Behavior, moreover, cannot be ex-

plained solely in terms of psychological predispositions; it also results from the situations in which people find themselves, including the formal and informal roles they are called upon to perform. See Fred I. Greenstein, *Personality and Politics* (Chicago, 1969), p. 7. The practice of law, we shall see, was strongly to influence Millerand's politics.

6. MP–JM. One hundred eighty-three letters have been saved. The *Mémoires* erred in stating that the family was sent to Brittany to escape the siege.

7. *Mémoires*, p. 5. The incident was recollected on several occasions.

8. *Mémoires*, p. 6.

9. *Mémoires*, p. 6.

10. One writer estimated that a single man could live on 850 to 1200 francs a year. Othenin d'Haussonville, 'La vie et les salaires a Paris', *Revue des deux mondes*, April 15, 1883, pp. 834–835. Millerand did not have to pay for room or full board.

11. Albert Guèrard, *Personal Equation* (New York, 1948), p. 84.

12. *Mémoires*, p. 9.

13. The house is owned by his cousin, Mlle. Suzanne Millerand.

14. MP–JM. There are 334 letters, bound and numbered, like those written during the siege of Paris.

15. MP–JM. March 12 (no. 165) and October 22, 1880 (no. 317).

16. *Mémoires*, p. 11.

17. Edouard Charton, *Dictionnaire des professions* 3rd ed. (1880), pp. 71–76.

18. *Statistique de l'enseignement supérieur, 1878–1888* (1889), Vol. I, pp. 103–104. Also see Louis Liard, *L'Enseignement supérieur en France, 1789–1893* (1894), Vol. I. p. 399.

19. Liard, II, p. 397; Pierre Sorlin, *Waldeck-Rousseau* (1966), pp. 87–92; F. H. Lawson, *et al.*, *Amos and Walton's Introduction to French Law* 2nd ed. (Oxford, 1963), pp. 6–7. René David, *French Law: Its Structure, Sources, and Methodology* (Baton Rouge, 1972), pp. VI–XV, 49–53.

20. Sorlin, pp. 89–94.

21. MP–JM. The letter was dated March 10, 1880.

22. *Mémoires*, p. 11.

23. AN, AB xix 3073, dossier 2, 'Conférence faite à la bibliothèque des amies de l'instruction du XIIIe arrondissement, May 7, 1881'.

24. *Mémoires*, pp. 11–12; Paul Acker, *Petites confessions, visites et portraits* (n.d.), p. 120.

25. MP–JM. His letter and Millerand's reply were not dated.

26. Laguerre never lived up to expectations. He supported the losing side in the Boulanger episode, and wasted his talents by a disorderly personal life. Alexandre Zévaès, *Ombres et silhouettes* (1928), p. 255.

27. *Le Droit*, December 15 to 24, 1882. AN, F7 12526, 'Les Troubles de Montceau-les-Mines'. The jury found extenuating circumstances for nine of the accused. Nine others were sentenced to a maximum of one to five years' imprisonment. For the description of Millerand, see *L'Avenir*, November 1, 1915; *Le XIXe Siècle*, January 18, 1892.

28. *Mémoires*, p. 13.

29. Barber, p. 321. Four letters sent by Roche to Millerand suggest the latter acted as a factotum. MP–JM.

30. Rochefort's letter of recommendation dated April 5, 1883, MP–JM. Also see Georges Renard, 'Millerand, Quelques souvenirs', RS, February 1950, p. 94.

31. *Mémoires,* pp. 17–18. De Bouteiller was defeated, the victim, according to Millerand, of his opponent's deceitful campaign practices.

32. MP–BN for election material. However, there is nothing to show how the money was raised.

33. *Mémoires,* p. 19; Alexandre Zévaès, *Jules Guesde* (1929), p. 77. For the relationship between depressed economic conditions and its political repercussions in the 1880s, see Jacques Néré, 'La Crise industrielle de 1882 et le mouvement boulangiste', unpublished principal thesis, Doctorat ès lettres, University of Paris, 1959, 2 vols. A precis may be found in his 'La crise industrielle et le mouvement boulangiste', *L'Information historique,* III (May—June 1959).

34. PP, Report to the Prefect of Police, March 8, 1883, B/A 339; Report of the Prefect of Police to the Sûreté Générale, March 16, 1883, PP, cited in Sorlin, pp. 281, 283–284. No municipally sponsored relief system was to be established until 1886.

35. *Almanach National: Annuaire officiel de la République française, 1884* (1886). *Mémoires,* p. 21.

36. Maurice Dommanget, *Edouard Vaillant: Un Grand socialiste, 1840–1915* (1956), p. 78. That Council was one of the first elected bodies of the Third Republic with a Radical majority. Vallès cited in Georges Lefranc, *Le Mouvement socialiste sous la Troisième République, 1870–1940* (1963), p. 77. The Labor Committee was approved the same session, and a nine-hour day was voted in 1886. The future subway (Metro) was declared a public utility, etc. See RS, January 1886, p. 58. In May, 1888 a minimum wage was voted for workers engaged on municipal projects, RS, May 1888, p. 545.

37. Sorlin, pp. 320, 322–323. Also see Louis Andrieux, *A travers la République, Mémoires* (1926), pp. 169–172.

38. *Bulletin Municipal Officiel de la Ville de Paris,* June 10, 18, 1884. (Hereafter referred to as BMO.) This committee handled the acquisition of property as well as relief problems.

39. *BMO,* July 29, 1884.

40. *BMO,* November 13, 1884.

41. *BMO,* December 4, July 26, 1884.

42. *BMO,* December 30, 1884.

43. *BMO,* December 22, 23, 1885.

44. *BMO,* June 25, 1885.

45. *BMO,* November 21, 26, 1885.

46. The *Almanach National* for 1885 lists Millerand's name on page 1379, although he was not fully certified until the end of his probationary period in 1887. Today, an examination is needed as well.

47. Fernand Payen and Gaston Duveau, *Les Règles de la profession d'avocat et les usages du Barreau de Paris,* 2 ed. (n.d.), pp. 167–168, 184–187, 216–217; *Mémoires,* p. 12.

48. Yvonne Geismar, 'L'Ordre des Avocats du Barreau: cet inconnu', RPP, February 1968, p. 72.
49. Jean Bernard, *La Vie de Paris, 1928* (1929), pp. 277-278; *Bulletin du Grand Orient de France. Procès-verbal du 21 septembre, 1883,* p. 176. Laguerre, Jules Roche and Millerand's colleagues on *La Justice,* like Camille Pelletan and Charles Longuet, were all Masons. After Millerand's denunciation of Combes' anticlericalism in 1904, there could be no question of his rejoining the Order. Masons condemned his efforts to reestablish diplomatic ties with the Vatican when Premier and President of the Republic.
50. *Mémoires,* p. 21.
51. *Mémoires,* p. 21. Of 347,089 votes cast on the run-off vote, Millerand received 159,957, placing him third on the Radical list of six. AN, Archives de l'Assemblée nationale, C 5309.

NOTES TO CHAPTER 2: THE RADICAL YEARS

1. *Mémoires,* p. 23. Conservatives, opposed to the regime, won 201 seats, Republicans, 383. Georges Lachapelle, *Les Régimes électoraux,* p. 76.
2. Our knowledge of parliamentary groupings in the Chamber during the early Third Republic is poor. More or less solid groupings were formed only after a Chamber ruling of July 5, 1910. Before that time they had no official existence; indeed, most were formed not before but after legislative elections. Their names, their very membership changed during the course of the legislature, and the same deputy could belong to two or three different ones. They can be identified only by comparing the biographical backgrounds and matching campaign platforms of their members. See the article by Jean-Marie Mayeur, 'Droites et rallies à la Chambre des députés au debut de 1894', *Revue d'histoire moderne et contemporaine,* April-June 1966, pp. 117-135.
3. J. Hampden Jackson, *Clemenceau and the Third Republic* (London, 1946), BN. Department of Manuscripts. The unpublished journal of Scheurer-Kestner, Vol. VI, *1883-1888,* N A fr. 12 709, p. 107.
4. Zévaès, *Notes et souvenirs d'un militant* (1913), p. 240-241. Gambetta's 'Belleville Program' of 1869 contained the political reforms called for by Radicals, but left undefined any social policy.
5. Zévaès, *Notes,* pp. 256, 237; Lefranc, p. 43.
6. Wormser, *La République...,* pp. 218-220.
7. For the social program of the 'leftwing' Radicals and its weaknesses, see the articles by Leo A. Loubère: 'The French Left-Wing Radicals: Their views on Trade Unionism, 1870-1888', *International Review of Social History,* VII (1962), pp. 203-230; 'Leftwing Radicals, Students and the Military, 1880-1907', *French Historical Studies,* III (1963), pp. 93-105; and 'Les Radicaux d'Extrême-Gauche en France et les Rapports entre Patrons et Ouvriers (1871-1900)', *Revue d'histoire économique et sociale* (1964), pp. 89-103.
8. *Kölnische Zeitung,* October 7, 1884. Cited in E. Malcolm Carroll, *French Public Opinion and Foreign Affairs, 1870-1914* (New York, 1931), p. 97.

9. Jean Juarès, *Discours parlementaires*, Vol. I: *Introduction sur le socialisme et le radicalisme en 1885* (1904), Edmond Claris, Ed., p. 121.
10. *Mémoires*, p. 15. Georges Suarez, *La Vie orgueilleuse de Clemenceau* (1930), pp. 125–126. Also see Camille Pelletan, *Georges Clemenceau* (1883), and Gustave Geoffrey, *Clemenceau, sa vie, son œuvre* (n.d.).
11. *Mémoires*, pp. 15–16; Léon Daudet, *Devant la douleur, Souvenirs des milieux litteraires, politiques...* (1915), pp. 176–179, credited Durranc with the line. Apparently it was the historian Aulard who told it to Durranc. See Jean Bernard, p. 422.
12. *Mémoires*, p. 15; Geoffroy, p. 56.
13. A. Zévaès, *Clemenceau* (1949), pp. 317, 53; Yves Guyot, *La Comédie socialiste* (1897), p. 180.
14. Henry du Basty, 'Les Hommes politiques français: M. Millerand', *Revue d'histoire contemporaine*, January 20, 1889, p. 10.
15. *La Justice*, August 15, 16, 26, October 29, December 1, 1886; April 17, 1887; June 28, 1885: March 16, December 9, 1886.
16. *La Justice*, January 2, 4, June 25, 1887; December 6, 1886. Hanotaux cited in Zévaès, *Ombres et silhouettes* (1928), p. 237.
17. JOC, January 12, 1886, p. 1. Speech reproduced in JOC, February 6, 1886 and in *La Justice*, February 7.
18. The speech was well received, but the bill failed to pass. *La Justice, Le Matin*, February 7, 1886. André Daniel [pseudonym for Georges Bonnefous], *L'Année politique*, 1886, p. 26.
19. Running accounts ot the strike appeared in every Paris newspaper, including *La Justice*. A detailed, if partisan, history may be found in Zévaès' pamphlet, *La Grève de Decazeville, janvier-juin*, 1886 (1938).
20. JOC, February 11, 1886.
21. *Le Temps*, April 18, 20, 1886. Also Maurice Garcon, *Histoire de la justice sous la IIIᵉ République* (1957), Vol I, pp. 196–200.
22. *Le Cri du Peuple*, April 22, 1886; Zévaès, *Decazeville*, p. 36. The Radical candidate, Gaulier, received 140,000 votes.
23. Carlo Sforza, *Makers of Modern Europe* (London, 1930), pp. 209–210. Also see Jean Maitron, *Histoire du mouvement anarchiste en France, 1880–1914* (1951), p. 141.
24. Dommanget, *Vaillant*, p. 203. The Perpignan Council sent potatoes, although most contributed cash. Zévaès, *Decazeville*, p. 29.
25. JOC, March 8, 1887; PR, March 26, 1887; Weill, *Histoire*, pp. 261–262; RS, April 1897, pp. 289–297; *La Justice*, March 15, 1887; RS, April 1887, p. 297, May 1888, p. 546.
26. Louis, *Histoire*, 4th ed., p. 234, or Albert Orry, *Les Socialistes indépendants*, Vol. VIII of *Histoire des parties socialistes en France*, 11 vols. Alexandre Zévaès, Ed. (1911), p. 13; Weill, *Histoire*, p. 262. Also see Jacques Néré, 'La Crise industrielle', Vol. II, p. 184.
27. Text and names in RS, January 1888, p. 87, and Orry, p. 13–14.
28. Both resolutions were defeated by one expressing confidence in the government. JOC, October 18, 1886; *La Justice*, October 19, 1886.
29. *La Justice*, May 31, June 1, 1887; Néré, II 'La Crise...', II, pp. 269–270. See

Frederic H. Seager, *The Boulanger Affair: Political Crossroad of France, 1886–1889* (Ithaca, 1969), p. 64; JOC, May 31, 1887.

30. November 26, 1887; Bernard Lavergne, *Les Deux présidences de Jules Grévy, 1879–1887. Mémoires de Bernard Lavergne* (1966), p. 471; JOC, November 17, 1887 and February 3, 1888. Millerand asked for a full investigation in *La Justice*, November 2, 1887, and on November 17 called for Grévy's resignation. Lavergne, *Mémoires*, p. 466.

31. *La Justice*, January 23, April 1, October 29, 1886; November 7, 1889; March 15, June 23, December 26, 1888.

32. JOC, February 25, 1885 and March 30, 1888. Also *La Justice*, February 26, 1885; December 19, July 11, 1887; February 1, 1889.

NOTES TO CHAPTER 3: TO SOCIALISM: THE BOULANGIST INTERRUPTION

1. *La Justice*, January 25, 1886. In the issues of February 2 and 11 he asked for the adoption of arbitration procedures.

2. *La Justice*, April 16, December 26, 1888; March 2, 1887; April 19, 29, May 20, 1889.

3. *La Justice*, May 17, 19, 1888; September 19, 1887.

4. Daniel, *1888*, p. 173.

5. Carl Landauer, 'The Origin of Reformist Socialism in France', *International Review of Social History* (1967), XII, Part I, pp. 84–85. Also Harold Weinstein, *Jean Jaurès: A Study of Patriotism in the French Socialist Movement* (New York, 1936), p. 8, Lefranc, pp. 80–95; Albert Orry, *Les Socialistes indépendants* (1911), p. 5. David Stafford, *From Anarchism to Reformism: A Study of the Political Activities of Paul Brousse...* (London, 1971), for Brousse's earlier years.

6. Marcel Prelot, *L'Evolution politique de socialisme français, 1789–1934* (1939), p. 102.

7. RS, January 1885, p. 1. N.E. Fry, 'Integral Socialism and the Third Republic: 1883 to 1914', unpublished doctoral dissertation, Yale University, 1964, Chapter 5.

8. Blum in *Le Populaire*, February 13, 1927. Cited by Prelot, who admitted, however, that it was not the only cause of Jaurès' conversion. Georges Renard, 'Millerand, Quelques souvenirs', RS, nouvelle série, February, 1950, p. 94.

9. RS, October 1885, pp. 881, 905; Lefranc, p. 85.

10. RS, December 1886, p. 1146; December 1887, p. 648.

11. Renard, 'Quelques souvenirs', RS, January–February 1950, pp. 94–95; RS, May 1888, p. 546; July 1888, pp. 54, 58; June 1888, p. 628.

12. RS, January 1888, p. 88. Pelletan was sympathetic to the Group, but refused to support any 'catechism'. See his editorial in *La Justice*, December 2, 1887; *Le Petit Troyen: La dépêche de Sâone et Loire*, December 27, 1887.

13. *Principes socialistes* (1896), p. xxiv. Cited in Lefranc, p. 86.

14. Renard, RS, January–February 1950, p. 95; 'Papiers de Gabriel Deville', AN, 51 AP 1, dossier 1. There are approximately seventy cards and letters from Millerand. Deville gradually withdrew from a revolutionary stand.

15. Acker, p. 120; RS, April 1903, p. 429. The speech was given March 14.

16. De Lanessan was a former *agrégé* at the Faculty of Medicine. For Millerand it was his 'independent attitude' that rendered him 'particularly congenial'. *Mémoires*, p. 26. Millerand claimed it was the first anti-Boulangist speech and, in a brief biographical account, the revue *Le Parlement et l'opinion*, agreed, September 23, 1920, p. 1678. See also the *Revue d'histoire contemporaine*, January 20, 1889, p. 9.

17. Scheurer–Kestner, 'Souvenirs d'un républicain alsacien', Vol. VI: 1883–1888; BN, Department of Manuscripts, N.A. fr; 12709, p. 201.

18. *La Justice*, May 22, 1887; *Mémoires*, p. 27.

19. *Néré*, 'La Crise', p. 120.

20. Adrien Dansette, *Le Boulangisme* (1946), appendix; Raymond Manevy, *La Presse de la IIIe République* (1955), pp. 89–90.

21. *La Justice*, March 18, 1888.

22. Lafargue to Engels, October 15, 1889, *Engels–Lafargue Correspondance*, II, pp. 123–124; Engels to Lafargue, August 27, 1889, *Engels–Lafargue Correspondance* pp. 311–312. Also see Goldberg, *Life*, pp. 54–56; Seager, pp. 169–170; and Fresnette Pisani-Ferry, *Le Général Boulanger* (1969), p. 239; Last quotation in Goldberg, *Life*, p. 56.

23. *La Justice*, April 24, 25, August 21, 1888.

24. *La Justice*, February 8, March 8, July 13, 1889.

25. Lefranc, p. 54.

26. Seager, pp. 218, 211.

27. *La Justice*, October 19, December 16, 22, 1888.

28. *La Justice*, May 4, 5, 1889; *Mémoires*, p. 25.

29. René Goblet, 'Souvenirs', RPP. November, 1931, p. 195; Georges Lachapelle, *Les Régimes électoraux* (1934), pp. 77–78.

30. Zévaès, *Jules Guesde, 1845–1922* (1929), p. 97.

31. Néré, 'La crise', Vol. I, pp. 485–486, 479. Georges Lefranc has mistakenly interpreted this as proof that Millerand was sympathetic to Boulangism, p. 88, Theodore Zeldin, that Millerand was 'neutral' to Boulangism. *France, 1848–1945* (Oxford, 1973), Vol. I, p. 770.

32. Daniel, *1889*, p. 186.

33. JOC, March 2, 1889. The vote rejecting it was 290–236. JOC, 1st session, March 14, 1889. Also see *Le XIXe Siècle*, March 14, 16, 1889. Cited in Néré, 'La Crise', I, p. 485.

34. See the article by Pelletan, *La Justice*, March 8, 1889. Cited in Seager, p. 219.

35. *L'Eclair*, May 14, 1889.

36. *La Justice*, May 12, 1889. Cited by Néré, 'La Crise', I, pp. 498–499. See the chapter entitled 'Le Desarroi des Radicaux et la scission Millerand'.

37. *Mémoires*, p. 26; Guyot, p. 181; René Viviani, 'Portraits contemporaines: M. Alexandre Millerand', *Revue des deux mondes*, November 1, 1920, p. 92.

38. *L'Eclair*, May 14, 1889.

39. Néré, 'La Crise', II, p. 503.

40. *Mémoires*, p. 28.

41. Le Conseil National du Parti ouvrier français, *Onze Ans d'histoire socialiste: Aux travailleurs de France* (1901), pp. 3–5.

42. *La Voix*, August 29, 1889.

43. *Mémoires*, p. 28.; PP B a/183–a/184. Report entitled 'Grève des ouvrieres terrass-
iers de 1888'.
44. MP–JM, Millerand's draft letter dated June 24.
45. *Mémoires*, p. 28.
46. G. Foëx, *La Viticulture, cours complet* (1888), MP–BN; J. Ernest-Charles, *Pratic-
iens politiques* (1899), p. 285.
47. *La Voix, La Justice*, September 23, October 7, 1889. The official final results were
5,358 to 4,277, AN, C 5326, Archives de L'assemblée nationale. Election material
in MP–BN.
48. *La Voix*, November 6, 1889.
49. Néré, 'La Crise', II, pp. 505, 632.
50. BN–VN, 'Trente Ans de République', p. 47; *Mémoires*, p. 14.

NOTES TO CHAPTER 4: THE SOCIALIST DEPUTY

1. The contrast was noted by Dr. Jacques Bertillon, head of the statistical section of
the Prefecture. His demographic survey of the city, *Résultats statistiques du dé-
nombrement de 1891 pour la ville de Paris*, based on census figures of 1891 was the
last able to use statistics based on each quarter; later census results were prepared
nationally and gave figures for the whole of Paris. See the discussion by D.R:
Watson, 'The Nationalist Movement in Paris, 1900–1906', in David Shapiro, Ed.,
The Right in France, 1890–1919: Three Studies. St. Antony's Papers, No. 13 (Carbondale, 1962), pp. 49–53.
2. Its birth rate was one of the highest. For every 1,000 married women between the
ages of fifteen and fifty, the annual number of births, including still-borns, for the
period 1886–1895 was between 139 and 152. The corresponding figure for the
VIIth was 0 to 64. For non-married women the figure was 68 to 79; in the VIIth
it was 0 to 12. Frequency of deaths from disease and alcoholism were also relatively high. Jacques Bertillon, *De la fréquence des principales causes de décès à
Paris pendant la seconde moitié du XIXe siècle et notament pendant la periode 1886–
1905* (1906), pp. 119–121, 141–142, 150, 154, 172, 217. The population of the *arrondissement* reached 112,684 in 1891. Millerand's constituency in that year numbered 55,847. *Annuaire statistique de la ville de Paris, XVe année* (1894), p. 124.
3. *Entrepôts* were places at which merchants were authorized temporarily to deposit
items subject to an entry duty without previously paying the duty. It allowed them
to submit their goods to potential buyers beforehand. See Jacques Hillairet, *Le
XIIe arrondissement et son histoire* (1972).
4. *Les Guides bleus: Paris* (1968), p. 430. Plans have been drafted to build in Bercy
a modern and self-sufficient quarter with numerous parks and highrises and no
automobiles, with the warehouses to be covered by suspended gardens.
5. Ernest Raynaud, *Souvenirs de police au temps de Félix Faure* (1924), pp. 30–33.
6. Lucien Lambeau, *Bercy: Histoire des communes annexées à Paris en 1859* (1910),
p. 330; Eugène Richard, *Le Marché du vin à Paris* (1934), p. 107. Repealed by the
law of December 29, 1900.

7. Charles Warner, *The Wine Growers of France and the Government Since 1875* (New York, 1960), pp. 14–15.

8. Enacted August 14, 1889, it defined wine as the exclusive product of the fermentation of grapes. Adulteration, however, was so difficult to detect that the law was practically unenforceable. JOC, July 12, 13, 1889.

9. JOC, March 24, July 3, 1890. Relating the event in his *Mémoires* (p. 32) Millerand wrote simply, 'I did not forget my constituents'. In 1892 the Méline Tariff raised the duty on foreign wines almost 60% and thus increased the amount of low-grade wine-manufacturing in France. Werner, p. 15.

10. A file listing his efforts is in the archives of the Ministry of Commerce. AN, F12 4847 (Projets, amendments, notes ministérielles, 1870–1905); JOC, June 16, 1894. He denied defending the interests of the Bercy merchants but claimed to be helping small café owners.

11. AN, F 2051 (Mouvement de la population de la France par arrondissement: Nord-Yonne, 1889); F 2063 (1893); F 2066 (1896).

12. Louis Chevalier, *La Formation de la population parisienne au XIXe siècle* (1949), p. 287. Charles Pouthas, *La Population française pendant la première moitié du XIXe siècle* (1956, pp. 148, 156. For a classic analysis of the relationship between local political organizations and immigration see Warren Moscow, *Politics in the Empire State* (New York, 1948), pp. 120–147.

13. Citations and statistics in this paragraph from Chevalier, pp. 263, 287–288.

14. Figures and lists in MP-BN.

15. Jean Melia, 'Portrait: Le caractère et la personnalité de M. Alexandre Millerand', *Le Parlement et l'opinion*, September 23, 1920, pp. 1657–58. If we include the elections of 1885 and 1919, in both of which he was returned by considerably larger constituencies, then Millerand represented Parisians from 1885 to 1920.

16. David A. Shannon, *The Socialist Party of America* (Chicago, 1967), p. 22. Before 1898 Millerand retained receipts for the campaign expenses incurred, and we may assume he paid them personally. There are no receipts after 1898, and presumably they were paid by the Committee, thus attesting its larger role. Unfortunately, no evidence has survived either to suggest how financial resources were obtained or to permit further generalization on the electoral sociology of the district.

17. See Manevy, p. 74, and Georges Weill, *Le Journal: Origines, évolution et rôle de la presse périodique* (1934), p. 258.

19. Daniel, *1889*, p. 207.

18. JOC, November 19, 1889; *Le XIXe Siècle*, November 21, 1889.

20. Claude Willard, *La Fusillade de Fourmies* (1957), p. 34. Zévaès also published a book under the same title in 1936, but Willard's is based on more extensive documentation.

21. Willard, *La Fusillade*, p. 41. There were disturbances in other cities as well, ranging from scuffling in Lyons to street battles in Saint-Quentin. In the latter city Millerand defended a party organizer named Langrand, who was sentenced to one year's imprisonment. A union organizer, who received a year's sentence at Charleville for organizing workers, had his sentence reduced to two months by the Nancy Court after Millerand had intervened. Maurice Garcon, *Histoire de la justice sous la IIIe République* (1957), Vol. I, pp. 200–201.

22. JOC, May 4, 1891; Zévaès, *Ombres,* p. 164. Also *Le XIXe Siècle,* May 6, 1891.
23. *Le XIXe Siècle,* May 10, 1891.
24. Lafargue to Engels, June 25, 1891, *Lafargue-Engels Correspondance, 1891-1895,* III, p. 67. In a letter to Laura Lafargue August 27, 1889, Engels said he saw Millerand as the embodiment of the 'new radicalism', but with Boulanger once out of the way, it would discredit itself like the Clemenceau variety, II, pp. 311-12. In a letter written September 1, 1889, to Laura Lafargue, he had voiced doubts over the radical potential of *La Voix;* II, (1956), p. 317.
25. A. Zévaès, *Notes et souvenirs d'un militant* (1913), p. 109; Millerand's letter to Lafargue June 6, 1891, Guesde Archives, IISH, 203/1.
26. *Paul Lafargue devant la cour d'assises de Douai, 5 juillet, 1891: Plaidoirie de Millerand* (Lille, 1891). The similarity with Zola's famous accusation seven years later is too close not to be mentioned.
27. Zévaès, *Notes,* p. 110; *Le Socialiste,* July 8, 1891; Goldberg, *Life,* p. 74; G. Renard, 'Millerand, Quelques souvenirs', RS. January–February 1950, p. 95.
28. Laura Lafargue to Engels, October 16, 1891, *Lafargue–Engels Correspondance.* III. p. 112. *Le Socialiste,* the Guesdist organ, was a weekly.
29. Zévaès, *Notes,* p. 112.
30. *Le XIXe Siécle,* November 6, 1891; JOC, October 31, 1891.
31. Paul Lafargue to Engels October 15, 1891, *Correspondance,* III, p. 111; also Zévaès, *Ombres,* p. 175, *Notes,* p, 120.
32. JOC, November 9, 1891; *Le XIXe Siècle,* November 11, 1891.
33. March 14, 1903. Text in RS, April 1903, especially p. 430.
34. April 14, 1903. Text in RS, May, 1903, especially p. 541.
35. Cited in Zévaès, *Notes,* p. 120.
36. Text in P.L. Berthaud, Ed., *Deux discours de M. Alexandre Millerand, Président de la République* (1923).
37. As an illustration of growing concentration of industry – and a future source of legislative concern – Millerand pointed to sugar refining. See J. H. Clapham, *The Economic Development of France and Germany, 1815-1919,* 4th ed. (Cambridge, 1963), II, 258-259.
38. Berthaud, *Deux discours,* Introduction, p. 7.
39. Emile Levasseur, *Questions ouvrières et industrielles en France sous la Troisième République* (1907), pp. 650-60; Goldberg, *Life,* pp. 97-99.
40. Léon de Seilhac, *Les Grèves* (1903), p. 235.
41. *Le XIXe Siècle,* September 20, October 5-7, 1892.
42. JOC, October 18, 1892. Summarized in RS, November, 1892, p. 593.
43. RS, November, 1892, p. 606; *Le XIXe Siécle,* October 28, 1892.
44. Text of letter in *Le XIXe Siècle,* October 29, 1892.
45. RS, November 1892, p. 609.
46. PR, January 11, 1893. Also see the issues of January 4 and 7.
47. Henry de Basty, in *Revue d'histoire contemporaine,* I, January 20, 1889, p. 10.
48. Jean Dietz, 'Un homme d'Etat français: M. Alexandre Millerand', *Revue de Belgique,* August 1, 1914 (46), pp. 808–809.
49. JOC, June 21, 1892.
50. RS, July, 1892, pp. 66-76. Ernest Charles, p. 286.

51. *Le XIXᵉ Siècle*, January 2, 14, April 24, 1891; PR, July 12, 1892.
52. Parker T. Moon, *The Labor Problem and the Social Catholic Movement in France* (New York, 1921), pp. 183–185, 191.
53. Fernand Payen, *Raymond Poincaré, l'homme, le parlementaire, l'avocat* (1936), p. 83; Conseil National, *Onze ans*, p. 28.
54. JOC, December 20, 1892; Seignobos, *L'Evolution*, p. 167.
55. PR, December 31, 1892; Paul Detot, *Le Socialisme devant les chambres françaises, 1893–98* (1902), p. 62.
56. JOC, February 16, 1893; Daniel, *1893*, p. 78; Detot, p. 63.
57. *Le XIXᵉ Siècle*, March 11, 1892.
58. Goldberg, *Life*, p. 108.
59. JOC, July 8, 1893. Text also in RS, August, 1893, pp. 214–219. For these events see Zévaès, *Notes*, pp. 57–58, and Seignobos, *L'Evolution*, pp. 170–171. On July 3, Millerand questioned the government on the 'police brutality' displayed in breaking up an entirely unrelated students' demonstration.
60. JOC, 2ᵉ séance, July 8, 1893. See *Le XIXᵉ Siècle*, July 9, 10, 1893; JOC, 1ᵉ séance, July 10, 1893.
61. RS, September, October 1893, pp. 352–354, 449.
62. RS, August, 1893, p. 231; Seignobos, *L'Evolution*, p. 171.

NOTES TO CHAPTER 5: LA PETITE RÉPUBLIQUE AND THE SOCIALIST UNION

1. Georges Lachapelle, *Les Régimes électoraux* (1934), p. 78. By 1892 only eight of the Groupe ouvrier remained in Parliament. Lefranc, p. 89.
2. RS, January, 1901, p. 86; A. Zévaès, *Les Guesdistes* (1911), p. 76; Willard, *Les Guesdistes*, pp. 68–71; Lafranc, p. 115.
3. Manevy, p. 174. Also Zévaès, 'La Presse socialiste', *Nouvelle Revue*, March–April 1973, pp. 23–40. Pellier's memoirs of the period appeared under the title, 'The Honeymoon: A History of Radical-Socialist Collaboration on La Petite République', *L'Ordre* from April 20 to May 4, 1932.
4. PR, October 27, 1892.
5. *L'Ordre*, April 24, 1932.
6. Speech reproduced in PR, November 8, 1892. For an analysis of the socialist desire to ally with Radicals see Georges Weill, 'Die Sozialistische Bewegung in Frankreich, 1893–1910', *Archiv für die Geschichte des Sozialismus und der Arbeiterbewegung*, (1910), I, p. 134.
7. RS, December, 1892, p. 749; Prelot, p. 16; Lefranc, pp. 90-91.
8. The article appeared in PR, February 15, 1893, the speech in JOC, February 16, 1893, and it was timed to coincide with the article. (The newspaper was dated from the following day until February 25, 1904.)
9. Daniel Halévy, *Essais sur le mouvement ouvrier en France* (1901), pp. 222–223. See also the analysis of A. Delon, RS, August, 1893, p. 204.
10. Hubert Lagardelle, 'Les origines du socialisme parlementaire en France', MS, September, 1909, pp. 82, 84.

11. Reproduced in *L'Ordre,* April 21, 1932. The Manifesto also called for 'an end to the capitalist regime'.
12. PR, January 16, 1893.
13. RS, March, 1893, pp. 365–66.
14. Jaurès' first article appeared on January 12.
15. *L'Ordre,* April 22, 24, 1932; Edmond Claris, *Souvenirs de 60 ans de journalisme, 1895–1955* (1955), pp. 14–15.
16. *L'Ordre,* April 22, 24, 1932. Millerand's letter to Deville, dated October 16, 1892, is in the Deville papers, AN, 51 Ap 1 dr. 1. Renard 'Quelques souvenirs', RS, January–February 1950, p. 95.
17. PR, July 6, 1893; *L'Ordre,* April 27, 1932.
18. *Le XIXe Siècle,* July 25, 1891; March 22, April 9, 1892; *L'Ordre,* April 27, 28, 1932, Pellier's letter assuring Millerand full control in MP–BN.
19. Paul Acker, *Petites confessions, visites, et portraits,* 2nd ed. (n.d.), p. 121. Also *Mémoires,* pp. 30–33.
20. *L'Ordre,* April 28, 1932.
21. *L'Ordre,* April 30, 1932.
22. *L'Ordre,* May 1, 1932.
23. References to the duel in *Le XIXe Siècle,* December 3, 1893; RS, January–February, 1950, p. 96; and in a memorandum, MP–JM.
24. *L'Ordre,* May 4, 1932.
25. PR, August 4, 1892. See *LE XIXe Siècle,* February 17 and March 24, 1895, and PR, March 23, 1895.
26. Text in *Le Petit Calaisien,* March 7, 1893.
27. *Le Petit Calaisien,* May 27, 1893; PR, March 27, 1893.
28. *Le Socialiste,* March 19, 1893, and Zévaès, *Jules Guesde,* p. 114 for Guesde's prediction. PR, August 6, 1893. Also A. Millerand, *Le Socialisme réformiste français* (1903), pp. 61–64 for Millerand's speech.
29. Cited in Compère-Morel, *Jules Guesde,* p. 387. Also see Carl Landauer, 'Erosion', *International Review of Social History,* VI (1961), p. 214.
30. Editorial opinion summarized in RS, April 1893, p. 400.
31. Millerand's speech was also reproduced in *La Ville,* August 26, 1893. MP–BN. *La Ville* was a weekly, sometimes bi-weekly, newspaper published by Millerand's Committee. Election material in MP–BN.
32. Millerand received 6,448 votes, Ribonnier, 1,195. René Samuel and George Bonet-Maury, *Les Parlementaires françaises, 1900–1914* (1914), p. 292; PR, August 22, 23, 1893.
33. Lefranc, p. 91. For Paris the 1893 election was the apogée of the left. Only four of the thirty-three deputies elected were on the right. Socialists, joined by former Boulangists, represented all of the 'U' belt of poorer Paris; Watson, p. 55. *La Petite République* (September 5) claimed that fifty-five socialists were elected. Most historians of French socialism place the figure at closer to fifty. But these figures were questioned by Aaron Noland (p. 32) as including Radicals and Boulangists running on socialist platforms.
34. Daniel, *1893,* p. 79; Ernest Labrousse, 'La Montée du socialisme, 1848–1945', RS, May 1946, pp. 23–24. Also see Rudolph Winnacker, 'Influence of the Dreyfus

Affair upon Political Developments in France', *Papers of the Michigan Academy of Sciences, Arts, and Letters* (Ann Arbor, 1936), XXI, pp. 467–78; Lachapelle, *Les Régimes électoraux*, p. 79.

35. Jacques Chastenet, *Histoire de la Troisième République*, Vol. IV, *Jours inquiets et jours sanglants, 1906–1918* (1955), p. 375.
36. *Le Socialiste*, August 26, 1893. Text also in Zévaès, *Jules Guesde*, p. 121.
37. Lefranc, p. 91; A Bertrand, *La Chambre de 1893, biographies des 581 députés* (1893).
38. Gabriel Mermiex, *Le Socialisme: Définitions, explications, objections* (1906), p. 162; Halévy, p. 228.
39. RS, March, 1894, p. 341; *Revue des deux mondes*, September 1, 1894, p. 201; *L'Ordre*, May 1, 1932.
40. In the first ten months of the new legislature there were sixty-one interpellations and thirty-one questions put to the goverment. The socialists were responsible for most of them. Daniel, *1894*, p.v., and Seignobos, *L'Evolution*, p. 181; Paul Louis, 'Une legislature', RS, March 1898, p. 299.
41. JOC, July 23, 1894. Cited in RS, August, 1894, pp. 215–216.
42. JOC, November 21, 23, 25, 1893; Daniel, *1894*, p.v.
43. *Le XIXe Siècle*, December 16, 1893; JOC, December 14, 1893.
44. JOC, May 22, June 4, 1894. The chief clauses and the names of those who signed may be found in Guyot, pp. 291–293.
45. PR, June 26, 28, 1894.
46. PR, August 12, 1893. Story in *L'Ordre*, May 1, 1932.
47. *L'Ordre*, May 4, 1932; *La Chambord*, September 29, 1894.
48. JOC, January 10, 1895.
49. JOC, January 14, 1895; Emmanuel Beau de Lomenie, *Les Responsabilités des dynasties bourgeoises*, Vol. II, *De Mac-Mahon à Poincaré* (1947), pp. 265–266.
50. Guyot, p. 278; PR, January 17, 1895.
51. JOC, October 26, 28, 1895.
52. Goldberg, *Life*, pp. 186–187. See the title page of Millerand's *Le Socialisme réformiste français*.
53. Renard, 'Millerand, quelques souvenirs', RS, January–February 1950, pp. 95, 97.
54. June 28, 1895. Printed in RS, July 1895, pp. 1–13.
55. Jaurès expressed and defended these views in an important article, 'Le socialisme français', *Cosmopolis*, January 1898.

NOTES TO CHAPTER 6: THE TRIUMPH OF REFORMISM

1. For the anti-German response on the part of French socialists, see Chapters I–IV of A. Zévaès, *La Question d'Alsace-Lorraine et le socialisme* (1917).
2. *Mémoires*, p. 34.
3. Letter dated September 20, 1893. *Fournière Papers*, IFHS, 14 AS 181, No. 1069.
4. Text in PR and *Le XIXe Siècle*, October 3, 1893, and RS, October 1893, pp. 499–503.
5. *Le XIX Siècle*, Ocotber 14, 19, 1893.
6. Conseil National, *Onze ans*, pp. 32–33. Also quoted in Compère-Morel, *Jules*

Guesde, p. 391, and Zévaès, *Les Guesdistes* (1911), p. 93. Also see Carroll, pp. 193–194.

7. Letter dated June 20, 1893. *Engels–Lafargue Correspondance,* III, p. 284.

8. Preface to J. Vingtras, *Socialisme et patriotisme* (Lille, 1900).

9. Dommanget, *Edouard Vaillant,* p. 222; AN, Archives of the Ministry of Interior. Reports to the Direction de la Sûreté Générale, 4e Bureau (hereafter referred to as Sûreté), F7 12886 (Parti socialiste: 1894–1906) dossier entitled 'Documents confidentiels relatifs au Parti Socialiste-Guesdiste', Report dated September 21, 1898.

10. JOC, June 10, 1895. Also see Frederick L. Schuman, *War and Diplomacy in the French Republic* (New York, 1931), pp. 151–52.

11. PR, June 12, 1895; A. Millerand, *Le Socialisme réformiste français* (1903); p. 31; Conseil National, *Onze ans,* p. 73; BN, Department of Manuscripts, Scheurer-Kestner, *Journal,* Vol. VIII, *1896–1898,* Na fr. 12 711, p. 167; AN, Sûreté, F7 12885 (Parti socialiste: 1894–1900), report dated September 2, 1897. Beau de Lomenie, II, p. 269.

12. JOC, November 21, 1896. *La Lanterne,* September 22, 1897.

13. JOC, February 22, 1897. See also PR, February 24, 1897. Millerand and Goblet interpellated the government on March 17. PR, March 18, 1897.

14. JOC, February 7, 1898.

15. Millerand said this at Firminy in 1902. Text in RS, February, 1902, pp. 228–31. Guyot, p. 277. For an example of Millerand's support see PR, January 14, 1896.

16. PR, November 16, 1895; Zévaès, *Notes,* p. 194; JOC, March 20, 1896; Hubert Lagardelle, 'Les Origines du socialisme parlementaire en France', MS, September, 1909, pp. 184, 186, 188.

17. Payen, *Poincaré,* p. 116; JOC, March 26, 1896; PR, March 28, 1898.

18. PR, May 2, 1896.

19. Georges Lachapelle, *Le Ministère Méline, deux années de politique intérieure et extérieure, 1896–1898* (1928), pp. 27–28, 35–38, 119–121.

20. JOC April 30, 1896, p. 765; PR, July 1, 1896.

21. JOC, November 26, 1896; March 12, 1898.

22. *La Lanterne,* April 14, 1897.

23. Campaign material may be found in the Guesde Archives, IISH, folio No. 638. It reflected patriotic sentiment for both the elections of 1893 and 1898, but more so for the latter. For the POF's agricultural program, see the discussion in Landauer, 'Erosion'. Also Paul Lafargue, *Programme agricole du parti ouvrier français* (Lille, 1895). For Deville's remark, see Paul Louis, 'Une legislature', RS, March, 1898, p. 308; Landauer, 'Erosion'. For Guesde's speech, JOC, June 15, 1896. Cited in Zévaès, *Notes,* p. 117. Guesde said that society could not be changed suddenly, 'with the use of a magic wand'. *Le Socialiste,* November 29, December 13, 1896; February 21, 1897, for Sarraute's articles. BN, Department of Manuscripts. Scheurer-Kestner, *Journal,* Vol. VII, p. 105; Ligou, p. 214.

24. Originally given to *Le Matin,* the interview was reproduced in *La Question sociale,* in Bordeaux, November 26, 1893. Cited by Michelle Perrot, 'Les Socialistes français et les problemes du pouvoir, 1871–1914', Michelle Perrot and Annie Kriegel, Eds., *Le socialisme français et le pouvoir* (1966), p. 55; Lefranc, pp. 173–175, 179. In 1912 Guesde was to say that he had been wrong in 1897 to vote for nationaliza-

tion of the Bank of France. It only reinforced the bourgeois state, and nationalization should follow the revolution. Lefranc, p. 173.

25. Lagardelle, p. 174. Guesde either sponsored these bills together with other POF deputies or with Independents like Jaurès. For his bill organizing the right to strike (requiring a majority vote on the part of the workers involved 'in order to prevent a collective right from being abandoned to individual usage') see JOC, annexe au procès-verbal de la séance du 8 février, 1894 (no. 358); for his bill to provide rural workers with a minimum salary and with delegates to be elected by them to oversee working conditions, see JOC, appendix to the session of February 15, 1894 (no. 385); for his bill to ensure an absolutely free vote, that of February 21, 1894 (no. 416); for a national maternity fund, that of November 14, 1896 (no. 2114); for minimum salary levels, that of January 20, 1894 (no. 356). Guesde also submitted bills designed to assure full freedom of campaign meetings, suppress residence requirements in voting, reform military courts and permit soldiers to vote. See the partial list in *Le Rappel*, September 4, 1894. His bill to establish grievance machinery was introduced February 8, 1894. See the *Journal officiel* for that date. The sum of his social legislative proposals may be found in his collection of speeches, *Quatre ans des luttes sociales à la Chambre 1893–98* (1901). See Ligou, p. 214, for Guesde's remark about the proletariat and its country.

26. RS, May 1895, pp. 628–69; JOC, June 13, 1898. Cited in Detot, p. 7.

27. *Le Socialiste*, January 19, 1896.

28. PR, January 29, 1896; *Le Socialiste*, January 12, 1896.

29. Electoral successes listed in Zévaès, *Ombres*, p. 267. Also see the introduction of R. L. Berthaud, Ed., *Deux discours de M. Alexandre Millerand* (1923); Prelot, p. 111.

30. A text may be found in PR, June 1, 1896, and in Millerand's *Le Socialisme réformiste français;* Halévy, *Essais*, p. 224.

31. RS, June, 1896, p. 748. Jacques Pinset, 'Quelques problèmes du socialisme en France vers 1900', *Revue d'histoire économique et sociale*, III (1958), p. 344. Lavy's letter dated August 30, 1896, MP–JM.

32. Lefranc, p. 100; PR, June 1, 1896. Yves Guyot pointed to Guesde's persistence in making Millerand come out for collectivism but also directed attention to Guesde's own full acceptance of reformism, Guyot, p. 128. See Goldberg, *The Life of Jaurès*, p. 185, for Guesde's confidence in Jaurès.

33. MP–BN. Millerand's draft lecture 'Trente ans de République', pp. 64–65.

34. Mirman's letter dated May 31, 1896, MP–JM. Also see *Le Rappel*, June 3, 4, 6 and 13 1896. The five Allemanist deputies, Avez, Dejeante, Faberot, Groussier and Toussaint all remained hostile. Orry, p. 30; For Richard, Sûreté, AN, F7 12886 (Parti socialiste, 1894–1906), Report №26, August 13, 1896; Raul Persil, *Alexandre Millerand: 1859–1943* (1949), p. 14.

35. Daniel, *1896*, p. 210; Guyot, pp. 93–94. There was, however, no move to bar dissident deputies, Lefranc, pp. 101–102. The four who refused were Independents; of the ten who abstained, five were Allemanists.

36. MP–BN.

37. James Joll, *The Anarchists* (New York, 1966 ed.), p. 195.

38. Goldberg, *Life*, p. 174. For the change in anarchist tactics see Maitron, pp. 245–

47, and Goldberg, 'French Socialism and the Congress of London', *The Historian*, Vol. 19 (4), p. 405.

39. PR, July 29, 1896.
40. Emile Vandervelde, *Souvenirs d'un militant socialiste* (1939), pp. 145–46.
41. Halévy, *Essais*, p. 225; Goldberg, 'French Socialism', pp. 420–23.
42. *Almanach socialiste illustré pour 1895*, p. 72; Melia, pp. 1656–59.
43. Romain Rolland, *Mémoires et fragments du journal* (1956), pp. 296–298. Cited in J. A. Lecourd, 'Romain Rolland, témoin de son temps', *Information historique*, 1959, XXI (1) p. 42.
44. Acker, p. 124.
45. Charton, 1882 ed., p. 73.
46. Payen, *Poincaré*, p. 47.
47. Zévaès, *Les Procès littéraires au XIXe Siècle* (1924), pp. 251–58; Garcon, pp. 272–74.
48. A. Millerand, *Plaidiorie... devant la cour d'assises de la Seine, audience du 15 mars, 1890.* Also appended to L. Descaves, *Sous-offs, Roman militaire*, 36th ed. (1892).
49. Letter to Millerand dated April 12, 1893, Brunellière Correspondence, IFHS, 14AS 102/13, folios 254–55 Letter to Millerand dated November 29, 1895, 14AS 103/15, folios 441–442. Also reproduced in Claude Willard, Ed., *Le Correspondance de Charles Brunellière, 1880–1917* (1968), pp. 22–24, 28, 91, 185–88, 213.
50. In a brochure entitled *L'Affaire des canaux agricoles, 1895*, MP–MR.
51. BN, Department of Manuscripts, Papiers et correspondence de Mme. Hermann Raffalovich, 3668, XXVII. Two letters are dated January 26 and April 21, 1891; a third letter is undated. MP–JM; Renard, 'Souvenirs', RS, January–February 1950, p. 93.
52. MP–JM. Offers came in 1896, when Millerand temporarily left *La Petite République*.
53. Charles Lyon-Caen, *Choix de plaidiories* (1921), pp. xiv-xvi.
54. Payen, *Les Règles*, p. 249.
55. Peter Nettl, 'The German Social Democratic Party, 1890–1940, as a Political Model', *Past and Present*, XXX, April 1965, pp. 68–69.
56. MP/JM. A letter dated April 12, 1889 to the tax office reveals he had recently moved to that address; Payen, *Poincaré*, p. 170.
57. 'Souvenirs', RS, May 1951, pp. 611, 615.
58. Letter dated October 20, 1898. Deville Papers, AN, 51 APT dr. 1. She survived her husband by seven years. Mme. Millerand died at Versailles October 23, 1950.
59. Letter dated May 24, 1897. Deville Papers AN, 51 APT dr. 1. The date would indicate there was a liaison before the marriage. Other letters to Deville reported the susbequent births.
60. Amélie-Mélanie died at the end of World War I, Jean-François in 1897.

Notes to Chapter 7: Prelude to schism

1. The value of the material gathered and the insights acquired has been acknowledged by French historians. See Michelle Perrot, 'Archives policières et militants ouvriers sous la Troisième République. Un example: Le Gard', *Revue d'histoire*

économique et sociale, XXXVII, (1959), 2, pp. 219–39. Also 'Le problème des sources pour l'étude du militant ouvrier au XIX siècle', pp. 21–34; Jean Tulard, 'La Prefecture de Police et ses archives', *Information historique,* 4, 1962, pp. 197–98. Willard, in *Les Guesdistes,* pp. 127, 219–220 and 667, praises at least those reports filed in Paris as 'precise' and 'truthful' and those on party life as 'indispensable'. See also Annie Kriegel, *Aux origines du communisme français, 1914–1920* (1964), I, p. 20. The American historian, Roger Williams, also called the use of police records 'indispensable'. He pointed out that some agents were very reliable, submitting reports confirmed by other observers and sometimes correcting themselves. Others, less sophisticated, were interested in pleasing their superiors or who seriously reported the 'prattle of cranks', *Henri Rochefort* (New York, 1966), p. 300.

2. Sûreté, F7 12886, Report dated August 13, 1896, no. 26. For one like Guesde, who devoted his life to a cause, it is almost impossible to distinguish between personal and party interests. But this is precisely the point. It is not his bad faith but his judgment that must come under consideration.

3. Zévaès, *Notes,* pp. 195–196.

4. Paul Lafargue to Engels, letter dated February 23, 1893; Engels to Lafargue, February 25, 1893, *Lafargue-Engels Correspondance,* III, p. 259; Engels to Paul Lafargue, October 13, 1893; Engels to Laura Lafargue, December 19, 1893; pp. 326, 349; Laura Lafargue to Engels, October 14, 1893; Paul Lafargue to Engels, March 8, 1894, pp. 326.

5. PP, Series B a/1472 (Socialisme en France, 1893–1896), report dated November 17, 1894; Zévaès, *Notes,* p. 196; Sûreté, AN, F7 12885 (Parti socialiste, 1894–1900) report dated October 20, 1897, no. 79.

6. Zévaès, *Notes,* p. 196.

7. Letter dated February 18, 1896, IFHS, Fournière Papers, 14AS 181.

8. Sûreté, F7 12886, reports dated August 3, 1896 (no. 14), and August 8, 1896 (no. 15); MP–BN. The letter was undated.

9. RS, January-February 1950, p. 97; May 1951, p. 622. Also see Weill, *Histoire,* p. 311. There is a description of a 'Marxist attack' in RS, February 1897, p 235.

10. A draft of the staff's letter is found in Millerand's papers, MP–BN. There is an unsigned explanatory 'circulaire confidentielle aux membres du POF concernant l'affaire de La Petite République' appended to a letter from Lafargue to Guesde, dated June 2, 1897, in the Guesde Archives, IISH, 275/1. It agrees substantially with the above account. However, it maintains that Guesde and Chauvin assumed control only after the departure of Millerand and Jaurès to *La Lanterne,* implying that Guesde was not involved in Millerand's departure and was only afterwards asked to replace him. It states, furthermore, that Guesde had insisted on working to retain socialist unity, had in fact asked Millerand and Jaurès to return, and only on their refusal agreed to become editor-in-chief. However, the same archives contain a Teilhard note to Guesde dated December 8, 1896, Guesde's reply the next day and a subsequent letter by Teilhard dated January 19, 1897. This reveals that the two men had in fact been communicating with each other before Millerand's resignation. Guesde Archives, IISH, 269/3 and 270/3; Sûreté, F7 12886, report dated January 30, 1897 (no. 143).

11. RS, February 1897, p. 236. An undated draft note from the new editors nevertheless promised that the newspaper would continue to work for socialist unity. Guesde archives, IISH, 274/9.

12. Sûreté, F7 12886, report dated February 4, 1897 (no. 146). The former Director-General of the Compagnie Générale Transatlantique, Eugène Péreire, had recently purchased *La Lanterne*. Presumably he and Millerand were negotiating before Millerand's first article was published.

13. Sûreté, F7 12886, report dated April 7, 1897 (no. 174). Guesde's criticisms in the 'Circulaire confidentielle aux membres du POF'. Guesde Archives, IISH, 275/1.

14. AN F7 12886; PP, B a/1125; Guesde to Liebknecht, June 20, 1899; Wilhelm Liebknecht Papers, IISH, 165/12. Also see Guesde to Liebknecht, July 29, 1900. Wilhelm Liebknecht Papers, IISH, 165/37–38; Willard, *Les Guesdistes*, pp. 129–30.

18. Lefranc, p. 95; Jean-Jacques Fiechter, *Le Socialisme français: De l'affaire Dreyfus à la grande Guerre* (Geneva, 1965), p. 79; Delroy to Guesde, May 29, 1897, Guesde Archives, IISH, 274/8.

16. *La Lanterne*, February 8, 1897. It was apparently more solvent, too. When Millerand became editor-in-chief, he drafted a list of salary payments (dated March 1, 1898). He gave himself, Jaurès and Pelletan 100 francs per article. Others were paid monthly: Baudin drew 500 francs, Léfèvre 300, and Briand 700. MP-BN.

17. IFHS, Fournière Papers, 14AS 81, letter dated September 6, 1896 (no. 1072); BN, Department of Manuscripts, 'Journal', N.A. fr. 12711, Vol. VIII (1896), p. 105.

18. Sorlin, pp. 354–364. My next two paragraphs are based on these pages. Also see Goldberg, 'French Socialism', *The Historian*, 19 (4), p. 408, and Alexander Sedgwick, *The Ralliement in French Politics, 1890–1898* (Cambridge, Mass., 1965), pp. 75–81.

19. *Almanach de la question sociale pour 1898* (n.d.), pp. 107–108.

20. Letter to Millerand dated February 14, 1898. Brunellière correspondence, IFHS, 14 AS 103/19 folio 129. Cited in Willard, *Brunellière*, p. 279.

21. Sûreté, F7 12496, 'Les diverses fractions du Parti socialiste et les elections de mai, 1898'.

22. Sûreté, F7 12886, Report dated October 8, 1897 (no. 234). The writer claimed that he attended a meeting of the Parti ouvrier's National Council. Report no. 237, dated October 25, 1897. Also no. 236 bis and no. 241, dated October 11 and October 30, 1897, respectively. According to this last report, at Guesde's suggestion he and other Guesdist editors agreed to drop their suit for 'damages' against *La Petite République* in the interests of unity. They also agreed not to ask for their salaries. September 2, 1897 (no. 219).

23. Sûreté, F7 12885, 'Parti socialiste, 1894–1900' (no. 84).

24. A. Millerand, *La Plateforme électorale* (1898). A report on the speech is in RS, February, 1898, pp. 72–85. Cited in Dietz, p. 807. A more anticapitalist sounding speech was delivered April 23; PR, April 24, 1898.

25. Samuel J. Eldersfeld, *et al.*, 'Research in Political Behavior', *American Political Science Review*, December 1952, pp. 1027–28.

26. Theodore D. Lockwood, 'French Socialists and Political Responsibilities, 1898–1905', unpublished doctoral dissertation, Princeton University, 1952, pp. 261–262. See Millerand's preface to Adrien Veber, *La Suppression des octrois* (1899).

27. Fifty-seven according to PR, May 10, 24, 1898. Lachapelle, *Les Régimes,* gave the Moderates an increase of only four seats. For Noland (p. 62) only forty-two legitimate socialists were elected, five more than in 1893.

28. According to Samuel (I, pp 292–293), 8,791 of 9,905 votes cast. Millerand admitted the seriousness of the loss of socialist chiefs in *L'Eclair,* May 30, 1898. For the socialist view of the result as a moral victory, see Prelot, p. 131, and G. Weill, 'Die Sozialistische Bewegung...', p. 195.

29. A. Millerand, 'Les socialistes et la législature nouvelle', *Almanach de la question sociale pour* 1899, pp. 61–62.

30. PR, June 2, 1898.

31. JOC, June 13, 1898. See also Daniel, *1898,* p. 234, and PR, June 15, 1898.

32. *La Lanterne,* June 29, 1898.

33. JOC, June 23, 1898. Guesde asked Millerand to press the attack in the Chamber. An undated letter written the beginning of July is in the Guesde Archives, along with supporting testimony and affidavits of irregularities. IISH, f° 640. For Millerand's optimism see AN F7 12886, Sûreté, report of June 7, 1898 (no. 330).

34. Also see Halévy, *Essais,* pp. 223–224; Willard, *Les Guesdistes,* p. 197; Sûreté, F7 12886, report dated June 7, 1898 (no. 336).

35. For a theoretical discussion of this 'deradicalization' process, see Robert C. Tucker, *The Marxian Revolutionary Idea: Essays on Marxist Thought and its Impact on Radical Movements* (New York, 1969), pp. 172–198.

36. Georges Suarez, *Briand: Sa vie, son œuvre, avec son journal et de nombreux documents inédits,* Vol. I: *Le Révolté circonspect, 1862–1904* (1938), p. 240.

NOTES TO CHAPTER 8: TO POWER

1. JOC, December 24, 1894. See Joseph Reinach, *Histoire de l'affaire Dreyfus,* hereafter, *Histoire,* Vol. I: *Le Procès de 1894* (1901), p. 478.

2. JOC, December 4, 1897.

3. Reinach, *Histoire,* Vol. III: *La crise: Procès Esterhazy–Procès Zola,* p. 145. Also Renard, 'Mémoires', RS, January-February 1950, p. 98.

4. Cited in James Joll, *The Second International, 1889–1914* (New York, 1966), p. 68.

5. MP–JM.

6. Manifesto dated January 19, 1898. PR, January 20, 1898; RS, January, 1893, p. 99; Reinach, *Histoire,* III, p. 254.

7. Halévy, *Essais,* pp. 232–234; Renard, 'Millerand, quelques souvenirs', RS, January-February 1950, p. 98.

8. Zévaès, *Ombres,* p. 272.

9. Reinach, *Démagogues et socialistes* (1896), p. 3.

10. A series of previously unpublished Péguy letters appeared in *Le Figaro Littéraire,* June 4, 1960. See his article, 'L'Affaire Dreyfus et la crise du parti socialiste', *Revue Blanche* (1899), p. 133.

11. *L'Amitié Charles Péguy,* June 15, 1960, pp. 27–28. See also Marjorie Villiers, *Charles Péguy: A Study in Integrity* (New York, 1965), p. 95, and Hans A. Schmitt, *Charles Péguy: The Decline of an Idealist* (Baton Rouge, 1967), p. 91. Renard,

RS, January-February 1950, p. 98. Péguy and Millerand drew closer when the former became disillusioned with anti-Dreyfusards in power after the turn of the century and when Millerand attacked Combes. Millerand was to eulogize Péguy after the latter's battlefield death in 1914 and write the preface to Péguy's collected works in 1917.

12. *Le Socialiste*, July 24, 1898; *Mémoires*, pp. 35–56. Millerand's letter dated May 15, 1898, cited in Renard, RS, January-February 1950, p. 98; Léon Blum, *Souvenirs sur l'affaire* 16th ed., (1935), p. 120.

13. *Mémoires*, p. 36; *Histoire*, IV, p. 222; Edouard Herriot, *Jadis: d'une guerre à l'autre* (1952), I, p. 205.

14. Mermiex, p. 103; Sûreté, AN F7 12496, report dated October 29, 1898.

15. Cited in Fiechter, p. 62.

16. JOC, December 17, 1900, 2e séance; BN, Reinach correspondence, Department of Manuscripts, N. A. fr. 24 888, dated May 23, 1903 (no. 94). In 1908 Millerand said he saw the affair in prespective and that the 'crimes, wickedness and hatreds were designed less to crush an innocent man than to protect a guilty one, by the need to hide the error'. June 14, 1908, N. A. fr. 24 882.

17. JOC, November 22, 1898.

18. PR, June 9, 1898. See also A. Zévaès, *Jean Jaurès* (1938), pp. 158–59.

19. PP B a/1125, dossier Jaurès, report dated June 30, 1898; Ligou, p. 140; Paul Desanges and Luc Meriga, *Vie de Jaurès* (1924), p. 82.

20. Fiechter, p. 59; Noland, pp. 75–76; D. Halévy, 'Apologie pour notre passé' (Cahiers de la Quinzaine, 11th series, no. 10), pp. 75, 78, cited in Fiechter, p. 59.

21. Orry, p. 37; Noland, pp. 76–77.

22. PP, B a/1620. (Comité de Vigilance du parti socialiste; Comité de rapprochement socialiste.) The term 'vigilance', or 'watch', committee was first used during the 1790s and hence in the best Jacobin tradition.

23. Orry, p. 42. Noland described how these committees stimulated unification, pp. 76–79.

24. Ligou, p 143.

25. *La Lanterne*, October 19, 1898; Sûreté, F7 12886, October 16, 1898, no. 357.

26. JOC, October 28 and 29, 1898; *L'Intransigeant*, November 30; *L'Echo de Paris*, November 30, 1898.

27. *La Lanterne*, December 3, 1898; *Mémoires*, p. 36.

28. JOC, December 19, 1898.

29. *La Lanterne*, February 2, 1899.

30. JOC, February 10, 1899.

31. Reproduced in *La Lanterne*, February 9, 11, 1899; MP/BN.

32. *L'Eclair*, February 22, 1899.

33. *La Lanterne*, March 2, 1899.

34. *La Libre Parole, Le Gaulois*, June 1, 1899.

35. PP B a/108, report dated June 2. Sorlin, p. 399.

36. Poincaré's disclosure came in a 1901 Nancy speech. MS, May 15, 1901, pp. 628–629; Payen, *Poincaré*, p. 232.

37. Payen, *Poincaré*, p. 236; Reinach, *Histoire*, Vol. V: *Rennes* (1905), p. 165; *Le Matin*, February 22, 1911.

38. Zévaès, *Ombres*, p. 276; Rouanet in RS, August 1899, pp. 202, 205–206; Breton, p. 9; J. Bourdeau, 'Revue du mouvement socialiste', RPP, August 10, 1899, p. 376.

39. Daniel, *1899*, p. 220; Payen, *Poincaré*, p. 233; Reinach, *Histoire*, Vol. V, p. 158.

40. Sorlin, pp. 391, 403. Ulrich's testimony was printed in *Le Matin*, February 6, 1911.

41. Published in *Le Matin*, February 6, 1911.

42. Bibliothèque de l'Institut (hereafter BI), Les papiers de Waldeck-Rousseau, 4, 579 (formation du ministère, juin, 1899); *Le Matin*, February 6, 1911.

43. Sorlin, p. 400.

44. Joseph Caillaux, *Mes Mémoires*, 3 vols., I: *Ma Jeunesse orgueilleuse, 1863–1909* (1942), p. 148.

45. Reinach papers, BN, N. A. fr. 24,887 (84); Sorlin, p. 401; Waldeck-Rousseau, *Questions sociales* (1900), p. 373; Sorlin, p. 403.

46. Reinach, *Histoire*, V, p. 162.

47. *Le Matin*, February 8, 1911; Reinach, V, p. 173; Sorlin, p. 400.

48. *Le Matin*, February 9, 1911; B.W. Schaper, *Albert Thomas, trente ans de réformisme social* (1959), p. 60. Simiand's testimony appeared in *Le Matin*, February 7–8. *Mémoires*, p. 38. Caillaux implies Millerand suggested his name, *Mes Mémoires*, I, p. 119. On p. 176 he acknowledged that he owed his 'recognition' to Millerand. He also admitted that much of his subsequent hostility toward Millerand was caused by the latter joining Caillaux's 'persecutors' in 1919 and 'passing them in the act of imbecilic accusation', which he could not forget.

49. *Le Matin*, February 9, 1911.

50. Sorlin, p. 401.

51. J. L. Breton, *L'Unité socialiste* (1912), p. 9; *Le Socialiste*, June 18–25, 1899.

52. Breton, pp. 9–10.

53. *Le Socialiste*, May 12–19, 1901. In a magazine article published early in 1898 Jaurès had written that socialists could cooperate with others for reform. However, anything short of complete power would only neutralize a party seeking the 'total reform' of society. Partial possession of power, he continued, would only make 'the great economic interests take fear without being harmed'. Jaurès warned that the 'error of 1848', when fear and counterreaction were aroused, must not be repeated. *Comopolis*, January 28, 1898, pp. 129–130. This article was to be cited by anti-ministerialists replying to Jaurès,' defense of Millerand as minister. See, for example, H. Lagardelle, 'Réponse à Jaurès', MS, June 1, 1901, pp. 688–689.

54. Jean Jaurès, 'L'Entrée de Millerand au Ministère', MS, April 15, 1901. In two private letters to Georg von Vollmar, a leader of the reformist faction of the German Social Decomratic Party, October 23, 1899, and February 15, 1900, Jaurès affirmed: 'under my responsibility as an honest man', Millerand consulted with the socialist group in the Chamber. In an undated letter, the Blanquist Dubreuilh acknowledged being informed of the ministerial overtures to Millerand; IISH, Vollmar Archives; Reinach, V, p. 171. Implicitly, Galliffet demanded *carte blanche* at the Ministry of War (as revealed in his letter to Princess Radziwell on June 22). He expected the Cabinet to last no more than three months and to be villified by the left. Henri de Rolland, *Galliffet* (1945), pp. 172, 173.

55. Charles Andler, *Vie de Lucien Herr, 1864–1926* (1932), p. 149. Also see Marcelle Auclair, *La Vie de Jean Jaurès, ou la France d'avant 1914* (1954), p. 335.

56. Jaurès, MS, April 15, 1901, pp. 454–55. He did not go to the heart of the debate probably because he did not expect the government to last three years; Rouanet, RS, August 1899, pp. 205–206; Vaillant, February 15; Dubreuilh, March 1; Jaurès, April 15; Vaillant, May 1.

57. Vaillant, MS, February 15, 1901, p. 205.

58. Zévaès, *Histoire du socialisme et communisme en France de 1871 à 1957* (1947), p. 279; Louis, *Histoire du socialisme en France, 1789–1945*, 4th ed. (1946), p. 239. See also Julius Braunthal, *History of the International, 1864–1914* (London, 1966), p. 257 and James Joll, *The Second International, 1889–1914* (New York, 1966), pp. 85–86.

59. The legitimate shock felt by Vaillant is illustrated by the following sentences: 'That appears to be so odious, so ignoble, that I cannot believe it, and I hope to be undeceived, reassured at the earliest. In short, in the hope that these alarms have been caused in vain...'. MP–JM. See Zévaès, *Histoire du socialisme...*, p. 308, and MS, April 15, 1901, p. 455. See *Le Socialiste*, July 2, 1899 for Vaillant's declaration.

60. Dommanget, *Vaillant*, pp. 185–186.

61. Jaurès, MS, April 15, 1901, pp. 454–456.

62. Letter dated March 1, 1901. Vollmar Archives, IISH. Vollmar's request to Millerand, his draft article for the *Sozialistische Monatshefte* and Millerand's draft reply to Vollmar in the MP–BN. For Millerand, it was the presence of Galliffet that made the difference.

63. Reinach, *Histoire*, V, p. 176.

64. Daniel, *1899*, p. 224. Editorial comment summarized in the *London Times*, June 24, 1899. Arthur Ranc, *Souvenirs, Correspondance, 1831–1908* (1913), p. 425. Jonnart's letter to Waldeck-Rousseau dated June 23, 1899. Waldeck-Rousseau Papers BI, 4568.

65. *Mémoires*, p. 38; MP–JM.

66. Noland, p. 94. Text in RS, August 1899, pp. 203–204. Breton, pp. 11–12.

67. Schaper, p. 60. Thomas would be the 'convinced partisan' of Millerand, defending him frequently, pp. 30, 64. In the Albert Thomas Papers, AN, there are copies of speeches by Millerand and numerous articles about him.

68. Text in *Le Socialiste*, July 2, 1899; PR, June 25, 1899.

69. Noland, pp. 94–95; Willard, *Les Guesdistes*, p. 422.

70. Testimony of both men in *Le Matin*, February 10, 1911.

71. Sorlin, p. 404.

72. JOC, June 26, 1899. Willard, *Les Guesdistes*, p. 423.

73. *Le Socialiste*, July 2, 1899.

74. The text is reproduced in Conseil National, *Onze ans*, pp. 76–79; *Le Socialiste*, July 16; RS, August 1899, pp. 207-208.

75. Willard, *Les Guesdistes*, pp. 424–425, 429, described the opposition in Guesdist ranks and identified the dissident federations, groups and deputies.

76. Pages listing unfavorable responses from socialist groups not affiliated with the Parti ouvrier contain twelve times as many. A third *cahier* contains letters from individuals, socialists both affiliated and not. Nearly all are unfavorable. A not

atypical response was that of the POF section in Etampes. It called the Manifesto an 'act of inexcusable gratitude' and found itself 'greatly surprised that such an important decision could have been taken by three or four personalities, who as respectable as they might be, had no right to engage the entire French workers' party without previously consulting it'. The section refused to submit to 'this work of socialist disunion' and gave its collective resignation. IISH, Folios 641/1–4.

77. Letter to Guesde dated July 16, 1899, IISH, Guesde archives. The second letter was sent to Fortin September 5, 1899. Lavigne wrote: 'Si on ouvrait le cerveau de Guesde, Vaillant et leur proches, et qu'on y put lire clair, on les verrait exclusivement hantés par *l'idée fixe de faire du mal* à Millerand, à Jaurès, et a *La petite République'*. Also cited in Willard, *Les Guesdistes,* p. 424, and Noland, p. 100.

78. Brunellière to Millerand, letter dated June 24, 1899, Brunellière Papers, IFHS, 14AS 104/21, folio 173; Brunellière to Millerand, letter dated July 13, 1899, 14AS 104/21, folio 202; Brunellière to Guesde, dated July 14, 1899, 14AS 104/21, folio 203–4; Also Willard, *Correspondance,* pp. 285–286, 299.

79. Sûreté, AN F7 12553 (Notes sur la situation politique, 1899–1905), June 29, 1899, nos. 876, 877; PP, B a/1473 (Socialisme en France: 1897–1914), July 15, 1899

80. Villiers, p. 119.

81. PR, July 19, August 2, 1899; G. Rouanet, 'La Crise du parti socialiste', RS, August and September 1899, pp. 200–215, 347–371, especially pp. 347 and 211.

82. Willard, *Les Guesdistes,* p. 424; PR, July 15, 1899; PP, B a/1473 (Socialisme en France: 1897–1914), July 15, 1899; IIHS, Liebknecht Archives, letter from Deville to Liebknecht, July 2, 1899.

83. Willard, *Les Guesdistes,* pp. 424–27.

84. PR, July 13, 17, 21, 22, 1898; Noland, p. 101. According to a police report, 'behind closed doors, Guesde had tried to impede the proposed gathering of socialists but encountered too much opposition', Sûreté, F7 12 496 (July 19, 1899).

85. PR, October 10, 1899; Citation in Sûreté, AN, F7 12 490. (Agissements socialistes, Congres ouvriers divers, 1876–1899), folio labelled '17ᵉ congrès national du Parti ouvrier à Epernay'. See especially the reports dated August 9 and August 12, 1899 revealing a proposed resolution censuring the party's executive committee for its Manifesto and the report of August 18 describing the struggle and divisions within the Congress. Also see RPP, October 10, 1899, p. 154; Willard, *Les Guesdistes,* p. 427.

86. Noland, pp. 101–102. The Congress acknowledged the right of the executive council to send the Manifesto but added that it 'had not intended to strike out at or excommunicate anyone'. Willard, p. 427–429; Zévaès pointed out that the Congress allowed greater representation of the provincial federations, which generally took a more moderate line, than did the National Council, *Les Guesdistes,* p. 107.

87. See the chronique of J. Bourdeau in RPP, October 10, 1899, p. 152; *Justice,*September 2, 1899. Cited in Chushichi Tsuzuki, *H. M. Hyndman and British Socialism* (London, 1961), p. 124.

88. Weinstein, p. 75, RPP, October 10, 1899, p. 150 for Kautsky; *Vorwärts,* July 27, 1899; cited in PR, August 27, 1899 for Liebknecht; Rosa Luxemburg, 'Sozial Reform oder Revolution', *Leipziger Volkszeitung,* July 6, 1899, published as 'Une

question de tactiques' in MS, August 1899, pp. 132–133. Also see Bourdeau's Chronique, RPP, October 10, 1899, pp. 150–160; PR, August 27, 1899 for Bebel; PR, October 10, 1899 for Vandervelde.

89. The replies were first published in the XIth *Cahiers de la Quinzaine,* lst series, 1899, and reproduced in Fiechter, pp. 69–75.

90. Lenin, 'Social Democracy and the Provisional Revolutionary Government' and 'On the Provisional Revolutionary Government', *Collected Works,* Vol. VIII, *January-July 1905,* 2nd rev. ed. (Moscow, 1965), pp. 82, 471. Participation, for the purpose of infiltration, however, came to be recognized as a useful tactic immediately after World War II.

NOTES TO CHAPTER 9: THE SOCIALIST MINISTER

1. Louis Lépine, *Mes Souvenirs* (1929), p. 223.
2. Lefranc, p. 113; Jaurès' letter dated January 1, 1901, MP–JM; Willard, *Correspondance,* p. 321; AN, Archives of the Ministry of Justice, BB 18 2134, dossier 1858 A99.
3. Sforza, p. 210.
4. MP–JM; MP–BN. The biography was that of Paul Reynaud, published in 1913.
5. Sorlin, pp. 46, 47.
6. Payen, *Anthologie des avocats français contemporains* (1913), pp. 137–43; Abel Combarieu, *Sept ans à l'Elysée avec le Président Emile Loubet* (1932), p. 111. Biographies include those of J. Ernest-Charles (1902); Gaston Deschamps (1905); Henry Leyret, which reaches only to 1889 (1908); and Paul Reynaud (1913). There is an American doctoral dissertation that covers his last decade: Boris Blick, 'Waldeck-Rousseau, 1894–1904' (University of Wisconsin, 1958). The most complete and most valuable, particularly in terms of the social, political and economic background, is Pierre Sorlin's *Waldeck-Rousseau* (1966).
7. Sorlin, pp. 209, 259, 301.
8. G. Renard, 'Portrait de Millerand', *La Vie,* February 24, 1912, p. 7; AN, Archives of the Ministry of Commerce, F12, 4846, Cabinet du Ministre du Commerce.
9. Violette's letter to Millerand dated May 17, 1896, MP–JM. See his article, 'Les Syndicats professionnels et le droit d'association', *Journal des économists,* February 1881, pp. 250–263; *Mémoires,* p. 41.
10. Schaper, I, p. 58; Bernard Lavergne, *Les Idées politiques en France de 1900 à nos jours; Souvenirs personnels* (1965), p. 132; Oral testimony of Maurice Baumont, 1967; Lefranc, p. 114.
11. Georges Noblemaire, *Carnet de route: Au pays des Parlementaires* (1923), p. 151; Oral testimony of Raul Persil, 1960.
12. As revealed in two letters, dated July 11, 1900, and January 18, 1901, in the Reinach correspondence, BN, Department of Manuscripts, N.A. fr. 24 882 (nos. 92, 94).
13. Jacques Bompard, 'Un Ministre de la Guerre, M. Alexandre Millerand', RPP, January 10, 1914, p. 36; Undated letter from Millerand, Reinach Correspondence, BN, N.A. fr. 24 882 (no. 85).
14. A. Millerand, *Travail et travailleurs* (1908), pp. 105–106.

15. *Mémoires*, p. 40.
16. These decrees and other Millerand achievements have been examined by Lavy, *L'Œuvre de Millerand, Un Ministre socialiste, juin 1899 – janvier 1902* (1902). See also Charles W. Pipkin, *Social Politics and Modern Democracies* (New York, 1931), Vol. II, pp. 54, 91, and Vincent Badie, *M. Alexandre Millerand* (Montpelier, 1931), p. 89.
17. Pipkin, II, pp. 55. Texts in *Bulletin de l'Officiel du Travail*, August, 1899, pp. 736–40; *Journal Officiel*, August 11, 1899; *Le XIXe Siècle*, November 3, 1891.
18. Maurice Charnay, 'L'Œuvre des municipalités socialistes', MS April 15, 1900, p. 485. Millerand's acknowledgement to the Municipal Council appeared in *L'Eclair*, March 24, 1899. As President of the Republic he was to introduce the decree of July 13, 1923, establishing the principle of compulsory family allowances in public contracts. Pipkin, II, p. 55. See also Paul Dramas, 'Les Conditions du travail et les décrets Millerand du 10 aout 1899', RS, September 1903, pp. 287–315, especially pp. 293–4; Henri Rollet, *L'Action sociale des Catholiques* (1947), p. 485; Dramas, p. 296.
19. Letter from Waldeck-Rousseau to Millerand, July 9, 1899, MP–JM. Sorlin, p. 462. The decrees consequently required only a weekly day of rest. They did not refer to hours and asked that prevailing salary rates of the area be respected. Legislative vindication of these decrees came with the minimum wage regulation of World War I.
20. *Mémoires*, p. 40; *Travail et travailleurs*, pp. 17–20; JOC, July 4, 1899. The Council of State approved in February 1904, Pipkin, II, p. 58; Daniel, *1899*, p. 23. Brunellière's approval reproduced in Willard, *Correspondance*, p. 299. Letters of support from provincial federations and newspapers were described in Willard, *Les Guesdistes*, pp. 428–429.
21. Caillaux, I, p. 138. Only after long questioning of the one civilian familiar with the activities of the 'statistical section' was Waldeck-Rousseau wholly convinced of Dreyfus' innocence; Sorlin, p. 412.
22. Reinach, *Histoire*, V, pp. 551, 560; Also Zévaès, *Clemenceau*, pp. 171–172. Waldeck-Rousseau Papers reproduced in *Le Matin*, February 10, 1911.
23. Georges Michon, *Clemenceau* (1931), pp. 85, 89; Wormser, *La République de Clemenceau*, p. 193.
24. Halévy, *Essais*, p. 253.
25. In the archives of the Minister of Commerce there is a file entitled, 'Voyages ministérielles', 1900–1902, AN, F12 4842; MP–JM for Millerand's draft letter; Waldeck-Rousseau papers, BI, 4579 (Papiers relatifs à l'année 1899) no. 12 for Millerand's undated letter; Waldeck's reply on September 30, MP–JM.
26. Text in *La Lanterne*, October 4, 1899; Daniel, 1899, termed it moderate', *La Nouvelle Revue*, October 15, 1899, p. 42.
27. Léon de Seilhac, *Les Grèves* (1903), pp. 152–176; PR, October 9, 1899; RS, November 1899, pp. 624–630. A copy of Schneider's telegram to Waldeck-Rousseau requesting arbitration in MP–BN. Both sides anticipated that another strike would break out. The writer referred to was Beau de Lomenie, II, p. 321.
28. Text and comment in PR, October 18, 1899; Also Lavy, pp. 392–398.
29. Combarieu, p. 40; Sorlin, p. 405. Galliffet, because of his long association with

Waldeck, and because the Premier felt that he could not afford to displease him, was exempted.

30. JOC, November 16, 1899.
31. *Mémoires*, p. 42.
32. Taken from the Bulletin de l'office du travail, October 1900, pp. 991–997; May 1899, p. 423; April, 1901, pp. 258–260. There were two million lost working days in 1901, Bulletin de l'Office du travail, February, 1903, p. 78. Also see Charles Rist 'La Progression des grèves en France et sa valeur symtomatique', *Revue d'économie politique*, March 1905, pp. 161–193. Also cited in Sorlin, p. 463. I have followed closely the arguments and data used by Sorlin, pp. 461–480.
33. De Seilhac, pp. 112–115. Jules Huret, *Les Grèves, enquête* (1902), pp. 166–167. Peter Stearns, 'Against the Strike Threat: Employer Policy toward Labor Agitation in France, 1900–1914', *Journal of Modern History*, (1968), pp. 479–481.
34. Sorlin, p. 468–469. See Joseph-Antoine Roy, *Histoire de la famille Schneider et du Creusot* (1962), pp. 97–99 on the Schneider holdings.
35. *L'Intransigeant*, October 10, 18, 1899; *La Libre Parole*, October 12, 17, 1899; *Le Journal*, September 25, 1899; *Le Gaulois*, September 23, 1899; *Le Journal des débats*, February 27, 1901; *La Croix*, September 26, 1899.
36. PR, October 6, 7, 9, 12, 1899; November 25, 1900; *La Lanterne*, October 6, 1899; July 2, 11, 25, 27, 1900; November 14, 1901; Goldberg, *Life*, p. 279; Sorlin, p. 470; PR, July 1, 1899; Pinset, pp. 359–360; Willard, *Les Guesdistes*, pp. 553–556; Sorlin, pp. 470–471.
37. Requests may be found in MP–BN and MP–VN. The latter contains 202 letters or petitions sent to Millerand by labor groups or individual workers between 1899 and 1902.
38. De Seilhac, p. 193. This interpretation in part explains the haste with which some strikes were declared, even before demands were formulated, as, for example, by the textile workers in the Loire, December 1900. Ministère de la Justice, Correspondance de la Division Criminelle, AN, BB 2183, dr. 315 A01. Also see the Prefectural Reports intended for the Minister of Justice, BB18 2202.
39. Sorlin, p. 472. The second letter was dated October 27, 1900. Both in MP–JM.
40. Text reproduced in Daniel, *1899*, pp. 403–410, and Lavy, pp. 233–240.
41. JOC, June 1, 1900; cited in Lavy, p. 229; Lavy, p. 230; *Bulletin de l'Office du Travail*, February 1900, pp. 190–193; April 1900, p. 390.
42. Figures in *Annuaire des syndicats professionals, seizième année*, cited in Weill, *Histoire*, p. 347. By 1906 there were 836,000, or less than one million out of five million potential members. Labor statistics, certainly during these early years, were not entirely reliable; they were based on payments of dues, which were never always met, and locals often understated their membership in order to pay less to the national office Pipkin, II, pp. 208–209; Clapham, 4th ed., p. 276. See Val Lorwin, 'Reflections on the History of the French and American Labor Movements', *Journal of Economic History*, XVII (1957), pp. 25–44, for causes of the slower growth rate of French unionism.
43. Sûreté, AN F7 12496. There is a dossier on the opposition to the bill. Maitron, pp. 282–283. Also see Edouard Dolléans, *Histoire du mouvement ouvrier en France* (1937), II, pp. 27–29, 139–141.

44. Sorlin, p. 461. Millerand reintroduced it as a *proposition de loi,* as compared to the government-sponsored *projet de loi.* His efforts were summarized in *L'Aide sociale,* March 15, 1909. See Henry Leyret, *De Waldeck-Rousseau à la CGT,* 2nd ed. (1921), p. 36.

45. JOC, November 23, 1899; June 15, 1896. Cited in Zévaès, *Une Génération* (1922), p. 43, as a plank in the POF program for 1897.

46. *Bulletin de l'Office du Travail,* February 1900, p. 190; Badie, pp. 98–99; Pinset, p. 365.

47. For Guesde's reaction, see Pinset, p. 365; for Vaillant's, Pinset, pp. 365–366 and PR, January 12, 14, 21, 1900.

48. Pinset, p. 367.

49. PR, January 16, 1900; Sûreté, AN F7 12496 (dossier entitled Scission socialiste à la suite de l'entrée de Millerand...), February 3, 1900, no. 152.

50. Levasseur, p. 442; text in Lavy, pp. 46–47; see also *L'Aide Sociale,* March 15, 1909, p. 117, and *Le Parlement et l'opinion,* September 23, 1920, p. 1680; PR, December 26, 1899.

51. Badie, pp. 120–121.

52. De Seilhac, *Les Grèves,* p. 230; Weill, *Histoire,* p. 261; Joel Colton, *Compulsory Labor Arbitration in France, 1936–1939* (New York, 1951), pp. 4–5.

53. JOC, February 8, 1894; Zévaès, *Une Génération,* pp. 41–42; see also Lagardelle, writing in MS, September 1909, p. 180; Caillaux, I, p. 180.

54. PR, July 1, 1900. The other speeches include that given to the Cooperative Producers Association and that delivered in Lens. Letter from Waldeck-Rousseau to Millerand dated September 12, 1900, MP–JM. Apparently the text of the bill was drafted by Millerand and revised by the Premier. Sorlin, p. 477.

55. *Journal officiel.* Documents parlementaries, Chambre, Session Extraordinaire, Séance du 15 novembre, 1990 (Annexe No. 1937). Text also in MS, May 1, 1901, pp. 561–570, and Lavy, pp. 150–172.

56. Lavy, p. 173.

57. Jaurès' letters and Millerand's draft replies in MP–BN.

58. PR, November 22, 1900; June 19, July 25, 1901. Also see Jaurès' article, 'La Réglementation des grèves et l'arbitrage obligatoire', RS, May 1901, pp. 513–538; his interview by Jules Huret, *Les Grèves,* pp. 149–154; and Goldberg, 'French Socialism', pp. 423–424. Jaurès had changed his mind; he had told the Chamber on November 21, 1895, that compulsory arbitration was only a 'clever manœuvre' that would absolutely suppress the right to strike and constitute the most formidable restraint that could be imposed on labor. JOC, November 21, 1895. The bill then proposed, however, lacked safeguards.

59. Caillaux, I, pp. 180–183.

60. *La Voix du Peuple,* January 6, 17, 1901. However, perhaps because the CGT was allotted fifteen of the twenty-two seats reserved for labor on the newly enlarged Superior Labor Council, it ultimately accepted the bill. See J. P. Bompiex, 'Le syndicalisme français et l'arbitrage obligatoire', unpublished thesis, 'Ecole des sciences politiques', 1954. Maitron, *Histoire,* pp. 282–283; Levasseur, p. 496.

61. PR, November 22, 1900; Jaurès' article, RS, May 1901, pp. 513–538. Articles in *Vorwärts* cired by MS, January 1, 1901, pp. 43–53. Other views reported on pp.

42, 54–55. Lagardelle's 'Réponse à Jaurès', MS, June 1, 1901, pp. 675–677. For similar socialist and syndicalist opinion on the government's intentions see Lagardelle's *La Grève générale et le socialisme, enquête internationale, opinions et documents* (1905), especially p. 125; and Georges Sorel, *Les Illusions du progrès*, 2nd ed. (1911), pp. 10, 307–309.

62. For the Rouen Chamber, see De Seilhac, *Les Grèves*, p. 243. For reference to the 'compulsory strike law', see Poincaré's, *Questions et figures politiques* (1907), p. 178; Levasseur, *Questions ouvrières*, p. 496, for management's response; Millerand, *Travail et travailleurs*, p. 101; Huret, pp. 21, 87, 106–110; PR, November 22, 1900; RS, May, 1901, pp. 517–18; Sorlin, p. 478.

63. For a summary of his efforts see *L'Aide social*, February 15, 1909.

64. Pipkin, II, pp. 108–109; Badie, p. 127; Lefranc, p. 116. A permanent and sound basis for collective bargaining relations was set in the laws of December 31, 1936, and March 4, 1938. Conciliation and arbitration procedures were to be resorted to before strikes and lockouts were permitted. No real sanctions other than that of public opinion were provided, and the measure was suspended by the war, but these laws were seen as 'one of the solid achievments of the government'. Joel Colton, *Leon Blum, Humanist in Politics* (New York, 1966); also see his *Compulsory Arbitration*, pp. 153, 165.

65. Fournière, *La Crise socialiste*, p. 67.

66. Millerand, *Le Socialisme réformiste français*, p. 112; *Travail et travailleurs*, p. 99.

67. There were also to be twenty-two employers' representatives and twenty-two civil servants and specialists, all of whom were required to consult with the government about needed social legislation. *Bulletin de l'Office du Travail*, April 1900, p. 390; Pipkin, II, pp. 62–68. Malon, *Le Socialisme intégral*, II, p. 350; I, p. 408.

68. Text in the *Journal Officiel*, September 18, 1900, and January 5, 1901. Described in Lavy, p. 80. For the history of the Superior Council and the regional councils in the twentieth century, see Pipkin, II, pp. 58–62.

69. Carl A. Landauer, *European Socialism: A History of Ideas and Movements* (Berkeley, 1959), Vol. I, p. 329; November 22, 1900; Millerand, *Travail et travailleurs*, p. 123; Lefranc, p. 115.

70. Georges Jalot, *Le Régime corporatif et les Catholiques sociaux* (1938), p. 184; Matthew W. Elbow, *French Corporative Theory, 1789–1948* (New York, 1953), pp. 91–92.

71. *Bulletin officiel du Ministre du Commerce*, Circulaire aux inspecteurs du travail, January 19, 1900; Lavy, p. 94; Sorlin pointed to Waldeck's support here, p. 475.

72. Pipkin, II, pp. 68–70.

73. The rival Exchange was being subsidized by a now nationalist Paris Municipal Council. Roger Picard, *Le Mouvement syndical durant la guerre* (n.d.), I, p. 12; Lavy, p. 247; Badie, p. 97.

NOTES TO CHAPTER 10: THE MILLERAND CASE

1. *Le Socialiste*, July 30, 1899; *Les Deux méthodes, Conférence faite à Lille le 16 novembre, 1900*. Cited in Fiechter, pp. 239–240, and Zévaès, *Histoire*, p. 308.
2. Lafargue's remark made at the Paris Congress of French Socialist Organizations on December 3, 1899, cited in Weill, *Histoire*, p. 323; Sûretè, AN, F7 12553, reports 1469 and 1472, dated November 14, 15, 1899.
3. PP, B a/1620, December 3, 1899; See Michelle Perrot and Annie Kriegel, *Le Socialisme français et le pouvoir* (1966), pp. 73, 75/76. According to the police report of December 7, a common position was arrived at only after 'stormy scenes'. Also see Halévy, *Essais*, p. 234.
4. Aaron Noland, *The Founding of the French Socialist Party* (Cambridge, Mass., 1956), pp. 102–11. PP, B a/1620, December 6, 1899.
5. Halévy, p. 235; Lockwood, pp. 196–197.
6. Halévy, pp. 24–41; Noland, p. 112; Feichter, p. 81.
7. Sûreté, AN, F7 12496, December 13, 1899.
8. Sûreté, AN, F7 12496, June 12, 1900 (nos. 722, 758); June 9, (no. 711).
9. Sûreté, AN, F7 12496, December 25, 1899 (no. 1666); January 12, 1900 (no. 46); February 3, 1900 (no. 152); February 7, 1900; Guesde's letters dated January 26 and February 4, 1900; IISH, Liebknecht archives, GE 50–52 and 42–44; Willard, *Les Guesdistes*, p. 443.
10. Sûreté, AN, F7 12496, June 7, 1900 (no. 701); PR, March 3, 1900; Willard, *Les Guesdistes*, pp. 445–446.
11. *Le Socialiste*, August 12, October 7, 1900; Willard, *Les Guesdistes*, p. 446.
12. A. Zévaès, *Henri Rochefort, Le Pamphlétaire* (1946), pp. 211, 215. Also see Roger Williams, *Henri Rochefort, Prince of the Gutter Press* (New York, 1966), pp. 241–242, 249, 265–267, and Willard, *Les Guesdistes*, pp. 410–411.
13. Sûreté, AN, F7 12496, February 26, 1900 (no. 266). *Le Socialiste*, March 26, 1899. *La Libre parole*, April 3. A Sûreté (F7 12496) report of April 9 (no. 496) described two of Guesde's colleagues, Ronsel and Zévaès, as doing their best to discourage him from furthering his *entente* with anti-Semites. Also see Sûreté, AN, F7 12496, July 7, 1900 (no. 972); March 15, 1900; June 2, 1900 (no. 684); February 28, 1900 (no. 276); June 30, 1900 (no. 782). Willard, pp. 556–557, Noland, 119–120, and Suarez, *Briand*, I, p. 294.
14. As an example of moderate socialist opinion, see the Belgian socialist newspaper, *La Réforme*, April 3, 1900. *Mémoires*, p. 43.
15. Richard D. Mandell, *Paris, 1900: The Great World's Fair* (Toronto, 1967), pp. 91, 103, 119. The dissertation from which the book came appears somewhat more comprehensive on the politics of the period: 'Politicians, Intellectuals, and the Universal Exposition of 1900 in in Paris', University of California at Berkeley, 1965. Millerand and Caillaux did sponsor legislation to subsidize workers' delegates to the Exposition, and the former asked the prefects in a circular letter to facilitate their going. AN, Minister of Commerce, F12, 5341; Letters from Schneider dated October 25, 30, 1899, MP-BN; J.-A. Roy, *Histoire de la famille Schneider et du Creusot* (1962), p. 90.
16. Andler, p. 150; Gustave Téry, *Jean Jaurès* (1907), p. 185; *La Suisse*, July 26, 1900;

Zévaès, *Histoire*, p. 301 for Mme. Renard; Brunellière's letter dated May 17, 1900, Willard, *Correspondance*, pp. 160–161; A. de Boisandre, *L'Etat-major socialiste: Millerand, Jaurès, et Cie* (1903). Millerand's Jewish background was especially denounced. *La Conférence*, July 5, 1901, for the comparison with Louis Napoleon.

17. JOC, March 23, 1900; Oral testimony of Raoul Persil, 1960; Charles Descoty, *Le Cabinet Dreyfus: Une Année du Ministère Waldeck-Rousseau* (1900), p. 113; originally published as articles in *Le Correspondant*, June and July 1900; JOC, March 26, April 3, 1900, for Zévaès' resolution.

18. Mandell, 'Politicians...', p. 59; *Le XIXᵉ Siècle*, April 22, 1900.

19. Daniel, *1900*, pp. 118/120.

20. A. Radziwell, *Lettres de la Princesse Radziwell au General de Robilant, 1889–1914*, Vol. II: *1896–1901* (1934). The appendix to Volume II contains the Galliffet letters.

21. *La Liberté*, August 6–7, 1909 (Recollections of the Comtesse de Mirabeau-Martel 'Gyp', a friend of Galliffet). Also Sorlin, p. 405. Galliffet spurned the rest of the cabinet. Joseph Paul-Boncour, *Entre deux guerres: Souvenirs sur la IIIᵉ République*, Vol. I: *1877–1918* (1945), pp. 99, 100, 94; MP-JM. Two notes from Galliffet (September 5, 1899, and May 1900) thanked Millerand for granting a commemorative medal and acknowledged Millerand's request to give a third party six month's leave.

22. MP-JM, undated letter from a Eugène Cross, whom I have been unable to identify; Lockwood, p. 304.

23. *Le XIX Siècle*, April 15, 1890, and September 22, 1891. A history of earlier efforts can be found in RS, September 1901, pp. 257–274.

24. JOC, June 13, 1901. Text also in Daniel, 1901, pp. 475–483. See Millerand, *Travail et travailleurs*, p. 161.

25. Lefranc, p. 116. Text in Lavy, pp. 222–223; Parker T. Moon, *The Labor Problem and the Social Catholic Movement in France* (New York, 1921), p. 218; Daniel, 1901, pp. 215–223, 232–233. The government, moreover, did not fight for a bill providing greater protection for railroad workers and permitted the Senate to cut back an inheritance tax passed by the Chamber.

26. RS, October 1901, p. 489; *Le Socialiste*, August 11–18, 1901.

27. *L'Aide Sociale*, March 15, 1909, p. 121; Paul Grunebaum-Ballin, 'La Tentative de Paix religieuse d'Aristide Briand', *Cahiers Laiques*, January–February 1956, p. 17 and oral testimony, 1964; Badie, p. 115; Pipkin, II, p. 174; *Mémoires*, p. 52.

28. Cited in *L'Aide sociale*, March 15, 1909; Viviani, 'Portraits contemporains: M. Alexandre Millerand', *Revue des Deux Mondes*, November 1, 1920, p. 94. Although voted by a huge majority, the law of 1910 had no teeth, and so employers as well as revolutionary workers hostile to state intervention were able to evade it.

29. Georges Scelle, *Precis élémentaire de législation industrielle* (1927), p. 80. Cited in Badie, p. 115; Pipkin, II, pp. 192–193, 199.

30. Noland, pp. 125–126; Rouanet, 'Le Congrès de 1900', RS, Vol. 32 (1900).

31. Dommanget, p. 196.

32. Noland, pp. 132–133.

33. Brunellière Papers, IFHS 14 AS 106 31, folio 217; PR, May 27–30, 1901; V. Sorge, *L'Unité révolutionnaire* (n.d.), pp. 11, 16, 24.

34. 'Consultation internationale sur l'Affaire Dreyfus et le cas Millerand', *Cahiers de*

la Quinzaine, nos. 5 (March 5, 1900, entire issue), 6 (March 20, 1900, pp. 45–72), 8 (April 20, 1900, pp. 27–42), and 11 (n.d., pp. 76–90); 1ᵉ série, cited in Fiechter, p. 85.

35. Noland, p. 140.
36. Brunellière Papers, IFHS, 14AS 11618, 14AS 10525, folios 157–58.
37. *Le Figaro,* August 15, 1901; copy in MP–BN.
38. A poem, commissioned for the occasion, was reflective of the widespread confidence and hopes placed in him:
    Salut à vous, ministre du commerce
    Vous qui vouliez semer l'egalité...
    Lens et Bruay saluez bienvenue de Millerand, père des ouvriers.   ₁
    Jetons-lui des fleurs partout et, dans la rue
    Si pleines mains, jetons-lui des lauriers.
    Cited in Louis Gaillard, *Le Royaume socialiste* (1902), p. 41; Text of the speech in *Le Reveil du Nord,* October 9; *La Lanterne,* and PR, October 10, 1900.
39. Daniel, *1900,* pp. 118–120; PR, October 10, 1900; MS, November 1, 1900, pp. 560–565; *Le Temps,* October 30, 1900.
40. JOC, November 6, 1900.
41. Speech given January 13, 1902. Text in Millerand, *Le Socialisme réformiste français,* pp. 36–42; RS, February 1902, pp. 228–231.
42. Daniel, *1902,* p. 7; MP–BN, dossier entitled 'Notes de M. Sarraute, 1901'. Lemaître's speech was delivered in Nancy, December 1, 1901, and reproduced in *L'Echo de Paris,* December 2.
43. Paul Louis, *Le Parti socialiste en France,* Vol. VII of *Encyclopédie socialiste, syndical et coopérative...* (1912), A. Compère-Morel, Ed., p. 63; Noland, pp. 140–141, 143; Lockwood, p. 327.
44. Badie, pp. 109–110, 131; Lavy, pp. 115, 250. A copy of the Code is in the Archives of the Ministry of Commerce, F12 4850 (Projets, Amendements, et Notes ministérielles, AN).
45. *Bulletin de l'Office du Travail,* May 1900, p. 506.
46. *Le XIXᶜ Siècle,* May 15, August 4, September 6, 1891; Smith, p. 1017; JOC, May 18, 1899; Lavy, p. 272.
47. Bernard Georges and Denise Tintant, *Léon Jouhaux, Cinquante ans de Syndicalisme,* Vol. I: *Des origines à 1921* (1962), pp. 13–14.
48. *Le XIXᵉ Siècle,* February 20, 1891; JOC, November 29, 1900.
49. Badie, p. 110–111; PR, February 3, March 10, 1904; *Travail et travailleurs,* p. 142.
50. *Le XIXᵉ Siècle,* August 22, 1890; JOC, October 29, 1901.
51. Lavy, pp. 314, 333–338.
52. PR, July 19, 25, 1901. See Lavy, pp. 362–388.
53. *Documents diplomatiques français (1871–1914),* 2ᵉ série (Paris, 1929), Vol. I, pp. 51, 232–33, 687 (April 16 and December 28, 1901). Millerand also proposed an undersea communications network to link France and her colonies.
54. *Le Temps,* July 27, 1901; January 15, 1902.
55. *La Vérité Républicaine,* April 20, 1902. However, when he received a letter of complaint from the Narbonne Chamber of Commerce about the watering of wine by Bercy distillers, he informed the Ministers of Agriculture, Finance and Interior.

See AN, Archives of the Ministry of Commerce, F12 6873. Text of his campaign speech in *Le Socialisme réformiste français*, pp. 68–72.

56. Sorlin, p. 481; Confidential report of Paul-Marius André, 'Contre Millerand', dated April, 1902, Guesde Archives, IISH, 337/53; Also Sûreté, AN, F7 12890 (Parti socialiste, 1902–1906). There is a folder containing 100 items under the heading, 'Une Affaire contre Millerand', nos. 3701–3800.

57. *Le Temps, Le Figaro,* April 14, 1902. Clippings, campaign receipts, posters, etc., in MP–BN; Sûreté, AN F7 12890. 'Le Socialisme, 1902'.

58. *Le Matin,* April 28, 1902. Millerand received 4,935 votes; Pechin, 4,185; Chauvin, 1,094; Mouthiez, 796.

59. MP–BN. Again, no evidence has survived to reveal the precise sources of his committee's finances.

60. Samuel, I, p. 292; Letter dated May 15, 1902, Brunellière Papers, IFHS, 14AS 105/27, folio 221, cited in Willard, *Correspondance,* pp. 346–47.

61. J. P. Charnay, *Les Scrutins politiques en France de 1815 à 1962, Contestations et invalidations* (1965), p. 103, cited in Sorlin, p. 482; Also G. Lachapelle, *Les Régimes électoraux,* p. 83.

62. PR, June 5, 1902; Daniel, *1902,* p. 146.

63. Millerand's copies in MP–JM.

64. Sorlin, p. 484.

65. See Lefranc's evaluation of Millerand's treatment by historians, p. 112; Fournière, 'La crise socialiste', RS, July 1905, p. 50; Pipkin, II, pp. 52–54.

66. Paul-Boncour, I, p. 94; Reaffirmed in his letter to this writer, dated September 19, 1960; Colton, *Compulsory Labor Arbitration in France,* pp. 164–165. It was also Blum who became Vice-President of a bourgeois cabinet to prevent the dissolution of the Popular Front coalition, James Joll, *Three Intellectuals in Politics: Blum, Rathenau, Marinetti* (New York, 1965 ed.), p. 46.

67. Reinach, *Histoire,* VI, p. 428.

68. David Thomson, *Democracy in France,* 2nd ed. (London, 1952), pp. 72–103.

69. Abel Combarieu, *Sept ans à l'Elysée avec Loubet, 1899–1906* (1932), p. 111. Millerand was puzzled by Poincaré's fears (Payen, *Poincaré,* p. 250), and one day in 1900, on the Eiffel Tower observation platform, told his friend that he was too reticent for a statesman. Miquel, *Poincaré,* p. 176; Sorel, *Les Illusions,* pp. 10, 307–309; Lagardelle, *La Grève générale,* p. 126.

70. Pipkin, II, pp. 53–54.

71. *Le Petit Sou,* March 6, 1902; Fournière, RS, July 1905, p. 68.

72. Halévy, *Essais,* p. 252; Lefranc, pp. 116–17.

73. Draft lecture, 'Trente ans de République, de Thiers à Waldeck-Rousseau', prepared by Millerand in 1936. MP–VN. This attitude is conveyed throughout his *Mémoires.* JOS, February 27, 1938.

74. RS, May 1902, pp. 507–511; Daniel, *1901,* p. vii; Paul Strauss, *Les Fondateurs de la République, Souvenirs* (1934), p. 225.

75. Blick, p. 600; *Le Temps,* April 7, 1902.

76. Sorlin, pp. 57, 480; Lépine, p. 240.

77. Sorlin, p. 455.

NOTES TO CHAPTER 11: EXPULSION

1. Waldeck-Rousseau papers, BI., Box 4615. There is a copy in MP–JM. The discussion between Waldeck and Loubet took place May 13, 1902.
2. *Le Temps,* October 30, 1900; Sorlin, pp. 424–25.
3. Auguste Soulier, *L'Instabilité ministérielle sous le Troisième République, 1871–1938* (1939), p. 425; R. W. Winnacker,' The Délégation des Gauches: A Successful Attempt at Managing a Parliamentary Coalition', *Journal of Modern History,* December 1937, pp. 449–470.
4. Malcolm O. Partin, *Waldeck-Rousseau, Combes, and the Church, 1899–1905: The Politics of Anticlericalism* (Durham, 1969), p. 135.
5. Many legal congregations assumed their own authorization carried over to their dependent establishments. Combes, however, interpreted the law of 1901 in the strictest possible sense. Partin, pp. 143, 79, 155.
6. Combes may have been driven to this change in procedure. Waldeck-Rousseau, who opposed requiring parliamentary rather than executive authorization, conceivably sought to 'inhibit the full effects of the law' by giving Parliament the 'formidable task' of having 'to prepare and vote upon bills both to accord and to refuse authorization', Partin, pp. 159–161.
7. Stationery and calling cards in the Department of Manuscripts, BN, N.A. fr 13 269, especially no. 342. A photograph of this office is in the possession of Mlle. Alice Millerand.
8. In his *Cahiers de la Quinzaine,* cited by J.J. Chevalier, *Histoire des institutions de la France de 1789 à nos jours* (1949–1950), Vol. II, p. 235.
9. Oral testimony of his children, Mme. Petite and Mme. Reinach. By merely possessing a sizeable family, Millerand differed from many Third Republic politicians. Ferry, Poincaré and Viviani had no children, Clemenceau never remarried and Briand was always something of a bohemian. Correspondence from the Nadars in BN, Department of Manuscripts, N.A. fr 24,278, nos. 338–58.
10. Viviani in *Revue des Deux Mondes,* November 1, 1920, p. 85; Renard, 'Souvenirs', RS, January–February 1950, pp. 101–102.
11. MP–JM, letters from Anatole France dated June 25, 28, 1901. There are numerous letters from Jonnart. MP–BN.
12. Oral testimony of Jacques Millerand; Renard, 'Souvenirs', RS, January–February, 1950, pp. 100–101.
13. Renard, 'Souvenirs', RS, January–February 1950, pp. 100–101.
14. F. J. Delasalle, *Les Congrégations non autorisées et leurs liquidateurs devant la loi de 1901* (1905). See Millerand's preface. This explanation was supported by Millerand's decision, on at least one occasion, to represent the government and not one of the *congrégations.* When no Grenoble lawyer stepped forward to represent the government-appointed receiver, in view of the passions aroused by efforts to liquidate the holdings of the Carthusian monks at La Grande Chartreuse, Millerand came from Paris to do so in April of 1903. Garcon, I, p. 287.
15. Millerand, *Politique de réalisations* (1911), pp. 349–353. Also see E. Nast, 'A propos de la liquidation des biens des congrégations', RPP, October 1907, p. 60. The writer, a former court-appointed receiver, stated that the sums allegedly gotten by

Millerand were enormously exaggerated. One example of a critic who revised his estimates sharply downward was that of Senator Riou. He had initially 'deplored' figures revealing that 115 *liquidators* returned only 190,000 francs to the state (by 1907) while 164,000 were spent for their fees; fees given to their lawyers came to over a million. Millerand questioned these figures, and Riou subsequently lowered them. In November of 1907 he told Millerand that he thought the attacks had been politically inspired and originated by Combes. Undated Riou memorandum and Millerand's reply, dated November 24, 1907, in MP–JM.

16. Delasalle's letter to Millerand dated October 20, 1903; Millerand's draft reply dated October 21, MP–JM; MP–BN. Delasalle's draft list of fees paid revealed that Millerand had, in fact, refused them. In the margin Delasalle had written: 'The truth should be known', and he then sent the list to Millerand. In reply to criticism of Millerand by *L'Action,* Delasalle wrote to the newspaper on June 23, 1904 (sending a copy of his letter to Millerand), stating that Millerand had always called for absolutely minimum fees. The receiver, E. Nast, in the article referred to above, agreed and called for an end to a 'campaign of slander'. He wrote to Millerand in this vein on August 19, 1907. MP–JM. In 1906 Millerand prepared a self-memo listing the fees received for defending the interests of various orders during the past four years; e.g., the Augustins of Ste. Marie, 10,000 francs; the Dominicans, 9,000; the Frères de Ste. Croix de Neuilly, 1000, etc. The list is apparently incomplete, but the letters received by Millerand suggest he refused much more. For example, Menage wrote on May 16, 1906, asking him to accept a larger fee. A letter from Delasalle dated two days earlier indicates that other lawyers, consulted by Delasalle, thought Millerand set his fees too low. MP–BN. These papers reveal no additional source of income other than occasional royalties for books and articles.

17. Letters and calling cards from various shipbuilders in MP–BN.

18. Draft speeches defending the pension bill in MP–MR. Millerand's speech to the Lyons section of the Comité républicain du Commerce et de l'Industrie, May 14, 1907, was reproduced in *Travail et travailleurs,* pp. 107–134.

19. There are six letters by Millerand in the Fournière Papers, IFHS, 14AS 181. Millerand sympathized with Fournière on the latter's defeat in the 1902 election. He tried to get him a chair in the Conservatoire des Arts et métiers in 1907 and persuaded General André to have him lecture at the Polytechnique. The article was entitled, 'Le Nationalisme. Lettre à M. Jules Soury', RS (36), 1902, pp. 1–30.

20. Anton Nyström, *L'Alsace-Lorraine* (1903), Carroll, p. 164, 194.

21. Marius-Ary Leblond, 'Patriotisme-socialiste', *La Grande France,* January 1902, MP–BN.

22. Bernhard Fürst von Bülow, *Denkwürdigkeiten* (Berlin, 1930), Vol. II, p. 8.

23. JOC, June 12, 1903; November 29, 1905; Also in *Travail et travailleurs,* pp. 150–56, 203–10; *Le Socialisme réformiste français,* p. 51.

24. *Le Socialisme réformiste français,* p. 56. Sarraute's book was published in 1901.

25. Lockwood, pp. 157–58.

26. Rappoport, *Socialisme de gouvernement et Socialisme révolutionnaire* (1902), pp. 29–30, 41, 44; *L'Union Républicaine de l'Herault,* March 30.

27. JOC, January 21, 23, 1903; MS, August 1, 1905, pp. 433–436.

28. JOC, January 26, 1903, January 29, 1903. As minister and with two other social-ists, Millerand had abstained in the vote on the *budget des Cultes,* December 17, 1901. Longuet said that Millerand's entry into the cabinet was the fruit of the policy practiced by the parliamentary group during the 1893–1898 legislature; 'Evolution du socialisme en France', *La Raison,* June 1908, pp. 11, 14. Millerand's voting record, as well as that of other socialists during these years, has been tabu-lated; Fiechter, pp. 95–108. It reveals that he systematically supported the Combes ministry before January 1903, including a bill covering the creation and utili-zation of congregational establishments voted November 11, 1902. But beginning in January 1903 and continuing until the end of the 1902–1906 legislature, Mille-rand refused to go along with the majority socialist vote on a dozen different occa-sions and in fact separated himself from his colleagues. The record indicates that he voted with the socialist majority on twenty-six other occasions; these votes, however, were not as vital as those on religious funds, legislation to curb anti-militarism, disarmament and, of course, giving confidence to the Combes ministry.
29. A colleague of Jaurès, who had worked on *La Petite République,* Gustave Téry, said that Jaures' policy was realistic and opportunistic. The word, however, car-ried an unfortunate connotation, and it was Jaurès and Millerand who invented the term 'reformism'. *Jaurès,* p. 265.
30. PR, March 14, 1903.
31. *Le Mouvement socialiste,* March 15, 1903, p. 487; *Le Parlement et l'opinion,* Sep-tember 23, 1920, p. 1702.
32. This line of argument was found logical by reformists like Albert Thomas. The *budget des Cultes,* he said, was the logical result of an existing situation, and the French proletariat was 'mature enough' to understand that. For Thomas, the mistake lay in not having thoroughly discussed the question in advance. The ob-jection to the 'Manuel du soldat' was more difficult and more serious, but social-ists had supported legal procedures, and to urge desertion was anarchy. Schaper, pp. 65–66.
33. RPP, May 1903, p. 381; *Le Temps,* March 5, 1903.
34. Major speeches printed in RS, May 1903. See also the excellent summaries in Noland, pp. 149–157.
35. The vote was 109 to 89 with 15 abstentions, MS, May 15, 1903, p. 135.
36. Lagardelle, 'La comédie de Bordeaux', MS, April 15, 1903, pp. 625–629; J. Bour-deau, RPP, May 1903, p. 386; MS, May 14, 1903, p. 138; RPP, August 1903, p. 403; Lockwood, pp. 99–100.
37. PR, May 29, 1903. For his defenses of the Pension and Arbitration Bills see RS, June 1903, p. 650; text, pp. 641–650. For the law prohibiting the use of lead in paint, p. 226. PR, June 16, 1903.
38. Draft in MP–BN. Also see PR, June 27, 1903.
39. Raoul Briquet, 'La Politique anticléricale', MS, August 15, 1902, pp. 1442, 1452.
40. PR, July 1, 1903.
41. Millerand had written to Brunellière on June 28. Brunellière to Millerand, July 4, 1903, Brunellière Papers, IFHS, 14AS 105/30, folios 273–274.
42. PR, October 2, December 19, 1903.
43. MS, December 15, 1903, p. 550.

44. Deville, however, abstained. JOC, November 23, 1903; See MS, December 15, 1903, p. 552; Brunellière to Lefebvre, January 3, 1904. Brunellière Papers, IFHS, 14AS 116 1B. Brunellière to Delasalle (former deputy mayor of Lille) in September 1903; Willard, *Correspondance*, pp. 355–356. Though sorely provoked, Brunellière had never tolerated attacks on Guesde's character and regularly pointed to the sacrifices made by the POF chief for the sake of socialism.

45. Lavy, pp. 68–69. The Resolution was voted on January 4. Text in *L'Aurore*, January 6. Account of discussion in PR, January 23.

46. PR, January 8, 1904.

47. PR, January 9, 15, 1904; Goldberg, *Life*, pp. 317–318.

48. Statements of support in MP–BN; Also PP, B a/1620 for additional testimony.

49. MS, February 15, 1904, pp. 218–219. The letter from the XIVe *arrondissement* was especially lyrical.

50. Debreuilh in *Le Socialiste*, September 24–31, 1904; cited in *L'Aurore*, January 6, 1904; Longuet to Kautsky, March 26, 1904. Kautsky Archives, IISH; Goldberg, *Life*, p. 317; Renard in *La Vie*, February 24, 1912; Brunellière's letter to Millerand dated January 8, 1904; Brunellière Papers 14AS 106/32 folios 125–26.

51. *Le Temps*, January 6, 1904. Millerand is quoted as saying: 'Besides, it does not depend on the Seine Federation or on anyone whether my friends and I are and remain socialists. I can no longer be a member of the Parti socialiste français or of the parliamentary socialist group, but no one has the power to render me unfaithful to my convictions and to my ideas. I am today what I was yesterday.'

52. *Le Temps*, January 6, 1904; MP–MR.

53. Louis Debreuilh, 'Encore le Cas Millerand', MS, February 15, 1904, p. 216. Millerand spoke on January 7, text in RPP, February 1904, pp. 226–247.

54. Andler, p. 148; Lefranc, p. 117; Paul-Boncour, I, pp. 193–195.

55. In 1931 Léon Blum wrote that France should take the initiative in arbitration and disarmament. Milorad M. Drachkovitch, *De Karl Marx à Léon Blum; La crise de la social-démocratie* (Geneva, 1954), pp. 117–118. He urged application of Jaurès' formula which defined the aggressor nation as the one refusing to submit to arbitration.

56. JOC, March 3, 1904; PR, March 4. Jaurès had regarded the church as the 'principle source of inspiration and organizer of the whole anti-republican campaign during the Dreyfus affair and greatest enemy of socialism'. *La Dépêche de Toulouse*, November 30, 1898, May 28, 1900; cited in Weinstein, p. 83. He thus viewed anticlerical legislation as 'the finest fruit' of the Radical and socialist coalition. *La Dépêche*, August 15, 1903; PR, March 8, 16, 1904; Louis Goulot, *Le Socialisme au pouvoir* (1910), pp. 50–51. For a discussion of the deeply rooted anticlericalism of the French working class, see Jean Bruhat, 'Anticlericalisme et mouvement ouvrier en France avant 1914', *Mouvement social*, 57 (1966), pp. 61–100.

57. Sûreté, AN, F7 12496, July 2, 1902 (no. M. 1439); Emile Buré, 'Les faits politiques', MS, August 15, 1902, p. 1464; Also R. Briquet, 'La politique anticlericale', MS, August 15, 1902, pp. 1442, 1452; 'Enquête sur l'anticlericalisme et le socialisme', MS, November 1 and December 1, 1902; Vandervelde's comment in the November 1 issue, p. 1924; Kautsky's in the December 1 issue, p. 2152.

58. Fournière, 'La Crise socialiste', RS, July 1905, p. 51; *L'Union Républicaine de l'Hérault*, July 6, 1905.
59. JOC, March 17, 1904. Also see PR, March 18, 19, 1904, and Daniel, *1904*, pp. 105–107.
60. Combarieu, p. 272; *Mémoires*, p. 48.
61. *Le Temps*, March 19, 1904.
62. MP–BN. Millerand was also expelled formally from French freemasonry which was closely supporting the Combes ministry. Renard, RS, January-February 1950, pp. 99–100.
63. *L'Humanité*, June 13, 1904; *Le Socialiste*, March 27, April 3, 1904; *Le Petit Sou*, March 19, 1904; PR, March 18, 1904; *L'Aurore*, March 19, 1904; Emile Combes, *Mon Ministère* (1956), p. 152; MP–MR. Millerand's documents included his March 8 letter to Combes and a copy of the latter's ministerial declaration promising to work for a pension bill.
64. Sûreté, AN F7 2553, reports dated March 15, 19, 1904.
65. This and other speeches reproduced in the pro-Millerand political weekly of the XIIth *arrondissement, Le Douzième*, March 29–April 4, 1904. Copies in MP–BN.
66. Combarieu, p. 250. There is less evidence to support the contention that the Waldeck ministers sought a crisis in order to return to power. Millerand, Doumer, Baudin, Lanessan and Leygues voted against Combes, and Caillaux abstained; Ries, p. 215.
67. Letter dated March 19, 1904, MP–JM. That Millerand remembered the advice is demonstrated by the almost identical words in his own counsel to Louis Marlio, his young *chef de cabinet* in 1910. Marlio, *Problèmes d'aujourd'hui* (Montreal, 1944), p. 181.
68. MP–MR.
69. MP–JM. There are eighteen letters, mostly undated, from Mme. Waldeck-Rousseau in Millerand's papers. She asked Millerand to help her select her husband's papers for publication. Some of these papers appeared in *Le Matin* in 1911. The last letter referred to was dated May 27, 1908. The biography was that of Henry Leyret.
70. On September 6. Text in *Politique des réalisations*, pp. 362–396.
71. Mme. Waldeck-Rousseau's letter was dated August 25, 1905, MP–JM; Combarieu, pp. 273–274.
72. Brunellière Papers IFHS, 14AS 106/33, folio 384; Willard, *Correspondance*, pp. 375–376.
73. *Le Socialiste*, November 9, 1900. Cited in Zévaès, *Une Génération*, p. 44. Lefranc, p. 158.
74. Sembat's resolution cited in *L'Union Républicaine de l'Hérault*, July 6, 1905. Antimilitarism was held up for special censure as only weakening the defensive forces of the nation. Zévaès, *Une Génération*, p. 44.
75. In subsequent sessions of the Chamber, at least throughout 1904, Millerand continued to concern himself with social reform and could still cooperate with socialists. Along with Jaurès, Basly, Breton, Rouanet and others he submitted legislation to increase the frequency of labor inspections, RPP, July 1904, p. 182. Together with Dubief, Chairman of the Chamber's Labor Committee, he introduced

a bill that would have increased state subsidies to private unemployment-benefit funds, the amount proportionate to the size of the organization, RS, July 1904, p. 103. He still represented the French section in the International Association for the Legal Protection of the Worker, RPP, April 1904, p. 194. And in November, he urged that the functions of mutual aid societies be extended to cover fully assistance to the unemployed, RPP, April 1904, p. 641.

76. Declaration of Principles of the SFIO, RS, January 1905, pp. 86–88; Lefranc, pp. 124–125.
77. Briand cited in A. Zévaès and Jacques Prolo, *Une Campagne politique: Le Parti républicain socialiste, 1910–1917* (n.d.), p. 5. Others refusing to join included Zévaès, Deville, Gerault-Richard, Briand, Hugues, Colliard, Augagneur, etc. Orry, p. 173; Fournière, p. 34.
78. Breton, *L'Unité socialiste*, pp. 31, 51.
79. The thesis of Fournière's book. See p. 73.
80. However, Jaurès' latest biographer argues that he became more radical in his later years, as demonstrated by his willingness to resort to the general strike, his struggle against the antilabor campaigns of the Clemenceau and Briand governments and his opposition to French colonial policy. Goldberg, *Life,* Chapter 12.

NOTES TO: EPILOGUE

1. JOC, June 10, 1904. Lapaquillerie, pp. 209–210.
2. *L'Humanité,* June 11, 13, 1904.
3. PR, June 13–22, 1904. *L'Union Républicaine de l'Hérault* published a series of in-depth articles in the spring and early summer of 1905. See the issues of April 27, May 8, 11, 18, 25, June 8, 15, 22, 29. Jean Bernard, *1904,* pp. 214–241.
4. Bernard, *1904,* p. 233. A Sûreté report dated July 5 described Millerand as especially angered by Cottingies' 'revelation', for he guessed that it was conceived by Combes, AN, F7 12533, no. 1343.
5. JOC, July 1, 1904. Cottingies resigned on July 6. For the growth of the opposition to Combes, also see Lapaquillerie, p. 244. The Chamber Committee cleared Combes and his son of bribery charges.
6. JOC, November 9, 1904. Millerand had used almost the same words to repudiate the Radicals' use of Boulangist tactics.
7. Daniel, *1904,* pp. 443, 492.
8. Combarieu, p. 285; Bernard, *1904,* p. 371.
9. Daniel, *1904,* p. 487. The resentment aroused by Combes' tactics has been described in Robert Cornilleau, *De Waldeck-Rousseau à Poincaré, 1898–1924* (1926), p. 108.
10. JOC, December 9, 1904; Reis, p. 217.
11. JOC, January 14, February 10, 1905; Daniel, *1905,* p. 21. Combes blamed the Waldeck-Rousseau ministers for his fall, *Mon Ministère,* pp. 248–49.
12. Orry, pp. 77–82.
13. *La Revue socialiste* continued to regard Millerand as an independent socialist, RS, August, 1909, p. 832. Also see Lefranc, pp. 80, 81 and Weill, 'Die sozialistische

Bewegung in Frankreich, 1893–1910', *Archiv für die Geschichte des Sozialismus...*, p. 153.

14. Zévaès, *Le Parti socialiste de 1904 à 1923* (1923), p. 32.
15. Zévaès, *Le Parti socialiste de 1904 à 1923* (1923), p. 57.
16. See, for example, the *Chronique* in the May-June 1906 issue of MS, p. 188. It was charged that the Socialist platform was virtually identical to that of the Radicals. Also see the article by C.G. Fages, 'La Crise socialiste', MS, April 15, 1906, pp. 377–389.
17. A well-documented case for the revival of reformism within the French socialist movement was made by Harold Weinstein. See especially pp. 156–160. More recent scholarship, however, makes his analysis appear somewhat oversimplified. In reality a new left wing was to emerge, sympathetic to revolutionary syndicalism and favoring insurrection. The Seine Federation was especially radical and was even to expel Brousse from its ranks. But a right wing favored the revisionism of Bernstein, and Jaurès' position may most appropriately be described as working to synthesize these divergent views and keep the party together, Lefranc, pp. 160–195.
18. MS, November 1906, p. 295; Zévaès, *Le Socialisme en 1912*, p. 40.
19. Weinstein, pp. 161–63. Thanks largely to Jaurès' willingness to keep his party 'flexible and realistic' and explore the merits of temporary alliances, the Congresses of 1909 and 1911 'conspicuously modified the spirit of Amsterdam'. Goldberg, *Life*, p. 399.
20. Eugen Weber, *The Nationalist Revival in France, 1905–1914* (Berkeley, 1959), p. 9. Millerand's remarks cited in *L'Aide sociale*, March 15, 1909, p. 116.
21. Undated letter from Maurice Bernard, MP–BN; Draft lecture 'Un Demi-siècle de politique français', MP–VN. *Mémoires*, p. 73.
22. Roger Soltau, *French Political Thought in the Nineteenth Century* (New York, 1959 reprint), p. 353.
23. Mermieux, p. 167. For the relationship between possiblism and reformism, see Carl Landauer, 'The Origin of Socialist Reformism in France', *International Review of Social History*, XII (1967), Part I, pp. 95–100. He demonstrated that Possibilists were very much committed to revolution in the early 1880s and did not become reformists until the last half of the decade.
24. Leroy-Beaulieu, *L'Economie français*, cited in RS, November 1900, p. 604. 'Because of MM. Millerand and Waldeck-Rousseau there will no longer be any room in the labor movement in France for anyone who remains apart from trade unions. This is the most colossal change which has taken place in France since 1789.' Halévy *Essais*, p. 292.

Sources

ORAL TESTIMONY

Details on Millerand's life were obtained during interviews with M. and Mme. Jacques Millerand, Mme. Alice Millerand, M. Jean Millerand, M. and Mme. Jean-Paul Alfassa (born Marthe Millerand), M. Raoul Persil, Mme. Sonia Balachovski Petit, Mme. Pierre Goujon (born Reinach), Mme. Suzanne Millerand and M. Stephane Garnery. I am also grateful for an interview with M. Paul Grunebaum-Ballin and for a lengthy and detailed letter from M. Paul-Boncour.

UNPUBLISHED MANUSCRIPTS

Private holdings. Millerand's public life reached from the early 1880s to well into the 1930s, and even those papers limited to his socialist years are considerable. The single most important collection of letters received by Millerand, many with draft replies that reveal at least his initial reactions, is that in the possession of his younger son, M. Jacques Millerand, who lives in Sèvres. There are several hundred letters from important people in all walks of French political life. There are also his father's unpublished memoirs, written in Versailles shortly before his death in 1943. Although Millerand had recourse to some documentary material in writing these memoirs – several sources are appended – they are based largely on memory and contain occasional errors of fact. The account presented is nevertheless coherent, but the memoirs are not very reflective, and, because they were written in an impersonal manner, they do not adequately reveal Millerand's inner feelings at such critical junctures of his career as his expulsion from the socialist party. M. Jacques Millerand also holds two collections of letters, the first set written during the siege of Paris in 1870–1871 between Millerand's father and relatives in Paris and the family in Dinard, the second between Millerand and his family during his year (November, 1879–November 1880) of service in Guingamp. Members of the family also possess numerous photographs.

There are two other privately held collections of Millerand papers. However, they contain relatively few letters; there are draft lectures and speeches, self-memoranda for articles, petitions received as minister, etc. All these papers were collected by Millerand's legal secretary in the 1930s, M. Lucien Vidal-Nacquet, who intended to write a biography but was deported to Germany during World War II. His son, Pierre Vidal-Nacquet, who lives in Paris, has retained the bulk of these papers but turned over most of those relating to the pre-1914 period to Mme. Madeleine Rébérioux, who is editing a collection of Jaurès' works.

Bibliothèque Nationale. The most extensive holdings (110 kilograms) of Millerand papers are in the Department of Manuscripts. They were donated by the family. Many of these papers are subject to the still stringent rules governing access to archival material in France, and none are sorted; consequently, I was granted permission to use them only as a result of the very active efforts of M. Jacques Millerand. Because he withheld most of the letters, the BN collection consists mainly of ministerial and legal papers, with numerous reports, memoranda and newspaper clippings. However, there are occasionally surprisingly important letters, such as the exchange between Jaurès and Millerand at the time the latter was Minister of Commerce and the former urged him to resign.

In the regular holdings of the Department of Manuscripts there may be found sixty-seven letters and cards from Millerand (and his wife) in the Joseph Reinach papers; *Nouvelles acquisitions françaises (N.A.fr)*, *24882* ff. 80–117. Some assorted and not very important letters to Millerand are filed under *N.A. fr. 13269*. Two important sources for the early history of the Third Republic are also found in the BN. One is the seven-volume unpublished journal of Auguste Scheurer-Kestner, 'Souvenirs d'un républicain alsacien', *N.A. fr. 12704–12711*. Especially relevant are volumes VI through VIII (*N.A. fr. 12709–12711*) which cover the period 1889–1898. The other is Bernard Lavergne, *Mémoires Politiques, 1881–1889;* much of this 1100-page manuscript has been published (see list of selected books), but that part which was not contains useful impressions of the political life of the early Third Republic by the longtime friend of Jules Grévy.

Archives nationales. Millerand communicated for many years with Gabriel Deville, Guesde's former lieutenant who became an Independent by the mid-1890s. The Deville Papers are in carton *51 AP I,* and dossier I contains seventy letters and cards from Millerand. I have already discussed the Sûreté Générale (national police) reports and their usefulness in research on the French socialist movement. They are available in the Ministry of the Interior papers, the F7 series. The following cartons were of especial significance:

F7 12486–12503: Agissements socialistes, especially *F7 12496:* Renseignements généraux sur le mouvement socialiste en France et à l'étranger 1893–1911; La scission socialiste en 1899 (crise Millerand); Le Comité général socialiste après Japy, etc.; Les diverses fractions du Parti socialiste et les élections de mai, 1898. *F7 12490:* Agissements socialistes, congrès ouvriers divers, 1876–1899. *F7 12526:* Les Troubles de Montceau-les-Mines. *F7 12553:* Notes sur la situation politique, 1899–1905. *F7 12560:* Notes de police, May 1900, May 1901, December 1902. *F7 12522–12525:* Congrès divers. *F7 12885:* Parti socialiste, 1894–1901, especially *F7 12886:* Documents relatifs au parti 'socialiste-guesdiste'. *F7 12562:* Notes de police, 1904–1905. *F7 13072:* Congrès socialistes, 1899–1909, (especially those of 1899–1900).

The archives of the Ministry of Commerce and Industry proved disappointing. Some information was made available in the following numbers of the F12 series: *F12 4842:* Voyages ministérielles; *F12 4846:* Cabinet du Ministère du Commerce, lettres et petitions, 1899–1901; *F12 4850:* Projets, amendements, notes ministérielles.

The few recorded appeals made by Millerand on behalf of socialists to Monis are in the archives of the Ministry of Justice: *BB18: 2134* (dossier 1858A99), *2183* (dossier 315/A01) and *2202:* Correspondance de la division criminelle.

Demographic statistics relevant to the Twelfth *arrondissement* may be found in the F20 series: Mouvement de la population de la France par arrondissement (*F20 51* for 1889; *F20 63* for 1893; *F20 66* for 1896; and *F20 832* for 1900). For election returns, series A and C should be consulted: Versements de l'assemblée nationale.

Archives de la Prefecture de Police. The following cartons were especially relevant: *B a/1472:* Socialisme en France, 1893–1896; *B a/1473:* Le socialisme, 1897–1914; *B a/1125*; Jean Jaurès; *B a/1620:* Comité de vigilance socialiste: comité de rapprochement socialiste.

Archives de la Seine. Paris. *75 GH 91,* folder labeled 'Alexandre Millerand'.

Institut français d'histoire sociale. The Eugène Fournière Papers, *14AS 181.* There are twenty-one letters from Millerand during the period 1893–1913 (nos. 1069–1089). The Papers of Charles Brunellière, *14AS 103–105* (for the period 1895–1903). The secretary of the Guesdist federation in Nantes exchanged several important letters with Millerand.

Bibliothèque de l'Institut. The Waldeck-Rousseau papers. Four letters from Millerand to Waldeck may be found in carton no. 4568; Letters reçues par Waldeck-Rousseau, J. à Z. For Waldeck's notes on the formation of the Ministry see carton no. 4579: Papiers relatifs à l'année 1899. The papers of Charles Benoist contain one letter from Millerand, carton no. 4556. Some letters from Millerand, accepting or declining invitations, are in the Marie Raffalovitch papers, cartons 3688 and 3669.

Archives of the International Institute of Social History (Amsterdam). The Jules Guesde papers contain some of Guesde's correspondence and part of the correspondence of the POF's National Council. Letters from various French socialists, including Guesde, are in the Kautsky and Liebknecht papers. There is a letter from Millerand in the Vollmar Papers explaining his entry into the Waldeck-Rousseau ministry.

DISSERTATIONS

Blick, Boris, 'Waldeck-Rousseau, 1894–1904', University of Wisconsin, 1958.
Fry, N. E., 'Integral Socialism and the Third Republic, 1893 to 1914', Yale University, 1964.

21*

Lockwood, Theodore D., 'French Socialists and Political Responsibilities, 1898–1905', Princeton University, 1952.

Néré, Jacques, 'La Crise industrielle de 1882 et le mouvement boulangiste', University of Paris, 1959.

Willard, Claude, 'La Correspondance de Charles Brunellière', Thèse complémentaire, University of Paris, 1965 (published in 1968).

PUBLISHED WORKS

Millerand's writings. Until his expulsion from the socialist party most of his writings consisted of newspaper articles. Many parliamentary speeches, lectures, courtroom defenses and campaign speeches, however, were also published. His clearest exposition of reformist socialism is contained in the preface and speeches reproduced in *Le Socialisme réformiste français*, 1903. Defense of his proposed bills may be found in *Travail et travailleurs*, 1908, and in *Politique de réalisations*, 1911. Published courtroom defenses include *Paul Lafargue devant la Cour d'assises de Douai, 5 juillet, 1891. Plaidoirie de Millerand, defenseur de Lafargue*, Lille, 1891 and *Plaidoirie devant la Cour d'assises de la Seine, audience du 15 mars, 1890* (for his defense of the Descaves novel, *Sous-offs*). Millerand's published reports to the Association international pour la protection légale des travailleurs may be found in a book by that title (1907); and in *La durée légale du travail: Des modifications apportés à la Loi de 1900*, 1905. An important campaign speech (1898) was published as *La Plateform électorale*, 1898. Two other articles may be found in A. Millerand, *et al.*, *Enseignement et démocratie*, 1950; and the *Almanach de la Question sociale pour 1899* ('Les socialistes et la législature nouvelle'). See his preface to Jules Huret, *Enquête sur la grève et l'arbitrage obligatoire*, 1901.

The newspapers to which Millerand contributed most extensively during his Radical and socialist years were *La Justice* (1882–1889); *La Voix* (1889); *Le XIXe Siècle* (1889–1893); *La Petite République* (1892–1897); *La Lanterne* (1897–1899); and *L'Eclair*, (1897–1899).

Official publications. Annuaire Statistique de la Ville de Paris. Bulletin Municipal Officiel de la Ville de Paris. Journal Officiel de la République française. Journal Officiel, Annales de la Chambre des Députés, Débats parlementaires. Almanach National, Annuaire officiel de la République française. Documents diplomatiques français, 1871–1914 (Ministry of Foreign Affairs). *Bulletin de l'Office du Travail* (Ministry of Commerce). *Statistique de l'enseignement supérieur, 1878–1888. Tableau des avocats de la Cour d'Appel de Paris.*

Relevant periodicals. (For dates and frequency of publication, names of editors, etc., consult P. Sorlin, *Waldeck-Rousseau*, 1966, pp. 546–547, and C. Willard, *Les Guesdistes*, 1965, pp. 695–697.) *L'Aide sociale, Almanach socialiste illustré, Archiv für die Geschichte des Sozialismus und der Arbeiter Bewegung, Bulletin du Grand Orient de France, Cosmopolis, International Socialist Review, Le Parlement et l'opinion, Le Mouvement socialiste, La Nouvelle Revue, La Revue des Deux Mondes, La Revue de Paris, La Revue Politique et Parlementaire, La Revue socialiste, La Vie.*

Relevant newspapers. (For dates, editors and frequency of publication, see P. Sorlin, *Waldeck-Rousseau*, 1966, pp. 541–545, and C. Willard, *Les Guesdistes*, 1965, pp. 695–697). The newspapers for which Millerand wrote may be found listed above. Others include: *L'Aurore, Le Bloc, Le Chambord, Le Cri du XIXe* (anti-Millerand), *Le Cri de Paris, Le Cri du Peuple, La Croix, La Dépêche de Toulouse, Le Douzième* (pro-Millerand), *Le Droit, L'Echo de Paris, L'Egalité de Roubaix-Tourcoing, L'Evénement, Le Figaro, L'Humanité, L'Intransigeant, Le Journal des débats, La Libre Parole, London Times, Le Matin, L'Ordre, Le Petit Bleu, Le Petit Calaisien, Le Petit Sou, Le Proletaire, Le Rappel, La Réforme, Le Reveil du Nord, Le Socialiste, Le Socialiste du XIXe Arrondissement* (Guesdist), *Le Temps, La Voix du Peuple, L'Union Républicaine de l'Hérault.*

Writings on Millerand. There is no adequate biography. That of Raul Persil, his longtime assistant (*Alexandre Millerand, 1859–1943*, 1949), is little more than a report of the author's relationship with his subject. A brief account by Vincent Badie, *M. Alexandre Millerand*, Montpellier, 1931, consists of a survey of his social legislation. The only useful biographical studies are in the form of articles, and they are not numerous before 1905. An early account was that of Henry du Basty, 'Les Hommes politiques français, M. Millerand', *La Revue d'histoire contemporaine*, January 20, 1889. Some information on his socialist years was offered by Jacques Bompard, 'Un Ministre de la Guerre, M. Alexandre Millerand', *La Revue politique et parlementaire*, January 10, 1914. A number of articles appeared when Millerand was Premier and President of the Republic in the early 1920s; their references, however, to his socialist years were sketchy at best. Perhaps the most important was that by René Viviani 'Portraits contemporaines, M. Alexandre Millerand', *La Revue des deux mondes*, November 1, 1920. Another article concerned with the pre-1905 period was that by Adolph Smith, 'Millerand, Briand, and the French Socialist Party', *Fortnightly Review*, June 7, 1921. Smith was the Anglo-French interpreter at the congresses of the Second International, and his focus was on the subordination of the French to the German party rather than on Millerand or Briand. The most useful articles for Millerand's early life were those of Georges Renard: 'Portrait de Millerand', *La Vie*, February 24, 1912; and 'Millerand, Quelques Souvenirs', *La Revue socialiste*, January-February 1950, pp. 94–110; March 1951, pp. 353–371; May 1951, pp. 610–628. The last two were published posthumously. A longtime friend, Renard broke with the family in the 1920s, leaving a bad taste on both sides, but his factual recollections, as contrasted to his speculations, appear reliable.

List of selected books and articles

Unless stated otherwise, place of publication is Paris. The notes should be consulted for detailed references and for a more complete bibliography. Good succinct comments on many of these works may be found in Aaron Noland, *The Founding of the French Socialist Party*, Cambridge, 1956, pp. 214–223. Lengthy bibliographies may be found appended to Pierre Sorlin, *Waldeck-Rousseau*, 1966, and Claude Willard, *Les Guesdistes*, 1965.

Andler, Charles. *Vie de Lucien Herr, 1864–1926*. 1932.

Badie, Vincent. *M. Alexandre Millerand, Socialiste réformiste. Son Œuvre sociale.* Montpellier, 1931.

Beau de Loménie, E. *Les Responsabilités des Dynasties bourgeoises.* Vol. II: *De Mac-Mahon à Poincaré.* 1947.

Blum, Léon. *Souvenirs sur l'affaire.* 1935.

Breton, J. L. *L'Unité socialiste.* Vol. VII of *Histoire des Partis socialistes en France.* A. Zévaès, Ed. 1912.

Caillaux, Joseph. *Mes Mémoires.* Vol. I: *Ma Jeunesse orgueilleuse, 1863–1909.* 1942.

Chevallier, Jean-Jacques. *Histoire des Institutions de la France de 1789 à nos jours, 2ᵉ cycle: 1870–1945.* 1950.

Claris, Edmond. *Souvenirs de Soixante Ans de Journalisme, 1890–1955.* 1955.

Colton, Joel. *Compulsory Labor Arbitration in France, 1936–1939.* New York, 1951.

Combarieu, Abel. *Sept Ans à l'Elysée avec Loubet, 1899–1906.* 1932.

Combes, Emile. *Mon Ministère, 1902–1905.* 1956.

Compère-Morel, Adéodat. *Jules Guesde. Le Socialisme fait l'homme, 1845–1922.* 1937.

– (Ed.). *Grand Dictionnaire socialiste du mouvement politique et économique, national et international.* 1924.

Conseil National du Parti Ouvrier Français. *Aux Travailleurs du France. Onze Ans d'Histoire socialiste.* 1901.

Cornilleau, Robert. *De Waldeck-Rousseau à Poincaré. Chronique d'une génération, 1898–1924.* 1926.

Daniel, André [pseud. of Georges Bonnefous] (Ed.). *L'Année Politique*. 1875–1906.

Dansette, Adrien. *Le Boulangisme*. 1946.

Daudet, Léon. *La Vie orageuse de Clemenceau*. 1938.

Delasalle, F. J., Burnet, G., and Duez, E. *Les Congrégations non autorisées et leurs liquidateurs devant la loi de 1901*. 1905.

Derfler, Leslie. 'Le cas Millerand. Une Nouvelle interprétation', *Revue d'histoire moderne et contemporaine*, April-June 1963.

– 'Reformism and Jules Guesde: 1891–1904', *International Review of Social History*, XII (1967), Part I.

Detot, Paul. *Le Socialisme devant les Chambres françaises, 1893–1898*. 1902.

Dommanget, Maurice. *Edouard Vaillant, un grand socialiste, 1840–1915*. 1956.

– *Histoire du Premier Mai*. 1953.

Duverger, Maurice. *Les Partis politiques*. 1951.

Earle, Edward (Ed.). *Modern France: Problems of the Third and Fourth Republics*. Princeton, 1951.

Engels, Fr., and Lafargue, Paul and Laura. *Correspondance. Textes receuillis, annotés, et presentés par E. Bottigelli*. Vol. II: *1887–1890;* Vol. III: *1891–1895*. 1956, 1959.

Fiechter, Jean-Jacques. *Le Socialisme français. De l'affaire Dreyfus à la Grande Guerre*. Geneva, 1965.

Fournière, Eugène. *La Crise Socialiste*. 1908.

Garcon, Maurice. *Histoire de la justice sous la IIIe République*, Vol. I, 1957.

Geoffroy, Gustave. *Clemenceau, sa Vie, son Œuvre*. n.d.

Goblet, René. 'Souvenirs', *Revue Politique et parlementaire*, November 1931.

Goguel, François. *La Politique des Partis sous la IIIe République*. 1946.

Goldberg, Harvey. *The Life of Jean Jaurès*. Madison, 1962.

Goulut, Louis. *Le Socialisme au pouvoir*. 1910.

Halévy, Daniel. *Essais sur le Mouvement ouvrier en France*. 1901.

Hubert, Louis-Lucien. *Ce qu'il faut connaitre des grandes journées parlementaires de la IIIe République*. 1928.

Huret, Jules. *Enquête sur la question sociale en Europe*. 1897.

Jaurès, Jean. *Discours Parlementaires*. Edmond Claris, Ed. (Preface by Jaurès, 'Le Socialisme et le Radicalisme en 1885'). 1904.

Joll, James. *The Second International*. New York, 1966.

Labrousse, Ernest. 'La Montée du socialisme, 1848–1945', *La Revue socialiste*, May, 1946.

Lachapelle, Georges. *Les Régimes électoraux*. 1934.

Lagardelle, Hubert. 'Les origines du socialisme parlementaire en France', *Le Mouvement socialiste*, September 1909.

Lambeau, Lucien. *Bercy, Volume d'histoire des communes annexées à Paris en 1859*. 1910.

Landauer, Carl A. *European Socialism: A History of Ideas and Movements*. Vol. I: *From the Industrial Revolution to the First World War and its Aftermath*. Berkeley. 1959.

– 'The Guesdists and the Small Farmer: Early Erosion of French Marxism', *International Review of Social History*, VI (1961).

– 'The Origin of Reformist Socialism in France', *International Review of Social History*, XII (1967), part 1.

Lavergne, Bernard. *Les Deux présidences de Jules Grévy, 1879–1887. Mémoires.* 1966.

Lawton, F. H., *et al. Amos and Walton's Introduction to French Law.* Oxford, 1963.

Lavy, Aimé. *L'Œuvre de Millerand, Un Ministre socialiste, juin, 1899–janvier, 1902.* 1902.

Lefranc, Georges. *Le Mouvement socialiste sous la Troisième République (1875–1940)* 1963.

Lépine, Louis. *Mes Souvenirs.* 1929.

Levasseur, Emile. *Questions ouvrières et industrielles en France sous la troisième République.* 1907.

Lorwin, Val. *The French Labor Movement.* Cambridge, Mass., 1954.

– 'Reflections on the History of the French and American Labor Movements', *Journal of Economic History*, XVII, 1957.

Louis, Paul. *Histoire du Parti Socialiste, 1871–1914.* 1922.

– *Histoire du Socialisme en France*, 5th ed. 1950.

Maitron, Jean. *Histoire du Mouvement anarchiste en France, 1880–1915.* 1951.

Manevy, Raymond. *La Presse de la IIIe République.* 1955.

Martin, Auguste. 'Péguy et Millerand', *L'Amitié Charles Péguy*, June 15, 1960.

Mermiex, Gabriel, [psend. of Terrail]. *Le Socialisme: définitions, explications, objections.* 1906.

Noblemaire, Georges. *Carnet de route, au pays des parlementaires.* 1923.

Noland, Aaron. *The Founding of the French Socialist Party.* Cambridge, Mass. 1956.

Néré, Jacques. 'La Crise Industrielle et le mouvement boulangiste', *L'Information historique*, III, May-June 1959.

Orry, Albert. *Les Socialistes Indépendants.* Vol. VIII of *Histoire des Partis socialistes en France*, II vols. Alexandre Zévaès, Ed. 1911.

Partin, Malcolm O. *Waldeck-Rousseau, Combes and the Church, 1899–1905: The Politics of Anticlericalism.* Durham, 1969.

Payen, Fernand. *Raymond Poincaré: L'homme, le parlementaire, l'avocat.* 1936.

– and Duveau, Gaston. *Les Règles de la profession d'avocat et les usages du Barreau de Paris*, 2nd ed., n.d.

Pelletan, Camille. *Georges Clemenceau.* 1883.

Perrot, Michelle, and Kriegel, Annie. *Le Socialisme français et le pouvoir.* 1966.

Pinset, Jacques. 'Quelques problèmes du socialisme en France vers 1900', *Revue d'Histoire économique et sociale*, III, 1958.

Pipkin, Charles W. *Social Politics and Modern Democracies*, 2 vols. New York, 1931.

Prelot, Marcel. *L'Evolution politique du socialisme français, 1789–1934.* 1939.

Ranc, Arthur. *Souvenirs, Correspondance, 1831–1908.* 1913.

Rappoport, Charles. *Socialisme de Gouvernement et Socialisme révolutionnaire.* 1902.

Reinach, Joseph. *Demogogues et Socialistes.* 1906.

– *Histoire de l'Affaire Dreyfus*, 7 vols. 1901–1908.

Renard, Georges. 'Millerand, Quelques souvenirs', *La Revue socialiste*, January-February 1950.

Richard, Eugène. *Le Marché du vin à Paris.* 1934.

Ries, J. 'Combes, Millerand et Jaurès en 1904', *La Revue socialiste*, July 1964., pp. 209–217.

Rochefort, Henri. *Les Aventures de ma vie*, 5 vols., n.d.

Samual, René, and Bonét-Maury, Georges. *Les Parlementaires français.* 1914.

Sarraute, Joseph. *Socialisme d'opposition, socialisme de govournement et lutte de classe.* 1901.

Scelle, Georges. *Précis élémentaire de législation industrielle.* 1927.

Seager, Frederic H. *The Boulanger Affair: Political Crossroad of France 1886–1889.* Ithaca, 1969.

Sée, Henri. *Histoire économique de la France*, 2nd ed. Vol. II: *Les Temps Modernes, 1789–1914.* 1951.

Seignobos, Charles. *Le Déclin de l'Empire et l'établissement de la 3ᵉ République, 1859–1875.*

– *L'Evolution de la 3ᵉ République, 1875–1914.*
Vols. VII and VIII of *Histoire de France Contemporaine*, 10 vols. Ernest Lavisse, Ed. 1920–1922.

Seilhac, Léon de. *Les Grèves.* 1903.

Sorlin, Pierre. *Waldeck-Rousseau.* 1966.

Soulier, Auguste. *L'Instabilité ministérielle sous la troisième République, 1871–1938.* 1939.

Strauss, Paul. *Les Fondateurs de la République, Souvenirs.* 1934.

Suarez, George. *La Vie orgueilleuse de Clemenceau.* 1930.

– *Briand: Sa vie, son œuvre, avec son Journal et de nombreaux documents inédits.* Vol. I: *Le Révolté circonspect, 1862–1904.* 1938.

Thomson, David. *Democracy in France: The Third and Fourth Republics*, 5th ed. New York, 1969.

Tucker, Robert C. *The Marxian Revolutionary Idea: Essays on Marxist Thought and Its Impact on Radical Movements.* New York, 1969.

Vandervelde, Emile. *Souvenirs d'un Militant socialiste.* 1939.

Vidal, Jacques. *Le Mouvement ouvrier français de la Commune à la Guerre Mondiale.* 1934.

Warner, Charles K. *The Wine Growers of France and the Government Since 1875.* New York, 1960.

Watson, D. R. 'The Nationalist Movement in Paris, 1900–1906'. In David Shapiro, Ed. *The Right in France, 1890–1919: Three Studies.* Carbondale, 1962.

Weber, Eugen. *The Nationalist Revival in France, 1905–1914.* Berkely, 1959.

Weill, Georges. *Le Journal: Origines, évolution, et rôle de la presse périodique.* 1934.

– *Le Mouvement social en France, 1852–1924*, 3rd ed. 1924.

Weinstein, Harold R. *Jean Jaurès: A Study of Patriotism in the French Socialist Movement.* New York, 1936.

Willard, Claude. *La Fusillade de Fourmies.* 1957.

– *Les Guesdistes: Le mouvement socialiste en France (1893–1905).* 1965.

– Ed. *La Correspondance de Charles Brunellière, 1880–1917.* 1968.

Williams, Roger. *Henri Rochefort, Prince of the Gutter Press.* New York, 1966.

Zévaès, Alexander. *Les Guesdistes: Le Socialisme en 1912.*

– *Conclusions et Annexes.*

Vols. III and **XI** of *Histoire des Partis socialistes en France,* II vols. A. Zévaès, Ed. 1911, 1912.

– *Notes et Souvenirs d'un Militant.* Rivière, 1913.
– and Prolo, Jacques. *Une Campagne politique, . . . 1910–1917.* n.d.
– *Une Génération.* 1922.
– *Le Parti Socialiste de 1904 à 1923.* 1923.
– *Ombres et Silhouettes.* 1928.
– *Jules Guesde, 1845–1922.* 1929.
– *La Grève de Decazeville, janvier-juin, 1886.* 1936.
– *La Fusillade à Fourmies.* 1936.
– *Henri Rochefort, le pamphletaire.* 1946.

Index